REGULATION

Politics, Bureaucracy, and Economics

REGULATION

Politics, Bureaucracy, and Economics

Kenneth J. Meier

University of Oklahoma

St. Martin's Press
New York

To W. O. Farber

ISBN: 0-312-66971-2
ISBN: 0-312-66972-0 (pbk.)

Library of Congress Cataloging in Publication Data

Meier, Kenneth J., 1950–
   Regulation, politics, bureaucracy, and economics.

   Bibliography: p. 303
   Includes index.
   1. Trade regulation—United States. I. Title.
HD3616.U46M39 1985   338.973   84-51842
ISBN 0-312-66971-2
ISBN 0-312-66972-0 (pbk.)

Contents

Preface

Regulation is essential to modern society. Without rules for acceptable behavior in relationships with other individuals, any complex society would rapidly collapse. Regulation provides a framework that defines acceptable behavior for individuals in a variety of situations. People in business must be concerned with the quality of products they produce, the safety of the workplace, and any pollution that results as a by-product. Other citizens also find their lives regulated: Restrictions are placed on how fast they can drive, what kind of products they can buy, even where they can live.

In the last two decades the amount of regulation in American society has exploded. At the federal level the Equal Employment Opportunity Commission, the Environmental Protection Agency, the Occupational Safety and Health Administration, the Consumer Product Safety Commission, the Commodity Futures Trading Commission, and the National Highway Traffic Safety Administration are just a few of the new agencies that were created. In addition, older agencies received new authority; bank regulators, for example, were given truth in lending laws, equal credit opportunity laws, and laws restricting insider activities. At state and local levels, regulation has expanded at an equal rate. State governments were given authority to implement federal regulations on environmental protection and workplace safety, while state legislatures sponsored numerous efforts in consumer protection, fair employment, and utility regulation. Local governments created their own regulatory agencies to oversee cable TV systems, local election practices, local cases of discrimination, and countless other areas.

Given the great increase in regulation, one would think that regulation was perceived as a universal good. In fact, the public perception of regulation is exactly the opposite. One of the increasing paradoxes in current American politics is that although regulation is heavily criticized, people still demand that it be extended to other areas of society.

In general, however, regulation continues to have a negative press. By reading such specialized journals as *Regulation,* one would get the impression that regulation accomplishes little good and produces great evils. This book addresses this misperception by examining several cases of regulation. Regulation in America is fairly complex, and simple generalizations such as those found in the popular literature or even the popularized economic literature are always incomplete and often wrong. This book will examine a wide range of regulatory situations to determine why regulatory policy exists as it does.

Regulation: Politics, Bureaucracy, and Economics uses a consistent conceptual framework to examine individual regulatory policies. Presented in chapter 2, the framework essentially combines the viewpoints of those who feel regulatory policies are determined by the social and economic environment and those who feel that bureaucracies are permitted the freedom to set policies without restriction. The economic and technological environment, along with macropolitical forces, sets the general parameters for regulatory policy. These elements provide both opportunities to make policy and restrictions on such activities. Within these forces, the specific policies are established by bureaucracies in interaction with their policy environments. Internal agency factors can be used to explain which of the specific policies an agency follows among those that the environment permits.

In this study of regulation, I have attempted to do three things. First, I have tried to integrate several approaches to the study of regulation that appeared to be useful. The result is a multidisciplinary view of regulation. At times concepts and approaches are taken from history, economics, law, and organization theory as well as from political science. Guiding this multidisciplinary approach, however, is a belief that regulation is a political process. I have emphasized political rather than economic or legal explanations for regulatory policy.

Second, I have addressed both empirical and normative issues. To encourage the reader to look at empirical questions, I have applied the conceptual framework introduced in chapter 2 to substantive regulatory areas in chapters 3 through 9. When we study regulation, avoiding normative issues is almost impossible. Our colleagues in economics have finessed this problem by accepting a normative viewpoint (that regulation is designed to enhance efficiency) and doing empirical research within that viewpoint. Such an approach strikes me as less satisfactory than simply admitting that certain questions are normative and discussing them as such. Consequently, in several places I have offered normative judgments about specific regulatory policies, and in chapter 10 the proposed reforms of others are subjected to an evaluation.

Third, I have made an effort to include a wide range of substantive regulatory policies that are rarely discussed by political scientists, including such areas as banking regulation, antitrust regulation, occupational regulation, and agricultural regulation. Balance was sought between regulatory policies that work fairly well and those that do not, between policies that are salient to the American people and policies that are not, and between social and economic regulation.

Chapter 3 discusses the regulation of financial institutions such as banks, savings and loans associations, and credit unions. Financial regulation is affected more than most areas by environmental forces outside the control of regulators, especially by the economic and technological forces that define the demand for a financial product.

Chapter 4 assesses several consumer protection policies, including those dealing with prescription drugs, food safety, automobile safety, consumer products, and deceptive advertising. Consumer protection policy puts more emphasis on political and bureaucratic variables, including the creation of consumer organizations and the activities of bureaucratic entrepreneurs.

Chapter 5 covers the economic regulation of agriculture. Agricultural regulation is of interest because it relies heavily on incentives rather than on coercion to get compliance with regulatory policy. I believe the results in agriculture indicate how well such policies would work in environmental protection and workplace safety.

Chapter 6 traces the development of environmental protection policy.

Although environmental policy illustrates several things, such as the role Congress can play in regulation or the impact of public interest groups, it was included primarily to illustrate the relationship between career staff and political leadership. The conflict between the former EPA administrator Anne Burford and the permanent bureaucracy and its allies is a classic case for students of bureaucratic power.

State regulation of occupations such as doctors, lawyers, and plumbers is discussed in chapter 7. It was included for two reasons: (1) to provide one case of state rather than federal regulation and (2) to illustrate an area where regulation is undertaken for the benefit of the regulated interest. State regulation of occupations, however, is probably the worst case; state efforts in other areas are much more effective, and some effort has been made to talk about these state activities in other chapters. In addition, even though regulation is designed to benefit the regulated occupation, the evidence shows that these regulatory agencies are not all that effective.

Chapter 8 deals with that reputed ogre of regulation, the Occupational Safety and Health Administration (OSHA). The chapter shows how OSHA policies can be explained by examining the professional values of the career bureaucrats; it also illustrates how a bureaucracy can learn from its mistakes. Antitrust policy is assessed in chapter 9. It provides an example of regulation that is enforced through the court system. Interesting issues exist in antitrust, and major policy changes have been introduced by recent antitrust administrators.

Several people deserve thanks for the effort they have contributed to this project. Dave Welborn rekindled my interest in regulation by providing me with a convention forum to express my views. He also provided a detailed critique of the entire manuscript, which improved it significantly. Paul Sabatier read several chapters of the manuscript; his comments on the conceptual framework were especially helpful and caused me to rewrite that chapter several times. George Edwards also read several chapters and raised many issues that were subsequently addressed.

Alan Stone read the banking chapter and provided helpful information on the policies and history of these agencies. The consumer protection chapter was improved greatly by the criticism of Paul Quirk. My colleague Steve Ballard provided an exceptionally detailed critique of the environmental protection chapter and, through these comments, encouraged the perspectives presented in the chapter. Paul Culhane, through more general discussions, improved my understanding of this area. William Gormley read and provided excellent comments on a previous version of the occupational regulation chapter and, through his own work, indirectly critiqued the conceptual framework. Anthony Brown on several occasions sharpened my thinking about regulation. I owe all these individuals a debt of gratitude for their assistance. Any errors that remain are mine, not theirs.

I would also like to thank all the people at St. Martin's Press for their encouragement, patience, and effort. Michael Weber deserves a special thank-you for giving me the flexibility to write the book I wanted to write and for tolerating the delays.

K. J. M.

List of Abbreviations Used

AAA   Agricultural Adjustment Act
AAM   American Agriculture Movement
ABA   American Bankers' Association
ABA   American Bar Association
AEC   Atomic Energy Commission
AMA   American Medical Association
AMS   Agricultural Marketing Service
APA   Administrative Procedures Act
ASCS   Agricultural Stabilization and Conservation Service
ATM   automated teller machine
BAT   best available technology
BPT   best practicable technology
CAA   Clean Air Act
CAB   Civil Aeronautics Board
CEQ   Council on Environmental Quality
CFTC   Commodity Futures Trading Commission
COWPS   Council on Wage and Price Stability
CPSC   Consumer Product Safety Commission
CUNA   Credit Union National Association
CWA   Clean Water Act
CWIP   construction work in progress
DIDC   Depository Institutions Deregulation Committee
DIDMCA   Depository Institutions Deregulation and Monetary Control Act
EEOC   Equal Employment Opportunity Commission
EFT   electronic fund transfer
EPA   Environmental Protection Agency
FCC   Federal Communications Commission
FDA   Food and Drug Administration
FDIC   Federal Deposit Insurance Corporation
FHLBB   Federal Home Loan Bank Board
FERC   Federal Energy Regulatory Commission
FIFRA   Federal Insecticide, Fungicide, and Rodenticide Act
FSIS   Food Safety and Inspection Service
FSLIC   Federal Savings and Loan Insurance Corporation
FTC   Federal Trade Commission
FWPCA   Federal Water Pollution Control Act
FY   fiscal year
GAO   General Accounting Office
GM   General Motors
GRAS   generally recognized as safe
HEW   Health, Education, and Welfare (Department of)

IBAA   Independent Bankers Association of America
ICC   Interstate Commerce Commission
INS   Immigration and Naturalization Service
MADD   Mothers Against Drunk Drivers
MMDA   money market demand account
MMF   money market fund
NAAQS   National Ambient Air Quality Standards
NAFCU   National Association of Federal Credit Unions
NAPCA   National Air Pollution Control Administration
NAS   National Academy of Sciences
NCUA   National Credit Union Administration
NEPA   National Environmental Policy Act
NFO   National Farmers Organization
NFU   National Farmers Union
NHTSA   National Highway Traffic Safety Administration
NIOSH   National Institute of Occupational Safety and Health
NMPF   National Milk Producers Federation
NOW   negotiable order of withdrawal
NPDES   National Pollution Discharge Elimination System
OMB   Office of Management and Budget
OSHA   Occupational Safety and Health Administration
OSHRC   Occupational Safety and Health Review Commission
PAC   political action committee
PCB   polychlorinated biphenyl
PIK   payment in kind
PMA   Pharmaceutical Manufacturers Association
PHS   Public Health Service
PSD   prevention of significant deterioration
R and D   research and development
RARG   Regulatory Analysis Review Group
S&Ls   Savings and Loans (Savings Associations)
SEC   Securities and Exchange Commission
UAW   United Auto Workers
UHF   ultrahigh frequency
USDA   U.S. Department of Agriculture
USLSA   U.S. League of Savings Associations.
VHF   very high frequency

1

The Myths of Regulation

WHAT IS REGULATION?

Regulation is any attempt by the government to control the behavior of citizens, corporations, or subgovernments. In a sense, regulation is nothing more than the government's effort to limit the choices available to individuals within society (Mitnik, 1980). Despite the simple definition, regulation can take numerous forms (see Daly and Brady, 1976).

First, the most commonly perceived form of regulation is price regulation. Price regulation means that a government regulator determines the minimum, maximum, or range of prices that an individual can charge for a good or service. State public utility commissions, for example, set the price that utility companies charge for a kilowatt hour of electricity. Numerous other state boards often set the price of haircuts, dry cleaning services, and even funerals. In the last few years, federal regulatory agencies have become less involved in price regulation; state and local governments, however, continue to regulate prices in many industries.

Second, franchising or licensing is a process by which regulatory agencies permit or deny an individual the right to do business in a specified occupation or industry. To operate a television station, for example, an individual must receive a license from the Federal Communications Commission. To open a bank, a person must obtain the necessary charter from either the Office of the Comptroller of the Currency or from a state banking commission. Along with licenses come regulations. Acceptance of a license to conduct a certain business normally implies that the government has an interest in how that business is operated.

Third, standard setting is a form of government regulation in which the government establishes standards for a product or a production process. Standards may be either performance standards or engineering standards. When the U.S. Department of Agriculture (USDA) requires that exported grain contain no more than a certain percentage of foreign matter, it is setting a performance standard. USDA's concern is the level of foreign matter, not how any excess foreign matter is removed. On the other hand, when the Occupational Safety and Health Administration (OSHA) requires that factory workers be exposed to no more than two parts per million of cotton dust particles, it often tells the business how to meet this standard. OSHA with an engineering standard specifies both the goal and the means.

Fourth, government can regulate by the direct allocation of resources. Under energy policies that grew out of the energy crisis of 1974, the federal

1

government directly allocated crude oil to various refiners and to various end products. Although direct allocation of resources by government is fairly uncommon in the United States, it may become more frequent if tradable pollution permits become a part of national environmental policy (see chapter 6).

Fifth, government can regulate by providing operating subsidies. Such subsidies can be direct as they were when the Civil Aeronautics Board granted subsidies to airlines to encourage them to serve small cities or when the Agricultural Stabilization and Conservation Service offers loans and subsidies to farmers not to plant crops. Subsidies can also be indirect; the national gasoline tax may be thought of as an indirect subsidy of the trucking industry because proceeds from the tax are used to improve the roads used by the trucking industry. Even though subsidies look like a direct benefit rather than regulation, they become regulation when they are used for the purpose of changing the behavior of the individuals who receive the benefit.

Sixth, government can regulate to promote fair competition. Free markets are so essential to the American economic system that certain regulatory agencies are created simply to monitor the marketplace for fairness. Regulations against deceptive advertising by the Federal Trade Commission and antitrust regulation are two prominent examples.

As the various types of regulation illustrate, not all regulation is coercive. Much regulation is done through inducements offered by the government or its agencies. The objective of regulation, however, is the same—to change the behavior of individual citizens, corporations, or governments.

THE REGULATORY EXPLOSION

Twenty years ago regulation was a fairly minor part of the federal government. The major political issues were redistributive issues such as medicare and tax reform or were foreign policy issues. Regulation was rarely on the national agenda, and little was being done to study the impact of regulation on society.

The last two decades have changed that situation. According to the Center for the Study of American Business, regulation became a major growth industry in the 1960s and 1970s. The number of federal regulatory agencies increased from 28 in 1960 to 56 in 1980 (Penoyer, 1981: 3). A series of major regulatory agencies were created in these two decades. The National Highway Traffic Safety Administration was established in 1966 to regulate both automobile and highway safety. The Environmental Protection Agency was created in 1970 to coordinate the federal efforts to protect the environment. To eliminate harmful and hazardous products from the marketplace, Congress formed the Consumer Product Safety Commission in 1972. Equal employment opportunity was placed under the jurisdiction of the Equal Employment Opportunity Commission in 1964. Workplace health and safety were delegated to the new Occupational Safety and Health Administration in 1971. Nor was the federal government alone in creating regulatory agencies. State governments created a variety of consumer protection agencies and were required by federal law to establish agencies to regulate air and water pollution.

Other indicators of the growth in regulation also exist. The funds budgeted for the federal regulatory agencies tripled in real dollars between 1970 and 1980 (Penoyer, 1981: 5). The number of regulatory employees increased to almost 90,000 by 1980. Because this figure included only federal employees, it was a significant underestimate because many federal regulatory programs are implemented by state and local governments (e.g., environmental protection, workplace safety, equal opportunity). The regulatory critics' favorite indicator of regulatory activity, the size of the *Federal Register,* increased from 14,479 pages in 1960 to 65,603 pages in 1977.

Not only was regulation growing, but the form of regulation had also changed. Early regulation was generally termed "economic" regulation; a regulatory agency regulated the price, entry, exit, and service of an industry. The Interstate Commerce Commission, for example, granted licenses to truckers, set the price that truckers could charge, and established their routes. Economic regulation had a negative reputation; it was characterized as regulation in the interests of the regulated industry only (see Stigler, 1971; Bernstein, 1955).

The regulatory activities of the 1960s and 1970s were different from this earlier form of regulation. Rather than prices, it concerned safety, health, employment fairness, and a variety of noneconomic issues. The new regulation was termed "social" regulation. Although social regulation dates back to at least nineteenth-century efforts to limit water pollution discharges, during the last two decades it became the predominant form.

Social regulation differed greatly in its approach to regulation. Economic regulation was often undertaken because the industry requested it (e.g., the Federal Communications Commission, the Civil Aeronautics Board) and often protected the regulated industry from the ill-effects of competition. Social regulation, on the other hand, was rarely demanded by the regulated industry and was more likely to be forced on it by a Congress that responded to nonindustry groups.

Regulation became an issue on the political agenda. First placed there by various consumer and public interest groups pressing for additional regulation, it was later opposed by business organizations that felt that the effort had gone too far. Regulation became salient enough to be an issue in both the 1976 and 1980 presidential election campaigns. Regulatory reform occupied the attention of both Congress and the president.

After the 1980 election, significant changes were made in regulatory policy by the Reagan administration. At the most general level, the rapid increase in the volume of regulation was slowed. No new regulatory agencies were created. Staffing for regulatory agencies, which had leveled off in 1978 at approximately 90,000, was reduced by 11 percent by 1983 (*Regulation,* 1982: 9), and the expenditures by the regulatory agencies were reduced both in real dollars and in 1970 constant dollars.

Although the Reagan administration stopped the growth in regulation, it did not make any significant cutbacks in regulatory structure. For the most part, laws were left unchanged. The initial efforts to rewrite environmental protection statutes, for example, were abandoned in the face of strong congressional opposition. If the political environment would again change to favor regulation, the regulatory agencies were in a position to renew the growth of regulatory activity.

THE MYTHS OF REGULATION

The study of regulation is clouded by several myths of regulation. These myths are widely accepted by politicians, students of the regulatory process, and even the general public. Because these myths are inaccurate or only partially accurate, they limit serious regulatory reform. Reformers often respond to the myths rather than the true shortcomings of regulation. Four prominent myths should be noted.

Regulation Is Ineffective

Regulation is often charged with failing to achieve its goals. When Penn Square Bank failed in 1982, the Office of the Comptroller of the Currency was charged with ineffective regulation to prevent the failure. The Occupational Safety and Health Administration (OSHA) is frequently denounced for regulating without improving the safety of industrial workplaces. The Food and Drug Administration (FDA) is condemned for not approving drugs that would benefit the American public.

To be sure, regulatory agencies have their share of failures. Failures are to be expected, however, given the high standards set for regulatory agencies, the almost impossible goals set for them by Congress, and the limited resources given to the agencies. The Consumer Product Safety Commission, for example, is charged with regulating 10,000 consumer products produced by 2 million firms with approximately 600 employees. Such a task is simply not possible. In addition, many regulatory tasks require activity at the cutting edge of science. In 1972 the Environmental Protection Agency (EPA) was tasked with cleaning up water and permitting "zero discharges" of untreated waste into the nation's waterways by 1984. In retrospect, the task was impossible.

Less visible than failures are the successes of regulatory agencies. The Consumer Product Safety Commission's regulations on childproof caps and baby cribs are credited with significant reductions in accidents and deaths (see chapter 4). The Federal Trade Commission's optometrist rule resulted in greater competition and a lowering of the prices of eyeglasses. No person has ever lost money deposited in a federally insured account at a depository institution.

Regulatory agencies are like all other large scale bureaucracies; they have some successes, and they have some failures. Because they are public sector organizations open to public view, their failures receive more attention than their successes. Because successes prevent problems, they are often obscured from public view. Failures such as a major bank collapse or an airline crash are always newsworthy.

The myth of regulatory failure is perhaps the most detrimental to reforming regulation. Citizens can benefit from efforts to reform the regulatory process if such an effort is built on an understanding of regulation's strengths and weaknesses. Reforms triggered by the belief that all regulation is ineffective will do more harm than good.

Regulation Is Out of Control

A second myth is that regulation is no longer under the control of the American people or their elected representatives. Faceless bureaucrats without authorization from Congress or the president are imposing their own political values on the American public. EPA bureaucrats tried to ban automobile traffic in downtown Los Angeles. The National Highway Traffic Safety Administration (NHTSA) attempted to require that no car be able to start without a seatbelt. Academic researchers must file long reports about the protection of human subjects to survey people about political attitudes. The Office of Education proposed that all father-son and mother-daughter functions be banned as sexually discriminatory.

Although some of these actions and others might appear to be irrational or to impose hardships on the American public, they do not indicate that regulatory agencies are out of control. In many cases, the actions of regulatory agencies reflect the guidance that Congress, the president, or individuals in the area give to them. The Los Angeles traffic rule was proposed because EPA was required by Congress to establish a plan for each air quality region to meet national pollution standards; the plan illustrated a point—without significant changes in traditional transportation methods, Los Angeles would not attain the national goals. NHTSA vigorously pursued passive restraints because Congress urged it to do so.

No better illustration that regulatory agencies are not out of control exists than the Reagan administration. Regulators appointed by Reagan have been able to change the regulatory priorities of a great many regulatory agencies. Thorne Auchter was able to greatly improve OSHA's standing with industry. The FDA approved a record number of new drugs for the pharmaceutical industry in 1981 and 1982. The NHTSA withdrew some 20 rules governing automobile safety to assist the auto industry.

President Reagan has had little problem in asserting control over the regulatory agencies (see Ball, 1984). Clearly, if regulatory agencies are out of control, this would not have been possible. Regulatory agencies in reality are highly responsive to the pressures of the political system. When a critic charges that a regulatory agency is out of control, he or she may really be stating that the regulatory agency is responding to political values different from those of the critic.

Regulatory Agencies Are Captured

A charge heard frequently among public interest groups and in the past by a variety of scholars is that regulatory agencies are captured by the industry that they regulate. The charge was initially presented by Samuel Huntington (1952) in a study of the Interstate Commerce Commission (ICC). Later such individuals as Marver Bernstein, George Stigler, and Sam Peltzman expanded on the idea.

In some cases, this charge has an element of truth. The Federal Communications Commission (FCC) was created at the request of the industry and regulated in many cases to protect it (Sabatier, 1976). Similar conclusions can be drawn about the Civil Aeronautics Board and the airline industry. On the other hand, many regulatory agencies are definitely not captured by the industry. The Environmental Protection Agency has a strong reputation for independence from the industry (reinforced after the departure of Anne Burford). Arguments could be made that federal bank regulators, the Occupational Safety and Health Administration, and the Food and Drug Administration frequently act contrary to industry demands.

In fact, the relationship between a regulatory agency and the industry or industries it regulates is an important political question and one that will concern us throughout this book. Agencies vary a great deal in their relationship with the regulated; some are fairly close, and some are fairly distant. One purpose of this book is to find out what variables affect the relationship between the regulator and the regulated.

The Purpose of Regulation Is Efficiency

A large volume of regulatory analysis by economists has evaluated regulation against the standard of economic efficiency. Much of this literature claims to be empirical rather than normative; that is, it claims that the goal of regulation is efficiency and that it is simply examining regulation against this standard. Judged against the efficiency standard, regulatory agencies often come up short.

Unfortunately for this approach, however, efficiency is rarely ever the prime goal of regulation and, in some cases, is not even a secondary goal. The idea that efficiency is the prime goal of regulation is taken from economic public interest theory, which contends that because a perfectly competitive market allocates goods and services efficiently, regulation should be undertaken only when the market fails (see Stokey and Zeckhauser, 1978 for an excellent summary of this position). Monopoly, imperfect information, and externalities are situations where the market operates less than efficiently; regulation should correct these problems.

Regulation in the real world is often undertaken for political reasons rather than for economic reasons. The Interstate Commerce Commission was created to counter the economic power of the railroads; the Food and Drug Administration was established to make the consumption of food and drugs safer; environmental protection statutes were adopted to restrict efficient operation of the unregulated market; The Civil Aeronautics Board was established to protect the airlines from competition. Although one might dispute whether or not these goals are the primary reasons each of these regulators was created, one rarely ever finds efficiency mentioned in the legislative history of these agencies' statutes. In fact, the economic concept of efficiency was fairly undeveloped at the time the early regulatory agencies were created. Only when economists began serious studies of regulation after World War II was the concept of efficiency stressed.

Arguing that efficiency is the goal of regulation is essentially a normative argument; it is an argument that efficiency *should be* the goal of regulation. To be sure, agencies can have more than one goal, and regulatory objectives should be accomplished in the most efficient way possible. But when efficiency conflicts with other goals, efficiency is often a second priority.

The Environmental Protection Agency, for example, often specifies the exact pollution control equipment to be used to clean up discharges. Such rigid specification is inefficient (see Crandall, 1983a), but it also facilitates EPA's compliance inspections. Some agencies such as the Occupational Safety and Health Administration are not required to consider costs when regulating; in such agencies, efficiency can be no more than a secondary goal.

The argument for efficiency as a regulatory goal also concerns the locus of regulatory decisions. Efficiency advocates usually demonstrate that if a business must be regulated, incentives (e.g., effluent fees, injury taxes, and so on) are preferable to traditional regulation. Incentive systems may well be more efficient, but they also shift the decision locus from government agencies to private business. Whether government or industry makes decisions concerning regulatory compliance will clearly affect the type of decisions made.

Efficiency is often a useful concept and plays a role in current regulatory policy. It is not the primary goal of regulation, however, and treating it as such results in a distorted view of regulation. If regulatory agencies are judged by a standard they do not have, they are bound to fall short.

THE STUDY OF REGULATION

Numerous ways exist to study regulation. Legal approaches focus on the law and such legal concepts as due process and fairness. Economic approaches are centered on efficiency and the role of regulation in correcting market failures. Historical approaches set regulation within the broader forces in society. The approach in this book, though decidedly political, has some distinct differences from traditional political science as well as from the preceding approaches given. These differences should be noted.

Regulation Is Complex

Simple generalizations about regulation will almost always be wrong. Regulation and regulatory agencies vary significantly on many dimensions. Some agencies are fairly effective; others are not. Some policy areas are controlled by the regulatory agency; others are not. Some agencies are known for expertise, cohesion, and dynamic leadership; others are not.

With so much variation, simple explanations of regulatory policy are rarely possible. The conceptual framework used to explain regulation in this book (see chapter 2) is fairly complex. Regulatory policy is the product of a regulatory agency operating in an environment that places demands on it. Both factors within the agency (e.g., expertise, leadership) and factors in the environment will affect regulatory policy. Among the other actors involved in regulatory policy are legislators, the chief executive, the courts, interest groups, state governments, journalists, and other bureaucrats.

Regulatory policy actors interact in a political, economic, and technological environment. These environmental forces place demands on the regulatory system, provide it with opportunities to act, and limit the scope of its actions. The relative impact of each factor varies from area to area. Understanding the complex relationship between the various actors and the environmental forces will enable a person to explain why a specific regulatory policy exists as it does.

Multidisciplinary Focus

Regulation has been fruitfully studied by a wide variety of disciplines because regulation contains facets amenable to study in different ways. Determining the relationship between market concentration and competition in antitrust is an economic exercise. Assessing the procedural requirements necessary for rule making is a legal question. Discovering the reasons why an agency was created is a political and historical question.

This study of regulation will borrow from such disciplines as law, economics, history, organization theory, and political science. Although the general focus is on politics, each of the other disciplines has useful contributions to make. Law can be used to analyze the role that the judiciary plays in regulatory policy, an especially important factor in an area such as antitrust. Economics allows us to assess the role economic forces play in shaping policy responses; banking regulation, for example, responds to economic forces that set interest rates. Organization theory illuminates the processes within the bureaucracy such as how organizational ideologies develop and how they affect policy decisions.

Of the various disciplines, perhaps as much attention is given to history as to any other. The political forces present at the creation of a regulatory agency often persist. Agency personnel take decision cues from the organization's history. Interest groups active at the creation will probably remain active. If Congress has historically resolved disputes in a regulatory area, it will be expected to resolve future disputes. The history of a regulatory agency contains the explanations for many present decisions.

Above all, however, regulation is a political process involving political actors seeking political ends. Economic and legal arguments are often used to define the problem in such a way that a given outcome occurs. Such activity is a political effort. Economics, law, history, and a variety of sciences can provide the justification for many public policies; only politics, however, can explain why the policies are what they are.

Normative Judgments

This study has two goals that are sometimes in conflict. One goal is to explain regulatory policy outcomes. The other goal is to suggest specific changes in regulatory policy. Although positivist tradition holds that empirical analysis should be separated from value judgments, in regulatory policy this rarely occurs. Most regulatory analysis has either normative objectives or was instigated by normative concerns. This is as it should be. Social sciences, as Herbert Simon (1969) argued, are sciences of the artificial, concerned as much with how things might be as how they actually are.

Accordingly, this book will not ignore normative issues, nor does it expect the reader to do so. Regulatory policy determines who benefits from government intervention into the marketplace, a topic on which few people can claim neutrality. Rather than disguise normative presentations as empirical arguments, as much of the literature does, this book will make its normative contentions explicit. Although normative and empirical arguments cannot always be separated, some effort has been made to do so by keeping the normative arguments in separate sections and labeling them as such.

2

The Regulatory Process

The study of regulatory policymaking is dominated by two perspectives (Weingast and Moran, 1983). One view holds that regulatory agencies are vested with vast discretion and are the major force in regulatory policy. Among the agency characteristics that affect policy outputs are professional values, policy expertise, bureaucratic enterpreneurs, and agency structure (e.g., see Wilson, 1980; Katzman, 1980). A second view suggests that regulatory agencies are dominated by their environment. Interest groups, legislative committees, economic forces, and technological change are among the determinants of policy (e.g., see Stigler, 1971; Lowi, 1969; Mazmanian and Sabatier, 1980). Both views are essentially incomplete. Regulatory policy is a product of both regulatory bureaucracies and environmental forces. This chapter develops an outline of the regulatory process that integrates both these explanations. Although the conceptual framework developed is moderately complex, so is regulatory policy. Little is gained by introducing simple views of regulation that are not linked to the real world.

REGULATORY POLICY OUTPUTS

The study of regulation is important because it is part of the policy process that allocates values among members of society. It is, as Lasswell (1936) described politics, a determination of "Who gets what, when and how." In short, what is important about regulatory policy from a political perspective is, Who benefits from regulation?

Although much regulation literature has focused on who benefits from regulation, this focus has been muddied by relying on the concept of the public interest. Bernstein's (1955) theory that regulatory agencies in the long run were captured by the regulated industries contrasted reality with an ideal standard of regulation in the public interest (see also Stigler, 1971; Peltzman, 1976). Unfortunately, defining the public interest in regulatory policy has been as elusive as it has been in other areas of politics (see Schubert, 1960). Even the most self-serving appeal by a regulated group is now phrased as a quest for the public interest.

In a perceptive essay, Paul Sabatier (1977) proposed an alternative to the public interest theory of regulation; regulatory policy can be arrayed on a continuum from self-regulation (regulation in the interests of the regulated) to aggressive regulation (regulation of one individual in the interests of another).[1] Sabatier's thesis can be divided into two separate dimensions—the degree to which regulation benefits the regulated industry and the degree to which it benefits nonregulated individuals such as consumers. These are two separate dimensions rather than poles on a single continuum.

As figure 2.1 reveals, the two dimensions of beneficiaries produce four extreme types of regulation. Cell 1 contains policies designed to benefit the regulated but not the nonregulated, the traditional "captured" regulation. Regulation by state occupational regulators is a classic example of cell 1 regulation (see chapter 7). Cell 3 contains those policies whereby an industry is regulated for the benefit of another party. Occupational safety and health regulation, for example, restricts industry behavior in an attempt to benefit workers (see chapter 8). Cell 4 contains those policies that benefit both the regulated and some portion of the nonregulated. Bank regulation and deposit insurance following the Great Depression benefited both depositors by guaranteeing the safety of their funds and the banks by encouraging the use of banks (see chapter 3). Finally, cell 2 includes policies that benefit no one. Current antitrust policy concerning price discrimination appears to harm both businesses that wish to compete and consumers (see chapter 9).

Although who benefits from regulatory policy is not always easy to discover, the question provides a focal point for comparing unlike regulatory policies. This text will examine two aspects of regulatory policy—what is the current set of regulatory policies, and who benefits from them? The conceptual framework in this chapter permits us to explain why regulatory agencies act as they do and why regulatory policies benefit whom they do.

SUBSYSTEM POLITICS

Although regulatory policies can be produced directly by legislatures, the chief executive, or the courts, in general, regulatory policy is implemented via bureaucracy. Typically, broad areas of regulatory discretion are granted to a regulatory agency by these political institutions of government. The Interstate Commerce Commission, for example, is charged with regulating interstate commerce with only a vague goal (the "public interest") as a guide. The policymaking activities of bureaucratic agencies can best be understood by examining the subsystem in which these agencies operate.

That public policy is made in semiautonomous subsystems composed of government bureaus, congressional committees, and interest groups has been a basic tenet of political analysis since the 1950s (see Freeman, 1965; McConnell, 1966). Subsystems exist because the American political system fragments political power (Long, 1962). With its division of federal authority into three branches—executive, legislative, and judicial—each operating with constraints on the other two, political power at the national level is fragmented among numerous political actors. Power is further divided by the federal system and informally kept that way by broker political parties that seek electoral success rather than unified political government. As a result, political power is not concentrated enough to dominate the policy process.

1. I have taken some liberties with Sabatier's (1977) work here. His intent was to distinguish between managerial and policing types of regulation. His work results in three types of regulation along a single dimension rather than four types along two.

Figure 2.1 Dimensions of regulatory policy

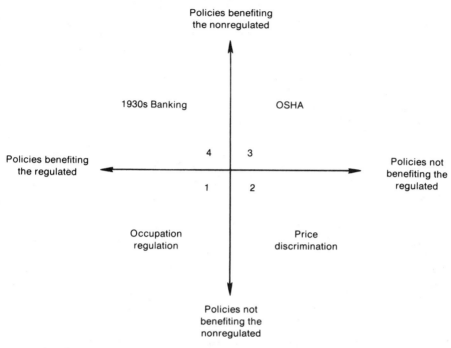

The fragmentation is exacerbated by the numerous policy issues that compete for attention on the policy agenda. Major political institutions must constantly jump from crisis to crisis—social security today, gasoline user fees tomorrow, MX missiles next week. Power in a given issue area flows to those who retain a continuing interest in it. In American politics a continuing interest usually means the permanent bureaucracy, specialized congressional committees, and the interest groups affected by the issue.

Policy subsystems can operate in a relatively independent fashion from the major political institutions *if* the members of the policy subsystem can satisfy each others' needs. The bureaucracy makes policy. It issues the permits, exceptions, and punishments; but to do so it needs resources and legislative authority. Congressional committees can provide the funds and authority needed by the bureau to operate, but the committee members need to be reelected. Reelection requires political support and campaign contributions. The interest groups affiliated with the regulated industry need the outputs that the bureaucracy is creating, especially if the outputs are favorable; and they have the political resources to commit to members of congressional committees. In combination, the members of the subsystem can often supply the needs of the other members. If all the needs of the subsystem members are satisfied, then subsystem members make no major demands on the macropolitical system. In turn, the subsystem is given autonomy.

Although subsystems have been fruitfully applied to numerous areas of political research (see Ripley and Franklin, 1980), recent work suggests that subsystems are not the homogeneous "iron triangles" that they are portrayed to be (see Heclo, 1978; Sabatier, 1983). First, interest groups, even industry groups, rarely agree completely about regulatory policy. Dissension among airline companies permitted deregulation of airline fares in the 1970s (Behrman, 1980); broadcasting interests are fragmented into several groups with vastly different goals, including groups representing networks, independent stations, religious broadcasters, ultrahigh frequency (UHF) stations, frequency modulation (FM) stations, and countless others (Krasnow, Longley, and Terry, 1982). Second, interest groups other than industry groups actively participate in the regulatory subsystem. Consumer groups are active in the auto safety, drug regulation, and consumer products subsystems; labor unions are active in safety regulation and sometimes in environmental regulation. Rarely do industry groups have the opportunity to operate without opposition.

Third, subsystems are often divided among several different subcommittees each with different policy objectives. Environmental protection programs, for example, are under the jurisdiction of seven committees in the House and five in the Senate (Kenski and Kenski, 1984: 111). Even with only a single committee involved in a subsystem, policy conflict occurs. Conflicting positions by the Commerce Committees at different times during the 1970s resulted in a series of policy changes by the Federal Trade Commission (Weingast and Moran, 1982). Fourth, a variety of other actors penetrate the subsystem to urge policy actions, including journalists and scholars who generate important information on policy options. Such issues as acid rain, pesticide regulation, drug safety, and others were placed on the agenda by such actors.

Fifth, one subsystem will sometimes overlap one or more other subsystems, thus adding additional actors to the political battles and creating greater conflict. Environmental protection subsystems collided with energy subsystems following the Arab oil embargo; insurance subsystems and automobile regulation subsystems came into conflict following the Reagan administration's relaxation of automobile safety regulations (see chapter 4).

Finally, the subsystems concept ignores the vital role of state and local government officials in the regulatory process. In many areas, federal regulatory programs are implemented by state governments; environmental protection and workplace health and safety are prominent examples. In a variety of other areas such as consumer protection, antitrust, and equal employment opportunity policies, both the federal government and state governments operate programs. Often the policy goals of state regulators can differ significantly from those of federal regulators (see Rowland and Marz, 1982), resulting in policy outputs different from those intended by the federal government. This conflict can result in either more vigorous regulation or less vigorous regulation depending on state objectives. California's aggressive mobile source air pollution regulation in the 1960s and 1970s, for example, often preceded federal efforts, but state-run workplace safety programs lag behind federal-run programs (see chapter 8).

In figure 2.2 an expanded version of the subsystem is shown that includes other (i.e., nonindustry) interest groups, significant others (e.g., researchers, journalists), and state governments in addition to the "iron" triangle. Paul Sabatier (1983) argues that policy subsystems can best be viewed as opposing advocacy coalitions; a coalition of industry and its allies (members of Congress, other groups, and so on) is opposed by other interest groups and their allies. Under such a conceptualization, the traditional iron triangle becomes a special case of a policy subsystem with only one advocacy coalition.

Figure 2.2 The regulatory policy system

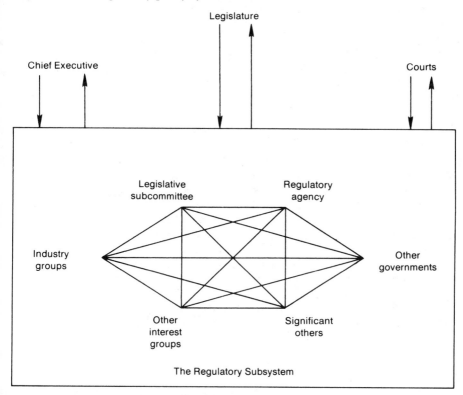

Among the most important aspects of policy subsystems is how open the subsystems are to outside influences via the chief executive, the legislature, and other nonsubsystem actors. Policy subsystems are perceived as fairly consensual, and in areas of distributive politics—health care research, agricultural policy, and educational aid—they are (Ripley and Franklin, 1980). The distribution of tangible benefits paid for by general tax revenues ties the members of the subsystems closely together. Consensual subsystems resolve policy issues internally and present a unified front to the larger political system. As a result, consensual subsystems are usually allowed to operate without outside interference.

Regulatory subsystems are not as consensual as those in distributive policy and, therefore, are more likely to be affected by outside influences for several reasons. First, regulatory policy restricts choice so that an industry is likely to see regulation as a mixed blessing. Regulated industries may defend their regulator when it is attacked by other political actors (e.g., the airlines and the Civil Aeronautics Board (CAB) circa 1976), but they are slower to come to the defense and less committed when they do so. Second, members of Congress are likely to be less committed to a regulatory subsystem than to a distributive subsystem. Unlike other policies, regulation often imposes direct costs. A member of Congress from a rural district will receive far more credit from constituents if he or she is on the soil conservation subcommittee distributing benefits than if he or she is on the environmental committee limiting pesticide use. Third, regulatory subsystems are likely to have more nonindustry groups that want to participate in the subsystem. The Federal Communications Commission (FCC), for example, cannot operate in a consensual, autonomous subsystem because numerous interests other than the television industry are also interested in regulating television. Politicians, the movie industry, cable operators, the phone company, and many others see television as important to their interests; accordingly, they will seek to participate in FCC decisions.

REGULATORY AGENCIES: INSIDE THE BLACK BOX

Government agencies are not passive actors pushed along at the whim of other subsystem members. They shape as well as respond to pressures from the subsystem (Rourke, 1984). The U.S. Department of Agriculture (USDA), for example, played a role in creating and developing the American Farm Bureau; Farm Bureau members, in turn, assisted the USDA in crop regulation. The Environmental Protection Agency funds academic research on pollution; such research is then used in debates over environmental protection. In a sense, both agencies helped create a portion of the subsystem. If bureaus can take an active role in structuring their environments, they need not passively respond to subsystem pressures. They can actively seek to influence the forces impinging on regulatory policy. To understand the policy actions of regulatory agencies, two variables—goals and resources—must be discussed.

Agency Goals

Every regulatory agency has goals including policy goals that agency employees wish to attain. Environmental Protection Agency employees seek cleaner air and water; FDA personnel pursue safe and effective drugs. Although this contention may seem trivial, many treatments of bureaucracy either assume an organization's sole goal is to survive or that the bureaucrats' goal is to maximize their income (e.g., see Niskanen, 1971). Both approaches provide a misleading view of regulatory agencies.

This distinction merits some discussion. If we assume, as Niskanen does, that bureaucrats are rational utility maximizers, regulators clearly seek goals other than income maximization. Because incomes are higher in the regulated industry, an income maximizer would choose to work for the regulated industry rather than the regulatory agency.[2] The choice to enter the public sector is not dictated by inferior skills because studies show that public sector employees in jobs similar to private sector ones have greater skills and better training (Guyot, 1979). A public sector bureaucrat, therefore, must be maximizing something other than income; the most logical thing to maximize is policy goals.

Ascribing regulatory policy goals to bureaucrats is consistent with motivation theory (e.g., Maslow, 1970) and empirical evidence. Employees

2. One might argue that working for a regulatory agency increases one's value to industry in the future. Such a calculation ignores both the careerist orientation of the regulatory agency's career staff (see McGregor, 1974) and the fact that regulators such as Joan Claybrook are unlikely to accept industry employment.

work for the Office of Civil Rights because they believe in racial equality (Romzek and Hendricks, 1982). Individuals work for OSHA because they desire to improve workplace safety (Kelman, 1980). In the long run, most agency employees become advocates of the agency and its goals (Downs, 1967). Those interested in higher incomes or in the goals of the regulated industry will probably leave the agency.

Having policy goals does not mean that bureaucrats would not like to see their organization survive, all things being equal. Survival, after all, is necessary to obtain most policy goals. In some cases, the present Civil Aeronautics Board bureaucrats, for example, are content to accomplish policy objectives that will eventually eliminate the agency. In sum then, regulators regulate because they wish to attain policy goals; without understanding that regulators are goal-seeking and without determining what those goals are, regulatory behavior will appear random to the outside observer.

Also important in terms of regulatory goals is the potential for goal conflict within an agency. Such lack of consensus might result from several different conflicts within the organization: central staff versus field personnel, professionals versus administrators, one profession versus another profession, career staff versus political appointees. The last source of conflict is especially important. Career staff are more likely to identify with the agency and be strongly committed to its programs (Heclo, 1977). Political appointees are more likely to see themselves as the president's representative (Welborn, 1977) and, therefore, hold different views.

Resources

In pursuit of policy goals, regulatory agencies have access to five resources—expertise, cohesion, legislative authority, policy salience, and leadership.[3] Access to such resources determines the value of the agency's participation to other subsystem members. The greater a regulatory agency's resources, the more likely the agency will be able to resist industry pressures for regulation solely in the interests of the industry.

Expertise.   Bureaucratic organizations are designed to develop and store knowledge. To a degree greater than legislatures or courts, bureaucracies can divide tasks and gain knowledge via specialization (Rourke, 1984: 16). An EPA employee, for example, could spend an entire career dealing with the intricacies of regulating the pesticide mirex. As part of specialization, American government bureaucracies recruit skilled technocrats as employees, and the agencies become professionalized. A professionalized agency often adopts the values of the predominant profession; the values of safety and health professionals in the Occupational Safety and Health Administration, for example, are the reason why OSHA relies on engineering standards (Kelman, 1980).

Professionalization and specialization permit an agency to develop independent sources of knowledge so that the agency need not rely on the industry (or others) for its information. Although the levels of professionalism and specialization in regulatory agencies cannot rival those of such

---

3. The section on bureaucratic variables relies heavily on Rourke (1984) and Sabatier (1977). The most applicable parts of the writings of each are used. In some cases, the impact of the variables reflects my interpretation of their work rather than their interpretation.

agencies as the National Institutes of Health, they are a factor. The Nobel laureate Glenn Seaborg's appointment to head the Atomic Energy Commission (AEC; now the Nuclear Regulatory Commission) increased the AEC's reputation for expertise. Similarly, the creation of a separate research arm for the Environmental Protection Agency provided the EPA with expertise it could use in its political battles (Davies and Davies, 1975).

Professionalism does not mean that an agency is dominated by a single profession. At times one or more professions may be struggling for control of the agency. In the Federal Trade Commission (FTC), for example, economists and lawyers have long fought over control of the FTC's antitrust functions. The professional conflict, in fact, has major policy implications. Lawyers prefer cases that can be quickly brought to trial like Robinson-Patman cases. Economists favor either major structural monopoly cases that will significantly increase competition or cases against collusion (see chapter 9).

Cohesion.   A second resource permitting the agency to affect public policy is the cohesiveness of the bureau's personnel. If agency personnel are united in pursuit of their goals, coalitions opposed to agency actions will need to develop their own sources of information to challenge agency decisions. A cohesive agency is far more difficult to resist than an agency that engages in public disputes over policy direction. Cohesion, in turn, is a function of an agency's goals and its ability to socialize members to accept these goals. Some public agencies such as the Marine Corps or the Forest Service even go so far as to create an organizational ideology for their members. Although no regulatory agency engages in the same degree of socialization that the Marine Corps does, they do seek consciously or unconsciously to influence the values of employees. Bureaucrats in the Environmental Protection Agency, for example, show much greater concern for environmental protection than for compliance costs. The Office of Education in the 1960s was a zealous advocate of school desegregation.

Legislative Authority.   All regulatory agencies must have legislative authority to operate, but all grants of legislative authority are not equal (see Sabatier, 1977: 424–431).[4] Five important differences in legislative authority exist and contribute to agency resources. First, policy goals as expressed in legislation can be specific or vague. Before 1973, Congress specified agricultural price support levels exactly, leaving little discretion for Agriculture Department regulators. In contrast, the Interstate Commerce Commission regulates interstate commerce with the general goal that regulation should be in the public interest. The more vague the legislative expression of goals, the greater the agency's ability to set regulatory policy. Specific policy goals should be correlated with regulation in the interests of whichever group has the best access to Congress. Consequently, specific goals are associated both with the regulation in the interests of the regulated (e.g., agriculture; see chapter 5) and with regulation for the benefit of the non-regulated (e.g., environmental protection; see Marcus, 1980).

Second, legislative delegations vary in the scope of authority they grant. Some agencies have jurisdiction over every firm in the industry (e.g., EPA).

---

4. The analysis of legislative authority follows that of Sabatier (1977). I have added the category of procedure and shortened his discussion of structure.

Other agencies might be denied jurisdiction over portions of their industry; OSHA's law, for example, exempts small farms. An agency with limited authority cannot affect the behavior of those outside its jurisdiction. The greater the limitations and restrictions on a regulatory agency, the more likely such an agency will regulate in the interest of the regulated industry.

Third, legislative delegations vary in the sanctions permitted to an agency. Bank regulators possess a wide variety of sanctions that can greatly influence the profits and viability of financial institutions. In contrast, the Equal Employment Opportunity Commission (EEOC) has no sanctions and must rely on court action to extract compliance. The greater the range of sanctions available to a regulatory agency, the more likely the agency will regulate in the interests of the nonregulated.

Fourth, regulatory agencies differ in their organizational structure. The two most common structural forms are the department regulatory agency (an agency headed by one person within a larger executive department) and the independent regulatory commission (a multimember board that reports directly to the legislature). Although the different structures do not appear related to performance (see Meier, 1980; Welborn, 1977), often independent regulatory commissions are subjected to other restraints. At the state level, regulatory commissions are often by law composed of members of the regulated industry (see chapter 7). When selection restrictions such as this occur, regulation in the interests of the regulated is a given.

Fifth, legislative grants of authority often specify agency procedures. The FTC must follow the lengthy *formal* rule-making process to issue rules, and the Consumer Product Safety Commission was handicapped until recently with a cumbersome "offeror" procedure (see chapter 4). Other agencies such as the EEOC and the antitrust regulators are limited further because they must use the courts to set policy and resolve disputes. The more restrictive an agency's procedures are, the less likely the agency will be able to regulate the industry closely.

Political Salience.   The salience of a regulatory issue (i.e., its perceived importance by the public) can be used as a resource in the agency's regulatory battles. Regulatory issues vary greatly in salience. Nuclear plant regulation after the Three Mile Island accident was a highly salient issue to political elites and the general public. State regulation of barbers, on the other hand, is rarely salient. Not only does salience vary across issue areas, it also varies across time within an issue area. Banking regulation was highly salient in 1933 but not so in 1973.

According to William Gormley (1983a), salience determines the willingness of political elites to intervene in the regulatory process. When issues become salient, the rewards for successful intervention are greater for elected officials. In salient issue areas, therefore, regulators will find their actions closely watched by political elites whereas in nonsalient areas regulatory discretion is likely to go unchecked. A lack of salience should be to the advantage of the regulated industry because it will have little opposition to its demands.

Leadership.   The final regulatory resource is the agency's leadership. Unlike the career bureaucracy, which is fairly stable, leadership positions turn over frequently. Two elements of leadership are important—quality and the leader's goals. Quality of leadership is a nebulous resource that, though difficult to define, is clearly a factor. The leadership abilities of Alfred Kahn as Civil Aeronautics Board chairperson were instrumental in deregulating airlines; the absence of strong leadership in Federal Trade Commission chairman Paul Rand Dixon was often cited as a reason for poor performance by the pre-1969 FTC (see chapter 4).

Essential to understanding the impact of leadership are the policy goals of regulatory agency heads. Through the leadership of Caspar Weinberger, Miles Kirkpatrick, and Michael Pertschuk, the Federal Trade Commission became less tied to the interests of the regulated industry and more interested in consumer issues. The appointment of Reese Taylor to head the Interstate Commerce Commission in 1981 signaled an end to the rapid movement toward deregulation of the trucking industry.

Leadership is especially important because the agency head is the focal point for interaction with the subsystem. In such interactions, the agency head is constrained by the expertise, cohesion, legislative authority, issue salience, and policy goals of the agency. An agency head who acts in opposition to the values and normal policy activities of the career staff risks political opposition from within the agency. Anne Burford's effort to alter environmental policy in the 1980s and the response of the EPA career staff is a classic example of this (see chapter 6).

Agency Discretion: A Recapitulation

Regulatory agencies, therefore, exercise some discretion in regulatory policy. This discretion is not limitless, however. The amount of discretion accorded an agency is a function of its resources (expertise, cohesion, legislative authority, policy salience, and leadership) and the tolerances of other actors in the political system. Each actor has a zone of acceptance (see Simon, 1957); and if agency decisions fall within that zone, no action will be taken. Because regulatory policy is more important to subsystem actors, the zone of acceptance for subsystem actors is probably narrower than that for macropolitical system actors (e.g., the president). Consequently, subsystem actors will be more active.

As long as the regulatory subsystem produces policies within the zone of acceptance of Congress, the president, and the courts, then these actors will permit the subsystem some autonomy. Actions outside the zone of acceptance will bring attempts to intervene. The size of the zones of acceptance should vary with both salience and complexity (see Gormley, 1983a). Salience increases the benefits of successful intervention to a political actor, and complexity increases the costs of intervention. All things being equal, therefore, political actors will be more likely to intervene in policies that are salient but not complex (Gormley, 1983a).

THE ORGANIZATION OF INTERESTS

Many regulatory analysts view interest groups, especially those from the regulated industry, as dominating the regulatory process. Bernstein (1955; see also Huntington, 1952) presented the "capture" theory of regulation. As the only political force in the agency's environment with any stability, the industry eventually forced the agency to accommodate its needs. The agency was captured and henceforth tried to regulate in the interests of the industry. George Stigler (1971), Sam Peltzman (1974), and Anthony Downs (1967) generalized this theory. They contended much as a pluralist (e.g., Truman, 1951) would that regulatory policy reflects the interests and the power of the concerned groups. Because this usually means only industry groups, policy should be responsive to the industry. Although versions of the capture theory have remained popular, they have been devastated by the empirical literature (see Meier and Plumlee, 1978; Mitnik, 1980; Quirk, 1981). The theory's most telling weakness is that in numerous cases regulatory agencies regulate the industry vigorously even though only industry groups are well organized (e.g., airline safety, banking, pharmaceuticals). Clearly interest group pressures are mediated and mitigated by other external pressures (e.g., from political elites) and internal pressures within the agency (expertise, cohesion, professionalism, leadership and so on).

Interest groups form part of the advocacy coalitions that seek to influence regulatory policy (Sabatier, 1983). These coalitions include bureaucrats, legislators, state and local government officials, researchers, journalists, and members of other subsystems in addition to interest groups. The value of both industry groups and nonindustry groups to advocacy coalitions is a function of the resources that the interest groups possess. These resources can be used either to persuade an agency to accept favored policy options or to convince political elites to intervene in the subsystem. Several resources merit discussion.

Size.   An interest group's size can be measured by its membership or its budget (Stigler, 1971; Zeigler and Peak, 1972). A great many members confer legitimacy on an interest group because interest groups claim to represent people and large membership figures legitimate that claim. In a crude sense, membership also means voters, and these individual voters can approach a legislator as constituents rather than as lobbyists. Studies show that legislators are more responsive to constituents than other petitioners (Ornstein and Elder, 1978: 88). For an interest group representing an industry, size has another aspect; the greater the size of the industry, the more important the industry is economically. Economic importance, especially in times of recession, is a powerful asset when petitioning policymakers worried about inflation and unemployment. Automakers, for example, were able to use the specter of widespread unemployment to convince policymakers to delay pollution controls (see chapter 6). All things being equal, therefore, a large group such as bankers are more likely to affect a regulatory policy than a small group like manufacturers of lawn mowers.

Resources.   Although size implies resources, those resources must still be mobilized and applied to public policy efforts. Consumers, for example, have massive resources but have only partially mobilized them (see Berry, 1977). Resources must also be applied. Some businesses are notorious for devoting few resources to public sector efforts. General Motors, for example, did not employ a full-time government lobbyist until 1969 (see Ornstein and Elder, 1978: 168). Groups must procure not only skilled analysts and lobbyists but also campaign contributions through a political action committee (PAC; see Ginsberg and Green, 1979). A lack of committed resources often explains why large corporations can be outmaneuvered by smaller public interest groups (e.g., the Clean Air Act or see Ornstein and Elder, 1978).

Dispersion.   Interest groups have an advantage if they are widely dispersed throughout the country rather than concentrated in a single geographic area. Dispersed groups can argue that they represent national rather than local interests. Dispersion also permits a group to appeal to many different members of Congress as constituents. Even though a major element of the economy, the steel industry was unable to get fast antidumping relief in the 1980s because the industry was regionally concentrated. In contrast, the savings and loan industry, a dispersed and locally controlled industry, was able to persuade Congress to pass the Garn-St Germain Depository Institutions Act of 1982 and to grant authority to issue All-Savers Certificates. Although many variables other than dispersion accounted for the differences between the steel industry and savings associations, dispersion was a definite advantage (Mulinix and Meier, 1983).

Cohesion.   Analysts of interest groups have long argued that the most effective lobby tactic is to provide technical and political information to allies (Zeigler and Peak, 1972; Milbrath, 1963). The value of information increases dramatically if it is the only information available. Cohesion among an interest's members is, therefore, a vital resource. If all automakers (including foreign manufacturers) would contend that achieving 29 miles per gallon for their entire sales fleet was impossible, they might have a good chance of convincing the EPA or Congress to ease such a requirement. Dissension, on the other hand, destroys the value of information. United Airlines' willingness to support airline deregulation in 1978 weakened the economic arguments of the other major airlines (Brown, 1981).

For those interest groups that rely on votes to persuade, cohesion is also important. Without cohesion, a group threatening electoral sanctions has little credibility. Organized labor's support for the Occupational Safety and Health Administration, for example, is backed by the unions' voting power. Recent evidence that union endorsements do not result in massive vote shifts, however, limits this resource (see Abramson, Aldrich, and Rohde, 1983).

Intensity of Commitment.   In distributive policy areas such as agriculture, health research, or education, interest groups are intensely committed to policy options. In general, few interest groups, especially industry groups, are intensely committed to regulatory agencies. Few industry groups, for example, even take the minimal effort necessary to appear at an agency's appropriations hearing. Regulatory agencies, for example, averaged 7.1 interest groups testifying on their behalf at appropriations hearings over a three-year period. Compare this figure to 14.7 for redistributive agencies and 58.1 for distributive agencies (Meier, 1979). Threats to deregulate an industry may be the only way to get intensity from an industry group and then only if the industry benefits from the regulation (e.g., trucking and the ICC).

Although they are rare, interest groups intensely committed to a regulatory agency or its goals do exist. Such nonindustry groups as auto safety advocates at the national level or Mothers Against Drunk Drivers (MADD) at the local level are two recent examples. Intensity translates into greater effort, which, depending on the agency's position relative to the group, could be a cost or a benefit to the regulator.

Prestige.   Francis Rourke (1984: 102) argues that the prestige of an interest group's members is a valuable asset. Physicians, according to Rourke, make better clientele than do ex-convicts. For most regulatory agencies, however, the prestige of interest group members varies little. All industry groups are usually comprised of producers with a vested interest in the regulation. Most nonindustry groups are likely to be professional consumer organizations. To be sure, a lobbyist from Chase Manhattan Bank may have slightly more prestige than one for the Land O' Lakes dairy cooperative, but these differences are relatively small. Prestige of interest group supporters, therefore, is unlikely to be an important variable in determining regulatory policy.

Number of Groups.   If the clientele of an agency are all organized into a single group, that group has the potential to dictate agency policy if the agency lacks other sources of support (Rourke, 1984). A regulatory agency, therefore, is more autonomous if the industry is divided into numerous small firms rather than a few large firms. With numerous firms, the opposition of one or two firms is not devastating. With a well-organized advocacy coalition opposing the industry, industry support is even less vital. The Federal Reserve System, therefore, should be less likely to conform to the dictates of 14,000 banks than the Interstate Commerce Commission is to the six major long-haul railroads, all other things being equal.

Coalition Breadth.   On specific regulatory issues, especially those before Congress, coalitional breadth becomes an important variable. Coalitional breadth is the number of different interests supporting a position.[5] A broad coalition links the regulated industry with interests outside the industry. In 1983 the American Bankers Association was able to attract the American Association of Retired Persons to its fight against tax withholding of savings' account interest (see chapter 3). Automobile companies coalesced with the United Auto Workers on a delay of Clean Air Act provisions (Ornstein and Elder, 1978); consumer groups and insurance companies both opposed the National Highway Traffic Safety Administration's 2.5 mile per hour bumper impact regulation (versus 5 miles per hour). Broad coalitions permit the coalition to argue it is seeking a broad public interest rather than a narrow self-interest; as a result, more political elites can be approached.

Interest groups, therefore, are more likely to intervene successfully in the regulatory process if they are large groups with resources and if they are dispersed, cohesive, intense, organized into a single group, and a member of a broad coalition, everything else being equal. To the extent that the interest group's opposition lacks these qualities, it is doubly strong. Even so, these resources are not sufficient for an interest group to dominate a regulator. The pharmaceutical industry has many of these characteristics, yet their dissatisfaction with the Food and Drug Administration indicates that they clearly do not dominate the FDA (Quirk, 1980). Interest group power is only one of the variables that in combination produce regulatory policy.

---

5. I am indebted to Robert Healy, a lobbyist for Atlantic Richfield, for pointing out the need for broad coalitions.

For nonindustry groups such as consumer groups, the resources just mentioned often must be supplemented by another—standing (see Berry, 1984: 199; Melnick, 1983: 10). Because regulations affect consumers indirectly, consumers may lack legal standing to intervene in the formal regulatory process. For example, the Federal Communications Commission held that the United Church of Christ lacked standing to challenge the license of television station KLBT. The church wanted the license revoked because KLBT had neither minority employees nor minority program content. The U.S. Court of Appeals (*United Church of Christ* v. *FCC*, 1966) reversed the FCC decision. Without standing, a nonindustry group is forced to abandon the administrative arena and fight its battles in political jurisdictions.

Interest group resources, then, are important in both pressing positions within the subsystem and in persuading political elites to intervene. The ability of an interest group to attain specific policy outcomes, in part, is determined by the political power of the interest group and its allies versus that of its opposition. The struggle between these advocacy coalitions occurs within the context of the macropolitical system, the next topic for discussion.

THE POLITICAL ENVIRONMENT

Although policy subsystems have been perceived as autonomous with the ability to operate independently from the larger political system, subsystems can be opened to the influence of political elites. Regulatory subsystems are especially permeable to political forces. Because regulatory subsystems generally impose costs rather than dispense benefits (Rourke, 1984: 53), regulatory subsystems lack the cohesion that other policy subsystems possess. The three main political forces in the environment of federal regulatory subsystems are Congress, the presidency, and the courts.[6] Each has the resources to intervene in the regulatory system if it desires.

Congress

Of all the actors in the political environment, Congress is the most concerned with regulatory policy. Regulatory agencies, especially independent regulatory commissions, are often perceived as congressional rather than executive agencies. Members of subcommittees that oversee regulatory agencies have always been heavily involved in regulatory policy. In the past, subcommittees operated with little interference from the entire Congress, but recent evidence indicates that norms such as deference to committees, specialization, and seniority that led to committee dominance have broken down. Deference to committees in the present Congress is far less than it was in the 1950s, and members of Congress are more likely to amend or reject a committee bill (Patterson, 1978: 160). Specialization, the conceded way to get ahead in Congress, has become less valued as members devote themselves to constituency service and, therefore, to more general roles. Even seniority was challenged with the 1974 freshman revolt. The impact of

6. The discussion in this section is limited to the federal level although the same forces apply at the state level.

changes in congressional norms is that individual members of Congress are more likely to be interested in the actions of a regulatory agency (especially if the agency regulates a constituent) and, therefore, more likely to intervene in the regulatory policy process.

Members of Congress have numerous avenues of influence if they seek to intervene in a regulatory subsystem. The most common methods are appropriations, legislation, hearings, legislative vetoes, and informal contact. Each has been used in the regulatory process to express displeasure to a regulatory agency or to encourage it to pursue a different path.

Appropriations.   Congress controls the purse strings of regulatory agencies through both the authorization and the appropriation process. Although across-the-board budget cuts are fairly blunt instruments, members of Congress have been creative in using the budget process to influence regulatory agencies. A prominent example is the use of authorization riders. When passing legislation that authorizes funds for an agency, amendments or riders are added that restrict agency actions. In the late 1970s and early 1980s, several members of Congress used this procedure to express displeasure with the Federal Trade Commission's consumer activism (Pertschuk, 1982). An authorization rider, for example, prohibited the FTC from pursuing its deceptive advertising case against children's cereal manufacturers. The appropriations process can also be used to assist an agency. Kemp (1982a) found that major airline crashes resulted in the appropriation of additional funds to the Federal Aviation Administration. The budget process, therefore, can be an effective method for members of Congress to attain specific regulatory goals.

Legislation.   Through the legislative process, Congress can issue instructions to regulatory agencies. Much regulatory legislation, especially the initial enabling legislation, is often vague, thus, vesting a great deal of discretion with the agency. In some cases, however, enabling legislation has been specific about goals and the timetables for achieving them (e.g., the Clean Air Act or the Clean Water Act; see Marcus, 1980; see also chapter 6).

Legislative actions can be used to alter agency procedures, change a single agency decision, or alter the agency's fundamental goals. The Magnuson-Moss Act of 1974, for example, required the Federal Trade Commission to use formal hearings in its rule-making process; the end result was major delays in issuing regulations (West, 1982). An example of Congress's intervening to change one decision is the FTC's initial attempt to regulate cigarette advertising (Fritschler, 1975). Responding to tobacco companies' appeals, Congress limited the FTC's actions in this area by substituting their own. Finally, the Airline Deregulation Act of 1978 fundamentally changed the goals of the Civil Aeronautics Board and moved the industry toward deregulation and the CAB toward its demise.

Hearings.   Part of the congressional oversight process includes hearings designed to determine what an agency has been doing or how new policy problems should be solved. In 1982, Senator Jake Garn's hearings on the savings and loan industry provided a forum for the S&Ls to plead their case. These hearings played a role in slowing down the deregulatory process of the Depository Institutions Deregulation Committee. Senate Judiciary

Committee hearings on airline deregulation, on the other hand, encouraged the Civil Aeronautics Board to continue its experimentation with deregulation under Chairman Alfred Kahn (Behrman, 1980). Similarly, hearings can be used to punish. Hearings in 1982 on implementation of the hazardous waste superfund law provided a forum to criticize agency actions and resulted in a contempt citation for EPA head Anne (Gorsuch) Burford for not supplying enforcement information. Eventually, Burford resigned under pressure.

Although hearings often result in legislation, they have an impact over and above any legislative activity. During hearings or in the committee report, specific instructions may be given to the agency about legislative intent (see Kirst, 1969). In addition, the simple fact that hearings are held cannot but affect an administrator's decision-making process. Hearings or the potential of hearings let the regulator know that actions will be subjected to public scrutiny. The anticipation of review may be as great a prod toward responsiveness to members of Congress than the actual hearings.

Hearings also enable Congress to influence regulation by participating in the appointment process. High-level agency personnel are subject to confirmation hearings. In such hearings, members of Congress can express policy positions or even refuse to confirm nominees. In 1983, Congress delayed approving President Reagan's ICC nominees, Paul Lamboley and Jane Holt, for policy reasons. To avoid such problems, presidents sometimes invite legislators to participate in selecting regulatory nominees. Conservative Senator Paul Laxalt, for example, was reportedly instrumental in the appointments of Interior Secretary James Watt and EPA administrator Anne Burford (see Greenwald, 1977:229 for earlier examples).

The Legislative Veto.   In past years the legislative veto was a popular method among members of Congress for controlling bureaucratic action. According to the Congressional Research Service, legislative veto provisions were placed in over two hundred pieces of legislation (Norton, 1976). The legislative veto operated as follows. Congress delegated the authority to make rules regarding some industry or activity to a regulatory agency. After these rules were issued but before they went into effect, the rules were sent to Congress. Congress, then, could veto these rules by voting to reject them. Although the veto process appears simple, in practice there were numerous types of veto. Some legislation provided veto by one house of Congress; others by both houses. Some vetoes required Congress to vote no whereas other rules were vetoed if Congress failed to vote yes. The constitutionality of the legislative veto is open to question; the Supreme Court declared legislative vetoes unconstitutional in an immigration case (*INS v. Chadha*, 1983). Congressional supporters are currently seeking a version of the veto that will pass court scrutiny (Cohen, 1983).

Even though a constitutional cloud hangs over the legislative veto, it has been used effectively to alter regulatory decisions. The Federal Trade Commission in 1982 had its used car dealers rule vetoed (a fairly modest rule that required used car dealers to specify if certain parts of the car were in working order or had not been checked). In fact, the anticipation of a veto may well have been the reason that the FTC used car rule was so modest. Legislative vetoes remain popular among members of Congress despite the constitutional question; Representative Elliot Levitas of Georgia has proposed that all regulations be subject to legislative veto provisions, and his proposal has attracted numerous cosponsors.

Informal Contact.   Informal contact is just that—any informal contact between a member of Congress and a regulatory agency. Informal contact exists and in all likelihood affects the direction of regulatory policy somewhat, but it is generally hidden from public view and, therefore, difficult to study. If informal contact in regulation resembles that in other policy areas (and there is no reason to think it does not), then the contact normally results from a constituent complaint and seeks an exception from current regulatory policy (see McCubbins and Schwartz, 1984). For example, a constituent might complain to a member of Congress that the Federal Energy Regulatory Commission (FERC) has been slow to respond to a petition for a rule exception. A call to FERC from the member will likely increase the speed of a decision although not necessarily change its content.

In sum, then, a member of Congress has numerous ways to intervene in regulatory policy. Subsystem members (e.g., member of the oversight and appropriations subcommittees) intervene frequently; other legislators are less active. Some interventions require the support of a majority of members (e.g., legislation, budgets) whereas others can be done by the individual member (hearings, informal contact). Because the avenues exist, the only question is whether or not the individual member has the resources and skills to intervene successfully.

The Presidency

The president is the political actor least likely to intervene in a regulatory policy subsystem. The press of foreign policy and major domestic issues means that presidents rarely have the time to focus on regulation, a fairly small portion of the overall federal government (Welborn, 1977: 146). Despite this situation and the historical avoidance of regulation, recent presidents have been involved in regulatory policy. Gerald Ford became an early advocate of deregulation. Jimmy Carter was perhaps the most active president in regulatory policy, recruiting consumer advocates to government posts and sponsoring numerous deregulation initiatives. Ronald Reagan stressed regulation in his campaign and established an institutionalized review process through the Office of Management and Budget.

Assuming that a president or his staff want to influence regulatory policy, what avenues are open to him or them? Terry Moe (1982) suggests that presidents can exercise influence in three ways—appointments, oversight, and leadership. Although Moe presented his argument for independent regulatory commissions only, it is appropriate for all regulatory agencies. To Moe's three avenues of influence, a fourth is added, budgeting (which he includes as part of oversight but which merits separate discussion; see Wilson, 1980; F. J. Thompson, 1982).

Appointments.   Through the appointment process, the president can name the head of every regulatory agency. In larger agencies such as the EPA, he can name several top administrators. Although, in theory, this power is limited in regulatory commissions with multimember boards and overlapping terms, in practice, it is not. The president can designate the commission chairperson who normally exercises the most power (see Welborn, 1977: 132), and early resignations often provide the opportunity to appoint a commission majority (Scher, 1960; Greenwald, 1977: 229).

The appointment power, even though subject in most cases to senatorial confirmation, provides the president with a major vehicle for influencing regulation. By appointing regulators who share his general political views, a president can change a key actor in the subsystem and influence the general direction of agency policy. Reagan's appointment of James Miller III to replace Michael Pertschuk as head of the Federal Trade Commission, for example, limited the consumer activism of the FTC. Similarly, Reagan's replacement of Darius Gaskins with Reese Taylor slowed the movement of trucking deregulation at the Interstate Commerce Commission. With agencies headed by one person, the impact can be even more dramatic. The appointment of Anne (Gorsuch) Burford as head of the Environmental Protection Agency resulted in major internal struggles over policy and the reduced credibility of the agency (Vig and Kraft, 1984).

Appointments only offer the potential to influence regulation. If regulatory appointments are used as patronage rewards (e.g., many state public utility commissions before 1970; Anderson, 1980) rather than for policy reasons, then the president will exercise little influence over the direction of regulatory policy (see Kemp, 1983).

Leadership. Simply because a person is president, that person's public policy views become legitimate. As a result even without direct contact, the president may influence a regulator to pursue given policy options. Reagan's general position on regulation as well as his criticism of the Occupational Safety and Health Administration provided enough incentive for Thorne Auchter to reduce the enforcement activities of OSHA; under Auchter the volume of fines dropped by 49 percent from 1980 to 1981. Similar arguments could be made about President Carter and consumer protection agencies. Carter's proconsumer views were pursued by several regulatory agencies.

A president's powers are not limited to persuasion. A president bent on influencing regulation has direct powers that allow it. When the then-Department of Health, Education, and Welfare proposed banning father-son and mother-daughter school functions as discrimination on the basis of sex, President Ford "vetoed" the regulation. Similarly when several Carter appointees attempted to promulgate new regulations on the last day of the Carter administration, President Reagan held up these regulations so that they could be evaluated by his people. The informal elements of presidential leadership are undergirded by the president's formal powers.

The formal powers of the president are not without limit. Presidential actions must conform to legal and constitutional restrictions. When the Reagan administration's National Highway Traffic Safety Administration abolished the 5 mile per hour bumper standard, for example, the Supreme Court rejected the rule withdrawal. Because NHTSA did not follow the procedures for promulgating a rule when they withdrew the rule, the action was illegal (*Motor Vehicle Manufacturers* v. *State Farm*, 1983).

Budgets. Just as budgets can be used by Congress to guide regulatory policy, so can they be used by the president. All "dependent" regulatory agencies and many independent regulatory commissions request funds via the executive budget. For an agency such as the Occupational Safety and Health Administration or the Agricultural Marketing Service, this means presidential appointees both in the executive department (in this case, the Department of Labor and the Department of Agriculture) and in the Office of Management and Budget (OMB) must pass on the budget request. The president or his agents, therefore, have ample opportunity to eliminate or add funds for a specific program or for the entire agency. Agencies favored by the administration may be given generous budgets so that they may pursue their objectives with greater vigor. Agencies out of favor may be limited in funds and, thus, prevented from taking aggressive actions opposed by the White House (see Kemp, 1982b; Stewart, et al., 1982).

Natchez and Bupp (1973), in their study of the old Atomic Energy Commission (AEC), an agency with some regulatory powers (now the Nuclear Regulatory Commission), found that the common perception of budgeting as incremental and without policy content was not correct. To be sure, the overall AEC budget changed in an incremental manner, indicating that budgets were used only infrequently as a policy control. An examination of budgets at the program level, however, revealed major year-to-year fluctuations, thus suggesting that budgets have sufficient flexibility to affect program direction (see Tucker, 1982 on incrementalism).

Oversight.   The management reforms of recent presidents (program budgeting, zero-base budgeting, cost-benefit analysis, and so on) can be viewed as efforts to increase the president's oversight capabilities. Although all presidents, by definition, exercise oversight over all federal agencies, regulatory agencies are targets of specific review mechanisms. President Ford required inflation impact statements for major regulations and subjected regulations to review by the Council on Wage and Price Stability (COWPS). President Carter created the Regulatory Analysis Review Group (RARG) to review major regulations. Similarly, President Reagan had formal regulatory oversight through the Task Force on Regulatory Relief (eliminated in 1983), headed by Vice-President George Bush, and required all major rules be subjected to cost-benefit analysis by OMB.

The existence of regulatory oversight in and of itself plays a role in influencing regulation. Regulators know that others will be looking at a regulation and its supporting analysis. The subsystem, therefore, is by definition open to outside influences. The rational regulator will seek to anticipate this oversight and be sufficiently responsive to avoid reversal (see Friedrich, 1940 on anticipated reactions). Even if the oversight organization cannot achieve its goals via anticipated reaction, it still has the option of formal intervention. At the very least, these oversight mechanisms can delay the promulgation of a regulation.

In sum, the president has at his disposal four avenues to intervene in regulatory policy. Given the weaknesses of regulatory subsystems, the president should be able to win many of these interventions. Moe (1982), for example, examined presidential influence on three regulatory agencies—the National Labor Relations Board, the Securities and Exchange Commission, and the Federal Trade Commission. He found that the policy outputs of these regulatory agencies varied systematically across presidential administrations. Implied in these findings is the conclusion that presidents can and do influence the actions of regulatory agencies.

The key variables, therefore, are the president's interest in regulation and his willingness to expend his political resources to intervene. No federal regulatory agency, not even the Board of Governors of the Federal Reserve, can resist the pressures of a president who devoted full time and all presidential resources to that pressure. Even the modest efforts of our three most recent presidents have contributed to major changes in regulatory policy.

Courts

In recent years courts, especially the federal court system, have been active in regulatory policy (see Melnick, 1983). Regulation has attracted numerous lawyers and as a result has turned much of the regulatory process into legal battles. Disputes that cannot be resolved between the various advocacy coalitions in a subsystem quite naturally end up in court. Initially, courts were hostile to the concept of regulation; the Interstate Commerce Commission, for example, lost 15 of the first 16 cases that it took to the Supreme Court (Belzoni, D'Antonio, and Helfand, 1977: 42). Over the past hundred years, the courts' position has moderated and stabilized to a more neutral role. Courts offer relief to regulatory "victims" under two general criteria—procedural violations and substantive wrongs.

Procedure.   An entire legal profession has grown up around regulatory agency procedure. Administrative law concerns the procedures that must be followed so that persons (and corporations are considered as persons) are not deprived of life, liberty, or property without due process of law. Because regulation by definition limits the choices of individuals, it, in a legal sense, deprives persons of full use of property. The Administrative Procedure Act of 1946 specifies proper regulatory procedures for most agencies.

Due process in administrative law is most detailed concerning adjudications—the determination of whether or not an individual has violated a government regulation. In such a case, a person must be given notice of the actions being considered and must be granted the right to be heard on the issue, the right to submit evidence on his or her behalf, the right to confront and challenge evidence against him or her, and the right to a decision by an impartial arbitrator. In addition, if found in violation, the person has some limited right to appeal. Although some agencies are exempted from the Administrative Procedure Act and others have more elaborate procedures, these are the basic procedural protections in administrative law (see Davis, 1972; Warren, 1982: 362 ff.; Heffron with McFeeley, 1983: 268 ff.; Cooper, 1983: 143 ff.).

Agencies are fairly adept at the practice of administrative law; after all, they have many years of experience. As a result, procedural challenges to agency decisions are unlikely to succeed. Studies have shown that some agencies win 90 percent of their cases in court (see Cannon and Giles, 1972). Despite agency dominance in the courts, some challenges on procedural matters do succeed and do result in policy change. The United Church of Christ sued the Federal Communications Commission over the ruling that the church did not have standing to challenge the television license of another party (*United Chuch of Christ* v. *FCC*, 1966). The Church of Christ was granted standing by the Court of Appeals and used the implied threat of this standing to negotiate greater minority hiring and minority program content in exchange for dropping the challenge (see Krasnow, Longley, and Terry, 1982). In general, courts have extended standing to a wide variety of individuals who wish to participate in the regulatory process (Melnick, 1983: 10).

Substance.   Courts have hesitated to address substantive regulatory issues. Because judges are generalists and bureaucrats are not, courts tend to defer to bureaucratic expertise. Individuals challenging regulations bear the costs of this deference because the burden of proof lies with the challenger, not with the regulator.

Despite this deference, one challenge has always been acceptable in a court of law—that the regulator has overstepped legislative intent. If the citizen can demonstrate that a regulation is contrary to statute or exceeds the authority that Congress delegated, then the court may void the regulatory action. Because many regulatory statutes are exceedingly general, urging regulation in the public interest, convenience, or necessity, overstepping legislative intent is difficult to do and equally difficult to prove. In addition, the agency need only demonstrate that its decision is supported by substantial evidence. This criterion is weaker than either the civil (preponderance of the evidence) or the criminal (beyond a reasonable doubt) standards for a factual decision. This vests greater discretion with the regulator.

According to Martin Shapiro (1982), however, recent Supreme Court and Courts of Appeals decisions suggest that the courts are going beyond the "legislative intent" criteria (see also Melnick, 1983: 11). Shapiro argues that courts are asking not only whether decision X was made correctly but also whether it was the correct decision. In a case involving the Occupational Safety and Health Administration regulation limiting workplace exposure to benzene (*Industrial Union Department* v. *American Petroleum Institute*, 1980), the Supreme Court voided the rule because OSHA did not produce sufficient evidence to support a conclusion that the specific standard would provide greater benefits. Although the Court later ruled that this did not mean regulation must provide more benefits than costs (see *American Textile Manufacturers* v. *Donavan*, 1981), it does broaden the focus of judicial review.

Courts have been criticized as ineffective checks on bureaucratic action because they are too slow, too passive, and too costly and because they lack appropriate remedies (Meier, 1979). Accepting this conclusion overlooks the obvious. Although courts cannot dominate the regulatory process, they can profoundly influence it. Over the last 50 years agency procedures have become heavily judicialized, thus slowing the process of regulation. Courts, by invoking their jurisdiction, can be of assistance to those who would benefit from delay. Every major health standard issued by OSHA except one, for example, has been challenged in court. Although OSHA has won all these cases but one (the benzene case), in each case the regulation's effective date was delayed pending the court decision. The regulated industry benefits from this delay because it postpones the day when expenditures must be made to comply with the regulation. As the myriad of lawsuits under the National Environmental Policy Act (NEPA) reveals, however, delay can also be used by the forces for greater regulation if delay penalizes the industry.

In sum, then, courts are a neutral weapon in the politics of regulation.

Figure 2.3 The environment of regulatory policy

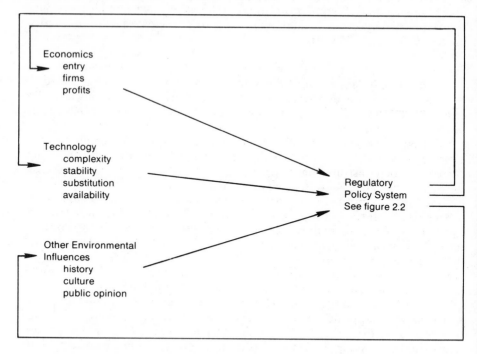

They offer a resource to those participants who would benefit from delaying changes in the status quo. Although courts offer a chance of reversing a regulatory decision, they usually only grant a delay. A delay, however, can be used to marshal other political resources to combat the regulation.

THE GENERAL ENVIRONMENT

The regulatory policy system made up of the regulatory subsystem and the set of immediate political forces that play on it is set in a broader environment that affects both components (see figure 2.3). Numerous forces in the environment influence regulation and the politics of regulation— history, political culture, public opinion, the legal system, public philosophy, and so on. Many of these influences are remote and indirect. Two environmental factors, however, directly impact on regulatory policy and limit the options of the regulators—economics and technology. Economics and technology structure the decisions that can be made by regulators and political elites. They limit the choices available to each decision-maker, and they also create opportunities for politicians and subsystem members to exploit.

Economics

Economics has played a continuous role in the literature on regulation. The classical justifications for regulation, for example, are economic; regulation is justified when the market system fails. Such market failures as monopoly, imperfect information, and externalities result in situations when government should consider the possibility of regulating (Stokey and Zeckhauser, 1978). Although market failures might be used to justify regulation in the economic version of the "public interest" theory, they are not the economic variables most likely to affect the direction of regulatory policy. The key economic variables for this purpose are ease of entry, number of firms, and profitability.

Ease of entry.   Both ease of entry and number of firms relate to the market structure of an industry. Ease of entry is defined as the difficulty in starting a new firm in the industry. For example, entry into the railroad industry is difficult because large capital investments are necessary to construct track and purchase equipment. In other areas such as the establishment of a genetic research firm, the barrier to entry is expertise. Not included as barriers to entry in this framework are political barriers to entry. For example, numerous professions use state-granted licensing powers to restrict entry to their profession. This is a political barrier to entry, not an economic one.

Ease of entry is a key variable in regulation because it determines the potential of adding new firms to the industry. Adding more firms to an industry may increase its competitiveness. When an industry is competitive, a regulator has more options available, including efforts to deregulate. For example, the trucking industry has some 18,000 licensed carriers, and entry was easy during the last year of the Carter administration. Deregulating and the benefits of spirited competition are more likely in trucking than in the railroad industry, where only six viable long-haul railroads currently exist. The greater the ease of entry, therefore, the less likely that regulation will be in the interests of the regulated.

Number of Firms.   The number of firms in an industry affects the regulator's options in two ways. Similar to the case of ease of entry, the greater the number of firms in an industry, the more likely it is that the actions of one or more firms cannot affect price or overall supply. In situations similar to this, a semifree market exists that may optimally allocate goods among their best uses.

In addition, the existence of numerous firms means that the failure of a single firm is less likely to be noticed. The failure of Braniff in 1982, for example, subjected the airline deregulation efforts to the scrutiny of political elites. The economic failure of a law firm, on the other hand, would be unlikely to generate much interest from the state bar association. Because failures are a sign in a capitalist economy that weak firms are being eliminated, the ability to absorb some failures permits a regulatory agency to preside over a healthier industry.

Failures are especially important from a policy perspective when a firm is so large that its failure creates negative externalities for others. U.S. Steel, for example, is so integrated with the rest of the economy that its failure would have repercussions for thousands of other firms. In such a case, regulatory options are restricted.

The number of firms also affects such interest group variables as cohesion and the number of interest groups. As firms increase, cohesion should decline, and the number of competing interest groups should increase. The end result of more firms should be less regulation in the interests of the regulated.

Profitability.   Industries vary a great deal in their return on investment. The television industry, for example, in some years had a return on investment of over 100 percent (Strickland, 1980: 272) whereas the savings and loan industry had a negative return on investment for 1982 (see Carron, 1982). Although industries with low profits may create demands for regulation, a low profit structure limits the type of regulation that a regulator can undertake. From the 1950s to the 1970s, for example, dry cleaning was a declining industry as the result of innovations in clothes and fabrics. Efforts to regulate workplace safety in this environment were futile because any additional costs usually bankrupted the cleaners, and efforts to set prices were unsuccessful because profit-conscious (i.e., desperate) cleaners were always willing to undercut regulated prices to gain a larger share of the market (see Meier and Plumlee, 1979).

In an industry with ample profits, the regulators do not need to be as concerned about imposing costs on the industry. In the television industry, for example, imposing public service costs would be reasonably easy (if the FCC were so inclined) from an economic perspective because profits are large enough to absorb the costs. Many of those profits are, in fact, monopoly profits resulting from a government license. In sum, therefore, higher profits create the potential for regulation in the interests of the nonregulated. Whether this potential is realized, however, is a function of numerous other subsystem and environmental variables.

Feedback.   Although economic factors influence the direction of regulatory policy, they clearly do not determine it. One need only take a look at any economic analysis of regulation in the past 20 years to see that economic factors do not determine policy (see MacAvoy, 1979). In fact, more often the other argument is seen—that policy affects economics.

What occurs is a simple feedback mechanism. Much regulatory policy is an output into the environment. Much of this policy is intended to affect the economic system, and much of it does. The large profits in the television industry may be attributed to early FCC decisions about the allocation of very high frequency (VHF) and ultrahigh frequency (UHF) stations (see Krasnow, Longley, and Terry, 1982). Utility regulation before the energy crisis allowed sufficient return on investment to attract the necessary capital for expansion (Anderson, 1980). At the present time, industries continually complain about the costs that regulation imposes on them, a clear indication that policy feeds back to affect economic factors in the environment (see Weidenbaum, 1981, on the costs of regulation).

Technology

Technology encompasses the production technology of the industry. In large part, technology determines the economics of the industry; complex technologies create barriers to entry and thus determine if a market is competitive or not. The elements of production technology relevant here are complexity, stability, and substitutability. Similar to economic factors, each of these limits the options available to the regulator and influences the direction of regulatory policy.

Complexity.   Complexity is the closeness of the industry's technology to the scientific state of the art. Industries engaged in genetic engineering or computers, for example, have technologies that are very close to, if not actually at, the state of the art in genetic research and computer design. Barbers, on the other hand, have very uncomplex technologies that are readily apparent to the layperson.

Technological 'complexity discourages close regulation. The more complex an industry is, the more likely it will not be easily understood by the regulator without large research budgets. This complexity should yield regulatory policy that reflects deference on the part of the regulator because ill-advised regulation may be harmful to the industry. Regulation may even evolve toward self-regulation. Industries with simple technologies, on the other hand, can be subjected to greater scrutiny and more restrictive regulation.

Stability.   The stability of an industry's technology is the rate of change in the basic technology of production. Some industries' technologies are slow to change; the trucking industry, for example, has had little change in its basic technology over the past 50 years. Similarly, the American railroad industry has not adopted even the elementary technologies of other nations' railroads. Other industries have rapidly changing technologies. The banking industry, for example, although not an industry known for technologial complexity, has undergone rapid changes in the past ten years as the result of computerization. Broadcast communication is now entering an era of high unstability with the introduction of direct satellite broadcasting, low-power television, microwave distribution systems, and innovations in cable capacity.

The greater the instability of an industry's technology, the more opportunities the regulator has to change how the industry is regulated. Computerization and innovation in the securities industry, for example, made bank deregulation a feasible political proposition. Although instability provides opportunities, this does not mean that the opportunities will be taken. Industry may well mount large campaigns to restrict the introduction of new technology that might disrupt the status quo (Krasnow, Longley, and Terry, 1982).

Substitutability.   Substitutability is the extent that substitutes are available for the industry's products or services. Are there alternative technologies available in the industry or in other industries that would permit someone to offer a comparable good or service? For example, rail passenger service can easily be replaced and was replaced to a significant extent by intercity airline service and private automobiles. In the 1980s the spread of computer technology and access to international money markets allowed nonbank institutions such as brokerage firms, credit card companies, and major retailers to offer services previously available only through banks.

The greater the availability of alternative technologies, the more discretion the regulator has in implementing public policy and the less likely regulation will be used to benefit the industry. In fact, this may create the impetus to act. Alternative investment instruments for small investors offered by money market funds, for example, created the pressure to permit depository institutions to offer similar instruments (Meier, 1982). Again, the availability of alternative technology only provides the opportunity for action; it does not guarantee it. In fact, political pressures may well close off options as the FCC did for a period of time when microwave long-distance calls became a reality.

Availability.   A fourth aspect of technology is not part of the production technology of the industry. The availability of a technology refers to whether or not a technology is available to achieve a regulatory goal. For example, if Congress decreed that by 1987 all U.S. automobiles would achieve fuel efficiency of 65 miles per gallon of gasoline, the technology to attain this may not be available. On the other hand, the technology for producing cable systems with 100 channels is feasible.

The availability of a technology to achieve regulatory goals is a key issue in the regulation of the environment, energy production, automobile safety, worker health and safety, and other areas. If the feasibility of reaching a policy goal can be challenged, the industry has the potential to win regulatory battles. In anticipation of such challenges, the regulator may well push less vigorous regulation. Nothing detracts from the reputation of a regulator more than promulgating a standard that is impossible to achieve.

Feedback.   Similar to the case of the economic environment, regulatory policy also feeds back to the technological environment and influences its development. Regulatory policy may encourage new technology as the Environmental Protection Agency has done with its innovative bubble concept. Regulation may also restrict the development or the adoption of technology; the FCC restricted the development of cable TV for many years and currently may be similarly restricting stereo amplitude modulation (AM) radio; the ICC restricted innovations in railroad cars designed to improve efficiency (Fellmuth, 1970); and OSHA's reliance on engineering standards rather than performance standards is likely restricting development of new safety techniques.

SUMMARY

This chapter presented an outline of the regulatory process that will be used to analyze regulatory policy in the remaining chapters. Regulatory policy can be characterized by who benefits from the regulation; two dimensions of beneficiaries exist—the regulated industry and the nonregulated. Each are separate dimensions because regulatory policy can benefit both the regulated and the nonregulated, and it can also benefit no one.

To determine who benefits from regulatory policy, the locus of regulatory decision making must be determined. Essentially, the locus of regulatory decision making means whether or not regulatory policy is set within the regulatory subsystem with little guidance by macropolitical forces. Subsystems can be either relatively autonomous, or they can be affected by a large number of interventions on the part of Congress, the president, and other political elites. The key variables in determining the autonomy of the subsystem are the regulatory issue's salience and complexity. Issues that are complex and issues that are not salient are generally left to the subsystem. Issues that are simple and issues that are salient attract political intervention.

If a subsystem is semiautonomous, then the key question is whether or

not the regulatory bureaucracy dominates the subsystem or if the bureaucracy is reduced to a more passive role of mediating disputes among the
active interests. A subsystem is likely to be under greater control of the
regulatory bureaucracy if the bureaucracy has political resources such as
expertise, cohesion, strong legislative authority, and good leadership. If the
bureaucracy lacks these resources, regulatory policy is likely to be determined by the interplay of the various advocacy coalitions.

In a subsystem with the bureaucracy as the dominant actor, who benefits from regulation is determined by a variety of factors. If the regulatory
agency operates under specific goals, has universal authority (i.e., no limitations on its range of authority), has effective sanctions, and is not limited by
procedural restrictions, regulation is likely to be in the interests of the
nonregulated. Agencies with vague goals, limited authority, few sanctions,
and weak procedures are more likely to regulate in the interests of the
regulated. If the issue area is salient but not salient enough to limit subsystem autonomy, regulation is more likely to reflect the interests of the nonregulated. In addition, the policy goals of the regulatory agency staff and
leadership are extremely important. To the extent that regulators identify
with the industry rather than with regulation, regulation will benefit the
regulated industry.

In a subsystem where the bureaucracy plays a lesser role, policy is
determined by the interplay between the advocacy coalitions. In general,
two major coalitions will exist, one representing the interests of the regulated industry and one opposed to those interests. Which coalition gains the
upper hand depends on a series of variables. Coalitions that are large; have
resources; and are dispersed, cohesive, intense, and broad have advantages
over those that lack these characteristics. Because advocacy coalitions include bureaucrats, legislators, legislative staff, state and local government
officials, researchers, and journalists as well as interest groups, these variables must be applied to the advocacy coalitions as a whole, not just to the
interest groups.

In an advocacy-coalition-dominated subsystem, the direction of regulation is a function of two variables. The first is obvious; the goals of the
dominant advocacy coalition are the primary factor. If the industry advocacy coalition overwhelms all others, regulation will be in the interests of
the industry. If the nonindustry coalition overwhelms the industry coalition,
regulation will be in the interests of the nonregulated. When the coalitions
are relatively balanced, regulation will be balanced. Also important in such
subsystems is the cohesion of the regulatory industry because the degree of
cohesion affects the power of the industry advocacy coalition. When the
industry lacks cohesion, regulation in the interests of the nonregulated is
more likely.

In regulatory areas where subsystems lack autonomy, Congress and the
president play a greater role. Congress has access to legislation, appropriations, oversight, and informal contacts to influence the actions of regulatory
subsystems. The president can affect regulatory policy via appointments,
budgeting, leadership, and oversight. Courts perform a generally neutral
role, but they can be used by other political actors to delay and to attempt
to change regulatory outcomes.

The political forces take place within an economic and technological
environment that creates opportunities for some actors and places restraints

on others. This environment can also influence the direction of regulatory policy by strengthening the hand of those seeking greater regulation or those wanting to permit the industry to regulate itself. In economic terms, when entry to the industry is easy, when the number of firms is large, and when profits are generally high, regulation in the interests of the nonregulated is more likely. In technological terms, when industry technologies are simple, when technologies are changing, and when substitutes exist, regulation will likely be in the interests of the nonregulated.

In any area of regulation, having all the variables point in the same direction will be unlikely. In some cases, the environment might favor regulation in the interests of the regulated whereas the political and bureaucratic forces suggest regulation in the interests of the nonregulated. The hypotheses presented in this chapter, therefore, should all be qualified with this caveat: all other things being equal. In cases when all other things are not equal, the interplay of the various forces on regulation can be observed to determine the relative influence of each variable.

3

Depository Institutions: Banks, Savings Associations, and Credit Unions

Federal regulation of depository institutions is fairly strict. Because banks and thrifts take money from consumers, the federal government recognizes a public interest in the stability and safety of these insitutions. Without a stable system of banking, commerce as we know it is not possible. This chapter examines government regulation of depository institutions. After the structure of the financial industries is discussed, the various regulatory agencies will be described. The politics of creation in this area has set a general tone for regulation since the Great Depression. Understanding the historical antecedents of financial regulation goes a fair distance in explaining current regulatory policies. The industry underwent substantial economic deregulation in the 1980s. An examination of this period will focus the chapter on current politics and current issues. Finally, an effort will be made to link the regulation of depository institutions back to the regulatory framework in chapter 2.

THE FINANCIAL INDUSTRY

Reference to the financial industry is a misnomer; in fact, there are several financial industries. Each of these industries acts as a financial intermediary—it collects money from one group of individuals and lends it to others. In a generic sense, they all perform the same function; in actuality, each industry was created to fill a specific need not served by the others. Until recently, each industry was regulated within a separate subsystem by different government regulators. The barriers between these industries are dropping rapidly, thus creating some unique problems. This section will discuss the nine major financial intermediaries in the United States— commercial banks, savings associations, mutual savings banks, credit unions, finance companies, investment companies, pension funds, insurance companies, and money market funds.

Commercial Banks

Commercial banks are the full service institutions that people normally identify as banks. Ranging in size from the California-based Bank of America to the local bank in a rural community, approximately 14,000 banks with some 39,000 branches have assets in excess of $1.8 trillion (United States League of Savings Associations [USLSA], 1982). In a subdivided financial world (e.g., pre-1970), commercial banks serviced the day-to-day needs of depositors (usually checking accounts and large savings accounts) and loaned money on short-term notes to business. Commercial banks are usually formed as stock companies, an economic characteristic that distinguishes them from thrift institutions.

Commercial banks, as can be imagined, are a powerful political force in the United States. They have the prestige, resources, and dispersion that Rourke (1984) deems necessary for influence. Some 280 political action committees are bank related (Keller, 1982: 191). The banking industry is not monolithic; however, the large money center banks (e.g., Chase Manhattan, Citibank, Marine Midland) often have goals that differ from those of the small rural bank. The Redfield State Bank of South Dakota, for example, is more concerned with rural credit and agricultural policy than with Brazil's credit rating (a major worry for Citibank). Large banks often represent themselves, but recently the American Bankers' Association (ABA) has advocated their interest in deregulation.[1] Smaller banks are more likely to belong to the Independent Bankers Association of America and identify with its concerns about competition from larger banks.

Savings Associations

Savings asociations, normally called savings and loans, were designed as a specialized financial institution to provide funds for purchasing houses. A savings association, in the pre-1970s era, attracted long-term savings from the small saver and loaned this money to individuals to purchase homes under long-term mortgages. In the United States, some 4,300 savings associations with over 22,000 offices (similar to a branch for a bank) have assets of $664 billion (USLSA, 1982). With their heavy investment in home mortgages, savings associations are affected directly by the national economy and its impact on home construction. Savings associations also are adversely affected by rapid changes in interest rates because they loan funds for periods as long as 30 years. Savings associations may be organized as stock companies or as mutuals though most choose the latter.

Even though savings associations vary greatly in terms of size and the role they play in long-term finance, they have generally spoken with a unified voice in lobby efforts. The U.S. League of Savings Associations, (USLSA), originally founded to combat "unethical" business practices by "National Savings Associations" earlier in this century, now represents most of the nation's savings associations. Savings associations not only have

---

1. In fact, almost all banks belong to the ABA, but in recent years this organization has taken a decidedly large-bank viewpoint. Many of the largest banks represent themselves or work through the Association of Bank Holding Companies. Bankpac, the ABA's political action committee, contributed $650,000 to candidates during the 1982 elections (Keller, 1982: 191).

many characteristics of successful interest groups (e.g., size, resources, prestige), but they also never want for allies. Housing interest groups such as the National Association of Home Builders can usually be found in the same coalition with the savings associations.

Mutual Savings Banks

Mutual savings banks, like savings associations, originally developed because commercial banks were not interested in offering savings accounts to individuals (Mayer, 1974: 190). Based on a mutual system of organization (that is, they have no stockholders; depositors technically purchase an interest in the bank), mutual savings banks are state chartered and located mostly in the Northeast. They were designed to encourage saving (especially among the working class) and invested initially in government bonds and later in home mortgages (Spellman, 1982: 20). In 1981, 500 mutual savings banks had assets of approximately $176 billion.

Mutual savings banks have developed less political clout than other depository institutions for both resources reasons and motivational reasons. In terms of resources, mutual savings banks, because they are regionally concentrated, do not have access to a great number of legislators. In addition, mutual savings banks did not suffer a great trauma from the depression and, as a result, had no motivation to seek government help. In fact, they often declined government assistance (e.g., deposit insurance) to avoid regulation. Mutual savings banks were organized as the National Association of Mutual Savings Banks until 1982. At that time they merged with a small savings and loan association to form the National Council of Savings Institutions.

Credit Unions

Credit Unions are depository institutions that serve a defined group of persons based on a common bond of employment, association, or residence. Normally affiliated with an employer, credit unions accept deposits (they refer to deposits as the purchase of shares in the credit union) and make installment loans to members. Credit unions seek to provide cheap funds for member loans while at the same time earning higher interest for member deposits. They have the potential to do this because the common bond (knowing the member) reduces the risk of a bad loan and because operating overhead is pared to a minimum (often with volunteer labor). Credit unions are generally small; 23,000 credit unions have assets of $78 billion.

Credit unions are represented by the Credit Union National Association (CUNA). Although greatly dispersed throughout the country, credit unions have some organizational liabilities. Credit unions are generally small, and they do not produce the local political activists that banks and savings associations do. In addition, by providing services in a somewhat closed market, credit unions can escape the financial pressures that squeeze other institutions. If demand for loans dries up or interest rates are too low, credit unions often deposit their funds in commercial banks.

The four financial institutions just discussed—commercial banks, savings associations, mutual savings banks, and credit unions—are referred to as depository institutions and will be the major focus of this chapter. Savings associations, mutual savings banks, and credit unions are often collectively termed "thrifts" (from the early effort to encourage thrift among workers) to distinguish them from commercial banks. The economics and technology of depository institutions will be discussed in depth after a brief discussion of the other financial intermediaries.

Other Financial Intermediaries

Investment Companies.   Investment companies perform a service similar to that of a depository institution. They sell shares in their company to investors and use the proceeds to purchase stocks (e.g., a mutual fund). Before the 1970s realignment, the role of investment companies was to provide investors with the opportunity to earn a higher rate of return in exchange for a greater risk. On the output side, investment companies provide funds to corporations to conduct business. In 1981 approximately 900 investment companies had assets of $55 billion (USLSA, 1982).

Money Market Funds.   Money market funds are the newest financial intermediary. Operated similarly to an investment company, they sell shares to individuals and use the money to purchase commercial paper and government bonds. Essentially, these funds aggregate small savings so that individuals can gain access to investments previously reserved for large investors. Although the growth in money market funds from 1978 to 1982 was phenomenal, the funds appear to have leveled off with assets of $182 billion (USLSA, 1982).

Insurance Companies.   Insurance companies, especially life insurance companies that can plan their payouts actuarially, operate as financial intermediaries. They accept premiums from individuals (some policies actually have savings) and invest that money in corporate bonds, corporate equities, and mortgages until it is needed to pay claims (Johnson and Roberts, 1982: 298). In 1981, some 1,800 insurance companies had over $521 billion in assets (USLSA, 1982).

Finance Companies.   Finance companies specialize in consumer loans; approximately 45 percent of their loans are personal loans, and 32 percent are for automobiles. Finance companies often specialize; there are personal finance companies, business finance companies, mortgage finance companies, and sales finance companies (e.g., automotive finance corporations run by automobile manufacturers; see Johnson and Roberts, 1982: 302–304). Finance companies do not have depositors; they raise money via the sale of stock or borrow the money from commercial banks. Finance companies generally make more risky loans and charge higher interest rates than depository institutions. Assets of finance companies total $224 billion.

Pension Funds.   Pension funds act as a financial intermediary by attracting compulsory savings from individuals and companies and investing that money until it is needed to pay retirement benefits. Private pension funds have an estimated $311 billion in assets whereas state and local government pension funds have assets of $226 billion.

Although these are the major financial intermediaries and have been for

Table 3.1 Percentage of Assets Controlled by Different
Financial Institutions

Financial Institution	1960	1981
Commercial banks	43.1%	42.6%
Savings associations	12.0	15.6
Life insurance companies	20.0	12.2
Mutual savings banks	6.8	4.1
Finance companies	4.6	5.3
Investment companies	2.8	1.3
Credit unions	1.0	1.8
Private pension funds	6.4	7.3
State and local government funds	3.3	5.3
Money market funds	0.0	4.3
Total assets in billions	597.4	4,246.0

Source: USLSA, 1982.

several years (see Table 3.1), numerous other financial intermediaries merit mention. The federal government has created a variety of special banks that assist segments of the economy. These include banks of cooperatives (agriculture), federal land banks (direct loans to farmers), and federal home loan banks (credit for savings associations). Several other financial institutions operate by buying mortgages from depository institutions and financing these purchases by selling securities. These include the Federal Home Loan Mortgage Corporation (Freddy Mac), the Federal National Mortgage Association (Fanny Mae, a private corporation), and the Government National Mortgage Association (Ginny Mae). Other financial intermediaries range from corporations that refinance student loans, to the local pawnbroker. The number of different financial intermediaries is virtually endless (Johnson and Roberts, 1982: 288).

THE REGULATORY AGENCIES

Each financial industry developed by filling needs that the other industries did not want to fill. Government regulation has until very recently encouraged this separation, and separate subsystems developed for each industry. Even within a given industry, however, the regulatory apparatus reflects a series of historical accidents rather than a comprehensive effort to regulate.

Office of the Comptroller of the Currency

The United States maintains a dual banking system. A bank or any other type of depository institution can be chartered by either the federal government or any one of the state governments. Many times banks switch from national to state charters and vice versa. At one time regulation by the federal government was substantially different from state regulation. The differences between the regulations binding national banks and those binding state banks, however, have narrowed. If a state bank, for example, voluntarily affiliates with the Federal Reserve System, the bank is subject to federal regulation. Similarly, any bank accepting federal deposit insurance on its accounts is subject to federal law. With the passage of the Depository Institutions Deregulation and Monetary Control Act of 1980 (DIDMCA; see later), other advantages of being a state bank are being phased out. Recently, however, several states have dramatically relaxed their banking statutes (see further on) to encourage state rather than national charters even though federal regulation will be present for both.

The Office of the Comptroller of the Currency, an agency in the Department of the Treasury, regulates all national banks. Included in its regulatory scope are both financial soundness requirements and consumer protection statutes that apply to banks (e.g., the Truth in Lending Act). It grants charters to national banks and examines them. It also regulates the activities of national bank operations overseas and the activities of foreign banks in the United States. The Comptroller's Office approves all bank mergers when the surviving institution is a national bank. Created in 1863, the Office of the Comptroller had a 1982 budget of $138 million and 3,300 personnel (Penoyer, 1981: 86).

The Board of Governors of the Federal Reserve System

The Federal Reserve System, or the Fed as it is known, administers the national banking system. Although only 29 percent of all banks are Federal Reserve members, those banks contain 52 percent of the assets. The Fed regulates, examines, and approves mergers for those state banks that are also members of the Federal Reserve System. It also administers the reserves that all member banks must maintain with the Fed and regulates the activities of bank holding companies. In addition to its banking powers, the Fed has substantial monetary powers that have made the agency a major player in national economic policy.

The Federal Reserve System is one of the most powerful and independent agencies in the entire federal government. The system is governed by the Board of Governors of the Federal Reserve System. Members of the board are appointed for 14-year terms and can only be removed via impeachment. Budget controls over the Fed are totally lacking because it receives no money from the Treasury. The Fed operates at a profit and in a recent year turned back over $11 billion to the U.S. Treasury. Staffing and expenditure figures for the bank regulation aspects only of the Fed are not available.

Federal Deposit Insurance Corporation

The Federal Deposit Insurance Corporation (FDIC) is a government corporation that insures bank deposits up to $100,000 for each account. Any state bank may opt to insure its deposits with the FDIC, and insurance is compulsory for national banks. Virtually all state banks (96.3 percent of deposits) are insured by the FDIC. With insurance comes regulation. The FDIC regulates all state banks that receive FDIC insurance but are not members of the Federal Reserve System. Its regulation covers the same economic soundness, consumer protection, and merger laws that the Fed and the comptroller cover for other banks.

The FDIC is governed by a three-member board, which includes the comptroller of the currency and two members appointed by the president for six-year terms. Similar to the Fed, though not to that degree, the FDIC is an independent agency. By assessing member banks for insurance, the FDIC operates at a profit and has never touched the $3 billion that it can borrow from the Treasury. Over the years the FDIC has presided over the liquidation of nearly 600 banks; it has paid out $6 billion in insurance claims but regained $5.1 billion from the assets of the liquidated banks (Lammers, 1983: 209). The operating budget for the agency in 1982 was $141 million with 3,791 employees.

State Banking Commissions

Those banks not insured by the FDIC avoid federal regulation. Such banks are state-chartered institutions regulated by the banking commission in the state they are chartered. State institutions that purchase FDIC insurance are regulated and examined by both the FDIC and the state regulator. In approximately half the states, the FDIC and state regulators by agreement rotate responsibility for inspections.

State regulation of banks preceded federal regulation, which dates from 1863. In general, states have a reputation for lax regulation of banks (Spellman, 1982: 23). Many differences between federal and state regulation have been documented, including definitions of what constitutes a loan or capital; restrictions on underwriting securities or purchasing stock; and restrictions on mergers, foreign affiliates, and branches (Stone, 1979: 25). Not all states practice lenient regulation. New York closely regulated banks early in the nineteenth century and served as a model for the national regulatory laws. The giant Marine Midland Bank even gave up its New York charter in 1978 because federal merger policy was less restrictive than New York's policy.

The Federal Home Loan Bank Board

The Federal Home Loan Bank Board (FHLBB) is the savings association equivalent of the Federal Reserve. The FHLBB maintains a series of regional banks to assist savings associations with liquidity problems and to loan funds to savings associations. All federally chartered savings associations and mutual savings banks are required to be members of the Federal Home Loan Bank system; state institutions may join at their option. The incentive to accept regulation is again federal insurance. The FHLBB operates the Federal Savings and Loan Insurance Corporation (FSLIC), which insures deposits similar to the FDIC. Approximately 95 percent of state institutions' funds and all federal institutions' funds are insured through the FSLIC (Lammers, 1983: 487).

The FHLBB has the broadest powers of any financial regulator and perhaps even the broadest powers of any federal regulator. It charters federal savings institutions, regulates all federally insured institutions (under the same laws that govern the bank regulatory system), operates the insurance fund, operates savings associations in cases of default, and de facto controls the Federal Home Loan Mortgage Corporation (Freddie Mac), which buys and sells home mortgages. The FHLBB is governed by a three-person board nominated by the president and confirmed by the Senate. One member is designated as chairperson. The board acts as the board of directors for Freddie Mac. Granted independent status in 1955, the board operates fairly independently though not to the extent that the Federal Reserve does. Operating expenses are self-generated, not through congressional appropriations. In 1982 the FHLBB had operating expenses of $62 million and approximately 1,500 regulatory employees; these expense figures do not include funds expended to assist the merger of failing savings associations (Penoyer, 1981: 44).

The National Credit Union Administration

The National Credit Union Administration (NCUA) was established in 1970; from 1934 to 1969 authority for regulating credit unions was shifted among several different agencies. NCUA generally enforces the same acts (e.g., Truth in Lending Act) that the Federal Reserve and the FHLBB do. NCUA charters federal credit unions, operates the National Credit Union Share Insurance Fund, operates a fund to assist credit unions with liquidity problems, and regulates all credit unions (some 70.5 percent) that have federal insurance.

NCUA is governed by a three-person board appointed by the president and confirmed by the Senate. Although NCUA does not have the formal independence of the Federal Reserve and the Federal Home Loan Bank Board, by the nature of its small size, it often avoids the attention of the president and Congress. In the last few years, NCUA has been given more autonomy than the other regulators; the Depository Institutions Deregulation and Monetary Control Act of 1980 (DIDMCA; see further on for a discussion), for example, permitted NCUA to withdraw from the deregulation process, which it did. The regulatory functions of NCUA are budgeted for $22 million with a staff of 718.

The Other Regulators

The regulators just discussed are the subject of this chapter because it focuses on depository institutions. A variety of other regulators, however, operate in the financial institutions area. For banks, savings associations, credit unions, and mutual savings banks, state regulatory agencies regulate those that are state chartered. Finance companies are regulated in terms of consumer protection by the Federal Trade Commission and by the state regulation. Investment companies and money market mutual funds are governed by the rules of the Securities and Exchange Commission. Some aspects of private pension funds are regulated by federal law. Insurance companies are regulated by state agencies. These other regulators occasionally play a role in the federal financial institutions subsystems.

Agency Resources

Because financial regulation is fairly complex, the various federal regulators have all developed a reputation for expertise. Each has the cohesion to operate in secrecy; sometimes institutions are closed, for example, before any outsiders know the institution is being examined. Leadership is less positive. Although many regulatory heads have effectively managed these agencies, few have become known for innovative leadership outside the regulatory subsystem.

Salience. Financial regulation in normal times is not salient. The state of the financial industries in the 1980s, though dynamic, was of little interest to the general public except when major banks failed. At times in the past, however, banking was highly salient. The political concerns with cheap money in the late nineteenth century, the fights over the Bank of the United States, and the depression collapse of banking are three instances when banking was a major political issue. Financial institutions regulation becomes salient when the system fails; a lack of salience reflects the success of federal regulators at preventing major crises.

Legislative Authority. Financial regulators have a generous grant of legislative authority. First, legislative goals are more specific than the vague "public interest" standards of transportation regulation but less specific than the detailed goals of agricultural policy. This grants the agencies a good deal of discretion but also sets standards. Second, each agency covers only a portion of the industry, thus fragmenting power; but within the specified portion, coverage is almost universal. All financial regulators have generally unrestricted rule-making powers. Third, the agencies have a wide variety of sanctions. Institutions that violate regulations may be required to write off loans, individuals may be forced out of a relationship with an institution, and institutions may be closed by the regulators. The discretion is unlimited. Fourth, agency procedures place no specific limitations on the activities of the agencies (e.g., special hearings, and the like).

THE REGULATORY ENVIRONMENT

The Economic Environment

Ease of Entry. Although regulation creates barriers to entry for financial institutions by establishing minimum capital requirements and other "fitness" concerns, entry into the industries is not especially difficult. To be sure, starting a bank or a thrift is more difficult than opening a dry cleaning establishment or other "nonbank" business, but most barriers are political rather than economic. A state banking application is more likely to be denied because other banks protested the new bank than because the bank did not meet the legal requirements.

Entry varies among the different types of depository institutions. Credit unions are without a doubt the easiest institution to open whereas commercial banks appear to be the most difficult. At times, however, entry is fairly easy. Under Comptroller of the Currency James Saxon in the 1960s, national bank charters were granted freely with little effort to restrict entry. In recent years, other industries (e.g., insurance, brokerage firms) have entered banking by purchasing existing financial institutions (see further on).

Number of Firms. The depository industries are potentially competitive. With 15,000 commercial banks, 500 mutual savings banks, 4,000 savings and loans, and 22,000 credit unions, there are sufficient depository institutions to be competitive. In fact, the number of firms has been kept large by the McFadden Act, which prohibits interstate banking, thus fostering local financial institutions. Even within local market areas, however, competition still exists. One small city of 70,000 in Oklahoma, for example, has 6 commercial banks, 6 savings associations, 12 credit unions, and numerous other financial intermediaries. Financial services are not a natural monopoly and show all the signs of an industry capable of competition.

Profitability.   The profitability of depository institutions varies by the type of institution and the time frame being considered. Commercial banking must be considered fairly profitable if the number of other institutions that wish to get into banking is any indication. Banks in 1982 averaged 0.71 percent return on their assets. Although this might not look like an impressive profit, bear in mind that assets include all the funds in a bank. Banks are heavily leveraged institutions; the average bank has capital equal to only 5.8 percent of assets (Johnson and Roberts, 1982: 175) and two-fifths of that is in the form of retained earnings. As a return on investment, 1982 bank profits were an attractive 12.2 percent after taxes (Opper, 1982: 489).[2]

Thrift institutions are greatly affected by current economic conditions. Savings associations and mutual savings banks generally make long-term loans and cover these loans with short-term deposits. During periods of high inflation, therefore, these thrifts may pay more for funds than they are earning. In the 1960s and 1970s this was not a major problem; savings associations returned 0.7 percent on assets or approximately 12 to 16 percent on equity; mutual savings banks returned 0.43 percent on assets or 7 to 10 percent on equity. In 1981 and 1982, however, with interest rates in the 18 to 20 percent range and many mortgages paying 9 percent or less, savings institutions lost money (Carron, 1982: 12). With the drop in inflation in 1983, they returned to profitability (Pauly and Ipsen, 1983: 59). Credit unions are not as susceptible to economic fluctuations because they specialize in shorter-term loans. When loans are not demanded or are unprofitable, credit unions often deposit funds in a commercial bank. Over the past 20 years, credit unions have returned 0.67 percent on their assets, an excellent return given their low capitalization.

In short, the profit picture of depository institutions is attractive. Even in the area of home mortgages, it is attractive to new firms because a new firm need not bear the burden of old mortgages with low returns. Potential competitors for entry into the industry, therefore, should not be difficult to find.

Technology

Complexity.   The technology of depository institutions is not complex. At a rudimentary level, the process of taking deposits and making loans does not differ significantly from that of the moneylenders of the middle ages. To be sure, present-day banks and thrifts have become highly automated, but they are a long way from the state of the art in computer technology and lag behind similar industries such as brokerage firms.

2. Bank profits show amazing stability. From 1960 to 1980 the return on assets never fell below 0.7 percent or rose above 0.9 percent (Carron, 1983: 76).

Stability. The key to banking technology is stability. Until the 1960s, banks and thrifts had a stable technology that had changed little in the previous 100 years. Rapid changes in this technology, however, fundamentally changed the industries. The changes are of such a magnitude that they merit further discussion.

The depository institutions from the 1930s to the 1960s were paper-intensive industries. Reliance on paper and currency did its part to keep banking localized. Transporting paper was expensive, and, in a fast-moving money market, delays of several days might mean that the reason for transporting the funds no longer existed. Large amounts of float permeated the system, and liquidity was restricted. As the increase in financial transactions grew, banks and other financial institutions became inundated with paper. Three technological changes—internal computerization, electronic fund transfers (EFT), and automated teller machines—resulted in a changed market for financial services in the 1980s.

Because banks and thrifts are traditional organizations that change slowly, automation came late in depository institutions. The systems used to automate the internal operations of banks were those developed elsewhere, primarily in the securities industry under the innovative leadership of Merrill Lynch and others (G. C. White, 1980). As depository institutions became familiar with electronic applications within the institution, possibilities for external use became obvious.

The electronic transfer of funds—the debiting of one account and crediting of another without any paper—is the key element in the changing technology of depository institutions (Bequai, 1981). Although EFT payments, both for regularized payments (e.g., loan payments) and for special payments via telephone, were slow to catch on with customers (Mayer, 1974), large corporations, governments, and other financial institutions were quick to use the system. Large corporations found it easier to send a computer tape to the local bank than to issue hundreds of payroll checks. To process EFT transactions, the National Automated Clearing House Association was created, linking 11,000 commercial banks, 3,500 thrifts, and 21,000 private companies. In 1983 this network processed 410 million transactions evenly split between the private sector and government (Lordan, 1983: 38).

One form of EFT that became popular with regular customers was the automated teller machine (ATM). Using a bank card, customers could withdraw cash from either checking or savings accounts, make deposits, or receive information about their accounts. ATM use has exploded. In 1982, 36,000 ATMs (a 38 percent increase over 1981) were operating with 3.1 billion transactions. Some 68 percent of the population had access to EFT-tied accounts, and one-fifth had access to telephone bill payment (Schroeder, 1983: 396). In many states, ATMs permitted banks to circumvent laws against branch banking (ATMs are not technically branches because they do not offer the full services of a bank such as loans). With first statewide and then nationwide systems of ATMs honoring the cards of all members, a form of interstate banking was established. Financial services companies such as American Express also tied into ATM networks to provide services for their members. The importance of the ATM is that it introduces the regular customer to new technology and breaks down resistance to more advanced technology in banking (e.g., telephone banking, at-home banking, and other EFT uses).

The result of internal computerization, EFT, and ATMs was that depositors could cut down on their float and minimize the working balances in their accounts. The freed-up funds could then be invested in interest-bearing assets. The result was an influx of money into the short-term money markets; corporations could then use these short-term funds rather than longer-term sources if long-term debt was unattractive. These funds became part of a national market for money because technology has linked the depository institutions to the money markets through a variety of networks. Bank Wire II linked correspondent banks; Fed Wire permitted quick trading in federal funds; CHIPs was used to clear transactions in New York; SWIFT linked U.S. banks with Europe (see G. C. White, 1980: 27). Private companies such as VISA, American Express, and others established information networks. By 1980, banks and thrifts were tightly linked with international money markets via technology (see Colton and Kramer, 1980).[3]

The new technology, with faster transactions, less float, and a tightly linked network of financial institutions, transformed the market for money from a local market to a national and international market. Funds deposited in a savings and loan in Midland, Texas, for example, might be transferred to Frankfurt, Germany, the next day, where they would be loaned to a Brazilian company. The market for money closely resembles the economists' free market; money flows to individuals who will pay the highest price (interest) for a given level of risk. As will be discussed later, the internationalization of money markets played a large role in deregulating the financial industries in the 1980s.

Substitutability.   In a technical sense, the technologies of commercial banking, savings associations, credit unions, mutual savings banks and other financial intermediaries are easily substituted for one another. Each industry collects money from one group of individuals and loans it to another. Restrictions on substitution are artificial barriers created by political decisions reinforced by geographic isolation. As technology changed in the 1970s, the technologies of each industry became substitutable for the others.

THE EARLY HISTORY OF DEPOSITORY REGULATION

Banking Regulation

Early Efforts.   The early political history of the United States is marked by a fear of political and economic concentration. Major political battles were fought over the creation of a national bank for the United States.[4] In

3. Commercial banks were more enthusiastic about networking technology than were thrifts. Thrifts might well have ignored the technology and the automation if they had had the choice. When the national money markets became a major competitor for funds, however, thrifts were forced to adopt the technology or suffer a major loss of deposits.

4. The political battle over the first bank was an extension of the political fights between Hamilton and Jefferson over the role of the national government. Private banks had little impact; in fact, there were only four private banks in the nation when the National Bank was chartered. The demise of the second bank was a battle between the bank and Jackson, with private banking supporting Jackson (even though Jackson was hostile to all banking; see Hammond, 1957).

fact, Congress twice created national banks in 1791 and 1816, both authorized for 20 years. Neither the first nor the second bank was a central bank
in a modern sense; both were essentially private banks licensed by the
national government (Johnson and Roberts, 1982: 315; for an opposite
view see Timberlake, 1978: 213). In both cases, Congress permitted the
authorizations to lapse, and both national banks were disbanded. Political
considerations played a major role in the demise of both (see Hammond,
1957: chapters 5, 10).

For a modern nation state, a central bank is essential. Governments
need a place to store funds, they need a way to finance wars and other
projects, they need a mechanism to sell bonds, and they need a way to
regulate the amount of currency in circulation. With a political culture that
distrusts economic concentration, the United States came late to central
banking. England had a central bank in 1694; France, in 1800; Japan, in
1882; but the United States did not until 1914. The origins of the central
banking function in the United States, however, had their roots much earlier
in the Civil War.

At the beginning of the Civil War, all banks were state-chartered institutions. These institutions issued their own paper currency backed by specie
held in the bank. Such currency might or might not be honored by merchants, especially merchants in other towns. Regulation was haphazard, and
bank failures were a common phenomenon. President Lincoln's motivation
for change, however, had little to do with the status of banking but rather
was tied to his need to finance the Civil War.

Two statutes marked the entry of the federal government into banking
regulation, the Currency Act of 1863 and the National Bank Act of 1864.
These laws authorized the comptroller of the currency to charter national
banks. National banks were authorized to sell government securities (e.g.,
Civil War bonds) and to issue uniform national bank notes. All national
banks were required to purchase a minimum of $30,000 in government
bonds and were issued currency for them (Klebaner, 1974: 81). As an
incentive to seek a national charter, a 10 percent tax was levied on all state
bank notes. The impact of this tax was to eliminate state bank notes as a
form of currency in the United States (see Hammond, 1957: 118 ff). The
architects of the national banking laws felt that without the ability to issue
bank notes state banks would fade from the scene (Hammond, 1957). They
did not because a new banking instrument, the check, permitted state banks
to issue a "currency" that was not subject to the 10 percent tax. The
invention of the check preserved the dual banking system of the United
States (Stone, 1979: 20; Spellman, 1982: 7).

Federal chartering began what is known as the era of free banking in
the United States. Because the purpose was to raise money for the Civil
War, charters were liberally granted to anyone who met the minimum capital requirements. From less than 2,000, the number of banks grew to
27,000 by 1913. Free banking resulted in numerous small, undercapitalized
banks rather than a centralized banking system with branches (branches
were prohibited by federal law; see Klebaner, 1974: 55–59; E. N. White,
1983: 223). Government policy was little concerned with regulation.

The United States struggled through industrial development with no
central banking system. The Panic of 1907, however, altered the thinking of
many political leaders on the need for a central bank. Essentially, the panic

started when numerous English citizens withdrew their gold deposits from American banks (English capital was a critical ingredient of the Industrial Revolution). With the withdrawal of gold, banks began to call in loans because they lacked assets to cover them. Calling in loans signaled to depositors that something was amiss, and depositors began runs on the banks to withdraw funds. Because banks often held insufficient reserves for such contingencies and had no source of additional reserves, the banks then collapsed.

In response to the Panic of 1907, Congress appointed a national commission to study the banking problem. With Wilson's election as president, the executive branch also supported reform legislation. Similarly, most business interests and some commercial bankers favored legislation designed to stabilize the banking industry. The Federal Reserve Act of 1913 created the Federal Reserve System. Twelve regional banks were established in major cities with the entire system governed by the Federal Reserve Board. The legislation required all national banks to keep on reserve a certain proportion of their funds with the regional federal reserve banks. These reserves created a pool of money that could be used to avoid liquidity problems. In addition, a bank facing liquidity problems had access to the Fed's discount window so that, rather than call in loans, a bank might sell the loans to the Fed. The act also authorized inspections by the Office of the Comptroller of the Currency, established common accounting procedures, and set up a check-clearing system through the Federal Reserve Banks. The United States had finally created a central bank and the rudiments of a regulatory system (Klebaner, 1974: 98).

The Depression.   The current system of regulating commercial banks was established in the New Deal as a response to problems of the depression. The regulatory climate established in the 1930s set the pattern for bank regulation down to the present time; without a conscious effort, an organizational ideology for bank regulators was created. Understanding the New Deal reaction to banking, however, requires some background in pre-New Deal banking.

Banking in the 1920s was far less restrictive than it is today. Banks could underwrite stocks (investment banking). Often banks loaned money to customers to purchase stocks that the bank was selling. Many times such purchases were made on margin, and the bank loaned the margin money also. A bank that underwrote a poor stock had an incentive to unload it as fast as possible. When the stock market collapsed in 1929, so did much of the business of the banks; 34.6 percent of commercial bank loans at this time were for stock purchases (Klebaner, 1974: 117). Loans made for stock purchases were defaulted, and the banks owned many shares of worthless stock. Consumer runs on the banks overwhelmed the meager bank reserves. The depression's impact on the commercial banking industry was devastating. In 1921 the United States had 29,788 banks; by 1934 only 15,484 remained.

The crisis in banking was not recognized as such initially. During the 1920s some 6,000 new bank charters (mostly state charters) were issued; the number of banks actually decreased by 6,600 by 1930 as small institutions merged or folded. The failure or merger of numerous small banks during the 1920s was not considered serious because only "weak" banks were failing. With the major crisis of 1929, the Hoover administration was unprepared to act quickly. Eventually, the Reconstruction Finance Corporation made loans of $900 million to 4,000 banks during Hoover's presidency, but he was unable to restore confidence in the banking system (Kennedy, 1973: 224). Withdrawals at banks were up to 10 percent of assets per week by March 1933 (Klebaner, 1974: 133).

The collapse of the banking industry can be attributed in part to government banking policy prior to the depression. With free banking and restrictions on branch banking, government policy encouraged a large number of small banks. The banking industry, as a result, was overbanked and undercapitalized as well as inadequately supervised by a fragmented regulatory system (Kennedy, 1973: 224). Although better bank regulation would not have prevented the depression, it may well have avoided the collapse of the banking system (E. N. White, 1983: 226).

Banking was among the first industries that Franklin Roosevelt addressed. To avoid a complete collapse of the industry, Roosevelt declared a bank holiday to buy time to mold a response to the problems. The holiday, plus Roosevelt's promise that only sound banks would be allowed to reopen, regenerated confidence in the banking system. When the banks reopened (six to eight working days later), deposits exceeded withdrawals (Kennedy, 1973: 230). In three weeks deposits had increased by $1.2 billion (Klebaner, 1974: 134).

A long-run solution was offered in June as the Banking Act of 1933 (often called the Glass-Steagall Act of 1933). The Banking Act of 1933 created the Federal Deposit Insurance Corporation (FDIC) to insure the deposits in banks. All national banks were required to carry FDIC insurance, and state banks could do so at their discretion. With federal insurance came federal regulation. Commercial banks had their loan powers restricted and were barred from investment banking completely. Multibank holding companies were subjected to Federal Reserve Board regulation. The Banking Act of 1935 authorized federal regulators to impose ceilings on interest paid by banks and prohibited interest on demand deposits (checking accounts). More important, the Banking Act of 1935 put a permanent end to free banking by requiring that the regulators consider the survival potential of new banks (Klebaner, 1974: 156; see also Peltzman, 1968). The general intent of all the depression legislation was to ensure financial soundness of banks by limiting risks including the risks of competition (Spellman, 1982: 27).

The depression set the tone of bank regulation. Because bank failures were to be avoided at all costs (bank failures undermine consumer confidence in all elements of the national economy), federal bank regulation became fairly stringent. Unlike other regulatory areas where the regulated can usually do anything that is not prohibited, in banking regulation the regulated can only do things that they are authorized to do (see Mayer, 1974). The apparent success of the New Deal legislation reinforced the agencies' perceptions that their view of the world was correct. The number of bank failures dropped from 1,000 a year before the FDIC to from 50 to 60 a year until 1940 and to ten or fewer a year from 1941 to 1981 (Whether failures have increased recently or we have witnessed a fluctuation in the curve remains to be seen).[5] From this period onward, bank regulation

5. Recent failures have hit prewar levels. In 1983, 48 banks failed, and 33 savings and loans failed. In 1982 the figures were 42 banks and 47 savings and loans. These were the highest figures since 1939 and reflect greater competition in the industry (Bank Failures, 1984: 26).

is characterized by banks' searching for loopholes in the law and the consequent regulators' efforts to close the loopholes.[6]

Mutual Savings Banks: Early Development and Regulation

Thrift institutions—mutual savings banks, savings and loan associations, and credit unions developed because commercial banks of the nineteenth century ignored the developing needs for credit. Commercial banks specialized in large deposits and showed little interest in small savings accounts, consumer loans, or home mortgages. The void in financial services was exacerbated by the development of a money economy and urbanization. With urbanization, age-old ties to land and housing were severed, and new needs for loans were created. With the money economy, savings of a liquid nature became possible (Teck, 1968: 4–5).

Suggestions for a new type of bank to encourage thrift among the working classes had been made by such people as Daniel Defoe and Jeremy Bentham. Several quasi-bank institutions developed in England during the nineteenth century, including Christmas banks, penny banks, and Sunday banks (the names descriptive of the function or service). The first mutual savings banks with reliance on small savings, mutual organization, and unrestricted loan powers were created in 1804 (the Tottenham Benefit Bank) and 1810 (the Ruthwell Bank; see Teck, 1968: 7–8).

Some three hundred mutual savings banks were in operation in England by 1819, when the first U.S. savings banks were opened in New York, Philadelphia, and Boston (Teck, 1968: 10). Chartering mutual savings banks required a major change in state banking laws because mutual savings banks required a perpetual existence whereas laws often limited banks to a term of years.

Mutual savings banks grew slowly with only 108 chartered by 1850. (Commercial banks on the other hand grew from 4 in 1790 to 300 in 1820; Hammond, 1957: 145) The post-Civil War industrialization proved a boon to savings banks as their numbers grew to 652 by 1900. Expansion after 1900 was hindered by two factors. First, mutual savings banks were chartered only by state governments, and only 18 states permitted this form of banking (Teck, 1968: 16). Second, the rise of alternative thrift institutions (e.g., savings associations, credit unions) mitigated some of the need for the services offered. Mutual savings banks have remained a Northeastern phenomenon (over half are in Massachusetts or New York).

Mutual savings banks followed policies of high liquidity and conservative investments. As a result, not a single mutual savings bank went bankrupt during the Great Depression. That record plus a streak of independence has limited federal regulation of mutual savings banks. With the creation of the FDIC in 1933, all mutual savings banks were insured for a 90-day

---

6. To be sure, the U.S. government has engaged in periods of more liberal banking policies. When James Saxon was comptroller (1961–1966), he liberally granted national bank charters and encouraged innovation in the banking industry. This period corresponded with the introduction of the certificate of deposit (CD) and aggressive bank pursuit of savings deposits (Klebaner, 1974: 180). In addition, for goals other than economic soundness, federal regulators have been less stringent. They did not become advocates of economic deregulation until the 1980s and, according to Greenwald (1980: 83), were slow to enforce the consumer protection legislation of the 1970s.

period. With their proven safety record, however, most mutual savings banks saw no need for federal restrictions and withdrew from the system. Even today many mutual savings banks are insured through state insurance agencies such as the Mutual Savings Bank Central Fund of Massachusetts rather than the FDIC (Teck, 1968: 123). Unlike other depository institutions, therefore, mutual savings banks do not have a long tradition of dealing with the federal government.

Credit Unions

Similar to mutual savings banks, credit unions also had their origins in Europe, this time in Germany. The first credit union in North America was opened in the French Canadian town of Levis by Alphonse Desjardins in 1901 (Moody and Fite, 1971: 18). Relying on the common bond of members, this credit union loaned over $200,000 in its first six years without any losses. From Canada, Desjardins was instrumental in encouraging credit unions in the United States. In Manchester, New Hampshire, St. Mary's Catholic Church established the first U.S. credit union, St. Mary's Cooperative Credit Association (Moody and Fite, 1971: 36).

Desjardins also influenced Edward A. Filene, who was instrumental in getting Massachusetts to adopt the first state credit union law. A true believer in credit unions, Filene encouraged other states to pass similar laws. Through his National Credit Union Extension Bureau, Filene and Roy Bergengren, the bureau director, organized other state movements for credit union laws. Even with an active organization and funding by the Twentieth Century Fund, progress was slow (Moody and Fite, 1971: 88). Some 32 states had 1,100 credit unions by 1932.

Despite the depression, credit unions grew in numbers although deposits declined (one reason for growth was the failure of other credit-granting institutions). Many credit unions closed, but the numbers were far fewer than those for commercial banks. Filene and Bergengren used the depression to press for federal chartering of credit unions. Through Filene's connection with the Democratic party and Franklin Roosevelt, the Federal Credit Union Act of 1934 was passed late in the 1934 legislative session (Moody and Fite, 1971: 88). The law permitted federal charters for credit unions; administration was lodged in the Farm Credit Administration.

Savings Associations

Savings associations were originally created to permit working-class people to buy homes and to encourage thrift. The idea was transplanted from Europe, and the first U.S. savings association was founded in 1831 in Frankfort, Pennsylvania (Ewalt, 1963: 373). The Oxford Provident Building Society, as it was named, operated as a terminating society. Each member made regular monthly payments. The society then loaned money to first one, then another member until every member had acquired a home. When all debts were paid, the society ceased to exist.[7]

---

7. One interesting aspect of the Oxford association is that its first loan, to a person named Comly Rich, became deliquent. Foreclosure has been with savings and loans from the beginning.

Savings associations gained permanence by enrolling new groups of participants every three months. Until 1920, this "serial association" was the predominant form. By 1893, 5,000 savings associations had been founded; this number grew to 12,000 by 1929 (Ewalt, 1963: 391).

The depression hit savings associations hard. The failures of savings and loans (S&Ls) were related to bank failures because S&Ls often placed their liquid assets in commercial banks. When a commercial bank failed, a depositing S&L lost its reserves. It was unable to make loans, and few people had money to deposit. The S&L became frozen; in some 1,700 cases during the 1930s, frozen S&Ls failed (Teck, 1968: 119). Foreclosures grew, and by 1935, 20 percent of the assets of savings and loans were in foreclosed real estate (Ewalt, 1963: 21).

Savings associations, through their trade association, the U.S. League of Savings Associations (then called the U.S. Building and Loan League), were an early petitioner for government assistance. Savings associations borrowed heavily ($118 million) from Hoover's Reconstruction Finance Corporation and pushed for the creation of the Federal Home Loan Bank System in 1932. Hoover's efforts to revitalize the industry, however, were unsuccessful.

The New Deal approach to savings associations stressed housing, tying the industry's future closely to the housing industry.[8] The Home Owners Loan Act of 1933 created the Home Owners Loan Corporation, which provided $3.1 billion in loans to depository institutions and home owners (Ewalt, 1963: 38; assets of S&Ls were less than $9 billion before the depression). The corporation was successful in stabilizing home ownership and ceased operations in 1951. More permanent were the provisions of the National Housing Act of 1934. This act provided for federal chartering of savings associations and insurance through the Federal Savings and Loan Insurance Corporation. With the acceptance of insurance came federal regulation restricting the activities of S&Ls. Other provisions of the National Housing Act created the Federal Housing Administration loan programs that became a major stimulus to home building and, thus, to savings associations.

Early Regulation: A Summary

Depression era politics in financial institutions is consistent with the process described in chapter 2. Financial regulation was extremely salient. Resolution of policy issues accordingly took place in the macropolitical system with Congress and the president playing major roles. Banking regulation of the 1930s could almost be characterized as "public interest" regulation. Consumers benefited because savings were protected; financial institutions benefited because regulation restored public confidence in the institutions, permitting them to attract funds.

As the salience of banking declined, the bureaucratic regulators became dominant in the subsystems because financial regulation was highly technical. Bureaucrats perceived themselves as technocrats working to prevent

8. One reason why the New Deal aided S&Ls only indirectly through housing might have been the industry's ties to the Republican party. S&Ls were the beneficiaries of much assistance during the Hoover administration.

another depressionlike failure. This orientation meant that the only issues that would escape from the subsystem were those causing a great deal of disagreement among the subsystem members. As technocrats, the regulators expected Congress to resolve these issues.

SEPARATE AND SPECIALIZED

Federal policy toward depository institutions during the depression ratified the separate functions performed by the various institutions before the depression. Separate regulatory subsystems were created for each industry with separate regulators, congressional subcommittees, and advocacy coalitions. Unlike the previous situation, however, separation was now maintained by law rather than by the economic preference of the institutions. The depository institutions, as well as the other financial intermediaries, had defined roles in the financial system. Commercial banks were to service the daily needs of depositors (e.g., checking accounts) and make short-term loans to local businesses. Savings associations and mutual savings banks were to service the long-term needs of savers and loan money for mortgages. Credit unions were to service long-term saving needs and make low-risk personal loans. Finance companies absorbed the surplus capital of banks and serviced higher-risk loans. Brokers served the needs of individuals who wished to take greater risks with their savings and invested their proceeds in business. Insurance companies funneled their long-term "savings" into stocks, bonds, and other investments.

Federal policy was designed to limit competition both between these industries and within individual industries. Competition led to failure, the reasoning went, and failure destroyed the confidence necessary for a healthy economy. Most legislation was aimed at the commercial banking industry rather than at the thrifts. Commercial banks were affected more by the depression because they took greater risks prior to the depression and suffered more failures. Commercial banks also showed more initiative in seeking loopholes to engage in prohibited activities. Thrifts operated in a more conservative manner and in a protected, yet profitable, sector of the financial industry.

A predepression law, the McFadden Act of 1927, began the efforts to limit competition by restricting interstate banking. A national bank could not open branches in another state if that state did not authorize such expansion (none did at the time). In addition, national banks were subject to state laws on intrastate branch banking. If the state did not allow branch banking by state banks, then national banks were also prohibited from branching. Although the McFadden Act was a liberalization of the existing federal policy that national banks were not allowed to branch, it was not a significant liberalization (Jessee and Seelig, 1977: 6; Klebaner, 1974: 129). The intent of this legislation was to prevent large money center banks from competing with small-town banks for deposits and loans.

Further restricting the competitive aspects of commercial banking was the Glass-Steagall Act of 1933 (also known as the Banking Act of 1933). One perceived cause of the depression was the interrelationship of banks and the stock market. Glass-Steagall prohibited commercial banks from engaging in investment banking (underwriting corporate stocks and bonds).

Essentially, Glass-Steagall shielded investment companies from competition from commercial banks.

The Banking Act of 1935, part of the second New Deal, gave the Board of Governors of the Federal Reserve the power to set interest rates on time deposits. The intent was to prevent competition for deposits (and thus raise the cost of money), which would require banks to take greater risks to earn higher returns. In addition, no interest could be paid on demand deposits (checking accounts). The interest rate ceilings (known as Regulation Q after the Federal Reserve Board's regulation implementing the ceiling) had little impact on competition for deposits until the 1950s because the ceilings were set well above the interest offered on most accounts (some savings accounts in the 1930s paid less than 1 percent interest). The prohibition of interest on demand deposits gave the commercial banks a cheap source of funds because other depository institutions were not permitted to offer demand deposits.

Laws restricting competition encouraged commercial banks to look for loopholes to circumvent stringent banking regulation. One such loophole was the holding company. By creating a holding company that purchased two or more banks, banks in the 1950s were able to circumvent both the McFadden Act and Glass-Steagall. A holding company merely established a subsidiary to engage in nonbank activities while operating banks through other subsidiaries. Similarly, a holding company might purchase banks in more than one state and thus "branch" across state lines. Aggressive holding company activities by Transamerica, at the time the holding company for the Bank of America, brought a congressional response. The Bank Holding Company Act of 1956 closed this loophole by subjecting multibank holding companies to the interstate branching restrictions (existing interstate companies were allowed to continue) and by subjecting holding companies to restrictions on operating nonbank businesses.

The holding company loophole was not finished, however. Within a few years, banks discovered that the holding company law applied to multibank holding companies only. A single bank could still be owned by a holding company that engaged in nonbank business with other subsidiaries. (The Federal Reserve actually recognized this potential loophole in 1956 and advocated a definition of holding company that included one-bank holding companies; see Jessee and Seelig, 1977: 10.) Linking banking to subsidiaries in securities, real estate, development, and other activities is highly profitable. Between 1965 and 1968 some 400 single-bank holding companies were established. In 1970, Congress closed this loophole by subjecting single-bank holding companies to the Bank Holding Company Act. A holding company is allowed to engage in a business if it is "so closely related to banking or managing or controlling banks as to be a proper incident thereto." The Federal Reserve has the discretion to determine what business functions fall within this definition (Jessee and Seelig, 1977: 34).

A final illustration of regulation designed to restrict competition is the extension of Regulation Q to savings associations. In 1966 savings associations were first subjected to interest rate ceilings via Regulation Q. Essentially, this regulation was undertaken with the support of the savings industry. With funds tied up in long-term mortgages, savings associations can be hurt badly by high short-term interest rates. An interest rate cap on savings limits competition for funds. Savings associations believed that limiting competition would allow them to procure funds when needed at a reasonable price. To give preference to S&Ls and the housing industry, thrifts were permitted to pay ¼ of 1 percent more for savings than commercial banks were.

That regulation of depository industries was designed to limit competition is beyond doubt. One other aspect of this regulation is also important to understanding financial regulation. Because regulation was stringent, that is, because regulators believed in enforcing the law to the letter, loopholes created problems. Although regulators exercised a great deal of discretion in determining if a bank or thrift were complying with regulations (especially during inspections), such compliance regulation is not suited to regulating a task that the law does not mention. As a result, Congress played a major role in setting policy because conflicts between the regulators and the regulated would be presented to them, often by the regulator. Given the economic importance of depository institutions (as opposed to merchant marine shipping for example), access to the congressional agenda was not difficult.

THE DESTRUCTION OF BARRIERS BETWEEN THE INDUSTRIES

The 1970s saw the carefully constructed separate industries and the federal policies that separated them destroyed. Advances in technology and changes in the economic environment eliminated the barriers separating the financial industries. The environment created a situation that required that Congress either accept the changes as inevitable or attempt to resurrect the old barriers. Changes in the political environment of Congress foreclosed one of these two options.

Technological Changes

The technological changes in the banking and thrift industries were discussed earlier in this chapter. Essentially, computerization of financial industries and the linking of financial institutions via networks eliminated any physical barriers to the transfer of funds over long distances. An international money market was created with funds flowing to whoever was willing to pay the highest interest. If funds could attract a greater return in bonds than in savings accounts, funds were moved from savings into other investments (the flow of funds out of depository institutions is called *disintermediation*).

Economic Changes

Technological changes alone could not have created the environment that led to the financial deregulation of the 1980s. Had interest rates remained low or even dropped (say to 6 or 7 percent), then there would have been no incentives to compete for small savings. Small savers in the 1970s were locked into low-yield investments. Commercial banks could only pay 5.25 percent, and savings associations were limited to 5.5 percent. Even eight-year savings certificates were limited to 7.75 percent interest.

Low interest rates were disrupted in August 1979, when the Federal Reserve committed to monetarism. Rather than attempt to control interest rates, the Fed announced that it would focus its efforts on controlling the aggregate supply of money. Interest rates would be permitted to fluctuate in response to supply and demand. The result of the Fed's policy was highly volatile interest rates. The prime rate hit 20 percent in early 1980, fell back to 11 percent by November, returned to 20 percent in early 1981, and dropped to 10 percent in early 1983 before beginning another climb.[9]

High interest rates created a different economic environment for depository institutions. First, large depositors withdrew their funds. Large deposits are highly sensitive to interest rates because a large depositor can purchase T-bills and other instruments directly if these pay significantly more than bank-thrift deposits. During the late 1970s and early 1980s, funds flowed out of depository institutions and into other investments; disintermediation was a major problem. This was an especially severe problem for savings associations because their assets were tied up in long-term mortgages. If a savings association fails to attract deposits equal to its outstanding loans, it must borrow the difference on the money markets. A thrift may be in the unenviable situation of paying 20 percent for money to support a 9 percent mortgage.

Second, passbook savings became a cheap source of funds for depository institutions. By lending passbook funds at the prime rate (say 16 percent), passbook savings became a profitable business. Other financial institutions (e.g., investment companies, insurance funds) viewed the large pool of passbook savings with envy. The spread between passbook interest rates and market lending rates greatly increased the rewards of finding a way to attract these funds from banks and thrifts.

Third, demand deposits became an envied source of funds. Because commercial banks by law pay no interest on checking accounts (and no one else was authorized to have checking accounts), the spread between the cost of demand deposits (costs of servicing a checking account) and the return the bank could get on the deposits made demand deposits an attractive and profitable source of funds. Banks even began competing with each other for these funds by offering free checking accounts or other inducements.

The economic situation can be summarized as follows. Demand for money was strong, inflation rates were often in double digits, and a large supply of money in passbook savings and demand deposits was earning substantially less than market rates. All that was needed was an entrepreneur to figure out a way to link supply with demand. Surprisingly, the linkage was slow in coming for two reasons. First, investors and other principals obviously expected the era of cheap money to return. Long-term treasury bills, as an illustration, sold for significantly less than the rate of inflation. If the economic conditions did not last, the risk of linking the supply of money with demand was too high. Second, as a conservative and highly regulated set of industries, neither banks nor thrifts were especially known for innovation. In such circumstances, innovation is likely to come from marginal firms or firms on the fringe of the industry.

9. The Federal Reserve actually belongs to two subsystems, one regulating banks and one establishing monetary policy. Its decision to let interest rates float was part of its monetary policy function. This decision affected not only banks but the entire U.S. economy.

Entrepreneurial Innovation

Both the economic and the technological environment provided incentives to innovate. Deposits were earning far less than their market value, and the technology was available to put deposits to better uses. Because the financial industry is composed of several industries—each facing different technology, economics, and, most important, different regulatory restrictions—innovations can come from a variety of directions. Three innovations—the creation of money market funds, methods of permitting interest on demand deposits, and the dissolution of geographic barriers to financial transactions—fundamentally changed the financial industry in the late 1970s and set the stage for Congress to pass the Depository Institutions Deregulation and Monetary Control Act of 1980.

Money Market Funds.   Neither banks nor thrifts had any incentives to pay higher rates for small savings accounts because they made good profits by loaning these funds at market interest rates. Among investment companies in the 1970s, however, pressures to innovate were great. Until 1975 brokers' commissions on the sale of stock were set by the Securities and Exchange Commission (SEC); commissions were set high to avoid competition and firm failure. On May 1, 1975, the SEC deregulated commissions. The result was strong competition, and commission rates dropped 15 percent (Stoll, 1981: 39). The introduction of competition coincided with a prolonged slump in the stock market (lasting until 1982). As stock earnings declined relative to other investment possibilities, two million persons withdrew their money from mutual funds between 1970 and 1978 (Dougall and Gaumnitz, 1980). Three hundred brokerage firms either merged or went out of business. Faced with a declining and unprofitable industry, innovation in the securities industry was a necessity.

In response to such industry problems, one manager, Henry Brown, founded the Reserve Fund in 1972. The Reserve Fund was the first money market mutual fund; it operated like a normal mutual fund except that it invested in T-bills, government bonds, certificates of deposit, commercial paper, and short-term debt. By permitting small investors ($10,000+) to pool their assets, the money market fund (MMF) provided access to instruments normally restricted to the large investor ($100,000+).

Despite higher interest rates, money market funds did not become a serious competitor to depository institutions until 1978. Before January 1978, money market funds totaled less than $5 billion in assets. One reason for this was that interest rates remained variable so that safe, but low, interest rates were preferred to slightly higher but unstable and uninsured rates (Kalogeras, 1981: 68). In 1976 and 1977, the six-month T-bill rate averaged less than 5.5 percent, hardly a sufficient rate to attract funds. The second reason was the unfamiliarity of the American public with money market funds. This changed with the entry of Merrill Lynch, the nation's largest broker with offices throughout the United States, into the money market fund business (Frank, 1981: 39).

In 1977, Merrill Lynch took the money market fund one step further with its cash management account (CMA). The CMA blurred the distinction between a money market fund and a depository institution. For a minimum deposit of $20,000, a CMA holder was permitted to write checks on the account, get cash advances via the account's VISA card, and borrow money while receiving market level interest rates (Frank, 1981: 39). Only such commercial bank services as auto loans and safe deposit boxes were not provided by Merrill Lynch.

Following the lead of Merrill Lynch, other investment firms offered other innovations in money market funds. Midwest Income Investment offered a fund with only a $500 minimum investment, thus opening up the MMF market to the smallest investor. Check-writing minimums fell to as low as $50 or were tied to a bank that serviced the checks with no minimum. Other funds specialized in guaranteed government securities, tax-free investments, or high-risk/high-yield investments.

Money market funds became serious competitors to banks and thrifts for the savings dollar. They grew until they topped out at approximately $180 billion in 1982 (the leveling out resulted from efforts taken to phase out Regulation Q). Money market funds would not have developed had not the spread between depository institutions' interest rates and market rates been so high and had not the technology permitted short-term investments in high-yield securities by aggregating funds. Like thrift institutions, therefore, money market funds developed because the current financial institutions failed to respond to consumer needs.

The initial reaction of the regulatory subsystem to money market funds was to restrict them. In response to bank pressure that MMFs were competing unfairly because they did not have to maintain reserves as the banks did, the Federal Reserve imposed a 15 percent reserve requirement on MMFs in the spring of 1980. Because reserve funds do not draw interest, this action would reduce the yield of the MMFs. So-called 'clone" funds were established to circumvent the reserve requirements; a clone fund, for example, might be offered through a broker's foreign office outside the reach of U.S. regulatory agencies. By late summer of 1980, the Federal Reserve accepted defeat and eliminated the reserve requirements.

Interest on Checking Accounts.   In 1933, Congress prohibited banks from paying interest on checking accounts as they had prior to 1933. Only commercial banks were permitted to offer checking accounts with thrift institutions restricted to time deposits (savings accounts). Several different reasons have been used to justify this prohibition even though the legislative intent is vague. One possible reason was to discourage rural banks from maintaining large deposits in urban banking centers, thereby reducing locally available funds. Because federal policy often distinguished between rural and urban banks, this reasoning was probable (Campbell and Campbell, 1975: 141). The second possible reason was that the interest prohibition provided banks with a cheap source of funds and, therefore, removed pressures to make risky high-yield loans (but see Mingo, 1981). A third possibility was that Congress saw it as a way of compensating banks for the deposit insurance payments that they pay.

Whatever the reason for the prohibition on paying interest on demand deposits, no interest was paid for 40 years. Competition for checking accounts was limited to premiums (gifts for opening accounts), offers of better service (permitting overdrafts), or lower service charges for check writing. Ron Hazelton, president of Consumer Savings Bank of Worchester, Massachusetts, decided that his bank, a state-chartered mutual savings bank, needed to attract more deposits by offering a service that no one else did. Because current savings accounts permitted the withdrawal of funds by signing a withdrawal form, Hazelton proposed that these forms be made negotiable so that people could use them to pay debts directly. In effect, Hazelton proposed check-writing privileges for a savings account. Because Consumer Savings Bank was a state institution and did not have FDIC insurance, it applied to the Massachusetts Banking Commission for authority to offer what Hazelton called negotiated order of withdrawal or NOW accounts. After being turned down, Consumer Savings sued in state court and won in 1972 (Mayer, 1974: 184).

Other state savings banks in Massachusetts followed Consumer Savings in offering NOW accounts. As these accounts began attracting funds from other banks, state-regulated institutions in New Hampshire were also allowed to offer NOW accounts. In response to pressure from national banks in Massachusetts and New Hampshire, the U.S. Congress authorized NOW accounts for banks in these two states as an experiment. Congress passed this experiment as part of 1973 legislation that extended ceilings on interest rates. In 1975 and 1978, Congress authorized banks in the rest of New England and New York, respectively, to offer NOW accounts. Both situations were in response to competitive pressures from state savings banks.

Federal regulatory agencies encouraged the experimentation in interest-paying demand accounts. The National Credit Union Administration in 1974 permitted credit unions to offer "share drafts" that were, in effect, checks drawn against credit union accounts. In the same year, savings associations were authorized by the Federal Home Loan Bank Board to set up remote service units in commercial locations. Such units allowed depositors to withdraw cash from ATM machines, thus enabling savings accounts to perform the same function as checking accounts (which savings associations could not offer). In 1975 the Federal Reserve approved telephone transfer accounts for commercial banks; a telephone transfer account allowed a depositor to shift money by phone from a savings account to a checking account in time to cover checks written. In 1978, the Federal Reserve went further and permitted automatic transfer of funds from a savings account to cover checks written in a checking account.

These federal regulatory efforts were all deregulatory in nature but should not be viewed as planned deregulation. Because the federal regulatory effort was fragmented and because each regulator was more sensitive to the needs of the industry it regulated, the efforts can best be treated as efforts to equalize the rules for competition. Each industry, through its regulator, sought a portion of the new interest-paying checking accounts. In addition, each industry viewed the others as attempting to infringe on its own turf. The various financial regulation subsystems were coming into conflict.

Geographic Barriers.   Under the McFadden Act commercial banks were prohibited from interstate banking. The McFadden Act was a political barrier to entry that restricted the action of large financial center banks and reserved a restricted territory for local banks (Wines, 1981: 2057). Within states, prohibitions against branch banking had a similar impact. Geographic boundaries were undergirded by other boundaries. The Glass-Steagall Act of 1933 barred commercial banks from investment banking and other nonbank businesses.

As noted earlier, the politics of banking since the depression is a history of attempts to circumvent these barriers. Holding companies were created to own banks and engage in other business simultaneously. In Texas, holding companies were used to circumvent laws on branch banking. The First Bank System of Minneapolis acquired 92 banks in several states as did the now-termed First Interstate Bank System in the Western states (M. White, 1982: 45). Holding companies also purchased a variety of businesses along with banks. Although these practices were ended for multibank holding companies by the Bank Holding Company Act of 1956, some of the activities were exempted via a grandfather clause.

In 1968, First City Bank of New York (now Citibank) found a loophole in the law; it applied only to multibank holding companies. To circumvent the law, therefore, First City formed a single-bank holding company (Citicorp) and purchased a 40-state chain of finance companies. By the time this loophole was closed, some 1,300 one-bank holding companies were formed with interests in almost every industrial sector (Wines, 1981: 2060). In addition, banks established loan origination offices (more than 7,000) in other states to service loans and attract business; because these offices did not accept deposits, they were not technically branches (deposits, however, could be made through any nationwide ATM system).

Bank efforts to circumvent geographical restrictions were minor, however, compared to efforts by other financial institutions that were not geographically restricted. These institutions used their dispersed bases to move into banking functions. Money market funds accepted deposits and made loans without any regard for state boundaries. Financial services companies such as American Express used ATMs to permit interstate loans. Prudential Insurance purchased Bache Group, Inc., a company owning a brokerage firm to move into the same business. Savings and loans became an attractive investment to some companies because savings and loans were not prohibited from establishing branches within a state. By 1980 the barriers that prevented interstate banking were beginning to dissolve just as the barriers between the financial industries were crumbling. Both technology and economics had made the regulatory distinction between Oregon and Idaho as obsolete as that between banking and investment companies.

The regulatory subsystems were unable to contain the innovations in money markets, NOWs, and geographic dispersion because the subsystems were fragmented along industry lines. No regulator had sufficient political authority to resolve the disputes. In attempts to counter innovations by granting additional freedom to their regulated institutions, each regulator exacerbated the problem.

Court Intervention

By 1979 the course of financial deregulation had been set. The economy demanded that restrictions on interest rates be lifted, and the technology permitted this to be done. The financial industries would have moved toward greater economic deregulation even if Congress had done nothing. Congress was not permitted this luxury, however, because the U.S. Court of Appeals for the District of Columbia intervened.

Each of the depository institutions attempted to invade the turf of the others while protecting its own during the 1970s. Each had successfully persuaded its regulators to ease up on some restrictions. These relaxations were challenged in court by the other institutions. The U.S. League of Savings Associations (USLSA) sued the Federal Reserve because the Fed approved automatic transfer of funds to checking from savings accounts to cover checks. The American Bankers' Association sued the National Credit Union Administration over its rule authorizing credit unions to issue share draft accounts. The Independent Bankers Association filed suit against the Federal Home Loan Bank Board because the FHLBB authorized savings associations to open remote service units.

The D.C. Circuit Court of Appeals consolidated all three cases in *ABA v. Connell* (1979) and vacated district court decisions that held for the agencies. The circuit court gave the Congress until December 31, 1979, to authorize the services in question (Conte, 1979: 1364). The court ruling affected only automatic transfer of funds by banks, share drafts by credit unions, and remote service units by savings associations. These accounts were no small matter; in 1979, automatic transfer accounts contained $6.4 billion, share draft accounts held $720 million, and 200 savings and loans had remote service units with access to $2.6 billion (Conte, 1979: 1366). Given the investment these institutions had in the innovations, pressure on Congress to pass some legislation was automatic.

THE DEPOSITORY INSTITUTIONS DEREGULATION AND MONETARY CONTROL ACT OF 1980

The Interest Groups Line Up

Each of the depository institutions had its own legislative agenda in 1980 based on the self-interest of that industry. The American Bankers' Association, in theory representing all commercial bankers, had adopted the viewpoint of the large commercial banks. The ABA wanted power to compete directly with the money market funds. Power to compete meant economic deregulation and the ability to pay money market rates on deposits. Although the ABA would have preferred to keep the restrictions on thrifts (limits on their loan powers, checking accounts, and so on), it was willing to accept these powers if the 0.25 percent differential that savings associations paid on time deposits (Regulation Q) were eliminated.

Smaller banks, represented by the Independent Bankers Association of America (IBAA), did not support the proderegulation stance of the ABA. Small banks hold more of their assets in long-term mortgages than do large banks and are not affected as directly by money market funds. The IBAA preferred the status quo. eliminating Regulation Q and creating NOW accounts would only increase their costs. Small banks did not wish to compete with savings associations for checking accounts or with the large banks and money market funds for the national investor.

Among savings associations, the National Savings and Loan League, representing the larger, urban S&Ls, wanted broader powers for its members, including checking accounts, broader ability to make loans, and fewer distinctions between banks and S&Ls. The U.S. League of Savings Associations, representing the smaller S&Ls, endorsed NOW accounts and strongly opposed the elimination of Regulation Q and other measures designed to increase competition. Savings associations also saw the legislation as a way to address fundamental problems of the industry (high interest rates and low yielding mortgages) and pushed for innovative methods of home financing such as variable rate mortgages and renegotiated mortgages.

Credit unions, represented by the Credit Union National Association (CUNA) and the National Association of Federal Credit Unions (NAFCU), pressed for broader powers for credit unions. They wanted share draft accounts (their version of NOW accounts) for all credit unions and freedom to make a wider variety of loans. Because credit unions already had authority to pay interest above Regulation Q limits, interest rate ceilings were not an issue.

The federal regulatory agencies were already on record as favoring deregulation because their administrative decisions resulted in *ABA* v. *Connell*. President Carter encouraged Congress on May 22, 1979, and in his 1980 State of the Union Address to pass a comprehensive financial reform bill that would permit NOW accounts nationwide, repeal Regulation Q, allow variable rate mortgages, and broaden the loan powers of savings associations. With the exception of the Federal Reserve, all the federal agencies supported these administration policies as enunciated by Treasury Secretary Blumenthal.

The Federal Reserve perceived deregulation as a mixed blessing for the Fed and its monetary control efforts. If the financial industry were to be deregulated, the Fed reasoned, competition would greatly increase. Banks that were members of the Federal Reserve System (all national banks and some state banks) were required to hold reserves at the Fed; these reserves paid no interest. Non-Fed members had state-imposed reserve requirements, but these reserves could often be held in interest-bearing securities. In short, non-Fed members, by receiving interest on their reserves, had a competitive advantage. Banks responded by withdrawing from the Federal Reserve System. Because reserves are one method of controlling the growth of the money supply, the monetary powers of the Fed were weakened. The Fed supported reserve requirements for all banks, both members and nonmembers.

Banking deregulation also attracted a variety of nondepository interests. Consumer groups, led by groups representing the elderly, appeared to argue that Regulation Q discriminated against the small saver. The National Association of Home Builders and the AFL-CIO opposed eliminating Regulation Q, stressing the essential need that the housing industry had for a long-term source of inexpensive funds. A variety of scholars also played a role in the advocacy coalitions. A long series of government studies dating from 1971, including the Hunt Commission and the FINE study, urged restructuring of bank regulation. Two broad but shifting coalitions formed, one around deregulation and one favoring the status quo.

The Legislative Battle

The battle for the deregulation of financial institutions reflected the access each advocacy coalition had in the House and the Senate. The House, with its smaller constituencies, was more accessible to small bankers and savings associations. As a result, the House could be expected to take a conservative approach to deregulation. The Senate not only had fewer local influences but also had Senator William Proxmire (Democrat, Wisconsin) as chair of the Senate Banking Committee. Proxmire had long supported economic deregulation of the financial industry.

Under the leadership of Fernand St Germain (Democrat, Rhode Island), the chair of the Subcommittee on Financial Institutions of the House Banking Committee, the House acted first. St Germain's bill (HR 4986) simply repealed the prohibition against paying interest on checking accounts and allowed all depository institutions to offer them. The bill passed quickly on September 11, 1979, by a large vote (367 to 39).

On the Senate side, Senator Proxmire had his own bill; it would phase out limits on interest payments over a ten-year period, permit NOW accounts, and reduce the minimum deposit for a money market certificate to $1,000. Proxmire argued to the Senate committee that the pending legislation was a significant opportunity to restructure the financial industry. Such a fundamental change affecting several subsystems drew opposition from savings associations, small banks, and housing groups.

One indicator of the conflict over the Senate bill was the four days the bill spent on the Senate floor. More than 20 amendments were offered. After failing to substitute a far more conservative bill, Senator Morgan (Democrat, North Carolina) deleted the requirement for reserves on non-Fed-member NOW accounts. Various other senators pressed special interests. Senator Thad Cochran (Republican, Mississippi) inserted a provision to override state usury limits on business and agricultural loans greater than $25,000. Senator Jake Garn (Republican, Utah) sponsored a noncontroversial amendment to simplify the requirements of the Truth in Lending Act. Alan Cranston (Democrat, California) had amendments passed that permitted S&Ls to issue credit cards and provide overdraft accounts and that increased deposit coverage to $50,000. Several other amendments concerned interstate banking, money market fund purchases, foreign banks, mutual savings banks' loan powers, and savings association reserves. The Senate bill passed November 1, 1979.

The House Banking Committee responded to the Senate action by taking HR 7, legislation on Federal Reserve membership for all banks, and attaching this bill to the NOW accounts bill (the Consumer Checking Account Equity Act). Committee Chair Henry Reuss (Democrat, Wisconsin) then requested a conference on both items. Reuss and St Germain, reflecting House views, were opposed to the "Christmas tree limbs" that the Senate had added. The House position, therefore, was to oppose issues other than interest on checking accounts in the conference (Gregg, 1979: 2546).

The conference immediately deadlocked. St Germain wanted to hold hearings on Regulation Q and other Senate-passed measures. The Senate conferees with bipartisan support were united behind the broader reform measure. With the December 31 deadline approaching, a temporary compromise was proposed. The law, PL 96–161, was passed quickly by both houses. The bill authorized the three accounts challenged by *ABA* v. *Connell* until March 31, 1980, thus giving the committee three more months to act. Some additional provisions, however, indicated that the Senate was winning over the House to a broader reform bill. PL 96–161 overrode state usury laws on mortgages and agriculture or business loans over $25,000 for the same 90-day period and authorized NOW accounts for New Jersey.

The 90-day delay permitted both houses to save face. It was sufficient time to hold hearings on some of the disputed points. Despite this time period, neither house formally polled committee members on the legislation or marked up alternative legislation. The key to the conference held on March 5 appeared to be Reuss's Federal Reserve membership bill because it gave the House side a positive proposal not included in the Senate bill.

Given all the disagreements, the conference reached a compromise quickly. In a single day, the conference agreed to a bill incorporating federal reserve membership conditions with the Senate provisions. The bill required all banks to hold reserves on transaction accounts at the Fed though it did not require membership. Although reserve requirements for nonmembers were to be phased in, NOW accounts and similar accounts were subject to reserve requirements immediately. Even though the reserve requirement is clearly a proregulatory element in a deregulatory bill, in one sense it can be considered a procompetitive effort. By equalizing the reserve requirements between members and nonmembers, the rules of competition were equalized. A bill designed to aid the Fed, therefore, promoted equalized competition.

Control over interest rates was transferred from the federal regulatory agencies to a Depository Institutions Deregulation Committee (DIDC). Composed of the heads of the Federal Reserve, the FDIC, FHLBB, and NCUA, the secretary of the Treasury, and the comptroller of the currency (nonvoting), DIDC was instructed to phase out all interest rate controls in six years. The committee's composition gave the commercial banking subsystem three of the five votes on the committee.

Thrift institutions were not left out; they received numerous additional powers to compete in the marketplace. They were permitted to invest in money market funds, issue credit cards, accept checking accounts, and loan money for a wider variety of purposes. Restrictions were not completely lifted; but savings associations, mutual savings banks, and credit unions became more like commercial banks. NOW accounts were authorized for all depository institutions effective December 31, 1980, and all the interest-based checking accounts challenged by the court's ruling were permitted.[10]

Given the environmental conditions of 1980, determining what the Depository Institutions Deregulation and Monetary Control Act of 1980 actually did is important. Even without the act, the financial markets were substantially deregulated. Savers willing to take a small risk could receive market interest rates on their deposits through money market funds. Interstate barriers to loans and deposits were fast becoming irrelevant as firms such as Merrill Lynch, American Express, and others conducted nationwide banklike activities.

In this environment, DIDMCA did not deregulate the financial industry. Rather, it permitted some depository institutions the opportunity to compete sometime in the future. With Regulation Q phased out, only commercial banks and credit unions were in a position to compete in a deregulated market. Both savings and loans and mutual savings banks had too many of their funds invested in low-yield, long-term mortgages. Survival for these institutions was not going to be easy even in a regulated market; in a deregulated market, the expectation was that many would fail (Wines,

---

10. Most of the Christmas tree limbs remained in the final version. State usury laws were preempted for mortgages and business or agriculture loans in excess of $25,000. Deposit insurance maximums were increased to $100,000; truth in lending requirements were simplified; banks were given more time to dispose of real estate (a vestige of the earlier Bank Holding Company Act); and the Fed was required to price its services.

1981: 2059; Carron, 1982). Because credit unions are generally small and because smaller banks were likely to remain localized, the net impact of the legislation was to allow the larger commercial banks to compete with non-bank financial institutions. The impact of the act, therefore, was marginal compared to the changes that had been determined by changes in technology and economics.

At a more localized level, however, greater competition resulted from the act. Within a given community, depositors now had more options for demand and time deposits. Savings associations became more like banks as did the credit unions. The true benefits of deregulation for the consumer would be noticed immediately only at the local level.

The Administrative Battle

As David Truman notes (1951), interest groups do not go home after legislation is passed and assume the battle is won. Rather, the battle shifts to the bureaucracy, where the policies of implementation are hammered out. Many DIDMCA provisions were self-implementing or implemented by the private sector. The exception was Regulation Q. The law only required DIDC to consider one-half percentage point increases in the Regulation Q cap every year until March 31, 1986. DIDC did not have to increase the rate, and it had the power to phase it out faster; the only restriction was that Regulation Q would be phased out on March 31, 1986.

The composition of DIDC favored the commercial bankers, but it permitted savings associations and credit unions to participate in this new subsystem. Commercial bankers as represented by the American Bankers' Association favored the rapid deregulation of the industry so that banks could compete with the money market funds. Savings associations, on the other hand, put their efforts into slowing deregulation. Savings institutions generally lost money in 1980 and 1981 because their long-term mortgages were paying less in interest than they had to pay to get deposits. Deregulation would only increase the cost of money to savings institutions, and they would have little opportunity to increase their earnings. The strategy of the savings associations was to delay deregulation while pursuing other options to support their industry (e.g., the All-Savers Certificate).

DIDC's approach to regulation in the last few months of the Carter administration was to pursue cautious but consistent deregulation. Federal Reserve Board Chairman Paul Volcker was elected head of DIDC. Interest caps on money market certificates (investment minimum $10,000) were tied up to the T-bill rate, and small-saver certificates were allowed to pay 12 percent. By September 1980 rules for NOW accounts were issued.

The 1980 election had little impact on the DIDC effort. The Reagan financial regulators were generally supportive of deregulation. Donald Regan, the new secretary of the Treasury, became the strongest advocate of deregulation (Clark, 1982: 713). In June 1981, DIDC adopted a plan to phase out Regulation Q by deregulating those deposits with the longest maturity first. All deposits for four years or more were to be deregulated on August 1, 1982. As August 1, 1985, drew nearer, the shorter-term deposits would be deregulated so that there would be no controls on interest rates by August 1, 1985.

The savings associations, displeased with the "rapid" pace of deregulation, counterattacked. Faced with an unsympathetic DIDC forum, savings associations tried to expand the scope of the conflict and strengthen their advocacy coalition. By bringing its members to Washington to lobby DIDC, the U.S. League of Savings Associations convinced DIDC to withdraw an increase to 6 percent on the interest cap on passbook savings (Carron, 1983: 75; Keller, 1982: 188). They also challenged DIDC's other actions in court and were successful in delaying the implementation of the DIDMCA. The delay tactic became so obvious that the National Credit Union Administration withdrew from the DIDC deregulation process (as the law permitted it to do) in March 1982 and immediately removed all interest rate controls for credit unions.

DIDMCA and Its Impact

In retrospect the DIDMCA of 1980 must be considered a failure. Consumers received many of deregulation's potential benefits before the act was passed because innovative nondepository institutions filled a financial void. Both market interest rates and interest-paid checking were available to the consumer.[11] Had DIDMCA been successful, it would have made the process slightly more convenient; but it would not have fundamentally changed the consumer side of financial institutions.

THE GARN-ST GERMAIN ACT

Just as environmental conditions dictated the deregulation of the financial markets in the late 1970s, changes in these environmental conditions dictated Congress's response to the failure of DIDMCA in the 1980s. Three environmental factors played a major role in shaping the 1982 Garn-St Germain Act—the continued outflow of funds to money market funds, the 1980 congressional election, and the change in the supply and demand for money.

Environmental Changes

Of the environmental changes, the political changes of 1980 promised to be the most important but turned out to be fairly mild. President Reagan did not appoint opponents of deregulation to the key financial regulator's positions. Administratively, therefore, little changed. The new Republican majority in the Senate, however, promised a greater impact. Senator Jake Garn replaced William Proxmire as chair of the Senate Banking Committee. Proxmire was a longtime critic of banks and a strong advocate of economic deregulation. Senator Garn was initially a cautious person on deregulation, preferring comprehensive oversight of DIDMCA to new legislation. In the next two years, however, Garn became a strong advocate of fundamental changes in the regulation of depository institutions, including economic deregulation. The Senate leadership in 1982, therefore, was as prochange as the Senate leadership in 1980 (see Miller, 1983).

---

11. Perhaps the small, unsophisticated consumer who felt secure only in banks did benefit from DIDMCA although safe instruments were available from other institutions.

The outflow of money to money market funds continued after the passage of DIDMCA. Money market funds attracted a total of $180 billion at their peak because depository institutions could not pay rates as high as the funds and still permit the liquidity and checking aspects of the funds. The large outflow of money motivated commercial banks to seek deregulation so that they could compete for these funds.

The most significant change in the environment, however, was the worldwide economic recession. With the recession, interest rates dropped dramatically. In early 1983, T-bill rates actually fell below 8 percent. The recessionary drop took some immediate pressure off the thrifts because they were profitable when the interest rate fell below 12 percent (Carron, 1982). At this time a complete economic deregulation would not be as major a shock to the thrift industry as it would have been in 1980. The recession, however, was a two-edged sword for the thrifts because housing sales dropped, and there was little demand for mortgages. With the immediate pressure for survival off, thrifts could afford to press for long-term changes in their industry.

Legislative Action

In a major change, the representatives of some 15 financial industry groups met in early 1982 to resolve their differences and push for new legislation (Wines, 1982d: 1500). Although a successful coalition was not built, the differences between the industries were such that just meeting was a major breakthrough. Senate Bill 1720 represented the results of this meeting; the bill would grant broader powers to thrift institutions (more freedom to make nonmortgage loans) in exchange for authorization of banks to engage in property and casualty insurance. The House under St Germain's leadership was considering a bill with provisions for federal aid to thrifts but no new powers for either institution.

The Senate Banking Committee, in response to pressure from the insurance and securities industries, reported out S 1720 without any new powers for banks. Both the ABA and the Independent Bankers Association of America denounced the measure as a "savings and loan sweetheart bill" and withdrew their support. Despite the differences between this bill and St Germain's (HR 6267), a conference committee compromise passed both houses and was signed into law on October 15, 1982. To gain support from banking interests, authority to offer market interest rate accounts immediately was granted (Puckett, 1983: 88).

The Garn-St Germain Depository Institutions Act of 1982 can be divided into three sections—those that affect both banks and thrifts, those provisions affecting banks only, and the provisions affecting thrifts only. For both institutions, the law authorized new accounts (called super-NOW accounts and money market demand accounts (MMDA)) that would pay market interest rates with checking and other services. The law also provided for a phaseout of Regulation Q by January 1984. This latter action was of little consequence because only uncompetitive accounts would be affected by Regulation Q after the implementation of the MMDAs and super-NOWs.

The law also provided the FDIC and its savings association equivalent, FSLIC, could provide cash assistance to troubled institutions and augmented their powers to assist mergers (the financial assistance provisions resembled those of the depression era Reconstruction Finance Corporation). Generally, federal policy has been to merge failing depository institutions with stronger ones rather than to close them. Over 450 savings associations were merged in 1981 and 1982. These provisions plus the override of state laws that bar "due-on-sale" clauses in home mortgages were designed to help the thrifts even though banks were also covered.

Bank powers were expanded only modestly. Banks could sell credit life insurance but not property or casualty insurance. Loan limits to individuals were eased, and bank service corporations (companies providing services to two or more banks) were permitted some additional powers. Despite the modest improvements, large banks were pleased because the super-NOW and MMDA accounts allowed banks to compete with money market funds (Keller, 1982: 189).

Thrifts came away the big winner. They could now offer corporate checking accounts and allow overdraft checking. Loan authority was expanded dramatically; thrifts could now use up to 5 percent of their assets for commercial loans, up to 40 percent for commercial real estate loans, up to 30 percent for consumer loans, up to 10 percent for equipment loans, and up to 5 percent for educational loans, and they can purchase government bonds with up to 100 percent of their assets.

Administrative Action

With the drop in interest rates, thrifts became profitable again in 1983 (Brownstein, 1983c: 1690; Pauley and Ipsen, 1983: 59). As a result, the pressure on DIDC to proceed slowly with regulation was eased. Two months after the Garn-St Germain Act, DIDC authorized both money market demand accounts and super-NOW accounts for January of 1983. These accounts were immediately popular. By April of 1983, some $340 billion flowed into MMDAs, and some $29 billion flowed into super-NOWs (Furlong, 1983: 319). The growth in money market funds stopped and, in fact, suffered a decline. In June 1983 with an October effective date, DIDC corrected an absurdity in the regulations that deregulated short-term funds (MMDAs) but kept an interest rate cap on some longer-term deposits. For all intents and purposes, the economic side of depository institutions was deregulated in terms of interest rates.

Garn-St Germain: An Assessment

Despite the popularity of the new instruments, Garn-St Germain did little for the consumer and could not hope to stabilize the condition of the financial industries. Consumers had more institutions offering money market returns and more places to seek nonmortgage loans, but they did not receive any new benefits. New loan sources basically add thrifts to numerous offerers already in place. Even the federally insured MMDAs are of marginal value because noninsured money market funds invest heavily in government bonds (and, therefore, in practice are as safe as the FSLIC) and are starting to offer their own forms of insurance. MMDAs have not yet offered the consumer the variety of funds offered by the securities industry.

For the second time in two years, therefore, Congress failed to recognize that the old barriers to financial competition have been leveled by economics and technology. On the liabilities side, depository institutions are no different from any other financial institution; that is, they must compete in the open market for deposits/investments. What remains is a restricted asset side. Banks and thrifts are still restricted in the types of loans and investments they can make. This limits the profitability of depository institutions, preventing them from earning the highest returns.

The various financial subsystems in the 1980s had been permanently opened to the influences of each other. Temporary political barriers could be erected, but the rigid pre-1970 separation was gone forever. Financial intermediaries will have to compete with each other both economically and politically. Because Congress refused to recognize this, it was faced with passing yet another financial deregulation bill in the mid-1980s.

THE BARRIERS CONTINUE TO CRUMBLE

Policy barriers to entry in banking as a generic industry can be divided into two types—barriers between industries (Glass-Steagall barriers) and geographic barriers (McFadden barriers). In both cases, these barriers to entry continued to crumble after the enactment of the Garn-St Germain Act of 1982. Even though the act had little to do with the decline in barriers, it served as a signal to federal regulators and to the industries that more freedom would be tolerated.

Interindustry Barriers

The days when commercial banks, credit unions, savings associations, mutual savings banks, securities firms, insurance companies, finance companies, and even retailers served distinct and separate elements of the financial market are over. The Garn-St Germain Act granted thrift institutions the powers to develop into commercial banks; credit unions actually were free to follow this course after the National Credit Union Administration withdrew from the DIDC deregulation process in March 1982.

The greater threat to homogenization of the financial service industry, however, comes from outside the depository institutions. The wave of innovation of the 1970s has continued with securities firms, insurance companies, and retailers entering areas that were at one time banking. Among securities firms, the major innovator has been Merrill Lynch. By entering the banking area with its cash management account (CMA), Merrill Lynch became a major force in depository industry. Merrill Lynch has 600,000 CMAs with deposits of $30 billion; if it were a bank, Merrill Lynch would be the ninth largest bank in the United States (M. White, 1982: 47). It offers a wide range of other financial services through its real estate subsidiaries and its mortgage banking subsidiaries. In 1983, Merrill Lynch formally moved into banking by purchasing a New Jersey state bank (Wines, 1983f: 909). Other securities firms have also been active. Dreyfus purchased a state bank in New Jersey under the nonbank loophole (see further on) and has begun to offer auto loans. Fidelity Daily Investment Trust became the first mutual fund to accept deposits via automated clearinghouses (EFTs from payroll deductions; see *ABA Banking Journal*, April 1983: 260).

Insurance companies have followed a similar pattern of invading the "banking" industry. The Prudential Insurance Company acquired Bache Halsey, a large brokerage firm, and offered financial services through it. In addition, in 1983, Prudential/Bache filed an application to acquire a suburban Atlanta bank under the nonbank loophole (Wines, 1983f: 909). Under loopholes in the regulation of insurance companies, some insurance companies have offered money market funds under the guise of insurance and, thus, subject to more favorable tax treatment. With their large cash flows, insurance companies could develop into a major competitor to the depository institutions.

Financial services corporations such as American Express and other bank card companies have originated banklike services. American Express acquired Shearson Loeb Rhodes, a major broker, to offer "banking" and investment services via their member network. Shearson/American Express offers money market funds to banks; and banks, in turn, sell them to their depositors (Aug, 1982: 49). Mastercard, in association with Fidelity Management Group, offers banks a sweep provision to permit excess funds in individual checking accounts to be swept into money market funds (Clark, 1982: 714).

Perhaps the largest threat to banks has come from major retailers led by Sears. Sears has announced that it will operate 600 financial network centers by 1986. Sears is in a unique position to provide financial services because it has systematically purchased a variety of components. It owns Allstate Insurance, recently purchased Dean Witter, the nation's fifth largest broker, and also acquired Coldwell, Banker and Co., the nation's largest real estate broker. Sears is, thus, in a position to accept deposits via money market funds, sell insurance, offer mortgages, provide consumer finance loans, and engage in almost all banking functions through a savings association it owns. With 860 stores, 1,200 Allstate offices, and 25 million holders of credit cards, it will be a major force in the industry (M. White, 1982: 47). Other retailers have followed suit. J. C. Penney, for example, has purchased a state bank in Delaware under the nonbank loophole (*National Journal,* July 9, 1983: 1468).

Depository institutions have not idly sat by and watched the invasion of their turf by securities firms, financial services companies, insurance companies, and retailers. With the aid of federal regulators, they have struck back. Specifically, the regulatory agencies have done four things to facilitate the banking counterattack. First, the Federal Reserve Board has broadened its definition of "bank-related activities" under the Bank Holding Company Act. At the present time 15 functions are accepted by regulation, and 20 others have been accepted on individual petition. Second, the bank regulators have not closed the nonbank loophole. By federal law an institution is a bank if it offers checking accounts and commercial loans. If a firm purchases a state bank, the bank can be turned into a nonbank by selling either the commercial loan portfolio or by eliminating checking accounts. This nonbank can then engage in insurance, investment banking, real estate purchases, or other functions that are prohibited to banks. In 1984 the Fed placed a temporary moratorium on nonbanks in the hope that Congress would act on this issue. Third, the FDIC has announced that state banks insured by the FDIC but not members of the Federal Reserve are not subject to the nonbanking provisions of the Glass-Steagall Act and may pursue nonbanking functions. Fourth, the FHLBB has authorized savings associations to engage in correspondent activities, offer consumer leasing services, and trade in financial market options (Pratt, 1982: 5).

Armed with the acquiescence of federal regulators, banks and bank holding companies have invaded the turf of other financial intermediaries. The two most active banks in this invasion were the nation's two largest, Bank of America and Citibank. Bank of America purchased the nation's largest discount broker, Charles Schwab; because a discount broker only buys and sells securities but does not give advice, this did not violate the Glass-Steagall Act. Bank of America also struck a blow at the McFadden Act (see later) by purchasing Seafirst, the bank holding company of Seattle First National Bank, the twenty-fourth largest bank in the United States.[12] Bank of America, in addition to normal banking functions such as credit cards, also leases computers and exercises futures contracts (Brownstein, 1983a; 1373).

Citibank, through its holding company Citicorp, engages in a wide variety of financial services, including travelers checks, credit cards, and insurance. Citicorp has purchased Fidelity Savings and Loan of California and operates 700 lending offices in 40 states (M. White, 1982: 94). Some 65 percent of Citicorp's income comes from nonbank sources (Brownstein, 1983a: 1374). Citibank and Bank of America are not alone. Security Pacific National Bank owns Fidelity Brokerage Services and offers brokerage services (M. White, 1982: 45). Northwest Bankcorp owns a chain of 500 consumer finance offices in 37 states. The most recent counterattack by the banks involves the insurance industry; by purchasing banks and turning them into nonbanks, commercial banks hope to engage in the insurance business. Citibank recently purchased American State Bank of Rapid City, South Dakota, for this purpose.

Although savings associations have not been as active as commercial banks in moving into other financial areas (to be expected given the financial situation in the industry), they have also made some inroads. More than 140 thrifts offer brokerage services to their depositors. In Phoenix, 25 thrifts formed a consortium so that they could pool their assets to make large commercial loans (Brownstein, 1983c: 1691).

Geographic Barriers

The McFadden Act prohibits interstate banking. The invasion of national companies from the securities industry, the financial services industry, the insurance industry, and retail trade into banking functions has eliminated the restrictions of the McFadden Act as far as consumers are concerned. The remaining restrictions are being chipped away by federal regulators, state regulators, and innovative depository institutions.

Federal regulators have moved against the McFadden Act as part of the deposit insurance function. Rather than liquidate an endangered thrift or

12. Perhaps the greatest force for interstate banking was the Penn Square Bank of Oklahoma. Before it was closed in 1982 by the FDIC, it made some $2 billion in questionable energy loans and sold these loans to other banks. Seafirst's collapse as well as the problems of Continental of Illinois (the seventh largest bank) were related to Penn Square loans. Large bank failures require mergers of the failed bank with a solvent bank. Normally, this means an interstate merger to find a bank large enough to absorb the failing bank.

bank, the FDIC and the FHLBB prefer to merge these institutions with stronger institutions. Although the Garn-St Germain Act gives preference to intrastate mergers, it permits interstate mergers. Home Savings of America, the nation's largest savings and loan with assets of $17 billion, has offices in California, Missouri, and Florida. Similarly, City Federal Savings and Loan has 98 offices in 12 states (M. White, 1982: 46).

Thrifts have not been the only ones to merge across state lines. Bank of America purchased Seattle First National Bank in 1983, when the Seattle bank got into trouble. Loopholes in the law have permitted other interstate operations. Banks often operate loan offices in other states to service loans. Some 7,383 interstate bank offices exist (Brownstein, 1983b: 1603). Nationwide ATM systems such as PULSE and CIRRUS permit the interstate deposit and withdrawal of funds. Nationwide toll-free numbers are being used to solicit deposits. Bank holding company purchases of consumer finance companies or savings associations also permit a form of interstate banking. Recently, banks with large credit card operations such as Citibank have moved these operations to states such as South Dakota that have less restrictive usury laws.

State regulators have been equally adept at encouraging the interstate expansion of banking. Banks are industries; and just like other industries, they contribute to the economic base of a state. States have adopted liberal policies to attract bank subsidiaries. Led by the state of South Dakota, states have repealed usury laws to attract credit card corporations and have allowed banks to sell insurance and perform other nonbank functions that the federal government prohibits (Brownstein, 1983a: 1376). In fact, a competition among states appears to exist to provide the most attractive environment for banking. Such competition is possible given the nonbank loophole and the recent FDIC position that state banks that do not belong to the Federal Reserve are exempt from Glass-Steagall restrictions.

State regulators have also encouraged more traditional interstate banking (e.g., opening a branch or owning a bank). Twelve states have passed some type of interstate banking law (Brownstein, 1983b: 1603). Four of the six New England states passed legislation granting interstate banking rights to the other New England states. The McFadden Act has become so riddled with loopholes that Dimension Financial Corporation applied for 31 national bank charters in 25 different states; of course, these would be nonbanks because they would not offer commercial loans. Richard Pratt, former head of the Federal Home Loan Bank Board, stated in 1983 that the McFadden Act would be dead by 1988 whether or not the act was repealed (Pratt, 1983: 100).

In summary, then, the momentum of the financial industry in breaking down barriers between industries and between states has continued. The technology of the modern financial industry is such that artificial restrictions will be circumvented. Regulations established in an era when banking was conducted out of brick and mortar buildings are no match for computer age technology. The numerous financial regulation subsystems now overlap. Richard Pratt is optimistic. Both the McFadden Act and the Glass-Steagall Act are dead; the only issue that remains is whether or not all financial institutions will be allowed to participate under rules that treat all institutions equally.

CONCLUSION

Who benefits from regulating depository institutions? Until recently, regulatory policy has sought one goal, economic soundness. Using stringent regulation coupled with deposit insurance, regulators made depository institutions a safe place to store funds. Economic soundness regulation benefits both the depository institution and individual depositors. Borrowers were indirectly subsidized by caps on interest payments at some cost to savers. The recent movement toward economic deregulation in the 1980s is a direct benefit to consumers with funds to invest; depositors can earn market interest rates on small amounts of money with little or no risk. The gains by depositors are offset by some losses to borrowers, who must now pay higher interest rates for loans. Among financial institutions, those large institutions with reasonably liquid assets will gain whereas smaller institutions saddled with long-term notes will lose. Deregulation, therefore, has benefited some consumers and some of the industry. Overall financial regulation, especially the emphasis on economic soundness, still benefits both the regulated industry and the nonregulated. Such benefits are possible because regulation maintains a sound financial system essential for commerce.

What determines the direction of regulatory policy? The key variables outlined in chapter 2 are summarized in Table 3.2. Financial regulation is

Table 3.2 Summary of Financial Regulatory Policy

Economy	*Banks*	*Thrifts*
Ease of entry	easy	easy
Number of firms	14,000+	25,000+
Profits	high	high/variable
Technology		
Complexity	low	low
Stability	low	low
Substitutes	high	high
Subsystem		
Bureaucratic control	strong	strong
Industry coalition	strong	strong
Nonindustry coalition	strong	strong
Bureaucratic resources		
Expertise	strong	strong/moderate
Cohesion	strong	strong
Leadership	moderate	moderate
Legislative authority		
Goals	specific	specific
Coverage	universal	universal
Sanctions	good	good
Procedures	good	good
Involvement of Macropolitical Actors		
Congress	strong	strong
President	weak	weak
Courts	weak	weak

normally characterized by low salience and a high level of complexity (regulation is complex even though the industry's technology is not). For short periods of time (e.g., 1907, 1933, 1980), banking became salient when the subsystem could not resolve its own problems and disputes. Regulatory policy in this area is characterized by long periods of subsystem operation interwoven with brief periods of macrosystem intervention.

Within the subsystem both the bureaucracy and the advocacy coalitions are fairly strong. The regulatory agencies have a reputation for expertise, professional values (stemming from the New Deal), and cohesion. Leadership has on occasion been innovative but not consistently. Such variables would indicate a dominant bureaucracy. The bureaucracy is not completely dominant because the industry advocacy coalition is large, well funded, and well organized and has substantial political resources. With the overlap of financial subsystems, more than one coalition arises on almost all issues, frequently pitting one financial industry against another. Subsystem outputs, therefore, are a compromise between advocacy coalitions. A second reason for the lack of bureaucratic domination is the dual banking system. By stressing lax regulation, state regulators can disrupt regulatory policies of the federal government.

The legislative authority resources of the regulatory agencies suggest that such compromises will often benefit the nonregulated. Regulatory goals are reasonably specific, regulatory authority is universal within a specific industry, sanctions are wide-ranging, and procedures are not limiting. In addition, agency goals forged during the depression collapse of banking strongly support stringent regulation to prevent bank failures. These factors explain why regulatory policy benefits the nonregulated just as the strength of the industry coalition explains why the regulated benefit also.

When conflict spills out of the subsystem, the normal forum for resolution is Congress. The industry has good access to Congress as do other groups. Congress accordingly plays a major role in resolving subsystem disputes. This process has happened often enough that the subsystem has developed a norm that Congress is entitled to resolve subsystem disputes. The Fed's willingness to place a moratorium on "nonbanks" in 1984 to give Congress a chance to act is a recent example. The role of the president and the courts is less significant although in exceptional cases (e.g., the depression), they can be mobilized.

The economic and technological environment contains factors that discourage regulation in the interests of the industry only. In economic terms, entry is easy, the number of firms is large, and profits are usually high. Technologically, the industries' technology is simple but unstable and substitutes exist. Turbulence in this environment forced the multiple subsystems together in the 1980s. The ability of one financial institution to enter the business of the others suggests that a broad, competitive subsystem is taking shape. Regulation that benefits one industry at the expense of the others is less likely in such circumstances.

4

Consumer Protection

Consumer protection was one of the fastest-growing areas of regulation in the 1970s and is currently among the most controversial. In a general sense, all regulation can be characterized as consumer protection to some degree, including such traditional economic policies as antitrust, railroad regulation, and airline regulation because consumers are often presented as among the intended beneficiaries of regulation (Meyer, 1982). This chapter, however, takes a more limited view of consumer protection and looks at the regulation of consumer products—protecting the consumer from deception and fraud in the marketplace and protecting the consumer from harmful products. Such consumer protection functions are shared by both federal and state governments. The programs of five federal agencies are examined: the Food and Drug Administration (FDA; drugs, food), the Food Safety and Inspection Service (FSIS; meat and poultry products), the National Highway Traffic Safety Administration (NHTSA; automobiles), the Consumer Product Safety Commission (CPSC; numerous industries), and the Federal Trade Commission (FTC; deceptive marketing). In addition, recent state consumer protection actions are briefly noted.

When examining consumer policies, one should keep in mind that two schools of thought exist on the proper strategy of consumer-oriented regulation (Creighton, 1976: 4). The consumer sovereignty position is based on the classical economics view that the consumer determines what will be produced in all industries if a perfectly competitive market exists. Of the common market failures (externalities, monopoly, and lack of information), absence of information is the major flaw in consumer product markets according to consumer sovereignty advocates. The solution to deception and hazardous products, therefore, is to give consumers as much information as possible and let them make their own decisions. Whether or not consumers actually use such information is irrelevant because consumers can rationally decide that such information has little utility and ignore it. Consumer sovereignty advocates try not to limit consumer choices but rather to give the consumer tools to make rational decisions. Examples include truth in lending laws and truth in packaging laws.

The consumer protection view rejects the rational economic man model of consumers and traces its roots to Thorstein Veblen rather than to Adam Smith. Information will never be equal, this view claims; and the profit motive creates incentives to provide ineffective, unsafe, and hazardous goods. This view holds that consumers must be protected. Hazardous products and low-quality goods are to be banned. This emphasis seeks to limit consumer choice to "acceptable" products (see Creighton, 1976: 10 ff). Examples might be the Consumer Product Safety Commission's lawn-mower standards or the National Highway Traffic Safety Administration's determination that all automobiles must have seat belts.

Both approaches claim the mantle of true consumerism. Many disputes over the effectiveness of current policy are, in fact, disputes between these two schools of thought over the appropriate strategy for government regulation.

THE FIRST ERA OF CONSUMER PROTECTION: THE PROGRESSIVES

The American political system has witnessed three eras of consumer protection—the Progressive era, the New Deal era, and the contemporary era. The eras contain numerous commonalities. Each is marked by the entrepreneurial ability of one or more consumer activists who succeeded in raising the salience of consumer protection. Each has a long period of struggle before the efforts culminate in federal legislation, and each was aided by a crisis or "media crisis."

Before the Industrial Revolution, little consumer protection was needed. For the most part, individuals produced their own goods and ser-vices. When goods were purchased, markets were local, and the sellers known to the buyer. Goods were usually simple enough so that a buyer could judge the quality (e.g., the sturdiness of a wagon wheel, the freshness of bread, and so on). If a product proved defective, the seller whose reputa-tion depended on word-of-mouth endorsements would usually repair the product without charge.

The Industrial Revolution ended the local markets where everyone was known and the quality of goods was easy to judge. Goods were manufac-tured elsewhere, and the proliferation of new goods was enormous. As a result, the buyer no longer had the ability to judge whether or not a product would perform as it was intended. If a good proved defective, rather than face a local provider, the buyer had to deal with a nonlocal manufacturer if the manufacturer could be located at all.

With the rapid growth of consumer products, three ills of the market-place were accentuated. First, deceptive advertising was common. Dr. Scott's electric hairbrush, for example, promised to cure nervous headache, baldness, dandruff, and premature graying of hair with only five minutes of daily use (Feldman, 1976: 8). Second, food products often contained harm-ful additives; a popular soft drink at the time traced its name to the fact that it contained cocaine. Third, patent medicines were often nothing more than powerful, but addictive, painkillers; many patent medicines, for example, were opium-based.

Within this context the chief chemist of the U.S. Department of Agri-culture (USDA), Dr. Harvey Wiley, began a campaign against adulterated food. Wiley used Senate hearings in 1883 and later years to expose common practices of adulterating food. Butter, for example, was mixed with pork fat and still sold as butter; chicory was a frequent additive to coffee. More alarming, according to Wiley, was the use of dangerous chemicals as food additives. Both boric acid and formaldehyde were used as preservatives in milk; hydrochloric acid was added to apple jellies. Perhaps the most effective method Wiley used to publicize this issue was his poison squad, a group of young employees in the Department of Agriculture who were fed controlled diets of food additives. The poison squad became famous (Nadel, 1971: 10).

Wiley's entrepreneurial actions increased the salience of food and drug issues. Under his influence, the Association of Agricultural Chemists proposed a food and drug law to Congress. Despite support from the American Medical Association, the Pharmaceutical Manufacturers Association, the Grange, women's organizations, grocers, and druggists,[1] the legislation failed to pass Congress. Senate opposition prevented passage. The legislative logjam was broken following the publication of Upton Sinclair's *The Jungle*, an exposé of the meat-packing industry in Chicago. Sinclair provided example after example of unsafe, unsanitary, and unhealthy conditions in the industry and in the food it produced. *The Jungle* and the resulting publicity given it by magazines of the day resulted in Theodore Roosevelt's backing the legislation and pressuring the Senate to pass the bill.

Probably of equal importance to Roosevelt's backing was the support of the large meat producers. Following publication of *The Jungle*, sales of meat and meat products dropped by 50 percent, and it appeared that export markets might be closed to U.S. meats. Fearing permanent loss of markets, the packers saw federal inspection as a way of reestablishing their reputation and their markets (Herrmann, 1978: 29).

In 1906, Congress passed the Pure Food and Drug Act. The act listed specific food additives that were banned, and it prohibited misbranding drugs (that is, making false claims). A precursor agency of the Food and Drug Administration was created in the Department of Agriculture to administer the law. Closer to the concerns of *The Jungle* was the passage of the Meat Inspection Act of 1907. This act provided for federal inspection of all meat sold in interstate commerce (currently about 70 percent of meat is sold interstate), and the responsibility was lodged in the Department of Agriculture.[2]

The passage of the Pure Food and Drug Act and the Meat Inspection Act marks the high point of the Progressive era consumer movement. Only one other action had lasting impact, the creation of the Federal Trade Commission in 1914, and that resulted from the perceived failure of federal antitrust policy rather than specific consumer protection goals (see chapter 9). The Federal Trade Commission did have authority to prohibit unfair competition through its antitrust powers, but the courts ruled in *FTC* v. *Raladam* (1930) that this power did not include jurisdiction over consumers.

The Progressive era of consumer protection ended with the start of World War I; national attention turned to other issues, and the public outrage supporting consumer legislation dissipated. The Pure Food and

1. The coalition behind the Pure Food and Drug Act of 1906 is interesting in that the Pharmaceutical Manufacturers Association and the American Medical Association both supported this bill. Both viewed the legislation as a way to eliminate the patent medicine business. For the PMA, this would eliminate competition; for the AMA, it was part of their attempt to assert monopoly control over the treatment of disease (see chapter 7).

2. The Meat Inspection Act of 1907 was supported by the major meat-packers of the time. Gabriel Kolko (1963) argues this support resulted because the meat-packers saw regulation as a way of achieving a competitive advantage over small packers, who could not afford the improvements necessary to comply with the law.

Drug Act of 1906 failed to live up to its expectations. By listing specific food additives as prohibited, the act was dated by the time of its passage. Food processors simply developed new additives that were not covered by the law. In addition, because the drug provisions prohibited only misbranding drugs, they did not eliminate dangerous drugs. An opium-based drug could still be sold if it was labeled as such. The Meat Inspection Act fared somewhat better as the Department of Agriculture began serious inspections of packing plants. Even this effort, however, was concerned as much with the benefits to packers as with the benefits to consumers.[3]

THE NEW DEAL ERA

After the war and the return to normalcy, thousands of new consumer products were introduced. Articulating a vague consumer discontent, Stuart Chase and F. J. Schlink published *Your Money's Worth* in 1927, documenting the ills of advertising and high-pressure sales. Chase and Schlink called for scientific testing and product standards to aid consumers in their purchases (Herrmann, 1978: 30). In response to thousands of letters from readers, Schlink established Consumer Research, Inc., to test consumer products.

The depression and other muckraking books (e.g., *100,000,000 Guinea Pigs* by Kallet and Schlink) again placed the issue of consumer protection on the national agenda. Assistant Secretary of Agriculture Rexford Tugwell was the policy entrepreneur; he authored a bill to increase the Food and Drug Administration's powers (The FDA was still located in USDA). The bill would have extended FDA powers to include not only labeling but also advertising in newspapers and magazines. The FDA would have been given broad seizure powers and authority over medical devices and cosmetics.

Support for the Tugwell bill grew slowly, increasing from just the American Home Economics Association and the PTA in 1933 to the League of Women Voters, the Pharmaceutical Manufacturers, and other groups by 1937. The reform proposal also drew opposition, perhaps as much from Tugwell's reputation as from its content (Nadel, 1971: 16). Consumers Union, founded in 1935 by Arthur Kallet, and the American Medical Association added their support for the FDA legislation. Despite some creative lobbying by the FDA, including its "Chamber of Horrors" revealing the ill effects of impure food and drugs, the bill failed to pass.

In 1938 one objection to the FDA bill was resolved when the Wheeler-Lea amendments to the Federal Trade Commission Act granted the FTC power over advertising. The FTC was perceived as more favorable to business and less likely to pursue regulation vigorously (Nadel, 1971: 18). This legislation became important during the revitalization in the 1970s of the FTC because it provided some of the legislative authority to engage in consumer protection.

In 1938 a medical disaster provided the catalytic event needed to

3. This does not mean the consumer did not benefit from USDA inspection of meat-processing plants; the improvements in sanitation were a direct benefit. Tolerances involving the amount of foreign matter (aesthetic benefits) that was permitted in meat products, however, illustrates that the consumer's benefits take second place to the needs of the packer (see further on).

muster majorities in Congress. The Massengill Company marketed without testing a liquid-based sulfa drug called elixir sulfanilamide. Although sulfa drugs had a long history of safe and effective use, the solvent used by Massengill, diethylene glycol, was toxic. Approximately one hundred persons died as the result of elixir sulfanilamide, thus revealing the dangers of not regulating drugs.

Congress responded to the disaster by passing the Food, Drug and Cosmetic Act of 1938. The act provided that new drugs could be marketed only with the approval of the Food and Drug Administration. The manufacturer must demonstrate that a drug was safe before the FDA would approve it. The law also spelled out criteria for judging the adulterating of food and expanded the jurisdiction of the FDA to cover cosmetics. With the passage of the Food, Drug, and Cosmetic Act of 1938, the FDA became a preventative agency charged with preventing harms to consumers rather than correcting ills after they occurred.

Although the Wheeler-Lea Amendments and the Food, Drug, and Cosmetic Act of 1938 are the only lasting efforts of the New Deal in terms of consumer protection, they were not the only efforts. The National Recovery Administration had a consumer advisory board even though it had little impact. Consumer counsels were established with the Agricultural Adjustment Act of 1933 and the Bituminous Coal Act of 1937. During World War II the Office of Price Administration attempted to do some consumer-oriented grading of food products. None of these efforts survived the war, and the war effort effectively ended the New Deal era of consumer protection (Creighton, 1976).

THE CONTEMPORARY ERA

The contemporary era of consumer protection has many things in common with the previous two. In all three cases, the entrepreneurial ability of individuals is important. The examples of Harvey Wiley and Rexford Tugwell are repeated in Estes Kefauver, Abraham Ribicoff, Warren Magnuson, and Ralph Nader. The important role of the media continues; *The Jungle* and *Your Money's Worth* find descendents in *Unsafe at Any Speed* and *The Hidden Persuaders*. Crises and disasters continue to be a factor; elixir sulfanilamide is replaced by thalidomide. The similarities should not blind one, however, to the important differences. The consumer movement of the contemporary era went beyond the food and drug focus of the earlier years to automobile safety, deceptive advertising, consumer products, and financial transactions. In addition, unlike the previous movements, the contemporary consumer movement became institutionalized with permanent organizations created to pressure for consumer interests. Finally, the consumer movement was not ended by the exogenous event of war but rather sowed its own opposition among business groups. The result was a series of political battles that slowed the pace of consumer protection policy. These similarities and differences will be illustrated in five areas of consumer protection—pharmaceutical regulation, food safety regulation, automobile safety regulation, consumer product regulation, and the regulation of deceptive and unfair trade practices. For each area, a brief discussion of the subsystem and the economic and technological environment will precede the analysis of regulatory policy.

REGULATING DRUGS

The Subsystem

The Agency.   Lodged in the Department of Health and Human Services, the Food and Drug Administration (FDA) regulates drugs (both prescription and over-the-counter), cosmetics, medical devices, and foods (but not meat and poultry). In these areas, the FDA seeks four goals: safety, purity (food and drugs only), sanitary manufacturing conditions, and effectiveness (drugs and medical devices only; see Greer, 1983: 427). The FDA had a fiscal year (FY) 1985 budget of $404 million (an increase of 24 percent over 1980) with 7,100 personnel.

Regulating drugs is a complex scientific task requiring knowledge on the cutting edge of science. FDA recruits heavily from the scientific disciplines, especially medicine. The agency has developed a high level of expertise and used its organizational ideology (see further on) to become a cohesive agency. Throughout FDA's history, its leadership has been competent but not outstanding.

The Food and Drug Administration has two other important resources, issue salience and legislative authority. Drug regulation is usually salient, especially after a well-publicized pharmaceutical disaster. Salience permits FDA to tap support from the macropolitical system. In addition, FDA has substantial legislative authority. Although its policy goals are vague, FDA has universal authority over marketing drugs and excellent sanctions; drugs cannot be marketed without FDA approval. FDA procedures are slow (see later), but this affects the industry more than the agency.

Advocacy Coalitions.   The pharmaceutical industry is represented by the Pharmaceutical Manufacturers Association (PMA). PMA was generally pro-regulation in its early years in hopes of using regulation to eliminate competition from unethical drug manufacturers (see Quirk, 1980: 193–196). In more recent times, PMA has opposed the FDA's more stringent regulation. Among the PMA's normal allies have been the American Medical Association and a variety of scholars (mostly economists) critical of post-1962 drug regulation.

A pro-FDA advocacy coalition has developed that is composed of scientists, legislators concerned with health care, journalists, and a variety of public interest groups (Noll and Owen, 1983: 15). Proposals for stronger regulation have received support from such diverse groups as the League of Women Voters, the American Pharmaceutical Association (representing pharmacists), the American Association of Retired Persons, and others. Ralph Nader's Health Research Group has frequently criticized the FDA for weak regulation.

The Environment

Economics: Firms, Entry, Profits.   As the result of elaborate drug-testing procedures, significant barriers to entry exist in pharmaceutical manufacturing. A $30 billion-a-year industry, modern pharmaceutical manufacturing requires large investments in research and development plus extensive marketing mechanisms. The number of firms is sufficient for competition; over 1,700 firms produce drugs (of these, approximately 20 are major manufacturers). Individual drugs, however, are often monopolies with only one or two firms producing a specific drug. Profits have historically been above average, but profits are similar to those in oil exploration. If a widely used drug is discovered, profits can be impressive; but most drugs never reach this state.

Technology: Complexity, Stability, Substitutes.   Industry technology is complex with research on the cutting edge of science. Change is rapid, but the process of change has been institutionalized so that it does not disrupt the industry. Medically, most drugs have both drug and nondrug substitutes.

The environment of pharmaceutical regulation is not amenable to close regulation. The economics limit competition, and technology does not provide new policy alternatives. The orientation of the regulator to the regulated, however, has been shaped more by political events than by the industry environment.

Agenda Setting: The Kefauver Hearings

The contemporary era of consumer protection, like previous eras, started with policy concerning drugs. Senator Estes Kefauver, troubled by the large profits and markups of pharmaceutical manufacturers, held a series of hearings in the late 1950s and early 1960s. As the hearings on the economic aspects of the industry progressed, defects in the safety and efficiency of drug regulation were revealed. Specifically, the hearings showed drug advertisements were frequently misleading, numerous drugs existed that had no clear advantages over other drugs, an excessive number of me-too drugs (drugs identical to a previously marketed drug) were on the market, and many drugs were of questionable safety and efficacy (Quirk, 1980: 197; Nadel, 1971: 122).

In 1961, Kefauver introduced a bill to amend the Food, Drug and Cosmetic Act. Although the bill contained provisions requiring that marketed drugs be safe and effective, some of the senator's economic priorities remained (Quirk, 1980: 198). Included were provisions aimed at limiting the life of patents and restricting profits (Nadel, 1971: 125). Kefauver's bill drew opposition from the American Medical Association and Senators Roman Hruska and Everett Dirksen. In addition, a weaker bill was introduced by the Kennedy administration.

By manipulating media coverage, Kefauver was able to get a relatively strong bill passed. The Merrell Corporation had applied to market a tranquilizer called thalidomide in the United States. Through the efforts of Dr. Frances Kelsey, an FDA bureaucrat, the drug was kept off the U.S. market despite strong pressure from Merrell. Evidence from Europe then linked thalidomide with a series of birth defects after the drug was used by pregnant women. When it appeared that the watered-down version of the bill would pass, Kefauver released the thalidomide story to the *Washington Post*. The *Post* ran a front-page story, and the salience of drug regulation increased dramatically. President Kennedy endorsed the Kefauver bill, and the bill passed both Houses of Congress unanimously (see Nadel, 1971: 128; Quirk, 1980: 199).

The Law and Agency Procedures

Essentially, the Kefauver-Harris Amendments, as they were called, provided that drugs must be proved effective before they are marketed and specified protections for human subjects used in drug research. All drugs that had been approved between 1938 and 1962 were to be reviewed for effectiveness. The 1962 amendments and the thalidomide case had a lasting impact on the FDA. From this point on, the agency adopted internal decision rules designed to limit the probability of approving an unsafe drug. Agency norms support requiring more evidence before approving a drug, and they accept foregoing the approval of a valuable drug if the process eliminates harmful drugs (Grabowski and Vernon, 1983: 10).

Reflecting this agency norm are the elaborate procedures used to approve new drugs. A new drug must undergo the following procedures: (1) therapeutic assessment in small-scale animal studies; (2) short-term toxicity studies in animals; (3) small-scale human testing for toxicity; (4) three-month animal studies to estimate the long-term impacts; (5) clinical studies on humans to determine efficacy, appropriate dosage, and any hazards; and (6) two-year animal studies to assess hazards of long-term treatment (Quirk, 1980: 219). The average length of time from initial application to approval of a new drug for marketing is eight to nine years. Approximately 86 percent of all new drugs fail to make it through this process although some 90 percent of those cases where marketing approval is requested (which occurs after testing) are approved.

The Impact of FDA Procedures

The extensive premarketing procedures of the FDA have several policy implications. First, the research and development costs of prescription drugs have increased dramatically. From 1960 to 1973 the research and development (R and D) costs of introducing a drug into the marketplace increased approximately 1,000 percent (Grabowski and Vernon, 1983). Although some of the rise in R&D costs reflects the low costs prior to the 1962 law and the large increases in inflation since 1960, new drugs have become more expensive to market. Second, the number of new drugs introduced into the United States has fallen (Peltzman, 1974). Third, when drugs have been introduced in both the United States and European countries, generally the drugs were introduced later in the United States (Wardell, 1973; Wardell, et al., 1978). Collectively, these implications have been termed "drug lag"; FDA critics argue that FDA regulation, specifically regulation undertaken since 1962, has delayed the introduction of beneficial drugs.

The Food and Drug Administration's response to such charges was predictable given the ideology developed following the thalidomide case. The FDA argued that the drop in the number of new drugs reflected the elimination of me-too drugs of little value, the exhaustion of the medical breakthroughs developed after the Second World War, and the requirement that drugs be effective as well as safe. In addition, some of the lack of innovation lies with the drug companies. From 1973 to 1979, R and D expenditures by U.S. drug companies increased by only 1 percent a year (Sun, 1983: 1157). All the FDA arguments can be tied to a belief that the American public is overmedicated (Quirk, 1980: 209). Although the FDA's belief of overmedication and its position on drug lag can be defended scientifically, they must be understood as the manifestation of norms developed after the thalidomide incident. Even though all drugs entail some risk, decision-making routines operate to keep harmful drugs off the market even if beneficial drugs are eliminated in the process.

Recently, the FDA has recognized the validity of some of its critics' arguments. The benefits of significant new drugs introduced in other countries have become evident (see Wardell, et al., 1978). As a result, the FDA adopted a fast-tracking procedure to speed up the introduction of "breakthrough" drugs. In 1981 the FDA approved 27 new drugs, twice the number approved in 1980 and the most since 1962 (Demkovich, 1982: 1250). In the next two years a total of 42 drugs were approved (Demkovich, 1984: 411). One drug, timolol, used to prevent repeated occurrences of heart attacks, for example, was approved on the basis of a single foreign study (Pauley, 1982: 52). Unfortunately, one of the new drugs, Oraflex, an antiarthritic medication, caused 11 deaths in the United States and at least 61 in England and had to be withdrawn from the market. Later Oraflex was linked to cancer in rats (Oraflex Linked, 1983: 26). Within the FDA, the Oraflex case can be viewed as support for the slow, careful procedures of drug licensing. Reinforcing this view was the stand of a House subcommittee. The House Government Operations Subcommittee on Intergovernmental Relations and Human Resources criticized the FDA for authorizing the drug and blamed the manufacturer, Eli Lilly, for not fully disclosing all the information about side effects (House Panel Raps, 1983: 15), including the deaths in Europe (see Oraflex Linked, 1983). The committee issued similar criticism of the FDA for approving the painkiller, Zomax, which was linked to 15 deaths (see Cromley, 1983: 1).

Withdrawing Ineffective Drugs

What outside critics of the FDA fail to realize is that the drug approval procedures reflect a bureaucratic decision to minimize risk via extensive analysis. This bias also explains why the FDA is often slow to remove drugs from the market when harmful side effects occur. For example, although the antibiotic chloromycetin was found to have harmful side effects for some persons as early as 1952, the FDA failed to place restrictions on the drug for 20 years (Consumer Reports, 1973). Most FDA resources are committed to premarketing evaluation with less effort devoted to postmarketing; this priority, plus the reliance on extended analysis, means that withdrawing a drug from the market takes a long time even though the FDA can order a withdrawal without a hearing in some cases (e.g., the Panalba withdrawal; see Quirk, 1980: 212).

The impact of extended analysis can be seen in the process of evaluation of those drugs approved between 1938 and 1962. Lacking the resources to do such extended analysis, the FDA contracted with the National Academy of Sciences (NAS) to evaluate prescription drugs and later to evaluate the contents of over-the-counter drugs. Under these procedures, some 6,000 different brands and products were removed from the market during the 1960s and 1970s (Greer, 1983: 430). Included were 600 prescription drugs (Quirk, 1980: 224) and more than 200 ingredients in non-prescription drugs (FDA Completes, 1983: 12). The process involved 58 reports issued by 17 NAS advisory panels and was not finished for nonprescription drug ingredients until October 1983.

Current Issues

Although the drug approval process is sufficient by itself to involve the FDA in controversy, in recent years two additional policy issues have become controversial. They are prescription knowledge and orphan drugs. In general, physicians rely on pharmaceutical sales personnel and the *Physicians Desk Manual* for their information about drugs. Even with FDA restrictions on new drugs, the growth of information in the area is rapid, and most physicians lack the time and the training to keep up with the latest developments in pharmaceutical research (this issue was first raised in the Kefauver hearings). If physician knowledge is limited, patient knowledge is even more so. In response, the FDA considered a rule that required pharmacists to place an insert in all prescriptions explaining the uses for the drug and possible side effects. Currently, prescription inserts of this nature are used for contraceptives. This rule was opposed by pharmacists on cost grounds and physicians on claims that it interferes with the doctor-patient relationship. During the Carter administration, a pilot project was designed to test prescription inserts in a small sample of cases. As part of President Reagan's general effort to ease the regulation of business, FDA Commissioner Arthur Hull Hayes eliminated the pilot project in 1982.

Orphan drugs are those drugs known to be effective for treating a specific illness, but the number of cases is so small that a company cannot manufacture the drug at a profit. In situations such as these, patients either do without the drug, or it is prepared by a local physician or pharmacist. Congress has endorsed efforts to manufacture orphan drugs by providing tax credits to companies that produce them. The FDA has embarked on a controversial program to "encourage" pharmaceutical companies to market orphans along with the other drugs that they wish to market.

Policy Direction

Assessing the direction of FDA drug regulation on the regulated and nonregulated dimensions introduced in chapter 2 is difficult. A review of the literature reveals that the FDA is charged with catering to the desires of the pharmaceutical manufacturers (see Nadel, 1971: 69, for a review) and that the FDA is denounced for needlessly harming the pharmaceutical industry (Grabowski and Vernon, 1983). By citing the FDA's slowness in withdrawing ineffective drugs from the market, the "capture" proponents can marshal evidence that drug companies benefit from FDA rule. By citing the "drug lag," the proponents of "harmful regulation" can marshal evidence that the FDA has imposed excessive costs on the industry.

Both these policies, as argued earlier, are a function of the FDA's organizational ideology. Reflecting both publicized drug scandals and congressional criticism, the FDA relies on elaborate testing and evidence to make decisions. Products currently on the market are given the benefit of the doubt until evidence is in whereas products seeking to be marketed are exposed to rigorous testing. The process is eminently predictable. With the evaluation of 1938–1962 drug approvals completed, the argument that the FDA is pro-industry is difficult to maintain. One careful scholar of the FDA concluded, "We can, however, say that the belief that the FDA is dominated by pressures from industry—as well as the belief that it is lacking any strong incentives to approve drugs—are equally wrong" (Quirk, 1980: 218).

The FDA's orientation to the drug industry has changed over time in response to changes in the political forces acting on the agency. The advent of the Reagan administration, for example, saw the introduction of "fast tracking" for breakthrough drugs and the elimination of the prescription insert pilot program. Changes in political forces, however, are limited by the bureaucratic norms of the agency, especially those developed after the Kefauver-Harris Amendments. Although the FDA's drug program will continue to make marginal changes as the political environment changes, the FDA will remain more concerned about protecting consumers and less concerned about the pharmaceutical industry.

FOOD SAFETY REGULATION

Regulating food safety and quality has always been a high priority of consumer protection movements. Concerns over food quality as expressed in *The Jungle,* for example, provided the momentum to pass the Food and Drug Act of 1906 and the Meat Inspection Act of 1907. The consumer movement today stresses both consumer sovereignty and consumer protection approaches in this area. At the local level, consumer groups use educational programs that encourage consumers to purchase nutritional foods. At the federal government level, these advocates favor protection measures to eliminate food hazards.

Three forms of food safety regulation exist at the federal level: health, aesthetic, and economic.[4] Health regulation concerns the regulation of food and food additives that might be dangerous for human consumption. A food additive that is carcinogenic, for example, is a health danger. Aesthetic regulation deals with problems that are not dangerous to a person's health if proper procedures are used to prepare the foods. A regulation limiting the amount of foreign matter (e.g., rodent hairs) in flour is an aesthetic regulation. Given proper cooking, such foreign matter is not dangerous, yet for aesthetic reasons individuals would prefer not to eat it. Economic regulation concerns those aspects of food production that are not health hazards regardless of how the food is prepared. Regulations that prohibit adding water to milk or soybean meal to hamburger, for example, are economic regulations.

The Subsystem

The Agency.   The food-processing industry is regulated by the Food and Drug Administration (discussed earlier) and the Food Safety and Inspection Service. Meats and poultry are regulated by the Food Safety and Inspection

---

4. State governments also regulate food products. One prominent example is the inspection of restaurants and the processors of milk and milk products. If approved by the FSIS, states can also inspect intrastate meat and poultry products.

Service, and other foods are regulated by the Food and Drug Administration. The Food Safety and Inspection Service (FSIS) is an agency in the Department of Agriculture. It monitors slaughterhouses and processing plants by placing inspectors in the plant on a daily basis. The FSIS also grades meat, poultry, eggs, and other products on a voluntary basis. Between the FDA and the FSIS, they regulate most food consumed in the United States except for fish (in the Department of Commerce) and dairy products (state governments). FSIS has 9,892 employees and an FY 1985 budget of $356 million (comparison to 1980 is not possible owing to a reorganization).

FSIS is a federal agency with little visibility. Most of its work consists of day-to-day plant inspections; scientific work on pesticide or chemical residues is done by other agencies. The agency's expertise, therefore, is not as well developed as that of the Food and Drug Administration. Similarly, the agency's cohesion and leadership do not stand out as exceptionally good or exceptionally bad.

Even without a strong bureaucratic base, however, the FSIS has two major resources—salience and legislative authority. Because food purity is an explosive issue if problems reach the media, processors have strong incentives to avoid the bad publicity of a contaminated products recall. Legislative authority is also strong. Although policy goals are general, FSIS has defined specific procedures to operationalize these goals. The agency's coverage is universal among meat-packers, and it has the administrative power to seize any contaminated products. Procedures do not limit the FSIS in any way.

Advocacy Coalitions.   Food processors are not a cohesive group. The meat-packing industry, for example, is represented by the National Meat Council; but firms such as Iowa Beef Packers, Wilson's, and Swift are such vigorous competitors that a single position is rarely possible. Large food processors generally represent themselves with some reliance on trade associations. Large firms are less likely to oppose regulation than are small ones.

Opposing the food-processing industry is an advocacy coalition composed of a variety of groups. Consumers are represented via such groups as the Community Nutrition Institute and the Center for Science in the Public Interest; hunger groups such as the Food Research Action Committee and Bread for the World are also active. At the state level, Ralph Nader's Public Interest Research Groups have been active (Berry, 1977: 68). The positions of these groups are often supported by research conducted by academic nutritionists.

The Environment

Economics: Firms, Entry, Profits.   The food-processing industry is generally a competitive industry. Producing food in over 90,000 plants owned by 22,000 firms, it is a $250 billion industry. Firms range in size from the local baker to the giant conglomerates (Beatrice Foods, General Foods, and so on). Specific food markets range from almost monopolies (Campbell's Soup has 85 percent of the market) to extremely competitive (meat-packing). Food processing has become more concentrated in recent years. From 1947 to 1977 the number of firms dropped from 47,000 to 22,000 (General

Accounting Office [GAO], 1981a: 5). The 93 largest firms control 67 percent of the industry's assets and 72 percent of its profits (GAO, 1981a: 7). Barriers to entry are low, but barriers to growth exist. Marketing foods nationwide requires nationwide distribution systems and nationwide advertising. Large firms have economies of scale in these areas. Profits vary greatly from firm to firm.

Technology: Complexity, Stability, Substitutes.   Food-processing technology is a large-batch and continuous-processing technology but is not complex. The rate of technological change is modest compared to that in other industries, and numerous substitutes exist for almost all products. In short, technology and economics do not limit the regulation of food processing.

The Food and Drug Administration

Plant Inspection.   The FDA has three areas of authority in food regulation—inspection of plants and food products, regulation of food additives, and programs that specify labeling content. The first of these areas—inspection of food and food plants—encompasses the bulk of FDA food regulation even though it is not a visible activity. The FDA is empowered to act whenever food is found to be adulterated. Food is adulterated if it is produced in an unsanitary plant; contains ingredients or additives harmful to human consumption; contains decomposed, putrid, or filthy portions; comes from a diseased animal; is packaged in a hazardous container; and so on (Hinich and Staelin, 1980: 7).

The amount of adulteration or contamination permitted varies somewhat given the source and type of contamination. Some foods contain health hazards naturally; coffee, for example, contains caffeine. Natural health hazards are regulated very little. Other foods contain contaminants that cannot be avoided; freshwater fish often contain high levels of polychlorinated biphenyls (PCBs), and peanut butter contains alphatoxins; both are hazardous to human health. Such contamination is regulated by threshold levels (e.g., a food can contain no more than x parts per million of a substance). Also regulated by threshold levels are unintentional food ingredients such as pesticide residues or packaging residues. Unintended food ingredients usually are restricted to extremely low threshold levels. In all three cases, the agency balances the hazards of exposure with the benefits of consumption (Pape, 1982; 162).

Faced with adulterated food, the FDA has a variety of regulatory options. The most common is to request that the producer voluntarily recall the hazardous or adulterated product. Several noteworthy examples exist, including the recall associated with the great cranberry scare of 1959 and the recall of Bon Vivant vichyssoise in the 1970s. If a producer does not voluntarily recall a product, the FDA can seize it. The FDA also has the power to seek injunctions and take other action against the offending firm. The major punishment facing a food adulterator, however, is not the FDA action but the publicity resulting from an FDA action. A publicized recall damages the producer's reputation and thus presents a future obstacle to marketing the food product. In addition, if the product caused injury, the publicity of an FDA seizure will probably increase the number of lawsuits filed for damages.

FDA food regulation is not as stringent as its drug regulation simply because it is not possible. Because every drug must be approved before it is marketed, the cases are limited to a manageable number. In food production, however, there are 90,000 plants located throughout the entire country. With approximately 1,000 inspectors, the FDA cannot possibly monitor food production closely. In a recent year, however, the FDA did inspect 33,000 plants and undertake 96,000 wharf inspections (Greer, 1983: 430). The records show that plants failing one inspection are more likely to be inspected again and that the time period between inspections is shorter for failing plants (Hinich and Staelin, 1980: 55).

Inspections place a great deal of discretion in the FDA's hands. With a stringent enough inspection, almost any food plant will fail. The time required for such inspections, however, would mean that many plants would not be inspected at all. At the current level of inspections some food prepared in unsanitary plants reaches the market. A General Accounting Office (GAO) audit found that 24 percent of the 90 plants that it examined were operating with serious unsanitary conditions (GAO, 1972).

The difficulty in obtaining total compliance with federal food processing regulations (a problem not unique to this agency) has raised the question of regulatory priorities. Hinich and Staelin (1980: 42), for example, argue that the FDA should stress only health-related regulations. Aesthetic regulations such as those that specify the allowable number of maggots in 15 ounces of mushrooms should receive fewer FDA resources according to Hinich and Staelin. Such aesthetic regulation, they argue, wastes food and could be handled by labeling (e.g., this package of mushrooms contains more than 21 maggots). On the other hand, health hazards are often notoriously difficult to find without extensive microbiological work, and labels designating the amount of foreign matter in a product might make the product unsellable (recall the drop in meat consumption following the publication of *The Jungle*).

Food Additives.   Food additives are substances added to food in processing to delay spoilage, improve nutritional value, enhance taste, reduce cost, or enhance other characteristics (color, foaming, sticking, and so on). Currently over 2,700 substances are used as food additives (GAO, 1980b: 1). The FDA regulates food additives to determine if they are safe and effective (that is, a preservative must preserve food).

Food additive safety is the most controversial area of FDA food regulation. Unlike other areas of food regulation where small traces of foreign matter or minute contamination is permissible, food additives can face an absolute standard. The Food Additive Amendments of 1958 (which contain the Delaney clause) require that all food additives be safe. If an additive is found to cause cancer in either animals or humans, the FDA must ban it. The FDA has no discretion (Gottron, 1982: 106; Greer, 1983: 427).

Food additives are regulated in a manner similar to the regulation of drugs. The FDA maintains a list of food additives that are GRAS or "generally recognized as safe." Additives may make the GRAS list in two ways. A new additive must be tested before it is submitted to the FDA for approval (Hinich and Staelin, 1980: 72). If found safe, it is added. In addition, substances in use and approved by either the FDA or USDA before 1958 were placed on the list by a grandfather clause (Pape, 1982: 169).

When the Delaney clause was passed, an absolute standard was a reasonable approach to regulation. Since 1958, however, the ability to detect minute substances has improved dramatically. In 1958 technology could detect substances in parts per million; today substances in parts per quadrillion can be detected (Pape, 1982: 172). In addition, research suggests that an array of nutrients may play a role in the carcinogenic process (Kessler, 1984: 1034).

The Delaney clause has involved the FDA in one controversy after another. In 1959 the FDA found that part of the cranberry crop was contaminated with aminotriazole, a weed killer shown to be carcinogenic in laboratory animals. Cranberry growers protested the FDA seizure and were eventually compensated for their losses by Congress. In 1976, the FDA banned red dye number 2, an additive used in ice cream, cookies, meats, and cosmetics. Again, the affected industry protested vigorously. In 1973 the FDA attempted to ban the cattle feed additive DES; a six-year court suit ensued before the ban became effective in 1979 (Gottron, 1982: 106).

None of the Delaney controversies, however, raised as much furor as the banning of artificial sweeteners. As the result of lab tests in animals, the FDA banned the artificial sweetener cyclamates (the American public consumed 17 million pounds of cyclamates in 1969). Although the experiments were widely criticized and some firms took major financial losses, the severity of this decision was mitigated by the existence of an alternative sweetener, saccharin. The cyclamates controversy, however, prompted President Nixon to order the FDA to evaluate all the substances on the GRAS list.

In 1977, on the basis of Canadian research, the FDA announced that it was banning saccharin. The reaction was vehement because no substitute was available. Critics argued that individuals would have to drink 800 cans of diet soft drinks a day to equal the amount of saccharin fed to the laboratory rats. Some health groups argued that saccharin could hardly be more dangerous than the substance it replaced, sugar. Congress responded to the uproar by preventing the FDA from banning saccharin and requesting that more studies be done. A warning label on all products containing saccharin was authorized. Saccharin continued to be consumed.[5] In 1981 the FDA authorized aspartame, an artificial sweetener, for use in dry foods and in 1983 for soft drinks. Although some questions about the safety of aspartame have been raised (see Randal, 1984), it is rapidly being substituted for saccharin.[6]

The regulation of additives demonstrates how a regulatory agency can become controversial through no fault of its own. Under the Delaney clause, the FDA lacks discretion. Any additive that causes cancer in animals or humans must be removed from the GRAS list and banned. The inconsistency of the Delaney standard is evident when it is viewed in the light of

5. Saccharin has a long political history. Harvey Wiley first proposed that saccharin was hazardous to health. This so enraged Theodore Roosevelt, whose doctor prescribed saccharin for him, that he created an advisory board to oversee and veto actions of Wiley and his agency (the precursor to the FDA). Conflicts with this board eventually caused Wiley to resign.
6. By 1984 some evidence accumulated that aspartame also was linked to health problems. Particularly troublesome was the inadequate procedure used by the manufacturer to test the additive for safety.

overall food regulation. Equally dangerous substances occur naturally in some foods or as the unavoidable result of processing. The risk of drinking one saccharin soda per day is less than the risk of eating four tablespoons of peanut butter (alfatoxin) or taking contraceptive pills, and it is significantly less than the risk from smoking (Greer, 1983: 435). Because none of these substances are "food additives," they are not subject to the rigid Delaney standard.

Actually the FDA has shown some creativity in skirting the Delaney clause. Selenium, a nutrient essential in low doses for normal growth metabolism, was found to produce tumors in lab animals at high doses. Selenium is used as an animal feed additive because animals cannot produce it themselves. Recognizing the benefits of the additive, the FDA claimed the Delaney clause did not apply because it knew the mechanism by which selenium was linked to cancer and because selenium was a secondary carcinogen (Kessler, 1984: 1034).

Although the Delaney standard is for Congress to keep or modify, the lack of action by Congress reflects a truism of politics. Whenever a policy is created, individuals favoring the policy will create pressures to retain the policy. A variety of consumer groups have supported the Delaney clause distinguishing between natural hazards that an individual can avoid and food additives that are consciously added to food. Given the development of laboratory sciences, the Delaney clause will continue to generate controversies.

Labeling.   Food labeling policies have two objectives—preventing deception and safety. To prevent deception, the FDA often prescribes the ingredients of a certain food. Orange juice, for example, must be composed of 100 percent of the juices of oranges whereas reconstituted orange juice must be juice prepared from orange juice concentrate, and orange drink may contain as little as 10 percent real orange juice. Recipe standards, as these are called, are an attempt to assure the consumer that a product contains the common ingredients that such a product would be expected to contain. As the technology has developed to produce "ice cream" without cream, eggless eggnogg, and nonmeat breakfast meats, recipe standards have become important (Hinich and Staelin, 1980: 2).

Although the antideception goals of recipe standards appear to be noncontroversial, they are not. In recent years, stories concerning the rigidity of recipe standards have surfaced. A ketchup manufacturer using all natural ingredients was denied the use of the label "ketchup" because the process used honey rather than refined sugar; the product had to be marketed as "imitation ketchup." In general, however, recipe standards receive little public attention.

Safety and nutritional labeling standards are subject to far more controversy. In 1974 the FDA required that any products containing added vitamins, minerals, or proteins and any products that made nutritional claims must have labels on their products. These labels list the number of servings per container; the size of a serving; the calories per serving; the amount of protein, carbohydrates, and fats; and the percentage of the recommended daily allowance of eight specific nutrients (Hinich and Staelin, 1980: 69).

Food labeling, however, has had little impact on consumer behavior. One review of six studies found that consumers do not comprehend the meaning of label information and do not use it in deciding what foods to purchase (Jacoby, et al., 1977). Although this lack of use might be cited by a consumer protectionist as a policy failure, a consumer sovereignty advocate would argue such findings are irrelevant. Consumers, after all, can decide for themselves if information contributes to product selection. A consumer can rationally decide that such information has little value and ignore it. Other consumers, even though a small percentage, may decide to incorporate such information in their food choices.

The Food Safety and Inspection Service

The Food Safety and Inspection Service (FSIS) performs food regulation responsibilities similar to those of the FDA but is limited to meat and meat products. Included in its jurisdiction are beef, pork, lamb, poultry, and eggs. These products are slaughtered or processed in 7,000 different plants (GAO, 1983c: 3). Since the publication of *The Jungle*, meat safety regulation has been more visible than the regulation of other foods. Ralph Nader in the 1960s was instrumental in getting Congress to pass the Wholesome Meat Act of 1967 and the Wholesome Poultry Products Act of 1968 (Feldman, 1976: 18). Gaining access to a USDA report on the inadequacies of state meat inspection, Nader gave the report to journalist Nick Kotz, who authored a Pulitzer Prize-winning series of articles. The increased salience generated efforts to pass the new laws (Nadel, 1971: 181).

Basically, the 1960s legislation subjected meat produced and sold in intrastate commerce to federal regulation. The previous legislation only permitted federal inspection of interstate meat. The FSIS may, however, permit states to inspect plants producing for intrastate consumption if state inspection systems are equal to the national system. Twenty-seven states are authorized by FSIS to conduct their own inspections (GAO, 1983b: 2). Only 3 percent of all meat is state-inspected. Under the law, packing plants, transporters, renderers, and warehouses are subject to regulation and inspection as is all meat imported into the United States. All animals are inspected prior to slaughter for diseases as is all meat after slaughter.

The food inspection processes of the FSIS are more exacting than those of the FDA. Unlike the FDA, the FSIS engages in continual inspection; that is, an FSIS inspector is present daily in every meat-processing plant. The FDA makes periodic inspections. As a result, the FSIS employs some 8,000 inspectors to oversee far fewer plants than the FDA does with 1,000 inspectors (Hinich and Staelin, 1980: 99). FSIS also has far broader authority over its industry than FDA does. FSIS-regulated products cannot be sold in interstate commerce without a USDA approval stamp; FDA products need not be approved. Meat-packers and meat processors must get FSIS approval for all plant construction; food processors do not. FSIS has a statutory right to examine all plant records; FDA does not. FSIS can condemn products and recall or seize products administratively; FDA must proceed through the Department of Justice and the courts.

Although the FSIS inspection program has not been as visible as other FSIS programs, it has not been immune from criticism. A General Accounting Office audit charged that 18 percent of packing plants had unacceptable sanitation procedures, 11 percent had unacceptable pest control problems, and 63 percent had water supply deficiencies (GAO, 1981b: ii). On the other hand, postslaughter procedures for eliminating unacceptable meat were considered effective.

In addition to inspection powers, the FSIS also issues recipe regulations similar to those of the FDA. A frankfurter, for example, can contain no more than 15 percent chicken or turkey; must contain spices as specified by USDA regulation; and may not contain hearts, tongues, fatty tissue, meat by-products, or unskinned pork (Hinich and Staelin, 1980: 103). The scope of FSIS regulation is so broad that the organization has been charged by some with overregulation. Hinich and Staelin (1980: 101), for example, argue that educational programs might provide a cheaper, but equally effective method to avoid problems with unsafe meats. As an example, they cite USDA efforts with trichinosis. Examining all pork for the trichina parasite would be prohibitively expensive (requiring microscopic examinations of all slaughtered swine). So owing to an education program that encourages people to cook pork thoroughly, public exposure to some 40 million servings of contaminated pork results in only 100 diagnosed human infections a year. Similar arguments can be made against FSIS regulation of bruised meat (an aesthetic regulation unrelated to health).

Before concluding that FSIS is guilty of overregulation, we should note that consumer groups have criticized the agency for not protecting consumers. The FSIS administers a voluntary grading program for companies that wish to participate. Beef, for example, is graded as prime, choice, good, standard, commercial, utility, and cutter. Consumer groups criticize these grades because they are not designed for consumer use. Beef grades are based on fat content (related to tenderness) rather than on nutrition. The grades were developed so that wholesalers could determine the quality of a shipment and pay a price based on that "quality." Not only are grading labels criticized for being unrelated to nutrition, but they are also criticized for being unrelated to taste. Studies have shown, for example, that beef grades are only weakly correlated with the taste of the beef (Miller, et al., 1976: 27).

Grading for marketing rather than consumer purposes can be traced to the origins of the grading program and the organizational incentives related to it. The FSIS was originally a series of programs in the Agricultural Marketing Service (AMS). AMS is the unit in the Department of Agriculture responsible for administering marketing programs designed to limit production and increase farm prices. The goal of AMS employees is to improve farm income and facilitate orderly marketing; the AMS has not developed norms of consumer protection.

One illustration of the AMS and its orientation occurred after the appointment of Carol Tucker Foreman to be assistant secretary of agriculture for marketing and consumer affairs in 1977. Foreman, the former head of the Consumer Federation of America, was a well-known consumer advocate. Opposition to Foreman among the agricultural establishment resulted in the transfer of the marketing programs from her jurisdiction and the creation of the FSIS. Marketing, in the eyes of the Department of Agriculture and its clientele, was to be kept separate from food and consumer issues. A second illustration of the FSIS connection with marketing rather than with consumer protection is its controversial 1982 decision to loosen labeling standards for mechanically deboned meat to allow more bone fragments than were previously permitted (Wines, 1982a: 97). Permitting more bone fragments makes meat cheaper to market; it does nothing for consumers.

Food Safety: Who Benefits?

FDA and FSIS food safety regulation should be the type of regulation that restricts business for the benefit of consumers. The regulatory agencies, particularly the FSIS, are concerned about the industry as well as the consumer. By easing consumer concerns about food safety and by standardizing production processes, regulation provides some benefit to producers. Large producers in particular benefit because small producers must invest in quality control equipment, thus limiting their ability to undercut prices.

That consumers also benefit from food regulation is also evident. Although no system of regulation can ever eliminate risk totally, food safety regulation has eliminated a great many unsafe and unsanitary practices. Criticizing the agencies for being unconcerned with nutrition is criticizing them for a goal they do not have. Their concerns are food safety, not food nutrition. The net benefits to consumers from food safety regulation in all likelihood exceed those to the industry.

AUTOMOBILE SAFETY REGULATION

Automobile safety regulation forms the classic pattern of contemporary consumer regulation. Regulation had its genesis with a political entrepreneur who skillfully exploited the media. Fairly stringent regulation resulted in political counterefforts by the regulated industry, and the industry's position received more consideration after the 1980 election.

The Subsystem

The Agency. The National Highway Traffic Safety Administration (NHTSA) is an agency in the Department of Transportation responsible for regulating automobile safety. It promulgates safety standards for automobiles sold in the United States and presides over the recall of vehicles determined to be safety hazards. NHTSA has jurisdiction over other traffic safety programs (e.g., it funds drunk-driver enforcement projects), but other agencies also regulate automobile production (e.g., the Environmental Protection Agency sets emissions standards). NHTSA had an FY 1985 budget of $217 million (an increase of 1 percent over 1980) and 617 employees.

NHTSA has funded a substantial amount of research on transportation safety, and it maintains hotlines to monitor safety problems. Accordingly, it has developed some expertise and usually presides over technical debates between auto companies and safety advocates. In terms of cohesion, NHTSA ranks in the middle of regulatory agencies. Agency leaders such as Joan Claybrook and Raymond Peck have been able to influence NHTSA policies forcefully.

A major NHTSA resource is the high salience of automobile safety. NHTSA recalls and reports generally make headlines. Although legislative goals are vague, NHTSA has broad authority. It can regulate safety by improving vehicles, improving roadways, or funding demonstration projects. Despite a modest range of sanctions and incentives, NHTSA usually relies on publicity as its major sanction against the automakers. NHTSA is not restricted by any unusual procedures.

The Advocacy Coalitions. Automobile manufacturers are all large enough to have their own lobby staffs in Washington. The industry rarely lacks resources for lobby efforts. Although the industry does not always agree about such issues as import quotas, it is reasonably cohesive on auto safety. On occasion, the automobile companies have been able to enlist the support of unions, particularly the United Auto Workers, when opposing regulation.

Perhaps the most active force opposing the automakers is Ralph Nader's Center for Auto Safety. The center receives all complaints to Nader about auto safety and has developed a large data base about automobile defects and safety hazards (Berry, 1977: 192). Joining the center in its lobby efforts have been a variety of state transportation safety regulators and many of the nation's insurance companies. Insurance companies have discovered an economic self-interest in strong automobile safety regulation.

The Environment

Economics: Firms, Entry, Profits. Only four American automobile manufacturers remain out of the two hundred or so companies that once produced automobiles. Barriers to entry are prohibitive in terms of capital; new automobile companies are simply not being formed. Profits vary greatly from year to year. Some years all firms incur losses, and other years significant profits are made. In 1983 the industry had record profits of over $6 billion.

Technology: Complexity, Stability, Substitutes. Automobile technology is no more complex than any other mass-production technology, but the government has increased the technology's instability. Government requirements for less pollution, better gas mileage, and safer vehicles have destabilized the technology of automaking. Substitutes for automobiles are available but in many cases are blocked by import restrictions (Japanese autos) or by accessibility (e.g., mass transit). The environment of automaking makes the regulator's task difficult. A small number of large firms constitute a significant portion of the economy and have the political skills to exploit this situation.

Setting the Agenda: Legislative Action

Concern with automobile safety regulation did not originate with Ralph Nader. Congressman Kenneth Roberts held hearings on automobile safety from 1956 to 1964; the muckraking book *The Insolent Chariots* by John Keats publicized safety problems with American automobiles. Minor legislation was passed during this period; it required that the General Services Administration set safety standards for automobiles purchased by the federal government (Nadel, 1971: 32). Automobile manufacturers generally opposed these early efforts, arguing that driver error was the major cause of accidents, a factor that could not be controlled by federal regulation.

The real push for change came in the early 1960s. With the introduction of high-powered muscle cars, traffic fatalities increased from the 1950s level of approximately 38,000 a year to more than 50,000 by 1965 (see Meier and Morgan, 1982: 161). Perceiving an issue that would generate favorable publicity, Senator Abe Ribicoff scheduled hearings on automobile safety (Nadel, 1971: 139).

Two factors generated a great deal of media attention for the Ribicoff hearings. The first was the presence on the committee of Robert Kennedy, perhaps the most visible senator of the time. Kennedy pressed General Motors' personnel into admitting that the company spent only $1.5 million on safety research the previous year despite profits of $1.7 billion. The second factor was the testimony of an obscure lawyer named Ralph Nader who had recently published a book called *Unsafe at Any Speed*. Nader argued that automobiles, the Corvair in particular, had designed-in safety defects. These safety defects became important during the second collision in an accident (the impact of the driver on the inside of the car).

The Ribicoff hearings might not have produced strong safety regulation if it were not for a political blunder by General Motors (GM). GM hired private detectives to investigate Ralph Nader. When news of the investigation was revealed, followed by GM's lame excuse that it wanted to know if Nader was behind the rash of Corvair suits filed against the company, sales of *Unsafe at Any Speed* skyrocketed. Hearings were reconvened, and automobile executives weakly submitted to embarrassing questions (Nadel, 1971: 141). Momentum built for legislation to regulate automobile safety.

The National Traffic and Motor Vehicle Safety Act of 1966 empowered the National Highway Safety Bureau (now the National Highway Traffic Safety Administration [NHTSA]) in the Department of Commerce (now in the Department of Transportation) to establish "reasonable, practicable, and appropriate" safety standards for automobiles and to create a systematic and open system of reporting safety defects. Over the next eight years, Congress passed a variety of other traffic safety laws. The Highway Safety Act of 1966 provided grants for states to operate highway safety programs resulting in such innovations as raised center-line bumps, breakaway sign posts, and sand-filled barrier cushions (see Menzel and Feller, 1977). The National Traffic and Motor Vehicle Safety Act was amended in 1969 to cover tires and in 1974 to require that all recalled vehicles be repaired free by the manufacturer. In 1974, NHTSA was given joint administration over the speed limit of 55 miles per hour (mph).

NHTSA Administration

The NHTSA approach to administration is two-pronged—regulations that apply to all cars sold and recalls of vehicles when safety defects are discovered. By 1982, NHTSA had issued more than 50 safety regulations for vehicles. Among the requirements of the regulations were dual braking systems, windshield wipers, seat and shoulder belts, child restraint systems, head rests, and collapsible steering columns (Greer, 1983: 436).

On the safety defect front, NHTSA conducts its own field tests and also provides a hotline for consumer complaints about automobile safety. NHTSA has the legislative authority for fining automobile companies that fail to conform to safety regulations, but it generally relies on voluntary recalls. A recall may be requested if a defect is safety-related and creates an unreasonable risk of accident or death (Tobin, 1982: 282). From 1966 to 1982, NHTSA presided over the recall of 82 million vehicles manufactured in the United States and 17 million foreign-manufactured vehicles.

Although the recalls are termed voluntary, they are hardly that. The automobile companies and NHTSA have frequently been at loggerheads over recalls. Automobile companies generally dispute claims of safety defects and then reluctantly agree to a recall after the evidence accumulates. One example of this process involves the braking systems of the General Motors X cars. The Department of Transportation (i.e., NHTSA) filed suit seeking $4 million in civil damages and the recall of 1.1 million cars in 1983. According to documents released before that suit went to trial, the brake defects of the X cars (marketed under the names Citation, Omega, Phoenix, and Skylark) were known to GM as the result of internal studies in 1978, a full year before production started (GM Knew, 1983: 3).

The impact of NHTSA recalls on safety has received little study. NHTSA determines recalls on a case-by-case basis; such a process usually results in bargaining with the companies about the content, scope, or wording of the recall (Tobin, 1982: 283). Although 84 percent of recalls were initiated by the manufacturers (consumer satisfaction and repeat purchases are a motivation), over half the total vehicles recalled have been in NHTSA-initiated recalls (Tobin, 1982: 289). For recalls to work effectively, vehicles must be repaired; studies estimate that only 60 to 70 percent of vehicles are repaired. No empirical data exist on the specific impact of recalls on the number of accidents or deaths.

The conflict between NHTSA and the automobile companies is also evident in the rule-making process. The automobile companies consistently testify before Congress that safety regulations greatly increase the price of automobiles for marginal safety gains. This conflict is best illustrated by the passive restraints controversy.

Active restraints (i.e., those that require the action of the driver or the passenger to use) such as seat and shoulder belts are an effective way to prevent some traffic fatalities. Estimates suggest that 16,000 lives a year could be saved if all passengers used seat belts (Gottron, 1982: 131). Because an overwhelming majority of people do not use seat belts, many lives are needlessly lost. Accordingly, NHTSA has investigated the use of passive restraints since 1968.

Passive restraints have been opposed by the automobile manufacturers since that time. NHTSA's first effort was the seat belt ignition interlock system that would prevent a car from starting if the seat belts were not fastened. This rule caused such protests that Congress in 1974 overruled NHTSA and prohibited such a rule (Gottron, 1982: 131).

NHTSA had two options—airbags (which inflate on impact) or automatic seat and shoulder belts (such as those in the current Volkswagen Rabbit). Fearing that individuals would disconnect automatic belts, NHTSA opted for airbags. The airbag rule-making process encompassed some 60 administrative hearings, two appeals to Congress and associated hearings, and two court challenges. In 1977, NHTSA required that automobile manufacturers phase in airbags during the 1982 through 1984 model years (Wines, 1983a: 1462). Citing costs of $1,000 per vehicle (other cost estimates were significantly lower), the automobile companies resisted and appealed to Congress and the courts.

The automobile companies' appeals were heard following the 1980 election, when Raymond Peck, the new administrator of NHTSA, began an effort to deregulate the automobile industry. Peck repealed the airbag rule.

Peck and the administration were promptly sued by insurance companies and consumer groups. In June 1983 the Supreme Court held that the Department of Transportation (NHTSA) could not withdraw a rule without going through the same process that was necessary to issue a rule (*Motor Vehicle Manufacturers* v. *State Farm*, 1983). As a result, the withdrawal of the rule was not permitted; NHTSA was told it could withdraw the rule only if evidence supported withdrawal. NHTSA interpreted this decision to mean that they must study the issue further, and, under Acting Administrator Diane Steed (who replaced Peck), the study process began again. In 1984 a new airbag rule was issued, but it would not become effective if states with two-thirds of the nation's population passed laws requiring seat belts by 1987. Because two of the three major auto companies terminated passive restraint research programs after the NHTSA rule change, fast implementation of a new airbag rule is unlikely (Wines, 1983b: 1536).

The passive restraint rule illustrates the changes in policy with changes in political administrations. By changing agency heads, a president can dramatically alter a subsystem's policy outputs. With the election of Ronald Reagan, NHTSA began a series of efforts to ease safety restrictions on the automobile industry. Consumer advocate Joan Claybrook, who headed the agency in the Carter administration, was replaced with Peck. Included in the Reagan administration's deregulation effort was the repeal or modification of rules regarding driver vision, fuel economy, speedometer tampering, tire rims, brakes, tire pressure, battery safety, tire safety, antitheft protection, vehicle IDs, and seat belt comfort (Wines, 1983b: 1535). The results were widely criticized by consumer groups and welcomed by the automobile industry.

The clear-cut nature of policy change was illustrated by NHTSA's 1981 attempt to eliminate restrictions on the impact an automobile bumper must take without damage to the car. NHTSA had required 5 mph bumpers front and rear. In May 1982, NHTSA announced a new standard of 2.5 mph, for which it claimed benefits of $300 million per year. Unlike other safety standards where cost-benefit analysis is mired in problems of estimating the value of human lives, the bumper standard dealt only with economic issues. Closer examination of the figures revealed that this benefit was, in fact, a reduction in costs to auto manufacturers. Even if such savings were passed on to consumers, they would have been wiped out by increases in automobile insurance. In short, the rule change simply redistributed costs from the automobile companies to insurance companies, who will, in turn, pass on these costs to consumers.

The Impact of NHTSA Policy

The impact of NHTSA on its environment has been controversial. Automobile companies contend that NHTSA rules have greatly increased costs with few compensating safety benefits. To support their arguments, they cite the economic studies of Peltzman (1975), who argued that these safety regulations impose more costs than benefits. What makes policymakers skeptical of these arguments, however, is the commonsense perception that automobile safety has improved. Traffic fatalities ceased their rapid increase after 1965 and leveled off at approximately 55,000 per year. Fatalities per 100 million vehicle miles have also dropped (see Meier and Morgan, 1982).

A study by the General Accounting Office estimated, for example, that safety requirements saved 28,000 lives between 1966 and 1970. Another study attributes a 39 percent drop in fatalities to the safety regulations (see Greer, 1983: 438).

One problem in estimating the impact of safety regulations exactly is that their impact occurs gradually. Only as older vehicles without safety equipment are sent to the junkyard can safety gains be realized. In addition, vehicle safety regulations have occurred simultaneously with improvements in highways, making the relative impact of each difficult to discern. Skeptics of traffic safety, however, are difficult to convince. Even the obvious, major safety impact of the 55 mph speed limit (see Meier and Morgan, 1982) has been questioned by some who argue that it imposes more costs than benefits.

The imposition of costs on the automobile industry is one aspect of safety regulation that cannot be ignored. From an economic standpoint, however, safety regulation simply incorporates the cost of safety into the vehicle price; safety is paid for up front rather than after the fact through injuries (whether regulation is the most efficient way to do this is an open question). Safety regulation has raised the cost of automobiles. To argue that safety regulation is the cause of the problems faced by the automobile industry from 1978 to 1982, however, is difficult to maintain. Economist Michael Levine (1982: 118) has argued that safety requirements actually help the American automobile manufacturer compete with foreign imports. Because the foreign manufacturer must spread safety investments over a smaller number of vehicles (only those that are sent to the United States) whereas the American manufacturer can spread the fixed costs over more vehicles, the net impact of safety regulations should be to lower the relative price of American-made vehicles. Recent ads extolling the safety features of American automobiles show that Detroit is now recognizing this fact.

Who Benefits?

Determining who benefits from automobile safety regulation is fairly easy. Regulation restricts the options of automobile companies for the benefit of people who buy cars. Because regulation increases the price of vehicles, consumers pay for the safety improvements they receive. Automakers actually experience a net economic loss from safety regulation. Although safety costs are passed on to consumers, the price of vehicles is higher, and this results in reduced demand. Automobile company profits are highly sensitive to the level of sales.

CONSUMER PRODUCT SAFETY REGULATION

The Subsystem

The Agency.   The Consumer Product Safety Commission (CPSC) is an independent commission; it is tasked with establishing safety standards for over 10,000 consumer products that are not regulated by other federal agencies. It can ban hazardous products as well as issue rules that standardize the production of certain products. Although the CPSC has economy-wide authority, it usually deals with one industry at a time. The CPSC had

616 employees with a budget of $35 million in FY 1985 (a decrease of 21 percent from 1980).

CPSC has not developed a reputation for expertise. Because the regulation of consumer product hazards is often complex, this lack of expertise has forced the agency to rely on industry for information. With the exception of Susan King, CPSC leadership has been generally poor. In combination, these factors produce an agency with little cohesion and high turnover.

Consumer product hazards could be a highly salient issue if CPSC skillfully used the media and targeted its efforts on the most pressing problems. It has not, however. Agency legislative authority is part of the problem. Legislative goals are vague. The agency's coverage is broad, perhaps too broad because it has only 600 employees to regulate 10,000 products. Sanctions exist, but they are rarely used. Finally, CPSC is severely handicapped by procedural restrictions; both the offeror process and the requirement of voluntary rules (see further on) have prevented strong action by the agency.

Advocacy Coalitions.   Because CPSC regulation is economywide, the regulated industry encompasses almost the entire manufacturing sector. The industry coalition varies, therefore, from issue to issue. A flammable fabrics rule will see action by textile manufacturers, a toy safety rule by toy makers, a lawn-mower rule by lawn-mower manufacturers. On a general level, the Business Roundtable has been active in opposing what they see as regulatory excesses on the part of CPSC.

Somewhat more stable, though spread thinly, is the consumer coalition. The Consumer Federation of America is a coalition of 200 local organizations. It has a permanent staff of about ten and a separate research unit (McFarland, 1976: 93). Consumers Union is a consumer product-testing organization that publishes *Consumer Reports;* Consumers Union spends a small portion of its time on advocacy. In fact, Ralph Nader resigned from the board of Consumers Union in 1975 over the lack of advocacy effort (McFarland, 1976: 90). The Nader organizations, especially the Public Interest Research Group, are also active in product safety. On any particular issue, these and other consumer groups are likely to be joined by state consumer protection officials, journalists, and product safety researchers.

The Environment

Because CPSC regulates several industries, generalizations about the economic and technological environment are not possible. More than 2 million firms produce thousands of consumer products. CPSC regulation has affected such divergent industries as lawn-mower manufacturers, home insulation producers, baby crib makers, and the children's toy industry. Foreign manufacturers are also affected; fully 30 percent of all products recalled by the CPSC are of foreign manufacture (Tobin, 1982).

Consumer Product Safety Legislation

In the 1960s, the number of products regulated for safety reasons was relatively few—food, drugs, airplane travel, cosmetics, medical devices, and pesticides. In other areas, product safety was "regulated" only by individuals filing lawsuits after some damages had occurred. To be sure, private organizations such as Consumers Research and Consumers Union tested consumer products, but no federal government agency was active in the field. Reflecting the concerns raised by consumer groups, President Lyndon Johnson appointed a National Commission on Product Safety in 1968 to investigate the problems of product safety. Included on the commission was future FTC Chairman Michael Pertschuk (Bureau of National Affairs, 1973: 19).

The National Commission on Product Safety in its June 1970 report documented numerous dangers involving consumer products. It found that 20 million persons were injured each year in using consumer products, 110,000 persons were permanently disabled, and 30,000 were killed. The annual monetary cost of these accidents was estimated to be $5.5 billion (Pittle, 1976: 131). The commission argued that industry self-regulation was "chronically inadequate" and that certification programs by independent laboratories were weakened because they depended on industry for operating funds (Bureau of National Affairs, 1973: 23). The commission's chairperson, Arnold Elkind, testified before Congress that an effective administrative agency could prevent as many as 4 million accidents and 6,000 deaths a year.

Immediately after the National Commission's report, bills to create a Consumer Product Safety Commission were introduced in both houses of Congress. No action was taken in 1970, when Congress adjourned early for midterm elections. In 1971, President Nixon tried to head off strong legislation by proposing educational programs in the Department of Health, Education, and Welfare (HEW) rather than a new regulatory agency (Bureau of National Affairs, 1973: 27). Nixon's proposal was ignored by Congress.

The major issue in 1971 was not whether to create a product safety regulator but what kind to create. The Nixon administration and business leaders favored regulation by existing departments (which was characterized by the National Commission as limited). Senator Magnuson and consumer advocates favored a new independent commission. Under Magnuson's leadership, the Senate Commerce Committee reported a strong bill that included not only consumer products but also transferred regulation of food, drugs, cosmetics, and meats to the new CPSC (Bureau of National Affairs, 1973: 29). In conference with the House, which passed a less comprehensive bill, the regulation of food, drugs, cosmetics, and meats was left in their original agencies. The bill's quick passage can be attributed to the noncontroversial nature of consumer protection in 1971. Serious opposition to consumer protection had not yet formed.

The Consumer Product Safety Act charged the CPSC with protecting consumers from "unreasonable risk of injury from hazardous products." The CPSC received jurisdiction over 10,000 consumer products that were not regulated by other federal agencies. Specifically exempted from CPSC purview were tobacco products, aviation and boating equipment, automobiles, food and drugs, cosmetics, and pesticides. In addition, jurisdiction over the Flammable Fabrics Act (1953), The Refrigerator Safety Act (1956), the Federal Hazardous Substances Act (1960), and the Poison Prevention Packaging Act of 1970 was transferred to the CPSC.

The Consumer Product Safety Act marked a change in the congressional approach to hazardous products. Prior efforts (fabrics, refrigerators, and so forth) were targeted at specific hazards. The 1972 act took a general position against hazardous products and vested authority to move against such hazards in a regulatory agency (see Pittle, 1976: 131).

CPSC administrative procedures were also innovative compared to those of other regulatory agencies. The commission was given broad powers to regulate consumer hazards by establishing standards, banning hazardous products, and recalling hazardous products from the market. The CPSC has used all three powers at different times; lawn mowers, for example, were subjected to standards, urea formaldehyde foam insulation was banned (reversed by a court decision), and asbestos hair dryers were recalled.

CPSC rule making followed an innovative process called the offeror system. CPSC did not issue rules by itself; rather, it advertised the area of rule making and received proposals (from offerors) to write the rule. One or more offerors were selected; and they were required to have participation by consumers, small business, and retailers in the process. The finished rule was then submitted to CPSC, which could either accept or reject it (Bardach and Kagen, 1982: 181). The congressional intent was to maximize participation in the rule-making process.

CPSC was also designed to be as independent as possible. Reflecting Nixon's opposition to CPSC (see Renfrow, 1980), procedures were established to prevent presidential domination of the commission. Unlike other regulatory commissions, where the chairperson serves at the pleasure of the president, the CPSC chairperson could not be removed from the position of chairperson during his or her term (in other agencies commissioners could not be removed, but the president was free to designate which commissioner would serve as chairperson). In addition, the CPSC was required to submit its budget to Congress at the same time it was submitted to the Office of Management and Budget. Dual budget submissions were designed to limit presidential budgetary control over the agency.

CPSC Administration

The actions of the Consumer Product Safety Commission were probably doomed to failure from the start. Like the Occupational Safety and Health Administration, CPSC was given an impossible task (regulating 10,000 consumer products) and limited resources. Avoiding the mistake of OSHA, CPSC did not adopt hundreds of voluntary product standards. Rather, it took a more cautious approach that was criticized by both consumer activists and the industries that were regulated.

With 10,000 products to regulate, some method of establishing priorities is essential. CPSC recognized this, in part, when it established an informal agency decision rule that "the vast majority of injuries, if they are to be reduced, must be addressed through changes in consumer behavior" (Staelin and Pittle, 1978: 58). Although many accidents were the result of consumer misuse, some products could be made safer by issuing standards. For example, many household accidents involve kitchen knives, but the overwhelming majority are not the result of design flaws in knives but rather in user carelessness. Accidents involving soft drink bottles (particularly from explosions), on the other hand, are often the result of design problems and can be addressed via standards (Staelin and Pittle, 1978: 58).

Even restricting itself to problems that could be corrected by using standards, CPSC faced a massive number of products. Initially, CPSC failed to set priorities and dissipated its efforts by trying to do too much. The tendency to overregulate was exacerbated by the agency's organizational ideology. Staffed with young consumer advocates, the agency was initially hostile to industry. As one CPSC commissioner said, "Ralph Nader isn't personally responsible for the Consumer Product Safety Commission—it was brought to you by those friendly folks who manufacture, import, or sell products that are difficult for the average consumer to use safely" (Pittle, 1976: 136–137).

Evaluation of Agency Policy

From its creation to 1977, the CPSC was characterized as at best ineffective and at worst a total failure. The agency was criticized for its slow response to consumer problems. In the agency's first four years it issued only three rules. These rules covered swimming pool slides, matchbook covers, and architectural glass. One illustration of its slow response is the children's sleepware issue. In 1972 standards for flameproofing sleepware were issued. Manufacturers achieved these standards by treating sleepware products with a chemical called Tris. Unfortunately, Tris proved to be carcinogenic; it was banned in 1977. In 1978, CPSC lost a court case holding that it could not ban the export of Tris-coated sleepware (Congress devoted substantial hearings and some legislation to this issue in 1978).

CPSC's failure to issue more standards and the slow nature of its actions were not entirely its own fault. The cumbersome offeror system with its emphasis on maximum participation slowed down the rule-making process greatly. In addition, by failing to set priorities, CPSC spread its resources too thin and attempted to regulate too much.

Numerous studies criticized the ineffectiveness of CPSC circa 1977. In 1976 the General Accounting Office criticized the agency for inefficiency, poor management, and poor enforcement. In 1977 the GAO revealed that the offeror process for rule making was taking approximately 2½ times longer than the 330 days permitted by law. A 1976 House Commerce Oversight and Investigations Subcommittee report found that the agency failed to set priorities and that participation efforts resulted in long delays in enforcement. A Civil Service Commission (now Office of Personnel Management) survey of CPSC employees discovered that only 43 percent of the agency's personnel felt the agency was doing a good job. Even an internal management task force found that the commission was falling short of reaching its legislative mandate (Lammers, 1983: 86). One journalist charged that the CPSC has "been such an abysmal failure that it is at least as responsible as any other government agency for the plummeting popularity of consumer protection" (Kurtz, 1977: 29).

CPSC's performance from 1972 to 1977 resulted in a loss of congressional support and only lukewarm consumer support. Contrasting with this support was strong opposition from sleepware manufacturers, swimming pool slide manufacturers, and other industries. The political environment of the agency changed dramatically in five years. Even President Jimmy Carter, a strong advocate of consumer protection, considered abolishing the agency in 1977 and assigning its functions to the Food and Drug Administration and the Environmental Protection Agency (Lammers, 1983: 86). As the result of some vigorous internal lobbying, particularly by Esther Peterson, Carter's special assistant for consumer affairs, the administration changed its mind and supported reauthorization of the CPSC.

After subjecting CPSC to a series of critical hearings, Congress grudgingly reauthorized the agency. In an effort to defuse the controversy surrounding the agency, CPSC Chairman S. John Byington resigned (Byington was accused of violating federal personnel rules). Congress also made several changes in the authorizing legislation. The CPSC chairman henceforth would serve at the pleasure of the president, the offeror process was modified, and the commission was encouraged to use voluntary industry standards. Implicit in the reauthorization was the threat that the agency might be abolished when its authorization expired in 1981.

The administration of CPSC improved after the 1978 reauthorization. Carter appointed Susan King to head the CPSC. Under King, CPSC emphasized voluntary industry standards. Of the 75 standards adopted between 1978 and 1981, only five were mandatory; the rest were developed voluntarily by the industries (Lammers, 1983: 90). CPSC began to set priorities for regulation based on the severity of risk involved, size of the population exposed, characteristics of the exposed population, and circumstances of the exposure. Even the agency's abysmal record in court improved. Prior to 1978 the agency lost almost every major court case it argued; after 1978 (until 1981) it won 17 of 21 cases (Lammers, 1983: 87).

CPSC's record on safety recalls also showed some results. Relying on toll-free hotlines, hospital injury room monitoring systems, and manufacturers for information about product hazards, it recalled millions of consumer products. The actual recalls, however, were of limited success because locating owners of consumer products is difficult. As a result, less than 50 percent of recalled products (up from 20 percent prior to 1977) were actually retrieved (Tobin, 1982: 295). CPSC estimated that these recalls prevented a million accidents between October 1977 and September 1980, approximately 1 percent of the total.

By the 1981 reauthorization, the agency could cite some regulatory successes. One notable success was CPSC's regulation of childproof caps for medicines and poisons. Rather than specifying exactly how such caps would be designed (as they did in their baby pacifier rules), CPSC subjected caps to performance standards. A cap could be marketed if 85 percent of a group of 200 children could not open the caps and 90 percent of adults could. The standards resulted in a 90 percent reduction in the number of children's deaths from ingesting medicines and poisons (Greer, 1983: 441; Child-resistant, 1984: 26). Similarly, the CPSC's standard that children's cribs could have slats no more than 2.375 inches apart (compared to the old industry standard of 3.5 inches) resulted in a 90 percent drop in the number of babies who strangled themselves by sliding their bodies between the slats until their heads were caught.

CPSC's performance under Susan King in all likelihood saved the agency. Following the 1980 election, President Reagan proposed that the commission be abolished. Had the agency's record in 1981 been similar to its record in 1978, the agency might not have survived reauthorization. In 1981, CPSC even received support from the regulatory critic Murray Weidenbaum, who stated that the agency was one of few that tried to weigh regulatory costs against benefits and act in an economically rational manner.

Despite improvements, CPSC faced a formidable array of enemies in its 1981 reauthorization. In addition to Ronald Reagan, the CPSC reauthorization was opposed by OMB Director David Stockman and Senate Oversight Chairperson Robert Kasten. The eventual reauthorization placed numerous constraints on CPSC. CPSC rules were subjected to one house veto (see chapter 2 on constitutional issues), the offeror process was abolished, CPSC was limited to performance standards regulation only (rather than design standards), and rule-making procedures were drastically altered. Since 1981, to issue new rules, CPSC must first invite proposals for voluntary standards. If a feasible voluntary standard is proposed, then CPSC must adopt it and end its own process. Mandatory standards could be adopted only if the voluntary standards were unlikely to reduce risk or would not result in compliance. The mandatory rule must also return benefits in excess of costs and be the least burdensome manner of reducing risk of injury (Lammers, 1983: 88–89).

The congressional restrictions placed on the CPSC were minor compared to the Reagan administration actions. With the resignation of King, Nancy Harvey Steorts was appointed chairperson. Unlike many 1981 appointees, Steorts had some consumer protection credentials (having served as a consumer affairs specialist in the Department of Agriculture from 1973–1977) even though much of her work had been with business. CPSC was subjected to massive budget and personnel cuts as part of the Reagan budget process. In fiscal 1982 the budget was reduced by 30 percent with a 27 percent reduction in agency staff. The agency continued to engage in setting priorities for consumer protection, but administered the priorities with reduced numbers of personnel. W. Kip Viscusi, an economist who authored a critical study of the CPSC's early years, recently criticized the Steorts' CPSC as being in chaos. "There is no clear vision from any of these people [at the commission] as to how they should change the agency" (Wines, 1982a: 94).

Who Benefits?

Consumer product regulation is intended to benefit consumers by restricting the behavior of business. In actual practice, determining the beneficiaries is not so easy. Given the performance of CPSC from 1972 to 1977, one could argue that no one benefited from regulation. From 1978 to 1981 some clear benefits to consumers were achieved, and producers were restricted. After 1981, CPSC has become an invisible agency, doing little. Similar to many other consumer agencies, the beneficiaries change in response to shifts in political pressures.

THE REVITALIZATION OF THE FTC

No agency more epitomizes the rise and fall of the consumer movement than the Federal Trade Commission (FTC). Rising from the ashes of a devastated agency in 1969, the FTC became the most aggressive advocate of consumer protection in the federal government by 1977. It also became the major target for the forces opposing consumer protection and the major battle ground after the defeat of the proposed Agency for Consumer Advocacy in 1978.

The Subsystem

The Agency.   The Federal Trade Commission is an independent commission charged with regulating unfair and deceptive trade practices; it also has antitrust functions, but these will be covered in chapter 9. The Federal Trade Commission has jurisdiction over all industries in regard to ensuring that the marketplace engages in fair competition. The activities of concern in this chapter are housed in the FTC's Bureau of Consumer Protection (Hinich and Staelin, 1980: 76). The FTC's budget in FY 1985 was $67 million (a decrease of 2 percent from 1980), and it has approximately 1,300 employees.

The FTC of the 1970s attracted many young consumer activists as employees. Reflecting the values of these persons, the agency developed a high level of cohesion and a consensus for vigorous regulation. Expertise, however, has generally been an FTC weak point because the FTC must cover all industries to check for unfair competition and deceptive advertising. Recent FTC leadership can be characterized as aggressive although not necessarily politically astute.

Although the issues addressed by the FTC are only moderately salient (e.g., advertising by professionals), the agency has the ability to increase its salience (not necessarily to the agency's benefit). The FTC's legislative authority has both pluses and minuses. On the one hand, the agency has a wide variety of sanctions ranging from rule making to antitrust suits, and it has a broad scope of authority (economywide). On the other hand, its goals are vague and probably contradictory (see chapter 9 on antitrust goals), and it has some cumbersome procedures. FTC rule making must follow a formal rule-making procedure that grants all parties extended rights to participate; as a result, FTC rule making is slow (see West, 1982).

Advocacy Coalitions.   Because the FTC regulates many different industries, the industry advocacy coalition varies from issue to issue. Recent industries that have protested FTC actions include agricultural co-ops, cereal manufacturers, oil companies, and professions (doctors, lawyers, and so on). In some cases, these advocacy coalitions are led by the National Association of Manufacturers and the U.S. Chamber of Commerce.

Advocacy coalitions supporting the FTC also vary from issue to issue. The same groups that are active in support of the CPSC (e.g., the Consumer Federation of America) are also active in support of the FTC. In addition, the agency often picks up the support of one industry or professional group that would like to see another regulated. Nurses, for example, opposed the American Medical Association's effort to be exempted from the FTC regulation. In addition, some labor unions, particularly the International Ladies Garment Workers, have been strong FTC supporters (Pertschuk, 1982: 100).

Environment

Because the FTC regulates a variety of industries, the economic and technological environment cannot be described in detail. Some industries have numerous firms and relatively easy entry (used-car dealers). Others have few firms with high barriers to entry (cereal manufacturers). Some affected businesses have complex and unstable technologies (oil companies) whereas others do not (funeral directors). Each FTC issue takes place in a slightly different economic and technological environment.

The Early Performance of the FTC

In the 1960s the FTC was among the least effective regulatory agencies in the federal government. Its reputation for ineffectiveness dated back to the 1920s, when its close ties to business were established. In fact, the famous court case *Humphrey's Executor* v. *U.S.* (1935), establishing the principle that independent regulatory commissions were to be independent of presidential control, concerned Franklin Roosevelt's effort to remove William Humphrey, a notoriously probusiness commissioner, from the FTC. Even Congress recognized the FTC's orientation. In 1938 the FTC rather than the FDA was given authority over drug advertising under the belief that the FTC would be more sympathetic to advertisers (see earlier).

In 1969, a group of law students under the auspices of Ralph Nader (they were termed "Nader's Raiders") released a highly critical report on the Federal Trade Commission (see Cox, et al., 1969). The commission and its employees were characterized as incompetent, lacking commitment, and often absent. The commission had poor personnel practices, failed to set priorities for agency action, and did not even have any full-time staff assigned to monitor deceptive advertising on television. Blaming Commission Chairperson Paul Rand Dixon for these problems, the study charged Dixon preferred mediocre attorneys from Southern law schools to those from prestigious Eastern schools. The Nader report suggested that the best thing Dixon could do for the FTC would be to resign (Feldman, 1976: 68).

The Nader report, written in part by President Nixon's future son-in-law Edward Cox, received widespread publicity. In response, Nixon asked the American Bar Association (ABA) to conduct a similar evaluation of the FTC. In September 1969 the ABA released its report with findings similar to those of the Nader report. The FTC was termed "a failure on many counts" with "many instances of incompetence in the agency, particularly in senior staff positions" (*Report of the ABA,* 1969).

The Revitalization of the FTC

Nixon then appointed Caspar Weinberger to head the FTC. Although Weinberger remained at the Federal Trade Commission for only seven months, he had a lasting impact on the agency. Weinberger reorganized the FTC, ostensibly for efficiency reasons but probably to justify his firing many senior people in the agency (Clarkson and Muris, 1981: 4). The two FTC bureaus, Competition and Consumer Protection, were then staffed with aggressive consumer advocates. With a massive amount of turnover in agency personnel, Weinberger was able to generate some enthusiasm for consumer protection and a cohesive spirit in the agency (Nadel, 1971: 40). A total of 18 of the top 31 FTC staff members were discharged in the Weinberger "reorganization" as were one-third of the mid-level and lower-level staff (Clarkson and Muris, 1981: 4).

Weinberger's successor, Miles Kirkpatrick, the head of the ABA committee on the FTC, continued these policies. The Federal Trade Commission became known as the place for consumer activists to work. Congress encouraged the FTC in this regard; in hearing after hearing, members of Congress urged FTC commissioners to be aggressive in pursuit of consumer protection (see Pertschuk, 1982). Perhaps the most forceful effort of Congress on the FTC's behalf was the Magnuson-Moss Act of 1974. The Magnuson-Moss Act set standards for warranties and also granted the FTC authority to issue industrywide rules. In addition, the Supreme Court augmented the FTC's powers when it held that the FTC could act if advertising were unfair (rather than according to the stricter standard, deceptive; see *FTC v. Sperry and Hutchinson*, 1972).

The FTC pursued its congressional mandate aggressively. In 1975 after the passage of Magnuson-Moss, the FTC announced 13 proposed rules (LaBarbera, 1977: 6). Unlike past FTC efforts that were designed not to offend anyone, the post-Magnuson-Moss efforts affected powerful economic interests. Professional regulation programs were targeted at price fixing by doctors, optometrists, and dentists. A major study of television advertising directed at children (the "kidvid" study) was started. An antitrust suit was filed against the major oil companies, and a similar suit was filed against cereal manufacturers, using the unique charge that the four largest cereal producers were a shared monopoly (see chapter 9).

The FTC issued a series of rules affecting major industries. In 1975 rules governing the holder-in-due-course of a note (e.g., the person who purchases a loan) and mail-order businesses were issued. In 1978 the FTC issued rules covering franchises, vocational schools, and eyeglasses. The year 1979 saw rules on octane posting for gasoline, R-values for insulation, and energy efficiency ratings for appliances. In all these cases, rules established regulation where none had existed and did so in the interests of the consumer. The FTC eyeglasses rule, for example, eliminated restrictions on advertising eyeglasses and required that optometrists give patients a copy of their prescription so that they could shop around for the best deal. The rule was widely conceded to have reduced eyeglass prices. Perhaps equally important was the effort to make sure that the consumer viewpoint was presented in the rule-making process. Under Chairperson Michael Pertschuk (a former Senate aide to Warren Magnuson), the FTC began to pay consumer groups so that they could come to Washington and testify on pending rules.

The Anticonsumer Backlash

Rarely in the history of bureaucracy has so small an agency provoked the ire of as many powerful interests in as short a time as the FTC did from 1974 to 1977. The quick rise of opposition to the FTC's consumer activities was the function of three variables. First, the industrywide rules changed dramatically the way businesses had to deal with the FTC. No longer was business entitled to a case-by-case adjudication before being penalized. And even worse from the business perspective, the ability to rely on the FTC for a favorable decision (as was the case in the 1960s) no longer existed. Several industries were subjected to real federal regulation for the first time. Second, the Commerce Committees of the House and Senate changed significantly between 1972 and 1977. Both committees went from being very liberal to being more conservative with the large turnover in the members of Congress (Weingast and Moran, 1982). No longer could the FTC rely on the protection of senators like Warren Magnuson. Third, Carter's FTC chairperson, Michael Pertschuk, was an aggressive and perhaps a not very politically skilled consumer advocate. His actions and statements did not calm the fears of people concerned about the FTC (Gottron, 1982: 81).

The effort to reign in the FTC centered in Congress. Industries concerned about the FTC quite naturally took their complaints to their member of Congress and sought relief. So strong was the disagreement concerning the FTC and what to do about it that Congress was unable to pass legislation authorizing the agency's budget from 1977 to 1980. The agency was funded via continuing resolutions. A major effort to restrict the FTC in 1979 failed, not because the legislators could not agree to limit the FTC but because they had a dispute over the use of the legislative veto (see chapter 2). Led by Representative Elliot Levitas, the House tried to subject FTC's rules to a legislative veto. Senate opposition to the veto killed a bill that would have significantly limited the FTC.

The 1980 session of Congress saw a formidable coalition of interests seeking restrictions on the FTC. Included in the coalition were the American Medical Association (AMA), the American Bar Association (both concerned about FTC efforts to encourage competition in these areas), the insurance industry (an FTC investigation), the television industry, advertisers (kidvid), automobile dealers (the used-car rule), drug manufacturers (an over-the-counter advertising study), Sunkist (the target of an antitrust suit), and Formica (the FTC petitioned to eliminate Formica as a trademark). These forces were led by the Chamber of Commerce and the National Association of Manufacturers. The professional associations alone contributed over $1 million in 1980 to congressional campaigns (Wines, 1982b: 993).

Opposed by consumer groups, the FTC, and the Carter White House, the anti-FTC coalition was able to pass a bill euphemistically called the Federal Trade Commission Improvements Act. The 1980 bill was far more moderate than the 1979 effort and led Pertschuk to conclude that the agency had weathered the attack (Pertschuk, 1982). The act effectively ended the FTC's insurance investigation, limited the use of funding for intervenors (e.g., consumer groups), restricted the kidvid study to questions of deception rather than questions of unfairness, required the FTC to engage in a form of cost-benefit analysis before issuing rules, prohibited the FTC from petitioning the Patents and Trademarks Office to repeal trademarks, and subjected FTC rules to a two-house legislative veto. The act did permit the FTC to continue to regulate agricultural co-ops if they violated provisions of the Capper-Volstead Act (an act granting some antitrust immunity to agriculture co-ops). Although the FTC was limited, the end result was a compromise that no one liked. It was denounced by FTC supporter Howard Metzenbaum as well as by FTC critic Jesse Helms (*Congressional Quarterly Almanac*, 1980: 236).

The Reagan FTC

Unlike regulatory agencies that are not independent commissions, the FTC changed its policy gradually after the election of Ronald Reagan. In part, this reflected the president's limited ability to appoint new commissioners. Economist James Miller III, briefly the head of the regulatory relief task force, was named to chair the FTC. Pertschuk remained on the commission as a commissioner.

Under Miller, the FTC made a series of decisions to indicate it was retreating from its aggressive consumer protection policies. Miller recruited numerous economists to the FTC so that he could rely on others with similar views to implement policy (Wines, 1982b: 992). Included among the personnel was Timothy J. Muris, a longtime FTC critic, to head the Bureau of Consumer Protection. During 1981 the FTC terminated its study of over-the-counter drug advertising, dropped its study of the automobile industry that it had begun in 1976, withdrew its shared monopoly case against the cereal manufacturers, and closed down the famous kidvid study (see Kosters, 1982: 15–18). Approximately one-fourth of the FTC's pending cases were dropped by the Miller FTC in 1981 alone (Wines, 1982b: 993).

As an illustration of the reliance of the Miller FTC on different remedies for market ills, the survival suit case is exemplary. The case involved hundreds of survival suits that had been sold to the government and private buyers to protect persons involved in ocean accidents. The suits leaked, and repairs would have cost no more than a few cents per suit. The FTC decided in December 1981 not to order a recall of the suits. The reasoning was that the free market would handle the problem because the relatives of drowning victims would sue the manufacturer for damages. After an investigation by the House Energy and Commerce Subcommittee on Oversight and Investigations publicized this case, the manufacturer voluntarily recalled the survival suits (Wines, 1983c: 223).

The Congressional Fight Continues

The congressional fight over the FTC did not end in 1980. Those who failed to achieve their goals continued to press their cases. Some of this battle centered on the legislative veto. In 1982 the FTC issued its long awaited used-car rule. The rule, a watered-down version of earlier proposals, basically required used-car dealers to disclose any major defects in a vehicle if known and to disclose any warranties on the vehicle. In overwhelming votes in both houses of Congress, the rule was vetoed May 26, 1982. This marked the first use of the legislative veto against a regulation issued by an independent regulatory commission (*Congressional Quarterly Almanac*, 1982: 346).

A second rule, this one concerning practices of funeral directors, was submitted to Congress by the FTC in late 1982. The rule survived a veto when it was not brought to a vote in either house. The status of the used-car rule remained in doubt. The Consumers Union challenged the veto as unconstitutional; and before the Supreme Court heard this challenge, the veto was declared unconstitutional in *INS* v. *Chadha* (see chapter 2).

The 1982 fight over reauthorizing the FTC contained many of the same political forces as the first fight, but this time the pro-FTC coalition was better prepared. The move against the FTC was headed by Senator Robert Kasten, the chairman of the Commerce Subcommittee on Consumers. Kasten introduced legislation that placed 14 specific restrictions on the FTC. The major limitations were to restrict the FTC's jurisdiction to deceptive advertising (as opposed to unfair advertising), to exempt agricultural co-ops from the FTC's control, and to eliminate FTC jurisdiction over professions.

The motivations behind the coalition supporting the Kasten bill were fairly obvious. In March 1982 the FTC won a Supreme Court case upholding its regulation of physicians; the FTC prohibited price-fixing (setting minimum fee schedules) and voided state prohibitions of advertising (*AMA v. FTC*, 1982). To build support for their cause, the American Medical Association along with the organizations for dentists and optometrists contributed $832,000 to members of Congress, including $300,000 to members of the Commerce Committees.

The other major force opposing the FTC was the dairy cooperatives. Under the auspices of the Department of Agriculture, large cooperatives have taken over milk marketing in the United States (see chapter 5). The Department of Agriculture had never really regulated co-ops in any serious way and had encouraged the growth of superco-ops. The political clout of the dairy co-ops dates back to the Nixon administration, when American Milk Producers, Inc., made headlines for huge campaign contributions while seeking higher price supports. The FTC filed an antitrust suit against Dairymen, Inc., a co-op with $1 billion in annual sales. The dairy co-ops responded by pressuring Congress to reign in the FTC (Wines, 1982c: 1594).

The FTC did not wage its lobby efforts alone in 1982; business organizations that benefited from the FTC's proconsumer stance defended the organization. Leading the coalition was the American Nurses Association, which favored greater FTC control over the actions of physicians. Also part of the coalition were the National Association of Chain Drug Stores (which profited from generic drug sales and the ability to advertise prices for eyeglasses and drugs) and the American Association of Retired Persons. Perhaps most important was the Washington Business Group on Health, an organization representing 200 of the *Fortune* 500 companies. This organization supported the FTC because it felt the FTC was playing a role in holding down health care costs (which all these businesses were paying for in employee benefits). These business and professional groups were joined by the FTC's consumer group allies.

Although FTC opponents were successful in attaching restrictions to the FTC authorization, the FTC proponents were able to win the battle by a parliamentary ploy. By striking the FTC authorization from a major authorization bill for several agencies, the restrictions were not enacted. In the end of the session rush, the FTC was funded by continuing resolution.

The 1982 election with its Democratic landslide provided some relief for the FTC. Seven new Democrats were added to the House Commerce Committee, and Senator Ernest Hollings replaced Senator Wendell Ford as the ranking Democrat on the Senate Committee. Hollings was a general supporter of the FTC whereas Ford had been a strong critic (Wines, 1983c: 221). In this environment, the AMA and the dairy industry found fewer supporters for their position. The National Association of Manufacturers still wanted to limit FTC rules and remedies but decided to sit out the fight over professional regulation and co-op regulation. As a result, the AMA struck a compromise with the FTC whereby the FTC could regulate only those activities of the professions that were not actively regulated by the states. Because state level regulation of professions does not actively regulate anything (see chapter 7), this compromise was widely viewed as an FTC victory (Wines, 1983d: 859). As a portent of challenges to come, however, the American Bar Association at its 1983 annual meeting passed a resolution to seek an exemption from the FTC's jurisdiction (Wines, 1983e: 1832).

Although the battle continues, the prospects for a further weakened FTC are not as great as they once were for several reasons. First, with James Miller in charge of the FTC, it is no longer the aggressive regulator it was during the Pertschuk era. Second, the political composition of Congress continued to change in 1982. The Democratic victory in the 1982 midterm elections meant fewer Republican votes to link up with conservative Democratic votes in an anti-FTC coalition. Third, the FTC and its allies are getting better at mobilizing not only traditional consumers but also business and professional organizations to support its programs. These factors do not mean the FTC will soon return to its 1970 pattern of action, only that further major restrictions on the FTC are not likely.

STATE CONSUMER REGULATION

Consumer protection is an area of regulation shared by the federal government and the states. With the de-emphasis of consumer protection under the Reagan administration, the role of state governments in protecting consumers becomes more important. Although states vary a great deal in the consumer activities they sponsor, collectively they have a broader scope and much more depth than the national government. Several areas of state-level consumer protection policies merit some discussion, including public utility regulation, sales and loan regulation, food regulation, drug sales regulation, and legal remedies.

Public Utilities

Public utility regulation, which is the regulation of prices charged for electricity, natural gas, or other public utilities, evolved as a consumer issue when utility prices began to spiral after the Arab oil embargo. Before the 1970s, technological advances and economies of scale permitted utilities to keep rates low while expanding service (Anderson, 1980). With major increases in the price of fuel, a series of consumer issues in public utility regulation has surfaced. Consumer issues have been pressed in these areas both by grass-roots citizen organizations and by state officials such as attorneys general willing to serve as proxy advocates (Gormley, 1983b).

Rates and the level of rates charged have been the major concern (Gormley, 1983b: 11). As rates increased and ratepayers were unable to make payments, utility companies cut off service. Some states have responded to this problem by limiting the ability of utilities to shut off service, by providing special funds for individuals who cannot pay bills, or by considering lifeline service rates (where a minimum level of service is billed at a low rate).

Related to rate problems have been supply problems. Until recent efforts at conservation and the decline in the economy, many utility companies were facing demand in excess of supply. Expanding supply by constructing either nuclear plants or fossil-fuel plants has been opposed by a variety of environmental groups. Especially related to consumers in this area is the question of construction work in progress (CWIP) allowances that permit utilities to raise rates by including the cost of construction on plants in progress in the rate base (Gormley, 1983b: 15). Northwestern states have addressed the demand problem another way by permitting utility companies to invest in conservation (e.g., home insulation, and so on) and to increase rates to pay for such investments.

Rate innovation is a third area of consumer concern. Traditionally, utility rates were based on the amount consumed, with large consumers given discounts. Encouraged by the federal Public Utility Regulatory Policies Act of 1978, several states have experimented with innovative rate procedures. Such reforms include inverted rates, which charge more as consumption increases; time-of-day rates, which charge more for consumption during peak daytime periods; seasonal rates, which increase charges during seasons of higher use; and interrupted-service rates whereby utility companies reduce rates if an individual will permit them to interrupt service during periods of peak demand (Gormley, 1983b: 19). Among the more innovative states in this regard (in most cases preceding federal encouragement) have been New York (under the leadership of Alfred Kahn), Wisconsin, California, and Michigan.

Sales and Loan Regulation

Federal efforts to enforce "fair practices" in both loans and sales were preceded by state efforts. In the loan area, states originated the ban on the holder-in-due-course rule. Under the holder-in-due-course doctrine, an individual who sells a good to a person on credit could sell the note to a financial institution. If the good were defective, the buyer's recourse would be on the seller, not on the financial institution. This prevented the buyer from withholding payment to get repair or replacement. Several states established regulations that eliminated the holder-in-due-course doctrine by extending liability to the financial institution; these institutions, in turn, could then take legal action against the person selling them the note. Twenty-four states passed holder-in-due-course legislation before the FTC acted on this issue in 1976. By 1981, 35 states had such laws (Meyer, 1982).

States also led the way in regulation that established a cooling off period for door-to-door sales. The FTC in 1974 issued a rule that permits a purchaser to return without penalty any items costing more than $25 in a purchase from a door-to-door sale. Eight states had cooling off legislation before the FTC acted (Oster, 1980: 43), and 47 had legislation by 1981 (Meyer, 1982: 544–545). State regulation of sales and loans in these areas remains important even after the FTC acted because the enforcement actions of the FTC are limited by budgets and time.

Food Purchases

Although food safety regulation has generally passed to the federal government, regulations affecting food pricing have been the domain of state governments. Some states have been fairly active in legislation designed to permit more intelligent food purchases on the part of consumers. Eleven states require food to be open-dated so that consumers can judge freshness;

17 states require that food prices be posted in price per unit or price per item so that comparisons between products of different sizes can be made. Federal regulation has been absent in this area.

Drug Sales Regulation

Although the Food and Drug Administration regulates health products at the national level, its concern is with safety and effectiveness. State governments have generally moved into more economic areas of health regulation. Advertising prescription drugs was prohibited by 30 states as late as 1974 (Oster, 1980: 44). Advertising prescription drug prices in theory generates competition and results in lower prices. In 1975 the FTC acted against these bans as anticompetitive. Only 9 states had retained advertising bans in 1981 (and thus were unlikely to enforce an FTC rule).

Related to prescription advertising are generic drug laws. Such laws require that pharmacists fill a prescription using a cheaper generic drug rather than a brand-name drug if the customer desires. Twenty-six states had adopted generic drug laws by 1981; the federal government has given signals that it supported such actions via decisions in its health care programs.

States also regulate a variety of health care products and health care professionals via state regulatory boards. The operation of these boards is discussed in chapter 7. In general, this regulation has not had consumer interests foremost. Under pressure from the federal government, anticonsumer practices such as price-fixing by these boards has been banned. Without federal pressure, state regulators are likely to become more protective of the professions they regulate.

Legal Remedies

The purchaser of a defective good always has the option of seeking legal remedies. Such action is usually limited to state and local courtrooms. Several states have passed laws that facilitate court action in consumer protection areas. Some states permit class action suits so that all purchasers of a good can be covered by a single lawsuit; other states permit the buyer to be awarded attorney's fees if he or she wins the case; still other states provide that treble damages can be awarded to the purchaser. The most common state action in the legal area is to provide small claims courts so that the expense and time of a product liability suit is reduced; every state but South Carolina and Mississippi have small claims courts (Meyer, 1982: 544–545).

Other Areas

The areas discussed here clearly do not exhaust all the aspects of state-level consumer protection. Landlord-tenant laws have specified the legal rights of both landlords and tenants. Laws have been passed requiring that insurance policies be written in plain English; no-fault insurance laws have been adopted in a variety of states. Mobile homes have been subjected to consumer-oriented regulation. The list of state actions in this area is virtually limitless.

The Forces Behind State Regulation

State-level regulation of consumer transactions varies greatly from state to state. Such states as California, Florida, Hawaii, and Oregon have been exceptionally active in the area whereas states such as Arkansas, Oklahoma, and South Carolina have done very little. Sigelman and Smith (1980: 67) found that the adoption of consumer protection legislation was related to political culture, family income, and legislative professionalism. Ford (1977: 180) found a relationship between consumer protection and income, education, and retail sales. The relationships found by both these researchers can easily be explained. Consumer movements have generally been characterized as middle class; as a result, states with higher income and education levels are more likely to have strong consumer group organizations. In addition, states with professionalized legislatures and with political cultures that support government intervention in the marketplace are more likely to be receptive to demands for consumer protection.

These findings and the decline of federal activity in consumer protection bode both good and ill for consumers. For those individuals living in states with active regulatory agencies, little difference will be noted in enforcement. Given the ability of innovative states to move before the federal government in these areas, these residents may even become better protected. Those individuals residing in states with few consumer protection laws and weak regulatory agencies will likely miss the activities of the federal government the most.

SUMMARY

Consumer protection policy has undergone dramatic changes in the past few years. Rising from the entrepreneurial ability of individuals such as Kefauver, Ribicoff, and Nader, the consumer issue became one of the most salient issues in government. From its peak, when consumer issues were noncontroversial, consumer protection issues are now openly fought. The decline of the consumer movement is usually dated from 1978, when legislation to create an Agency for Consumer Advocacy failed to pass Congress. Pressure for consumer protection has not declined, however, so much as opposition to additional measures has jelled and made further advances more difficult.

The beneficiaries of consumer protection policy change with the changes in political forces. During the 1970s, policy had a definite proconsumer orientation. The FTC aggressively regulated business practices; the NHTSA imposed safety requirements on automakers. Food and pharmaceutical companies faced inspections, recalls, and seizures. And after 1977 the CPSC had some positive impacts. After the 1980 election, aggressive regulators were replaced with passive regulators, and policy became more business-oriented. Coupled with changes in personnel were budget cuts and, therefore, less personnel to engage in regulation.

Consumer protection regulations, especially food, drug, and automobile regulation, are highly salient. Consumer products and deceptive advertising are moderately salient. As salient issues, the macropolitical system is often involved in setting policy. For the FDA, the NHTSA, and perhaps the

Table 4.1 A Summary of Consumer Protection

	FDA	FSIS	FDA*	NHTSA	CPSC	FTC
			Agency			
Economics						
Ease of entry	easy	easy	hard	hard	?	?
Number of firms	22,000	1,000	1,700	4	2 mil.	many
Profits	vary	vary	high	vary	?	?
Technology						
Complexity	mod.	mod.	high	mod.	mod.	mod.
Stability	vary	vary	low	mod.	vary	vary
Substitutes	high	high	mod.	mod.	high	high
Subsystem						
Bureau control	strong	strong	strong	mod.	weak	mod.
Industry Co.	strong	strong	strong	strong	mod.	strong
Nonindustry Co.	weak	weak	mod.	mod.	weak	mod.
Bureaucratic resources						
Expertise	mod.	mod.	strong	strong	weak	weak
Cohesion	high	mod.	high	high	low	high
Leadership	mod.	mod.	mod.	strong	mod.	strong
Legislative authority						
Goals	general	general	general	general	general	general
Coverage	all	all	all	all	all	all
Sanctions	good	good	good	mod.	mod.	mod.
Procedures	good	good	good	good	poor	mod.
Impact of Macropolitical Actors						
Congress	weak	weak	mod.	strong	strong	strong
President	weak	weak	mod.	strong	strong	strong
Courts	weak	weak	weak	mod.	mod.	mod.

*Pharmaceuticals.
See Appendix.

CPSC, regulation is also complex, indicating a bureaucratic form of regulation. These conflicting pressures explain why consumer protection issues are decided in both the subsystem and in the macrosystem.

Within the subsystems, some regulators exercise more control than others because they develop expertise, cohesion, or effective leadership. The FDA, the NHTSA, and perhaps the FSIS are known for expertise (see Table 4.1). The CPSC and the FTC are not. All the agencies (except for CPSC) have attracted consumer protection advocates and developed cohesion around an organizational ideology. When this orientation corresponds with good leadership (e.g., the FTC 1969–1980), consumers benefit. When it does not (e.g., CPSC 1972–1977), no one benefits. In recent years the FTC, the NHTSA, and briefly the CPSC had effective leadership; the other agencies had at least competent leadership.

Preventing bureaucratic dominance in these subsystems are usually two well-organized advocacy coalitions. In every case, the industry coalition is organized and well funded. Each subsystem also has an active consumer advocacy coalition. The consumer coalition cannot equal the industry coalition in size and resources, but it does not have to because the bureaucrats are predisposed to favor consumer interests. Both coalitions are quite willing to appeal to the macropolitical system for help.

Both the president and Congress have responded to these appeals. Appointments and budgets under both Carter and Reagan significantly affected the direction of regulatory policy. Carter's actions generated the largest bureaucratic effort on behalf of consumers in history; Reagan's actions effectively stalled that effort. Also playing a major role was Congress, first by passing proconsumer legislation and then by conducting oversight hearings. Many of the policy entrepreneurs have been members of Congress. The agencies have generally responded to congressional pressures but not as quickly as members of Congress would have liked. Recent changes in the direction of consumer protection policy have followed changes in the macropolitical system.

The nonpolitical environment of consumer protection (e.g., economics and technology) is relatively less important in explaining the direction of regulatory policy. In consumer products, food production, and pharmaceuticals, the number of firms is large, and profits are adequate. In addition, the technology experiences some changes, and substitute products are available. In general, then, economics and technology do not constrain regulatory actions. Only in the automobile industry with its high barriers to entry, few firms, and variable profits, is regulatory policy constrained.

In sum, then, consumer protection policy reflects its salience and is forged in the political environment. Agency activists must recognize the demands of Congress and the pressures of the president. The "political" branches of government will continually intervene in regulatory policy, and the agencies will not be able to resist intervention without political allies. Consumer protection policy, therefore, will reflect both bureaucratic and political roots.

5

Regulating Agriculture

Agriculture regulation is a microcosm of regulation in the entire economy. Parts of agriculture are highly regulated to the point of resembling government-sanctioned cartels (e.g., tobacco) whereas other parts operate almost completely free from government regulation (e.g., poultry). Within agriculture all six methods of regulation noted in chapter 1—price setting, licensing, standard setting, direct allocation of resources, subsidies, and promotion of competition—are used. Regulation sets prices either by setting support floors under prices (e.g., wheat and feed grains) or by specifying wholesale prices (milk). The equivalent of licensing exists when producers are granted allotments to grow and sell a certain amount of product or plant on a given acreage (e.g., tobacco, some marketing orders). Standards are set for such things as oranges marketed as fresh or almonds produced for domestic consumption. Direct allocation of resources is used when the government builds soil conservation projects for individual farms. Subsidies in the form of target price supports provide income to numerous farmers. To promote "fair" competition, farmers are urged to form cooperatives and market their products directly.

This chapter examines a variety of economic regulatory policies that affect animal and plant production, the traditional core of agriculture. Other regulatory policies that affect agriculture such as environmental protection and food-processing safety are discussed elsewhere. After an overview of the industry is presented, the economic, technical, and political environment will be examined, followed by an analysis of economic regulatory policies affecting agriculture.

THE INDUSTRY

As is true of financial institutions, agriculture is not one industry, but several. The production of fresh oranges, for example, is an industry totally separate from the production of eggs or the growing of wheat. Farms and the types of commodities produced on them are determined in part by natural conditions such as soil characteristics and weather and by the preferences of individual farmers. As a result, some agricultural industries can serve as substitutes for each other (e.g., soybeans and peanuts grow under similar conditions), but complete substitutability is not possible. Orange groves cannot be turned into wheat farms without great difficulty and would have only a marginal chance of success.

The Agricultural Sector

Despite the tremendous variety of production within the industry, a general description of the agriculture sector is possible. The United States has approximately 2.6 million farms (Schertz, 1979: 13). The number of farms is declining at the rate of 1.1 percent per year. Although this rate of decline (for the 1970s) was less than the rate for the 1960s (2.7), future projections suggest that the number of farms will decline by 3 percent annually in the 1980s (Tweeten, 1981: 119). Concomitant with the decline in the number of farms has been an increase in the size of individual farms. Although farm size varies dramatically depending on what is produced on the farm, the average size of farms has doubled to 400 acres since 1950.

In 1982 agriculture was a $148 billion industry dwarfing the size of most other industries in the United States (USDA, 1982). Sales within the industry, however, are not equally distributed. Some 64,000 farms (approximately 2.5 percent of the total) with sales of over $200,000 produced 39 percent of the total farm output. The smallest 44 percent of the farms (over 1.1 million farms) produced only 2 percent of the farm output (Penn, 1981: 21). Economist J. B. Penn (1981: 36) divides American farms into three categories. The largest category includes farms with less than $5,000 in sales; this 44 percent is characterized by off-farm income that greatly exceeds on-farm income. Penn refers to these farms as rural residences rather than farms. One-third of all farms are classified as small farms with sales between $5,000 and $40,000; these farms provide a marginal existence for full-time farmers. Finally, the largest 22 percent of farms, those with sales in excess of $40,000, are termed primary farms and account for three-fourths of farm output.

Individual Industries

Agriculture produces in excess of 300 products, and describing each of these industries is beyond the scope of this chapter. This section will briefly note several farm industries that fall into four general categories of regulation (see table 5.1). First, the major regulated crops—wheat (7 percent of total farm sales), feed grains (15.5 percent), cotton (2.8 percent), and soybeans (8.7 percent)—are the most visible regulated agricultural products. These crops are regulated by price support programs and occasionally by an effort to restrict the acreage planted. All these crops are not regulated equally, however, with wheat permitted high price supports whereas soybeans are supported far below their market price.

Second, three minor crops are heavily regulated to the point of being produced by government-sponsored cartels. Tobacco (2.4 percent of total farm sales), peanuts (0.7 percent), and sugar (both beet and cane 1.5 percent) are supported by government payments to processors and producer associations, which, in turn, pass these benefits through to individual producers. These arrangements have the economic characteristics of cartels with high prices and production limitations. As an example, tobacco can be grown only on land authorized to grow tobacco; the crop can be sold only in government-sponsored warehouses. Prices are maintained by the government's bidding the support price for all lots of tobacco (see Gardner, 1981a: 22). Each of the cartel crops has some unique characteristics. Tobacco is

Table 5.1 The Distribution of Agricultural Production

Major Regulated Crops		34%
Wheat	7.0%	
Feed grains	15.5%	
Cotton	2.8%	
Soybeans	8.7%	
Cartel Crops		4.6%
Tobacco	2.4%	
Peanuts	.7%	
Sugar	1.5%	
Market Order Controlled Crops		20.9%
Fruits, nuts, vegetables	8.5%	
Milk	12.4%	
Free Market Agriculture		39.5%
Cattle	19.5%	
Hogs	6.8%	
Eggs and poultry	7.0%	
Other	6.2%	
Other Products		1.0%

Source: USDA, 1982.

highly labor-intensive; allotments to grow tobacco are restrictive and profitable. Peanuts are a crop with little economic value because for most uses soybeans can be substituted for peanuts, and soybeans are generally cheaper. Sugar is protected by import quotas to prevent cheap foreign sugar from driving domestic sugar producers out of business.

Third, the market-order controlled crops include fruits, nuts, vegetables, and milk. A marketing order (see further on) is a government-sanctioned agreement among producers to provide for orderly marketing of a product and may include a variety of supply reduction mechanisms. In some parts of the country, fruits, nuts, and vegetables (8.5 percent of total farm production) are controlled by market orders whereas the same crop might not be controlled in another part. The California grapefruit crop, for example, is under a federal market order, but the Arizona grapefruit crop is not (see Anderson, 1982). The dairy industry (12.4 percent of sales) is also controlled via market orders, but these orders are supplemented by a complex subsidy system and federal government purchases of surplus products to support milk prices. All market order commodities are generally associated with large producer cooperatives that administer the marketing order (e.g., Sunkist, Sunsweet, Blue Diamond, Land O' Lakes).

Fourth, the nonregulated portion of agriculture includes livestock and its related functions such as the production of fodder. Such industries as beef cattle (19.5 percent of farm sales), hogs (6.8 percent), and poultry and eggs (7.0 percent) are subjected to little economic regulation by the federal government although there are some minor import quotas.

This brief discussion of the agriculture industry illustrates that the degree of federal economic regulation varies considerably from one farm sector to another. Table 5.2 shows the major agricultural products on a contin-

Table 5.2 Degree of Regulation for Various Agricultural Commodities

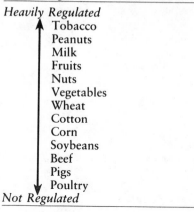

Heavily Regulated
- Tobacco
- Peanuts
- Milk
- Fruits
- Nuts
- Vegetables
- Wheat
- Cotton
- Corn
- Soybeans
- Beef
- Pigs
- Poultry

Not Regulated

uum that ranges from nonregulation to strictly regulated cartels. The reasons for this variation in the stringency of regulation will be discussed in the sections on regulatory politics.

Advocacy Coalitions

Agriculture learned early that influencing government was essential to its well-being. Numerous political organizations exist and can be divided into two groups—the general farm organizations and the commodity organizations. General farm organizations try to represent all farmers and speak for the entire agricultural sector. Five general farm organizations have attained some degree of political influence.

The largest general farm organization with over 2.5 million members is the American Farm Bureau Federation (Tweeten, 1979: 75). The Farm Bureau was created through the efforts of the USDA's Extension Service. Each county extension agent created a local farm bureau of progressive farmers to assist him or her in spreading the word about research and education. The Extension Service encouraged farmers through the local bureaus to adopt new agricultural techniques. These local farm bureaus were eventually joined to create state organizations, and in 1920 a national organization was formed (Tweeten, 1979a: 74). The Farm Bureau remains a federation with control by state units. The Farm Bureau is the most conservative of the general farm organizations, supporting free-market approaches to agriculture and allying itself with the Republican party. The organization's membership is dominated by Southern cotton farmers and Midwestern corn and hog producers (Anderson, Brady, and Bullock, 1977: 364).

The National Farmers Union (NFU) is a more liberal farm organization that supports active government intervention on behalf of agriculture. It has strong ties to the Democratic party and often forms coalitions with organized labor (Anderson, Brady, and Bullock, 1977: 365). The NFU's base of support is among Midwestern wheat farmers, and it has over 250,000 members (Tweeten, 1979a: 71). The NFU was greatly assisted in organizing by the Farm Security Administration during the depression (see Baldwin, 1968).

The Grange is the oldest general farm organization and can claim some credit for numerous reforms in the nineteenth century, including the Sherman Antitrust Act and the Interstate Commerce Act. In recent times, the Grange (with 300,000+ members; Tweeten, 1979a: 64) has not been aggressive politically and is not considered one of the major forces in agriculture policy. The Grange is composed of fruit, vegetable, dairy, and poultry farmers (Anderson, Brady, and Bullock, 1977: 365).

The National Farmers Organization (NFO) began as a protest movement by marginal farmers in the Midwest. It sponsored strikes and holding actions in the 1950s and 1960s in efforts to raise the prices paid to farmers for their products. The NFO has since developed into a traditional farm lobby organization with approximately 200,000 members.

The American Agriculture Movement (AAM) is the most recent general farm organization to grow out of a protest movement. Started in Colorado in 1977, the AAM sponsored farmer strikes and used tractorcades to dramatize the plight of farmers squeezed by low prices and high costs. Because AAM generally lacks a strong organizational structure, its permanence on the scene as a general farm organization is open to question (see Tweeten, 1979a: 84–85; Browne, 1983).

The general farm organizations are supplemented by commodity organizations that represent farmers' interests in regard to a single commodity. Commodity organizations are necessary because different types of farmers often disagree on agriculture policy goals, thus preventing the general farm organizations from advocating any position. For example, grain farmers advocate high price supports for grains whereas livestock producers who must feed this grain to their animals favor lower price supports. Similarly, grain farmers who are heavily dependent on exports favor free trade whereas livestock producers and sugar producers favor import limitations.

Almost every commodity is represented by a commodity organization. Among the more successful commodity organizations is the National Milk Producers Federation (NMPF). The NMPF is composed of dairy farmers and the giant cooperatives that market milk. It plays a major role in determining price support policies for dairy products (see Guth, 1980); and the giant co-ops such as American Milk Producers, Inc., Mid-America Dairymen, and Dairymen, Inc., are major contributors to political campaigns. The NMPF is not encumbered by the interests of nondairy farmers when pressing its policy goals. Among the other commodity organizations are the American National Cattlemen's Association, the National Wheat Growers Association, the National Turkey Federation, the National Cotton Council, the American Sugar Cane League, and the National Wool Growers Association. In 1981 and 1982 agricultural political action committees (mostly representing commodity groups) made $3.9 million in contributions to political candidates, about 5 percent of all political action committee or PAC contributions (Hagstrom, 1984: 422).

THE REGULATORY AGENCIES

Economic regulation of agriculture is conducted within the U.S. Department of Agriculture (USDA). Created in 1862, USDA has grown to 109,000 employees with an annual budget of $37.7 billion for fiscal year

1985. Employees of the Department of Agriculture generally do not think of themselves as regulators; rather, they perceive their role as assisting the farmer to receive fair prices and incomes. Recruited from the same state land-grant colleges of agriculture that produce the nation's farmers and agribusiness executives, USDA employees are technocrats with specific skills related to agriculture (see Talbot and Hadwiger, 1968: 240 ff). Consistent with the assistance rather than the regulatory view, the department is decentralized with well over 90 percent of its employees located outside the Washington, D.C., area. Every county in the United States, including the totally urban ones, has at least one USDA office. Decision making in USDA is also decentralized, with the power located in the individual bureaus and the field units.

The Department of Agriculture uses five specific tools to regulate the price of agricultural goods. First, the most commonly used tool to regulate prices is the loan. Numerous crops can be used as collateral for loans from the Department of Agriculture. For example, the loan rate for wheat is currently $3.40 per bushel. Rather than sell his or her wheat, a farmer may choose to use it as collateral for a loan. Such action makes sense if the price of wheat is less than the loan rate and prospects for an increase in price are promising. Agricultural loans are nonrecourse loans so that the farmer may default on the loan with no penalty, and the government then keeps the crop. If prices rise, the farmer normally redeems the wheat and sells it; if not, he or she defaults on the loan. The loan rate is a price floor for a commodity because no farmer would sell a commodity for less than the government would loan.

Second, target prices and deficiency payments are used to regulate prices and increase farm income. Crops such as wheat, corn, and cotton have target prices. With a target price of $2.30 a bushel for corn, for example, the system works as follows: The farmer sells his crop for whatever the market will bring. If the crop is sold for $2.10, the government pays the farmer $.20 a bushel so that the farmer receives the target price in income. Crops sold at prices higher than the target price receive no deficiency payments.

Third, for some crops the USDA has authority to limit production through restricting the number of acres planted or the amount of the crop that can be sold. Use of mandatory quotas or allotments is not common. Tobacco is regulated in this manner as are some fruits, nuts, and vegetables under marketing orders that limit production (see later).

Fourth, in times of great overproduction, the department can use set-aside programs. Essentially a set-aside program pays farmers not to grow crops on a portion of their land. In 1984 the department established a program for the first time to pay dairy farmers if they decreased milk production (Wines, 1983h). Set-asides are often used in combination with loans and target prices because only those farmers who participate in set-asides are eligible for loans and deficiency payments. Although such links create incentives to participate in set-aside programs, set-asides are essentially voluntary. The effectiveness of the set-aside programs as voluntary programs that rely on incentives (discussed later) may indicate how incentives programs would work in environmental regulation or workplace safety regulation.

Fifth, import controls are used to support the price of domestic production by limiting competition from foreign producers. Domestic sugar prices are kept high in this manner by limiting total imports via a series of national quota systems. Dairy products and—to a lesser extent—beef are also affected by import quotas.

Regulatory policies often combine a variety of these tools simultaneously. Dairy products, for example, are regulated by target prices, set-asides (in 1984), and import quotas. Each commodity is regulated in slightly unique ways by an administrative unit that is in either the Agricultural Stabilization and Conservation Service or the Agricultural Marketing Service.

ASCS

The Agricultural Stabilization and Conservation Service (ASCS) is the department's main price support regulator. It operates programs for wheat, corn, cotton, soybeans, peanuts, rice, tobacco, milk, wool, mohair, barley, oats, sugar beets, sugar cane, sorghum, rye, and honey. The specific mechanisms for supporting prices for these commodities is set by law; but normally loans, target prices, and set-asides are involved. ASCS programs are administered in the field. The secretary of agriculture appoints a committee to oversee each state program, and each county program is handled via an elected farmer committee supported by ASCS staff. The ASCS operates in conjunction with the Commodity Credit Corporation, a government corporation authorized to make loans and accept grain as collateral.

AMS

The Agricultural Marketing Service (AMS) is a multifunctional agency with control over agricultural marketing orders. A marketing order is a government-sponsored agreement among producers of a commodity that might specify quality controls, rate of flow to market, allocation of products to processors, or allocation of quotas to producers. Any group of growers can petition the secretary of agriculture to establish a marketing order. After hearings, such an order is adopted if passed by a two-thirds vote of producers. Although marketing orders vary in content, they are essentially a government authorization for establishing a cartel to control the marketing of a commodity. In 1981, James Anderson (1982: 99) identified 47 marketing orders for 32 different fruits, nuts, or vegetables. In addition, 56 milk marketing orders cover most of the major population areas except for California (MacAvoy, 1977: 7).

Resources

The major resource of both the AMS and the ASCS is technical expertise. The entire Department of Agriculture prides itself on the technocratic orientation of its employees. Reflecting this orientation plus a common background is a high level of cohesion. Leadership is known for cultivating political support with Congress and the interest groups.

Both salience and legislative authority also affect agriculture regulators. Agricultural regulation reflects the interests of the agricultural sector most strongly during times when few outsiders are concerned with agricultural issues. Then policy decisions are generally made within the agricultural subsystems. Unfortunately for agricultural interests, agriculture and related issues have become more salient for large numbers of Americans. The high rise in food prices from 1973 to 1975 motivated many urban members of Congress to intervene in agriculture policy. The interrelationship between agriculture and foreign trade and foreign policy as well as recent escalations in the price of subsidy programs (USDA's budget swelled to $46 billion in 1982) has meant that significant agricultural decisions are made outside the agriculture subsystems (see Youngberg, 1976; Barton, 1976; Peters, 1978).

Legislative authority consists of goal specificity, coverage of the policy, sanctions available, and procedures. The legislative authority of agencies regulating agriculture is distinctive in that it tends to be specific; the 1981 Omnibus Farm Bill runs over 182 pages. Congress actually sets the exact price support levels for some crops, a specificity rarely found in other regulatory legislation. The coverage of agricultural regulation is also limited. Agricultural policy has always reflected an element of volunteerism. If farmers wish to forego the benefits of regulation (e.g., price supports), they need not comply with any of the restrictions (e.g., set-asides). Although some exceptions to this generalization exist in tobacco production and marketing orders, these affect only a small portion of agriculture's output. Correspondingly, sanctions permitted to the Department of Agriculture are limited to the denial of participation in USDA programs. Finally, USDA procedures stress participation by farmers in local level decisions, thus turning the programs into a version of self-regulation.

Subsystems

Agriculture is not a single subsystem but rather many subsystems. Each major commodity has a specialized unit within the AMS or the ASCS to handle that commodity. Congressional subcommittees are also organized around commodity lines. The major battles with other advocacy coalitions do not occur within the subsystems but rather in the macropolitical system. The subsystems make a conscious effort to form a single agricultural coalition before pressing issues in the larger political system.

Although the ASCS and AMS programs are central to the operation of the Department of Agriculture, USDA has many additional programs. These programs are often the source of coalitional allies for the regulatory programs. The largest program in the department is the food stamp program, which, in years when agricultural prices are not depressed, constitutes more than half of the department's budget. Also included in the department are agriculture research and education programs, soil conservation programs, general loan programs via the Farmers Home Administration, and the Forest Service. Some units in USDA such as the Agricultural Research Service seek to increase production at the same time the AMS and ASCS try to limit it.

THE ENVIRONMENT OF AGRICULTURE

Economic Environment

Agriculture has many of the characteristics of a competitive market; no single producer or buyer is large enough to influence the price of agricultural goods (at least in the long run), the grain of one farmer is easily substituted for the grain of another, and information is readily available about the supply and demand for commodities. The number of farms is large; over 2.6 million farms exist in the United States. Even limiting the definition of farms to those that produce 85 percent of the goods leaves over half a million producers. Similar numbers are found within commodities; one million farms produce beef; 200,000 farms produce dairy products (Forste and Frick, 1979: 121). Even though some sectors of agriculture are more concentrated than others (e.g., feedlots, poultry producers), every sector has thousands of producers. Although agricultural economists note the concentration of agriculture today compared to agriculture in the past, when compared to other industries, agriculture is not concentrated at all.

Entry to agriculture, however, is moderately difficult, with a large capital investment necessary to become a farmer. A modest 400-acre corn farm in Illinois, for example, requires a capital investment of $1.78 million (Tweeten, 1981: 124). The ease of entry into agriculture characteristic of America's past during the Homestead Act no longer exists.

Profits in agriculture are attractive. From 1970 to 1978, Schertz (1979: 39) found that agriculture earned an annual return of 4.69 percent plus a capital gain of 11.59 percent for a total return of 16.28 percent. Few industries can match this return on investment. Unfortunately for farmers, however, not all this return is in usable income. The bulk of the return is in appreciation of land values. As a result, farms are often plagued by a problem of low cash flow (Gardner, 1981a: 11). Despite this problem, the median family income for full-time farmers in 1978 was $24,000, 36 percent above the national median for all families (Lee, 1983: 8).

Technological Environment

At one time in our nation's history, the technology of agriculture was fairly simple, and farmers were generally self-sufficient. In the twentieth century, however, this is no longer the case. The specialization of farmers to produce a single cash crop (monoculture) has turned agriculture into a complex industry. The farmer must make decisions on pesticides, fertilizers, plant and animal hybrids, and tillage. Special tax provisions for agriculture as well as futures markets make the financial side of agriculture equally complex.

Agricultural technology is highly unstable. The Department of Agriculture and numerous state agricultural colleges spend millions of dollars a year developing new technologies. Major breakthroughs in mechanization, plant and animal productivity, and other areas have tripled the productivity of agriculture in the last 100 years (Tweeten, 1979a: 133). The result has been major changes in the input mix of agriculture. Tweeten (1979b) found that agriculture inputs in 1940 were 17 percent land, 54 percent labor, and 29 percent capital; in 1976 these inputs were 22 percent land, 16 percent labor, and 66 percent capital.

Agricultural commodities have many substitutes for each other. Soybeans can be substituted for beef in our diets. One type of fruit can be substituted for another. Cattle can be fed corn, soybeans, or wheat (if the price is low enough) or be allowed to graze. Within limits farmers can shift production from one commodity to another.

THE POLITICS OF REGULATING AGRICULTURE

Preregulatory Policies

Before 1933, government policy toward agriculture was promotional rather than regulatory. Government encouraged individuals to become farmers by selling federal land cheaply or by giving it away. Under the Homestead Act of 1862, individuals who resided on 160 acres of land for five years were given title to that land. From 1868 to 1879 some 70 million acres were homesteaded; from 1898 to 1917 another 100 million acres were homesteaded. All totaled, the U.S. government either gave away or sold 500 million acres of land to individuals (Tweeten, 1979a: 99). The result of the cheap land policies was an overinvestment in agriculture, a problem not readily apparent in the nineteenth century because farmers were more self-sufficient. Overinvestment in farming becomes a major problem when farmers rely on cash crops as their sole source of livelihood.

After the Civil War, the federal government followed a policy of supporting research and education for agriculture. The Morrill Act established land-grant colleges, and research conducted at these schools was disseminated by the Extension Service. Social investment in research and education exacerbated the overinvestment in agriculture by increasing the productivity of individual farmers. Total output increased and prices fell.

Government policy also encouraged overinvestment in farming by providing subsidized credit to farmers. Federal land banks and the USDA and state government credit programs permitted farmers to borrow money at less than market rates. Consequently, more investment than optimal was made in farming resulting in overproduction and low prices (Heady, 1983: 26).

By the turn of the century the economic structure of agriculture was set. An institutionalized technological revolution (via research at land grant colleges) aggravated the overinvestment in agriculture resulting in chronic overproduction. Overproduction is joined by three other sources of chronic economic hardship in agriculture. First, the supply of agricultural goods is a function of weather, soil conditions, and numerous other factors outside the control of individual farmers. In years with poor crops, therefore, those farmers with good crops will prosper. Second, the demand for food is fairly inelastic. If the supply of food increases and prices drop, consumers usually do not increase their food consumption more than marginally. As a result, small increases in oversupply result in major drops in prices. Similarly, small shortages result in major price increases. Third, entry and exit from farm production are delayed. Exit from farming has no impact on supply and demand until the next crop year; similarly, entry has a delayed effect on supply. These economic conditions resulted in periodic recessions in agriculture, a situation made more harsh by the government's hard money policies in the late nineteenth century.

Chronic economic hardship in agriculture is coupled with a long tradition of political action to correct such hardships. Numerous political movements from Shays' Rebellion to the Patrons of Husbandry to the Granger movement to the Greenback party to the Populist party had roots in agrarian discontent (see Taylor, 1953). Political action was sanctioned by the Jeffersonian ideal that small farmers were somehow more deserving and more noble than their urban cohorts (for a discussion, see Talbot and Hadwiger, 1968). Economic problems were to be addressed with political solutions.

Modern Agricultural Regulation

The first efforts to regulate farm prices and income came in the 1920s.[1] The preceding decade was a good one for agriculture, with strong demand and high prices. Following the end of World War I, however, demand and prices dropped. Rather than run candidates for Congress as agrarian movements in the past had, the American Farm Bureau organized members of both political parties who represented agricultural districts. The Farm Bloc, as the political organization in Congress came to be known, stressed both self-help and exports as the solution to the farm problem.

Self-help centered on the use of cooperatives to purchase raw materials and to sell farm products. In 1922 the Capper-Volstead Act exempted agricultural co-ops from antitrust laws. Such co-ops were to be regulated by the secretary of agriculture rather than the FTC, thus ensuring that, as combinations in restraint of trade, they would not be bothered by the government.[2] Although the immediate impact of co-ops is minimal, in the long run they play a significant role in those commodities regulated by marketing orders.

Increased exports were the goal of the Farm Bureau's McNary-Haugen bills. The McNary-Haugen bills would have established a government corporation to purchase sufficient agricultural products to raise the price of farm goods to parity; parity is the price of farm goods that would be necessary to give farmers the same purchasing power as they had in the period 1910–1914. The government corporation would then dump any agricultural products not needed for domestic consumption on the world market at whatever price they would bring. Farmers would be paid a price for their production that represented a blend of domestic and international prices; these prices would be protected by import controls.

The McNary-Haugen bill was introduced in 1924 and actually passed both houses of Congress in 1927 and again in 1928. In both cases, President Coolidge vetoed the bill over concerns of cost and constitutionality. President Hoover's approach to declining farm incomes was the Federal Farm Board, authorized by the Agricultural Marketing Act of 1929; the Federal Farm Board had authority for $500 million in loans to cooperatives. By 1932 the board was an admitted failure, providing too little assistance too late; farm prices dropped 56 percent from 1929 to 1932 (Paarlberg, 1980: 20).

The New Deal

Franklin Roosevelt's solution to the depression problems of agriculture was similar to his initial solution for most industries—establishment of government-sponsored cartels to raise prices. The Agricultural Adjustment

1. The following historical sections on agriculture draw heavily from Anderson, Brady, and Bullock (1977) and from Tweeten (1979a).

2. As expected, the Department of Agriculture was a lenient regulator of co-ops. Essentially, the department granted co-ops a free hand (see Gardner, 1981a: 48). Only with the revitalization of the FTC in the 1970s was any regulation of co-ops contemplated (see chapter 4). The co-ops have had sufficient political clout to resist regulation so far.

Act (AAA) of 1933 encouraged farmers to join together in marketing and price agreements. In addition, processors of agricultural goods were taxed, and those taxes were used to pay farmers who voluntarily reduced their acreage in production. To assist cash-flow problems, nonrecourse loans were permitted, using crops as collateral. The initial AAA program covered cotton, wheat, rice, corn, hogs, tobacco, and milk; in addition, sugar and peanuts were subjected to acreage controls. The commodities covered reflected, in part, Democratic party strongholds in the South and parts of the Midwest. The AAA programs plus some bad weather were successful in raising the price of some agricultural products by 1936 (Tweeten, 1979a: 459).

The Supreme Court, however, brought an end to the first New Deal in Agriculture. In *United States* v. *Butler* (1936), the Court held that the first AAA was unconstitutional because agriculture was a state matter and because the act taxed processors for a special interest rather than a general interest (Anderson, Brady, and Bullock, 1977: 378). Congress immediately finessed the Supreme Court decision via the Soil Conservation and Domestic Allotment Act of 1936. Under this law, farmers were paid to take "soil depleting" crops out of production; soil depleting crops were defined by Congress as those in oversupply (i.e., corn, wheat, and such).

The Supreme Court's decision did not affect the marketing order provisions of the AAA (although Congress repassed them anyway in 1937). Under these provisions, some industries such as the dairy industry organized cartels. Milk marketing orders, for example, set the price and production amount of fluid milk (milk used for drinking) with all excess production assigned to manufacturing (processing into cheese, butter, and such). Surplus manufactured products were then sold to the government to maintain prices above a specified level. Producers were paid a blend of the price of fluid and manufacturing milk (MacAvoy, 1977; Guth, 1980).

In 1938, with the Supreme Court taking a more tolerant view of the New Deal, a second Agricultural Adjustment Act was passed. The second AAA is the base legislation for agricultural regulation with subsequent acts passed as amendments to it. The AAA authorized nonrecourse loans to support crops at 52 to 75 percent of parity and provided for payments to set aside acreage. In addition, the act provided for a variety of programs to dispose of any surplus the government might acquire, including a commodity distribution program, the school lunch and school milk programs, subsidized exports, and even a forerunner of the food stamp program.

Early experience with the second AAA revealed that government agricultural programs were working at cross-purposes. The regulatory programs were designed to increase income by decreasing the supply of agricultural goods whereas the research and education programs were designed to increase productivity and thus supply. As a result, in 1938, although farmers reduced acreage under the AAA, total output increased.

Before the second AAA had time to affect agricultural production, the war in Europe fundamentally changed agricultural goals from restraining production to encouraging production. During the war and for two years afterward, prices were set at 90 percent of parity with few controls on production. Only such crops as tobacco faced production limitations after the war. When the wartime legislation expired in 1948, prices were to drop back to from 52 to 75 percent of parity.

Party Conflict Within the Subsystem, 1948–1973

The wartime legislation was intended to prevent a sharp postwar drop in farm prices similar to that after World War I. Such a drop did not materialize because postwar reconstruction in Europe contributed to a strong demand for agricultural products. The 1948 expiration date of the war programs, however, permitted the government time to reexamine farm policy; several studies were commissioned (Cochrane and Ryan, 1976: 24), and a variety of different viewpoints were suggested.

Essentially, the issue was one of high versus low price supports with Democrats favoring the former and Republicans and the Farm Bureau favoring the latter. The year 1948 saw a compromise bill passed that extended the high price supports for two years to be followed by variable price supports established by the secretary of agriculture. After Truman's surprise victory over Dewey, however, the president reevaluated this position (Cochrane and Ryan, 1976: 29). Secretary of Agriculture Brannan proposed his famous Brannan plan designed to treat the farm problem as an income problem rather than a price problem. Under the Brannan plan, farmers would sell their goods at whatever price the market offered, and the government would then subsidize farm income with direct payments to farmers. All farm organizations except for the National Farmers Union opposed the Brannan plan, and it was defeated in Congress. Conflict over agricultural policy, however, was rendered moot by the Korean War, which greatly stimulated demand and increased farm prices.

The 1950s and 1960s saw an extension of the postwar farm politics with the parties taking similar positions. Under Secretary of Agriculture Ezra Taft Benson, the Republican party advocated a greater reliance on the market and low price supports whereas the Democratic party favored high supports. In general, prices in the 1950s were kept high, and the government owned large surpluses of various commodities.

In an effort to control the growing surpluses, President Kennedy advocated supply management—government efforts to impose real regulation to limit the supply of agricultural goods. The cornerstone of this policy was mandatory production controls. Unlike previous policies that permitted farmers to avoid regulation by foregoing subsidies, the Kennedy proposal would apply to all farmers. Congress, however, was unwilling to grant Kennedy all he wanted; instead, it authorized mandatory controls for the 1964 wheat crop if a referendum of wheat producers accepted such controls. The mandatory controls proposal was actively opposed by the American Farm Bureau, which campaigned against it during the referendum. The 1963 referendum rejected mandatory controls. President Johnson then sent agricultural policy back into the subsystem by inviting the various interest groups to write a Wheat-Cotton Bill. From 1964 onward, agricultural programs were considered in a group to facilitate the formation of an advocacy coalition to pass the bills.

Opening the Subsystems

By 1973 changes in the political system destroyed the careful efforts to resolve agricultural disputes within the confines of the agricultural subsystems. Four major changes occurred. First, as the nation continued to urbanize and as farms consolidated, the proportion of the population engaged in agriculture fell to less than 4 percent (and declined further to 2.7 percent by 1980). The farm sector became less and less important to the nation's politics. Second, the decline in voters was exacerbated by reapportionment. Before the Supreme Court's decision in 1962 (*Baker* v. *Carr*) requiring apportionment on the basis of population, rural areas were greatly overrepresented in Congress. The number of congressional districts with over 20 percent of the population in farming fell from 154 in 1965 to 12 in 1973 (Anderson, Brady, and Bullock, 1977). To pass farm legislation, therefore, the agricultural coalition needed urban votes (Barton, 1976).

Third, food and agricultural policy became a salient political issue. In 1972, faced with two crop failures in a row, the Soviet Union decided to purchase grain rather than slaughter herds as they had in the past. The unprecedented Soviet entry into the market coupled with poor worldwide harvests resulted in demand that greatly exceeded supply. In response, food prices jumped 20 percent in 1973, 12 percent in 1974 and 7 percent in 1975. Shortages developed, and consumers protested and boycotted some agricultural products.

Fourth, agricultural policy became important enough for presidents to be involved (Youngberg, 1976: 59). Food exports became crucial to the nation's balance of payments situation, and food aid was a significant part of foreign policy. Both exports and aid dictated increased rather than limited production. With the explosion in the cost of government entitlement programs, agricultural programs that limited production were an attractive place to cut the size of government. Earl Butz, secretary of agriculture under Nixon and Ford, was a hard-core free-market advocate favoring unregulated production and sales.

The battle over the 1973 farm bill marked a turning point in the passage of agricultural legislation. Never again would the passage of a farm bill be an easy task with participation restricted to the agricultural subsystem only. The agricultural coalition was forced to vote for raising the minimum wage (a policy not favored in agriculture) in exchange for urban votes needed to pass the farm bill (Barton, 1976). In addition, rural interests had to grant concessions; even the bill was entitled the Agriculture and Consumer Protection Act of 1973. Two noteworthy changes in the 1973 act were target prices and payment limitations. Major grains were placed in a target price system whereby farmers received a check for the difference between the sale price of their crop and the target price.[3] Target prices, as in the Brannan plan, supported farm income but allowed consumers to benefit from a lower market price. In addition, the total amount of subsidies that each farmer could receive was limited to $20,000 (raised in later legislation to $50,000).

The mid-1970s saw a brief free-market era in American agriculture. In general, prices were above targets so that few subsidies were paid except for milk, tobacco, and peanuts. Earl Butz eliminated set-asides and encouraged all-out production. Unfortunately, American agriculture responded so well that by 1977 large surpluses were again being produced. Policy again changed to reimpose regulation. One permanent legacy of the mid-1970s, however, was agriculture's increased reliance on exports. One-third of all

3. Loan programs were retained with loan rates set below target prices.

agricultural production is exported, some $40 billion in 1980 (six times the amount exported in 1970). Some crops are especially export-dependent; the nation exports 65 percent of its wheat, 65 percent of its cotton, 45 percent of its soybeans, 45 percent of its rice, 40 percent of its tobacco, and 30 percent of its feed grains (Penn, 1981: 18).

The 1977 farm bill (titled the Food and Agriculture Act)' again faced the problem of surpluses but in a changed environment. Depressed agricultural prices and presidential pressures to limit the budget created conflicting pressures on Congress (see Peters, 1978). The farm bill was able to pass only because it contained provisions for the food stamp program. Under the leadership of Representative Fred Richmond, rural legislators voted for increases in food stamps in exchange for urban votes for price supports. Several votes to delete such crops as peanuts from the program came close to passage. Despite the tenuous coalition and two weeks of floor debate in the House, the 1977 bill was essentially an incremental extension of the 1973 act.

The 1981 Farm Bill faced an even less promising environment than previous ones. With the 1980 election, the Republican party took control of the Senate. Republican control of the Senate coupled with the urban domination of the House provided a difficult environment for agriculture. In addition, President Reagan viewed agriculture as a promising area to target budget cuts and proposed that target prices be eliminated and that the secretary of agriculture have discretion in setting loan levels for all crops. Creating even greater difficulties was the Reagan proposal to cap all agricultural spending at $11 billion for four years and the separation of the food stamp program from the farm bill (Hagstrom, 1984: 424). The cap made agricultural groups compete for a fixed pie rather than logrolling to expand the pie, and eliminating food stamps hurt the urban-rural food coalition.

A stalemate developed between the Senate, supporting Reagan's position of lower price supports, and the House, favoring greater expenditures. Many urban legislators viewed the farm bill as a way to strike back at conservative Senator Jesse Helms for his advocacy of school prayer and human life legislation. Senator Helms represented North Carolina, a major tobacco producer, and was a strong supporter of tobacco subsidies. A compromise bill worked out between the administration, the Senate, and some members of the House proved so controversial that some of the House members on the conference committee refused to sign the conference report. The final bill passed the House by a slim two-vote margin.

Despite the difficult nature of passage, the 1981 bill was only a modest extension of the 1977 and 1973 policies. The changes were few. Most price support levels for crops were increased slightly, the dairy subsidies were reduced modestly, and some restrictions in the peanut program were eased. The 1981 conflict illustrated that portions of the farm coalition had become definite liabilities, especially when forming coalitions with urban legislators. The expensive programs for peanuts, cotton, and tobacco were alienating urban legislators and endangering the urban-rural coalition.

Two additional changes in agricultural regulation occurred after the 1981 farm bill (the 1981 bill expires in 1985). As a way to remove one of the irritants to successful coalitions, the tobacco subsidy program was removed from the budget in 1982 and funded by a tax on processors. Tobacco remained a heavily regulated crop, however, with strict production controls. By 1984 tobacco was in serious trouble; because tobacco price supports were kept high, imports took over 30 percent of the U.S. market. Additional attempts to protect tobacco farmers were predicted (Sinclair, 1984: 18). Second, the Reagan administration announced its payment in kind program (PIK) in 1983, whereby farmers who set aside a portion of their land would be paid in surplus farm products rather than cash. Neither action fundamentally changed the regulation of agriculture.

The increasing difficulty in passing farm legislation illustrates one difference between agricultural regulation and regulation of other industries. Unlike the situation in many other areas, in the regulation of agriculture there is a periodic congressional review of policy when major legislation expires. Failure to pass new legislation, however, would not deregulate agriculture but rather would reestablish the permanent legislation of 1938.

Who would benefit from reverting to the 1938 legislation is interesting. Because the AAA of 1938 expressed support levels in terms of parity, these levels are adjusted for inflation. As a result, the 1938 legislation is not unattractive to some commodities. Cotton, in particular, would be better off if new legislation failed to pass and the 1938 law were reinstituted.

The Failure of Farm Policy

The 1981 farm bill and other agriculture experiences of the early 1980s illustrate the hazards of writing detailed regulatory legislation without bureaucratic discretion. The 1981 farm bill assumed a continued demand for farm products and continued inflation. As a result, target prices were set to increase automatically every year. The wheat target price, for example, was set at $4.05 for 1982, $4.30 for 1983, and $4.45 for 1984, and $4.60 for 1985. Because target prices are guaranteed, these prices encouraged farmers to increase production.

The worldwide recession, on the other hand, caused a slump in the demand for grains. This slump was exacerbated by the strong showing of the U.S. dollar in foreign markets, which increased the price of agricultural goods to foreign purchasers. Total farm exports dropped from $43.8 billion in 1981 to $34.8 billion in 1983 (Brownstein, 1984: 271). Net farm income dropped from a record $32.7 billion in 1979 to $19 billion in 1982 (R. Thompson, 1983: 71).

Encouraged by high target prices, farmers produced a record crop in 1981 and a large crop in 1982. Government support payments soared from $2.7 billion in 1980 to $11.7 billion in 1982. Government ownership of commodities skyrocketed; in 1983 the Commodity Credit Corporation owned 1.5 billion bushels of wheat, enough for two years' U.S. consumption (Brownstein, 1984: 272). In an effort to reduce these inventories, the Reagan administration implemented the payment in kind (PIK) program. Farmers who had already set aside 20 percent of their land were eligible to set aside 10 to 30 percent more; rather than cash payments, these farmers would be paid in surplus government grains. Unlike normal set-asides, when 60 to 70 percent of farmers participate, the PIK program attracted over 80 percent of farmers, and nearly 20 percent of all cropland (82 million acres) was set aside. PIK's popularity could be traced to provisions guaranteeing 95 percent of wheat yields and 80 percent of other crop yields. With few marginal costs, potential profits were high.

Despite PIK payments valued at $9.7 billion in 1983, the price of other support payments ballooned to $18.9 billion for a total cost of $28.6 billion, ten times the cost in 1980. Huge surpluses and heavy subsidies were forecast for the next five to ten years. In less than ten years, U.S. agriculture went from nearly a free market to being heavily subsidized with large surpluses. The blame can be laid at the feet of inflexible regulatory policies that encouraged production as demand fell.

WHO BENEFITS?

Agricultural regulation is intended to benefit farmers; consumer benefits are considered secondary by agricultural regulators.[4] Despite the intent, not all agricultural producers benefit equally from regulation. Hog and egg producers, for example, are not regulated. The beneficiaries of the regulatory process are those sectors that are regulated—dairy products; wheat; feed grains; cotton; tobacco; sugar; and fruits, nuts, and vegetables. Other sectors of agriculture such as beef, pork, and chicken producers actually lose from regulation because regulation increases the price of the grains they use to feed their stock.

Among those commodity producers that are supported by regulation, some producers benefit more than others. Despite the often heard rhetoric about farm policies designed to protect the family farm, the benefits of regulation have gone to the large farmer. In 1971, Schultze (1971: 16) found that the largest 20 percent of farmers received from 46.8 to 83.1 percent of the subsidies (depending on the specific crop). Thirty percent of direct farm payments went to 1 percent of the farmers (Anthan, 1980). In many cases. the distribution of farm subsidies was less equal than the distribution of farm income. In other words, economic regulation has benefited the richer farmers; it has not assisted the poorer farmers. A 1980 study by the Department of Agriculture (Lin, Calvin, and Johnson, 1980) came to a similar conclusion. Recent historical research summarized by Kirkendall (1980) suggests that from the New Deal onward the *intent* of agricultural policy has been to benefit large farmers at the expense of small farmers. Such intent was predictable given the links of the USDA to progressive Farm Bureau members and the local autonomy of the programs (see Baldwin, 1968). Intended or not, the prime beneficiary of regulation has been the large farmer.

How do consumers fare in this process? The impact of agricultural regulation on consumers is fairly complex. Consumers gain in that they benefit from assured supplies, but they pay for assured supplies in terms of higher costs for agricultural products, 5 to 6 percent higher than in an unregulated market (Gardner, 1981b: 58). Benefits to consumers vary a great deal in terms of specific commodities. Federal dairy programs, for example, penalize those individuals who drink fresh milk and at the same time benefit those persons who consume cheese and butter (Gardner, 1981a: 53). The only clear thing about consumer benefits is that agricul-

---

4. Consumers might indirectly benefit from farm programs. If such programs ensure an adequate supply of farm commodities from year to year, consumers might benefit in the long run. Whether such benefits are worth the extra costs is an empirical question.

tural regulatory policy is not designed to benefit consumers directly, and it does not consistently benefit consumers.

The reasons why some farmers such as corn producers benefit from agricultural regulation and others such as livestock producers do not is a function of politics pure and simple. In the postwar years, the Agriculture Committees of the House and the Senate have been dominated by Southerners. Southern control of the key political posts plus the activities of the American Farm Bureau explain why Southern crops such as cotton, tobacco, and peanuts are heavily regulated in the interests of the producers. Other major beneficiaries such as the dairy industry can also be explained in terms of political activities. Milk is a highly organized industry with giant cooperatives handling the distribution of milk. These co-ops including such giants as American Milk Producers, Inc., MidAmerica Dairymen, and Dairymen, Inc., have devoted considerable resources to political influence ($1.7 million in 1982 PAC contributions alone). The infamous milk fund scandal of 1971 illustrates the co-ops' use of campaign contributions to influence congressional policy on milk price supports. As price supports are funneled through the co-ops to the individual farmers, individual dairy farmers are unlikely to protest co-op actions. The end result is higher prices and massive surpluses; at the end of 1983 the U.S. government owned 903 million pounds of cheese, 391 million pounds of butter, and 1.35 billion pounds of powdered milk.

The other major beneficiary of agricultural regulation has been wheat farmers. As Johnson (1981: 144) noted, the ratio of the support price of wheat to corn increased from 1.19 in 1964 to 1.62 for the 1979 crop year. Wheat farmers, generally represented by the National Farmers Union with its ties to the Democratic party, have been challenged less by urban Democrats than peanut, cotton, or tobacco programs. In sum, then, the beneficiaries of agricultural regulation reflect the political resources of each sector.

Overall, Gardner (1981a: 72) argues that agriculture regulatory programs result in a net loss to society. Gardner estimated farmers benefited by $6.4 billion in 1978. These benefits were offset by $5.85 billion in increased costs to consumers and $1.44 billion in direct costs to the taxpayers. In 1978, a year with relatively low support costs, agriculture regulation resulted in a net loss of $1.5 billion to society. In 1983, with direct costs close to $30 billion, the net loss to society must have been substantially greater.

Reforming the system of agricultural regulation requires a closer look at the economic reasons for regulation. Prices in agriculture are set by supply and demand. Supply is uncertain owing to forces beyond the control of the farmer, and demand is inelastic. This results in large fluctuations in farm income. The essential problem is that the market adjusts to changes in supply and demand faster than the industry can adjust. To withdraw from production or to enter production, a farmer must wait a year for such a decision to result in changes in supply. Prices, on the other hand, react immediately. The economic problem is that the market reacts too fast for individual producers to make rational decisions.

An effective government policy would attempt to deal with the great fluctuations in price without distorting long-run changes in price. This would permit individual farmers to withdraw gradually from the market without the trauma of bankruptcy sales. To stabilize the fluctuations in farm income, governmental policy needs to be flexible so that supports can be triggered in years with low farm prices and withdrawn in years of high farm prices. Establishing rigid price supports for four years in advance with built-in increases merely encourages overproduction. Supports based on a moving average of farm prices over a five-year period and set at a reasonably low level would permit farmers to make rational long-run decisions about farming. Such supports could also be related to current surpluses with support levels lowered as surpluses expand.

SUMMARY

The administration of agricultural regulation is significantly different from the administration of other forms of regulation. Most of these differences are reflected in the legislative authorization that guides the program operations. First, agricultural legislation is very specific; the level of price supports and the various types of price supports are set by law. Second, the agencies, as a result, exercise little discretion; their task is to encourage farmers to participate in such programs and administer the day-to-day details. Third, regulation relies almost totally on voluntary compliance by farmers. Restrictions on production except for a few crops are voluntary; participation is encouraged by subsidies, but in any normal year some 30 to 40 percent of farmers do not participate. Fourth, prices are supported by government payments rather than by raising the price to consumers. Target prices are direct government payments whereas such price supports as airline rates (prior to 1978) were reflected by higher consumer prices. Fifth, the regulation is for the benefit of farmers; little pretense of regulation in the interests of consumers is presented.

Given these differences, agriculture is a unique regulatory area. This uniqueness cannot, however, be attributed to differences in the economic or technical environment of agriculture. Agriculture's economic and technical environment resembles that of a perfectly competitive industry with a large number of producers and reasonably good sources of information (see Table 5.3). Some differences do exist, however. Production is uncertain, being in part a function of uncontrollable variables such as soil, weather, and other inputs. Demand is also uncertain, with high inelasticity of demand. Although barriers to entry exist in the form of large capital investments necessary for agriculture, these barriers to entry are not excessive.

The unique regulation of agriculture can be attributed to the political environment of the industry. Agriculture is populated by well-organized interest groups with a long history of using political means to solve the economic problems of agriculture. Agriculture groups do not need to be told how the political system works and are not hesitant about using it. This political efficacy is assisted by the Jeffersonian ideal of a nation of small farmers; farmers are somehow seen as more deserving than other interests. The dominant focus of agricultural politics is Congress, which controls the process by writing specific legislation every four years or so.

The regulatory bureaucracy in such a situation becomes a technocratic administrative arm. Although agriculture bureaus have a reputation for expertise and cohesion, they do not become independent political operatives. Congress and the interest groups keep a close watch on the actions of the bureaucracy.

Table 5.3 A Summary of Agriculture Regulation

Economics	
Ease of entry	Hard
Number of firms	2.6 million
Profits	High
Technology	
Complexity	Moderate
Stability	Low
Substitutes	High
Subsystem	
Bureaucratic control	Weak
Industry coalition	Strong
Nonindustry coalition	Strong
Bureaucratic resources	
Expertise	High
Cohesion	High
Leadership	Moderate
Legislative authority	
Goals	Specific
Coverage	Universal
Sanctions	Poor
Procedures	Fair
Involvement of Macropolitical Actors	
Congress	Strong
President	Moderate
Courts	Weak

See Appendix.

In recent years, the agricultural political system has been opened up to the participation of others. Agricultural affairs have been deemed too important to be left in the hands of the agricultural subsystems. The use of food as a weapon in foreign policy and the high cost of subsidy programs have attracted the interest of the president. The importance of food programs to urban consumers has provided a means of influence for nonrural legislators. The recent farm bills have reflected urban-rural coalitions, and farm interests have had to compromise their goals in the interests of passing legislation. Macropolitical trends are operating against the agricultural community; the increased costs of farm subsidies in the 1980s may well portend the last hurrah of the agricultural subsystems. At a price of $30 billion annually, deregulating agriculture becomes a salient political issue.

6

Environmental Protection

Environmental protection exploded on the national agenda in the late 1960s. Following Earth Day and other significant events, Congress responded with legislation that granted the federal government authority to regulate air and water pollution. Since 1972 new environmental issues have demanded a place on the agenda; noise pollution, drinking water pollution, and the disposal of hazardous waste have all become salient political issues. Reflecting the range of different pollutants, environmental regulation follows a variety of forms. In some cases, standards are set, and individual firms can determine how to comply (bubbles); in other cases, compliance is defined via engineering standards (water pollution); in still other cases, incentives are used (waste-water treatment grants); and in still others, the government allocates resources (funds to clean up hazardous waste sites).

THE ENVIRONMENT

All industries in the United States are affected by environmental regulation although the major impact is on manufacturing and on local governments. Because environmental regulation affects multiple industries, many of the economic and technological variables discussed in other chapters can only be applied to decisions affecting individual industries rather than to the entire policy area. Within a specific industry, economic variables such as number of firms, ease of entry, and profits affect the difficulty of implementing regulation. Industries with few firms, high barriers to entry, and low profits will resist regulation more than other industries. For example, the steel industry has strongly resisted environmental regulation and has the lowest compliance rate of any major industry. In part, this can be explained by economic circumstances in the industry.

The explanatory ability of technological factors such as complexity, stability, and substitutes is similarly affected. Industries are less likely to be regulated closely if they have complex and stable technologies with few available substitutes. One technological factor that is important in all areas of environmental regulation, however, is availability. Often environmental goals such as "zero discharges" are not met because the technology for meeting them does not exist.

THE SUBSYSTEM

The Agency

Most federal environmental regulation is vested in the Environmental Protection Agency (EPA), an independent agency that reports directly to the president. The Environmental Protection Agency is unique structurally; it is the only regulatory agency (that is, headed by a single person rather than a commission) that is not located in an executive branch department. The EPA has jurisdiction over water pollution, air pollution, drinking water contamination, hazardous waste disposal, pesticides, radiation, and toxic substances. In addition, the EPA administers a large grant program for local government waste-water treatment plants. In fiscal year 1985, EPA had 10,033 employees and a budget of $4.187 billion. This budget reflects a 25 percent decline from its 1980 budget of $5.6 billion. According to an Office of Management and Budget analysis, EPA's budget declined 43 percent in real terms from 1981 to 1984.

Because environmental regulation is complex, EPA has developed a reputation for expertise. EPA is one of the few regulatory agencies with its own research office so that the agency need not rely on industry for all its information. By recruiting employees who value environmental protection, EPA has also developed a high level of cohesion. Both expertise and cohesion have normally been augmented by talented political leadership.

EPA has two other resources, salience and legislative authority. Environmental protection has been a highly salient issue since 1970 (Resources for the Future, 1980; Mitchell, 1984; 52, 56). To be sure, at times environmental protection has taken a backseat to other issues such as energy, but the issue has consistently rated high in public opinion polls. Because the issue is salient, political actors have been heavily involved in environmental regulation. Congress prides itself on the leadership the legislative branch has shown in this area. Presidents since Richard Nixon have felt compelled to justify their actions in environmental policy.

The legislative authority of the Environmental Protection Agency is somewhat unique. The enabling legislation is detailed; the Clean Air Act and the Clean Water Act contain provisions normally left to agency discretion. Regulatory goals are highly specific with deadlines for meeting the goals (e.g., reduction of 90 percent of automobile emissions by 1975). The EPA's coverage is universal, and its sanctions rate as moderate among regulatory agencies (not so strong as the controls of the Food and Drug Administration and not so weak as the Equal Employment Opportunity Commission). The Environmental Protection Agency's legislation despite specific goals leaves considerable discretion in the administrative procedures to be employed in contrast to the rather specific requirements imposed on many other agencies.

EPA does not regulate in isolation. The normal pattern is for EPA to issue regulations and for state agencies to implement them. EPA, therefore, creates the basic regulatory structure whereas state agencies do the bulk of the work in writing and enforcing pollution permits. Although one might expect states to have no incentive to regulate vigorously (see Rowland and Marz, 1982), that is not the case. Several states have complained that federal regulation is too lax and have imposed more stringent regulation. Massachusetts, for example, has been critical of the federal effort in hazardous waste. The state had cleaned up 51 hazardous waste sites whereas EPA had cleaned only 16 nationwide (Stanfield, 1984: 1034). California has long had more stringent air pollution requirements than the EPA. Other states have taken the lead in toxic air pollution controls and pretreatment of industrial sewage (Stanfield, 1984: 1034).

Other federal agencies are also active in environmental protection. The Department of the Interior manages federal lands and along with the Army Corps of Engineers has jurisdiction over some waterways. The Department of Agriculture supervises the national forests, and the Bureau of Indian Affairs, in conjunction with Indian tribes, can exercise some environmental functions. These other federal agencies often play a role in the regulatory subsystem.

The Advocacy Coalitions

The subsystem contains two well-organized advocacy coalitions. The affected industry—specifically the manufacturing industries—is politically well represented. Large companies such as U.S. Steel represent themselves as they have for years. In addition, industry viewpoints are also presented by trade groups and the National Association of Manufacturers. Industry has been able to attract allies in its battles. Labor unions have occasionally joined with industry to protest pollution controls. A substantial number of scholars (mostly economists) and many politicians also participate on the side of industry.

A large number of proenvironment groups have also developed to support stronger regulation. Friends of the Earth (20,000 members, $970,000 budget), the Sierra Club (335,000 and $6.5 million budget), the Environmental Defense Fund (45,000 and $1.7 million budget), and the National Resources Defense Council (35,000 and $2.0 million budget) are only four of many active environmental groups (see Downing, 1984: 264). Mitchell (1984: 60) estimates environmental groups have 2 million members. Environmental group members are often political activists; some groups rate candidates, and in 1982 environmental PACs made contributions of $2 million (Mitchell, 1984: 67). Environmental groups have a major source of allies in state environmental regulators. State regulators and environmental scientists can marshal expertise equal to that of the EPA.

EARLY ENVIRONMENTAL POLICY

Contrary to popular belief, environmental protection did not begin in 1970 with the Clean Air Act. The environmental movement in America can trace its origins back to the conservationists of the nineteenth century (Enloe, 1975: 145). Although pollution was considered a state and local government problem, a federal presence in environmental policy was established as early as 1899. The federal role gradually expanded from technical assistance to funding to direct regulation by 1970.

Early Water Pollution Efforts

In general, efforts to combat water pollution predate air pollution efforts and set a general pattern for dealing with environmental problems. The Refuse Act of 1899 required that all individuals dumping waste into navigable waters have a permit from the Army Corps of Engineers (Davies and Davies, 1975: 24). Although the pollution aspects of the Refuse Act were ignored, it was rediscovered by the Environmental Protection Agency in 1970 and used in an unsuccessful effort to limit water pollution. In addition, the Oil Pollution Act of 1924 prohibited oceangoing vessels from dumping oil in coastal waters (Davies and Davies, 1975: 27)). Little enforcement of the 1924 act occurred, however.

The federal government's actual entry into water pollution control came in 1948 and was built on the federal government's public health function developed during the New Deal. The Water Pollution Control Act of 1948 authorized federal grants to local governments for the construction of sewage treatment plants. Efforts to prevent water pollution were left to state enforcement. Because sewage was viewed as a public health problem, the federal portion of the law was administered by the Public Health Service (PHS).

In 1956 the Water Pollution Control Act was readopted as permanent legislation. Although the emphasis remained on public health objectives via public works projects (a popular pork barrel program), the 1956 act marked the beginning of a regulatory effort by the federal government. If water pollution occurred, the Public Health Service was permitted to call a conference to discuss the problem. If the conference failed to resolve the problem, a public hearing could be scheduled. If the public hearing failed to convince the polluter to mend his or her ways, the Public Health Service could go to court to prevent pollution (Davies and Davies, 1975: 32). The law limited even this modest federal presence because states had to request that PHS intervene. In general, states were reluctant to ask the Public Health Service to act, and PHS felt little or no pressure to do so.

Changes in environmental policy during the 1960s reflect the actions of two political entrepreneurs who were able to redirect water policy from pork barrel projects to pollution. Representative John Blatnik from Minnesota and Senator Edmund Muskie of Maine identified environmental policy as salient early in the 1960s and were the source of many policy innovations (Davies and Davies, 1975: 32). Under Muskie's leadership, Congress passed the Water Quality Act of 1965. Although still tied to popular sewage treatment grants, the act stressed the establishment of clean water standards. Federal grant moneys were contingent on a state's developing state water-quality standards. If the state failed to develop standards, the federal government was authorized to promulgate them. To oversee the program, the Federal Water Pollution Control Administration was established (first in the Department of Health, Education, and Welfare and later in the Department of the Interior).

In retrospect, these early water pollution efforts had limited success. States resisted strong enforcement of water pollution standards for two reasons. They feared that industry would leave the state rather than clean up their discharges (Anderson, Brady, and Bullock, 1977: 76); and with the long history of state preeminence in water resources, the federal effort was viewed as an intrusion into state affairs. From 1956 to 1971 a total of 53 water pollution conferences were held; only four of these conferences progressed to the hearing stage; and only one, involving St. Joseph, Missouri, resulted in a court suit (Lieber, 1975: 20).

Early Air Pollution Efforts

Air pollution was recognized as a problem in the 1940s with the growth of smog problems in the Los Angeles area. In 1948, Denora, Pennsylvania, suffered a severe air pollution incident resulting in the deaths of 20 people (Ruff, 1981: 240). The fedeeral government's gradual response was to authorize research on air pollution via a 1955 law, the Air Pollution Control Act. Little occurred in this area until President Kennedy, in a special message to Congress, called for federal action against air pollution.

The federal response, led by Blatnik and Muskie, was patterned after the federal efforts in water pollution. The Clean Air Act of 1963, which passed by a partisan vote, authorized the Department of Health, Education, and Welfare (HEW) to hold air pollution conferences if requested to do so by a state. If the conference failed to solve the problem, a public hearing could be held. If the public hearing failed, HEW could go to court to impose a solution. The 1963 law was a weak one, authorizing only $95 million to air pollution for a three-year period.

In 1964 hearings conducted by Edmund Muskie, testimony targeted the automobile as a major source of air pollution (Davies and Davies, 1975: 46). The automobile industry even supported federal automobile emissions standards, fearing the possibility that each of the 50 states would follow California's lead. California had already developed emissions control standards for all cars sold in California. In response, Congress passed the Motor Vehicle Air Pollution Control Act, authorizing HEW to set emissions standards for new automobiles. In 1967, HEW did so, adopting the standards that had been set by the state of California and applying these standards to 1968 automobiles. Federal standards were then resisted by the industry; in 1969, for example, the Department of Justice found the three largest automakers conspired to prevent development of pollution control devices (Davies and Davies, 1975: 53).

Little progress resulted from the initial federal efforts. By 1970 only 11 air pollution conferences were held, and only one court suit was filed over air pollution (Anderson, Brady, and Bullock, 1977: 78). Pressure built among interest groups for national air quality standards and a serious federal effort to combat air pollution. Senator Muskie opposed national standards, believing that local variation was so great that national standards could not work (Davies and Davies, 1975: 49). President Johnson in 1967 called for the establishment of national air quality standards, and Congress responded by passing a law to study the problem. The Air Quality Act of 1967 authorized HEW to create air quality control regions and required states to adopt air quality standards (Lave and Omenn, 1982: 7).

CHANGES IN THE POLITICAL ENVIRONMENT

The 1970s saw major changes in the political environment, creating the opportunity for an enlarged federal role in environmental protection. First, environmental protection became a salient political issue. In part, this salience reflected a series of ecological disasters. In 1967 the oil tanker *Torrey Canyon* broke up off the coast of England and released over 100,000 tons of crude oil, contaminating 250 miles of English and French beaches. In 1969 a Union Oil Company well off the coast of Santa Barbara blew out, and 20,000 gallons of crude oil a day washed up on California beaches. Ohio's Cuyahoga River became so polluted that it caught on fire. These events were reflected in a growing concern about environmental problems. In April 1970, Earth Day raised the environmental consciousness of many. By 1970 public opinion polls showed that environmental protection was the most frequently cited public problem; it was listed by 53 percent of the population (Anderson, Brady, and Bullock, 1977: 74).

Second, politicians saw environmental protection as an issue to improve their political stature. Richard Nixon, in his 1970 State of the Union Address, devoted a great deal of attention to environmental problems. In February 1970, he sent a special message to Congress, seeking federal standards for industrial and municipal sources of pollution (Davies and Davies, 1975: 40). President Nixon's actions were viewed as a direct challenge to Muskie, who was at this time the front-runner for the Democratic nomination in 1972.

Third, the Nader organization published highly critical evaluations of the federal air and water pollution programs (Zwick and Benstock, 1971; Esposito, 1970). *Vanishing Air,* the title of one report, blamed Muskie for the sorry state of air pollution laws. *Water Wasteland,* the other report, criticized Representative Blatnik for the pork barrel nature of water pollution programs. In an effort to recapture this issue, Muskie began a concerted effort to strengthen pollution laws (Jones, 1975: 192).

LEGISLATIVE ACTION OF THE 1970s

Changes in the political environment, especially the competition between Richard Nixon and Ed Muskie, resulted in environmental action on several fronts. Among the most important events were the passage of the National Environmental Policy Act, the creation of the Environmental Protection Agency, amending the Clean Air Act, and amending the Federal Water Pollution Control Act. Each merits separate discussion.

The National Environmental Policy Act

Among the major threats to the environment in the 1960s was the federal government. The federal government operated hydroelectric plants, ran coal-burning utility plants, built thousands of miles of highways, managed millions of acres of public lands, sponsored research on pesticides, and so on. Under the sponsorship of Senator Henry Jackson, Congress passed the National Environmental Policy Act (NEPA) in 1969. The brief four-page law sailed through Congress without any serious opposition (especially once Jackson and Muskie settled their differences; see Andrews, 1976: 12).

NEPA established environmental protection as a goal of the federal government and created the Council on Environmental Quality to serve as the environmental equivalent of the Council of Economic Advisors. The act also required that all federal agencies prepare an environmental impact statement for major actions (Andrews, 1976: 9; Ruff, 1981: 242). The provision for an environmental impact statement attempted to do three things. First, it established a procedure so that federal agencies would at least consider the environmental ramifications of their actions. Second, it permitted federal agencies to comment on the environmental impact of another agency's actions. Third, it permitted citizen access to the environmental impact statement. The third element proved to be the most influential even though it was added to the legislation as an afterthought.

Citizens immediately took advantage of the opportunity to participate in environmental impact statements for major federal construction projects. In NEPA's first five years, some 400 court cases were filed to force agencies to comply with NEPA provisions. In one case, the Alaska Pipeline, environmental pressures caused so many delays that Congress in 1973 exempted it from further environmental impact delays.

Although the National Environmental Policy Act was initially important, its impact diminished over time. NEPA is essentially an act that changes agency procedures; it does not necessarily change their substantive actions. By altering agency procedures, however, the federal government's natural resources agencies gave greater consideration to environmental factors than they did before NEPA (Caldwell, 1982). By 1980 over 12,000 environmental impact statements were issued (Vig and Kraft, 1984: 16). Environmental impact statements became an effective short-term tactic for environmentalists, allowing them to delay federal construction projects (Andrews, 1976: 158). Some agencies such as the Army Corps of Engineers, for example, were profoundly affected by the act. The Corps changed from an agency little concerned with the environment to one that began to stress less environmentally damaging ways to control flooding (Mazmanian and Lee, 1975).

The Environmental Protection Agency

Before 1970 federal environmental protection efforts were scattered among numerous agencies. The two major programs, air and water pollution, were originally in the Public Health Service but were administered in 1969 by separate agencies, the National Air Pollution Control Administration (in HEW) and the Federal Water Pollution Administration (in Interior). Neither was a success. The National Air Pollution Control Administration by 1970 had not defined air quality regions, had dealt with only two pollutants, and had not approved a single state air quality plan (Ruff, 1981: 241). The Federal Water Pollution Control Administration had no better reputation.

As part of Richard Nixon's initiatives to take the leadership in this area away from Edmund Muskie, the president submitted reorganization plan number 3 to Congress in 1970 (Davies and Davies, 1975: 108). The plan proposed consolidating all pollution control efforts in a new Environmental Protection Agency (EPA). EPA not only received the air and water pollution programs but also was given programs on environmental radiation, pesticides, and solid waste. Illustrating the extent of the consolidation, the EPA pesticide program involved transferring separate programs from the Food and Drug Administration, the Department of Agriculture, and the Department of the Interior. Later Congress would add programs on noise pollution and hazardous waste.

Established in December 1970, EPA had as its first administrator William Ruckelshaus. Even though many EPA employees came from other agencies, Ruckelshaus was able to create a reasonably cohesive agency. As an attorney, Ruckelshaus stressed court action to enforce the law. In the first few months of the agency, some 185 law suits were filed against ITT, U.S. Steel, the City of Atlanta, and others. The announced agency policy was "to single out violators with the greatest visibility in order to get the message across" (Rosenbaum, 1973: 124). Ruckelshaus was able to establish a sense of mission in the EPA similar to that of such action agencies as the Peace Corps.

The sense of mission established by Ruckelshaus is especially impressive given the different types of EPA employees. Not only was EPA populated by individuals from different agencies, but they also represented different professions. Under Ruckelshaus the lawyers were dominant, but he also recruited numerous economists who played a greater role in later administrations (Marcus, 1980: 290). Also in the agency were large numbers of health specialists (from the days of the Public Health Service) and engineers (designers of pollution control materials). During the 1970s environmental scientists joined the agency. Although these professions had a more long-run focus than the lawyers, Ruckelshaus was able to blend them into a cohesive unit that identified with EPA's goals. This identification increased in the 1970's as the agency developed a sense of accomplishment. This cohesion would become especially troublesome for Anne Burford when she attempted to change EPA's orientation in the 1980s.

The 1970 Clean Air Act Amendments

The House of Representatives took the lead in passing amendments to the Clean Air Act in 1970 that made modest changes in the 1963 law. As the Senate was considering the House bill, the Nader organization released its report, *Vanishig Air,* criticizing the regulation of air pollution in general and Senator Muskie's role in particular. The report stated "Muskie is, of course, the chief architect of the disastrous Air Quality Act of 1967. That fact alone would warrant his being stripped of his title as 'Mr. Pollution Control.' But the Senator's passivity since 1967 in the face of an ever worsening air pollution crisis compounds his earlier failure. . . . Perhaps the Senator should consider resigning his Chairmanship of the Subcommittee and leave the post to someone who can devote more time and energy to the task" (Esposito, 1970: 290 ff).

According to Jones (1975), Nader's criticism was effective in mobilizing Muskie into action. Muskie pressed for a stringent bill that required automakers to reduce emissions by 90 percent by 1975, ordered EPA to establish national ambient air quality standards within a few months, required states to produce air pollution control plans that meet federal air pollution standards by 1975, and permitted citizens to sue the EPA for enforcement of the law. The state dominance in pollution control was to be passed to the federal government. States would be limited to designing a plan to meet national standards. If EPA approved the state plan, then the state would be in charge of enforcement. The Clean Air Act Amendments passed the Senate unanimously, were accepted by the House in conference, and signed into law by the president. The lack of opposition to the 1970 act illustrates that pollution control had become a motherhood issue with little organized opposition.

The Clean Air Amendments differed significantly from previous pollution legislation and for that matter from other regulatory legislation. Some of the amendments were technology-forcing. The technology for reducing automobile emissions by 90 percent did not exist in 1970. The act was designed to force the technological changes necessary to clean up pollution; as an incentive, the act authorized fines of $10,000 per car for failing to meet the 1975 standards. The act also began a series of efforts to write highly detailed legislation.

The 1972 Federal Water Pollution Control Act Amendments

After the 1970 Clean Air Amendments, Muskie turned his attention to the Federal Water Pollution Control Act (FWPCA). Challenged by President Nixon for leadership of the environmental movement, Muskie competed with the president to see who could provide the toughest pollution legislation. In 1971, Muskie proposed that the federal government establish a national policy of fishable and swimmable waters by 1981 and zero discharges of insufficiently treated waste into waterways by 1985. Federal standards were to be issued for pollution control equipment, requiring that industrial plants install the best practicable technology (BPT) for pollution control by 1976 and the best available technology (BAT) by 1981. Reflecting the long ties of water pollution policy to pork barrel politics, the Senate bill also provided $14 billion for sewage treatment grants.

The FWPCA Amendments proposed by Muskie as well as the Clean Air Amendments differed dramatically from normal regulatory legislation. Normal regulatory legislation sets vague standards such as "the public interest" and delegates all authority to the regulatory agency. Muskie's approach was to set specific standards (best practicable technology) with rigid deadlines for meeting the standards. The intent was to prevent the legislation from being subverted in the administrative process (see Marcus, 1980: 120).

Muskie's approach received support from William Ruckelshaus and the EPA (Lieber, 1975: 36) although the White House announced its opposition based on the cost of the sewage treatment grants program (Lieber, 1975: 56). The White House urged the House of Representatives to go slow and hold hearings on the legislation. Representative Blatnik opposed public hearings on the Senate bill and wanted to report out legislation immediately. During the committee debates, Blatnik suffered a mild heart attack; and in his absence other committee members voted to hold additional hearings.

The House hearings provided a forum for industry to attack the legislation as costly and impractical. In response, the House weakened the bill; the 1981 policy for fishable and swimmable waters and the 1985 policy for zero discharges were made contingent on the findings of a congressional study. The legislation passed the House by a lopsided vote of 380 to 14.

The conference committee immediately deadlocked over the House-sponsored changes. The conference committee held 40 meetings between May and September before a compromise was worked out. The compromise established "fishable and swimmable waters" and "zero discharges" as goals for 1983 and 1985 rather than as policies. The industries must use best practicable technology by 1977 and best available technology by 1983. Municipal treatment plants were subjected to less stringent requirements having to meet best practicable technology by 1983. Under the newly established National Pollution Discharge Elimination System (NPDES), states were to administer effluent permits, with the EPA exercising oversight over the permit process. The compromise provided strong penalties for noncompliance.

The FWPCA Amendments were then caught in a political battle between Congress and the president. After Congress failed to accept White House-sponsored legislation to raise the debt ceiling, President Nixon vetoed the FWPCA Amendments, citing their $24 billion price tag (Davies and Davies, 1975: 43). Congress easily overrode the veto. The FWPCA Amendments of 1972 fundamentally changed the federal government's role in water pollution. Prior to 1972 the federal government's role was primarily technical assistance and funding. After 1972 the federal government becomes a regulator and dominates this policy area (Lieber 1975: 11).

IMPLEMENTING POLLUTION POLICIES

The goals of Congress in 1970 and 1972 were ambitious. Never had Congress established specific goals that were nonincremental changes from current policy, that required the cooperation of 50 state governments, and that were to be accomplished in a short time period. As the policies were implemented by the Environmental Protection Agency and state pollution control agencies, problems occurred, pressures for change arose, different policies evolved, and new issues surfaced. Five areas of implementation merit discussion—automobile emissions, air pollution standards, water pollution programs, pesticides, and hazardous waste.

Auto Emissions Controls

The 1970 Clean Air Act Amendments established specific goals and rigid timetables for automobile emissions. Emissions of carbon monoxide and hydrocarbons had to be reduced by 90 percent (from 1970 levels) by 1975, and nitrogen oxides had to be reduced by 90 percent by 1976. Nitrogen oxides and hydrocarbons are elements that produce smog, and carbon monoxide is dangerous by itself. In 1970 motor vehicles produced 69 percent of all carbon monoxide, 36 percent of hydrocarbons, and 27 percent of nitrogen oxides emitted into the air (L. J. White 1982: 7). The law permitted the EPA administrator to delay these standards for one year.

The 90 percent standard resulted from earlier calculations by the National Air Pollution Control Administration (NAPCA). NAPCA took the highest carbon monoxide level (Chicago), the highest hydrocarbon level (Los Angeles), and the highest nitrogen oxides level (New York) ever recorded. Assuming a 3 percent annual increase in the number of vehicles, NAPCA then calculated the reductions that were necessary to bring these highest areas into compliance with national standards. Congress determined that this required a 90 percent reduction for hydrocarbons and applied this percentage to all three pollutants (Lave and Omenn, 1982: 30).

Unlike other pollution programs, the states have few responsibilities in the mobile source air pollution area. The federal government establishes the standards, enforces the law, and punishes the violators. States are generally limited to programs of inspection and maintenance of pollution control equipment, a controversial part of the program. Despite the stress on federal action, the state of California operated a more restrictive program and had lower emissions standards than the federal government (Stubbs and Cole, 1982: 494).

The automobile industry strongly opposed the pollution control standards. The industry had at its disposal substantial political resources; approximately 18 percent of the economy can be linked to automobile production (Mazmanian and Sabatier, 1983: 86). Immediately, the industry claimed that the standards were technologically infeasible and pressed the EPA for a one-year delay. When Ruckelshaus refused the delay, the companies sued (*International Harvester* v. *Ruckelshaus,* 1973); and the courts remanded the case to the EPA, stating that its refusal must be justified by the facts in the situation (Ruff 1981: 244).

The political environment changed dramatically with the 1973 Arab oil embargo. Pollution controls affect gasoline mileage, and with the embargo fuel economy became a competing issue with environmental protection. Ruckelshaus granted the one-year extension. Ruckelshaus' decision was probably influenced by Chrysler's failure to meet the standards. In part, Chrysler failed because it spent little on research, changed suppliers, and deliberately dragged its feet; General Motors had little trouble with the interim standards (L. J. White, 1982: 75). Rather than shut Chrysler down, Ruckelshaus capitulated.

The automobile industry, having accomplished all it could through the administrative branch, turned its attention to Congress. The industry's motivation for further relief from the Clean Air Act is clear. The mid-1970s were not good years for the auto industry. For the first time, the industry was being seriously regulated not only in terms of emissions and fuel economy but also in terms of safety (see chapter 4). Such regulation increased the cost of producing automobiles. At the same time, foreign competition became a serious threat to auto manufacturers. Imports rose, domestic sales dropped, and profits fell. The automobile industry faced the twin challenges of competition and regulation.

The automakers were fairly new at lobbying Congress (some did not even have full-time lobbyists before 1969, see Ornstein and Elder, 1978) and were not successful until they convinced the United Auto Workers (UAW) to take the lead. The UAW has more credibility with Congress because it has long ties to the Democratic party and has effectively engaged in lobby efforts since the 1940s. The UAW stressed the loss of jobs if automakers were forced to meet the emissions standards. Automakers threatened to close down assembly lines rather than produce cars that would result in $10,000 fines. In a direct challenge, General Motors (GM) produced 1978 vehicles according to 1977 standards. As the president of GM was quoted, "They [the federal government] can close the plants, put someone in jail— maybe me—but we're going to make [1978] cars to the 1977 standards" (quoted in L. J. White, 1982: 22).

The automakers-UAW coalition was successful in using the political environment of the mid-1970s to weaken the automobile emissions section of the Clean Air Act. In the Energy Supply and Environmental Coordination Act of 1974, emissions standards were delayed two years to 1977 for carbon monoxide and hydrocarbons and to 1978 for nitrogen oxides. As part of the 1977 amendments to the Clean Air Act, the hydrocarbon standard was delayed to 1980; and the carbon monoxide and nitrogen oxide standard, to 1981. For the 1977 amendments, the automakers and the UAW also had the support of President Jimmy Carter (Gottron, 1983: 134). In addition, the 1977 amendments lowered the nitrogen oxide standard from a 90 percent reduction to a 75 percent reduction (Mazmanian and Sabatier, 1983: 87).

Although emissions control policy has been successful in limiting emissions from mobile sources such as automobiles, the results of the law have been disappointing. Because the initial deadlines were short (the lead time for changes in the automobile industry is approximately two years) and because automobile companies were not known for their ability to make major engineering changes, a pollution technology was selected that minimized the changes required in the rest of the vehicle (Mazmanian and Sabatier, 1983: 107). All U.S. automobile manufacturers chose to use catalytic converters to control emissions. Catalytic converters are a high-cost method of controlling emissions because they reduce fuel economy and add hardware to the vehicle (see L. J. White, 1982: 63).

Catalytic converters also have other problems; they are easily tampered with, are prone to failure, and produce sulfur oxides as a by-product. Sulfur oxides are a pollutant in their own right (see later) and may cause as much damage as the pollutants the converter screens out. In addition, the EPA has found evidence of tampering in 50 percent of all converters, with serious tampering in 20 percent (EPA, 1978: ii). Tampering usually involves using leaded gasoline, which destroys the catalytic converter.[1]

The automakers were forced to rely on the unemployment arguments in seeking regulatory relief when events showed that the standard was not technologically infeasible. Both Honda and Volvo produced cars in the mid-1970s that met the final standards; other foreign manufacturers often met interim standards without catalytic converters (L. J. White, 1981: 27). In addition, economic analysis shows that pollution control requirements are more costly for foreign manufacturers because they must spread the fixed costs of such equipment over a smaller number of vehicles (see Levine, 1982).[2]

Despite the political controversy, emissions control standards were eventually met. Emissions from vehicles have been significantly reduced (L. J. White, 1982: 35) even though vehicles in use often fail to meet the standard. The decline in emissions per mile, however, is offset partially by an increase in the number of miles traveled (L. J. White, 1982: 55). But even with more miles driven, carbon monoxide concentrations decreased by one-third in urban areas from 1970 to 1978 (L. J. White, 1982: 56). This reduction has been achieved even though the benefits of controls are real-

---

1. The EPA has found evidence of tampering in 50 percent of all converters, with 20 percent of all converters seriously tampered with (EPA, 1978: ii).

2. The credibility of the automakers was further damaged in 1973, when Ford was fined $7 million for tampering with test engines so that they would meet pollution standards (Gottron, 1982: 133).

ized only as older vehicles are replaced. The results are especially impressive given the loopholes in the law. Trucks and farm vehicles received special treatment under the law as did diesel vehicles (L. J. White, 1982: 21). Special exemptions were granted to 30 percent of 1981 model cars for the carbon monoxide standard and to 5 percent (mostly diesel-powered cars) for the nitrogen oxide standard (Gottron, 1982: 134).

The political battles over emissions standards have not ended. As Congress considered the reauthorization of the Clean Air Act in the 1980s (see further on), the automakers pressed for additional regulatory relief. Specifically, they asked that the carbon monoxide standard be relaxed from 3.4 grams per mile to 7.0 grams per mile and that the nitrogen oxide standard be relaxed to 2.0 grams per mile from 1.0 grams. These requests reflected a new tactic because the proposed standard would permit automakers to produce vehicles with less pollution control equipment than current models. The proposals were caught in the politics that delayed the reauthorization of the Clean Air Act and have not been accepted.

Stationary Sources of Air Pollution

Among the more controversial pollution laws are the sections of the Clean Air Act concerning stationary pollution sources. Regulation includes both setting ambient air quality standards (i.e., the overall quality of the air) and emissions standards for pollution control at individual plants. Several aspects of EPA implementation have generated some controversy, including the establishment of National Ambient Air Quality Standards (NAAQS), pollution standards for existing sources, pollution standards for new sources, the prevention of significant deterioration of standards for areas meeting NAAQS, the special treatment of coal, and the Carter administration's innovations.

NAAQS.   The 1970 Amendments to the Clean Air Act required that EPA propose ambient air quality standards within 30 days and issue final standards within 120 days (Lave and Omenn, 1982: 7). Six pollutants were covered by the initial standards—suspended particulates, sulfur dioxide, nitrogen oxides, hydrocarbons, carbon monoxide, and photochemical oxidants. Suspended particulates are the soot and dust particles in the air; they have been linked to respiratory ailments. Sulfur dioxide is a waste product resulting largely from electricity generation and industrial combustion; it is associated with respiratory diseases and acid rain. Nitrogen oxides are major ingredients in smog and are associated with pulmonary edema; they come primarily from automobiles, electricity generation, and industrial combustion. Hydrocarbons include gasoline and chemical vapors; atmospheric reactions convert hydrocarbons into ozone, which affects individuals suffering from asthma, heart disease, and other ailments. Carbon monoxide is a product of automobile exhausts and various industrial processes; it is poisonous and aggravates numerous diseases. Photochemical oxidants are ingredients in smog.

Although Congress was fairly specific about EPA action, the agency still had discretion in setting ambient air quality standards for these pollutants. EPA was to define a population most susceptible to risk from these pollutants; then EPA was to find the threshold level below which risk from these pollutants was minimal. Finally, EPA was to build in a margin of safety and issue an ambient air quality standard (Lave and Omenn, 1982: 16).

EPA's discretion was virtually unlimited because the scientific study of pollutants was just beginning. In fact, the lack of scientific consensus about air pollution has plagued this regulatory area to the present day. The dangers of air pollution are from long-term exposure to low levels of pollution whereas most laboratory work is generated from short-term exposure at high levels (and generally with animals). At the present time, little scientific evidence supports the idea of a threshold below which pollutants are safe.[3] Despite the limitations of knowledge, EPA responded to Congress's mandate with six National Ambient Air Quality Standards in 1971. A standard usually specifies the maximum exposure level in a given time period; the carbon monoxide standard, for example, limits exposure to no more than 10 milligrams per cubic meter of air for any eight-hour period and no more than 40 milligrams per cubic meter for any one hour period.

The photochemical oxidant standard was later changed to a standard for ozone. In 1978 a NAASQ for lead was added. Under a separate section of the Clean Air Act, certain hazardous air pollutants such as asbestos or mercury are prohibited altogether, and others are strictly limited (e.g., vinyl chloride, inorganic arsenic, and so on). The scientific problems involving ambient air quality standards were illustrated in 1979, when EPA revised the ozone standard. Little research had been done, and that which had did not present consistent findings concerning ozone (see L. W. White 1981: 48–68; Kimm, Kuzmack, and Schnare, 1981; Hoel and Crump, 1981). The revision effort was controversial, with environmentalists pressing to retain the current standard, EPA supporting a slightly weaker standard, and the president's Regulatory Analysis Review Group advocating an even weaker standard. The end result was a relaxation of 50 percent (from 0.08 parts per million to 0.12 parts per million) that left everyone dissatisfied.

Existing Sources.   Existing sources of air pollution were to be contolled through state implementation plans designed to upgrade the air quality in EPA's 247 air quality control regions to national ambient standards. Most states passed legislation implementing such plans although state plans were generally not as stringent as EPA would have liked (only 26 state plans had been approved by the EPA by 1983; see Andrews, 1984: 172). State plans, however, were only the first step; enforcement then proceeded on a plant-by-plant basis. With some 200,000 plants, progress in controlling pollution was slow (Ruff, 1981: 246).

Case-by-case enforcement met significant resistance from industry and resulted in negotiations over how much pollution had to be removed (see Bardach and Kagan, 1982). In general, state pollution agencies were hesitant to regulate industries aggressively because industries often argued that they would be forced to close if they had to invest in costly pollution control equipment.

Despite the resistance, the Environmental Protection Agency found that 94 percent of all plants were in compliance with Clean Air Act regulations

---

3. Thresholds are perceived as a conservative way to regulate pollutants because a margin of safety is usually built in.

by 1977 (Ruff, 1981: 247). In many cases, however, this did not mean significant improvements in air quality because many plants were in compliance before the regulations were issued. In addition, some 57 percent of these plants involved the plant voluntarily certifying that it was in compliance with the law without any monitoring by the EPA (Crandall, 1983a: 29). Some 1,200 known noncompliers were identified in 1977.

The enforcement problems in this area are best illustrated by the worst case, the steel industry. Only 13 percent of all integrated steel plants were in compliance with emissions standards in 1977. The steel industry had generally dragged its feet on pollution control, stressing that the poor profit picture in the industry prevented investments in pollution control. This defense was weakened in 1982, when U.S. Steel, a major noncomplier, found the capital to purchase Marathon Oil. Both state and EPA officials, however, were reluctant to force large industries with marginal profits to invest large sums in pollution control.

New Source Standards.   Pollution control standards for new plants were issued by the Environmental Protection Agency. New source standards are fairly stringent, requiring the best technology available to control pollution. New source standards, therefore, are more stringent than standards for existing sources. EPA accepted this policy under the belief that incorporating pollution controls into new plants would generally be less expensive than retrofitting pollution controls in old plants.

The new source policy has resulted in a bias against new construction because greater investment is required. A second-order consequence of this policy is that older and dirtier plants are kept in operation longer than they would be without the policy (see Crandall, 1983a: Lave and Omenn, 1982). Rather than improving air quality, therefore, stringent new source standards may contribute to a worsening of air quality in the short run. In the long run, this standard should improve air quality because pollution control costs are not a large percentage of new plant construction costs.

Preventing Deterioration.   In 1970, Congress was not specific as to what national policy would be toward areas where the quality of the air exceeded National Ambient Air Quality Standards. Could such regions attract industry away from areas that failed to meet the standards by offering relaxed emissions controls? Congress did not specify the amount of deterioration in air quality that would be permitted in these regions.

In 1974 the Sierra Club sued the EPA on this issue. The Supreme Court in *Sierra Club* v. *Ruckelshaus* (1974) ruled that the EPA must prevent significant deterioration of air quality in areas conforming to NAAQS. EPA responded by issuing rules that divided clean air areas into three classes. Class I regions, including areas such as national parks, were allowed no significant deterioration; such areas were to be kept pristine. Class II regions were allowed some deterioration if the new sources applied the best available control technology. Class III areas were allowed to let air quality deteriorate to the National Ambient Air Quality Standards. Initially, all areas were placed in Class II, with state governors and Indian tribes authorized to move land into either Class I or Class III.

As part of the 1977 amendments to the Clean Air Act, Congress essentially adopted the EPA rule into law and required best available con-

trol technology for all new sites in regions that attained the national stan-
dards (Ruff, 1981: 250). The law also designated several areas as Class I.
The 1977 amendments were part of a congressional effort to fine-tune the
1970 amendments. They permitted nonattainment areas to delay meeting
NAASQ until 1982 and, in severe cases, until 1987 (Mazmanian and
Sabatier, 1983: 87).

Regional Coal Conflict.   Coal is a major source of air pollution in the
United States (Lave and Omenn, 1982: 39). In fact, much of the improvement in air quality between 1940 and 1970 resulted from the switching of
utilities and other industries from coal to cleaner burning oil or natural gas.
With the Arab oil embargo, national energy policy mandated a shift back to
coal, which the United States had in substantial quantity.

In 1971, EPA regulations set sulfur dioxide emissions from burning
coal at 1.2 pounds of sulfur dioxide per million BTUs of heat (Crandall,
1983b: 86). The EPA standard could be met in two different ways: plants
could either switch to low sulfur coal, or plants could continue to burn high
sulfur coal but use scrubbers to remove sulfur dioxide emissions. Such a
decision was not without ramifications. High sulfur coal is generally found
in Eastern states and is mined by traditional deep mines; low sulfur coal is
found in the West and is strip-mined. The rational utility would switch from
Eastern to Western coal if the transportation costs were less than the scrubbing costs.

The 1977 Clean Air Amendments provided a forum for Eastern coal
interests to impose a political solution on what promised to be an economic
problem. Unlike Western coal mines, Eastern coal mines are highly unionized. A coalition of Eastern coal miners, the United Mine Workers, and
environmentalists proposed that all coal be scrubbed regardless of source
(see Ackerman and Hassler, 1981); otherwise, the coalition argued, Western
coal would have an unfair competitive advantage. Congress responded to
this pressure by requiring that all coal-burning plants use scrubbers.

In regulations implementing this portion of the law, the EPA required
that high sulfur coal be scrubbed to remove 90 percent of the emissions and
that low sulfur coal be scrubbed at 70 percent. The policy imposes significant costs on Western industries with little real benefit in air quality to the
West. Reducing Western emissions of sulfur dioxide, however, benefits Eastern states suffering from acid rain. Although the initial decision reflected
political pressures, it may result in long-run pollution control benefits.

Carter Administration Innovations.   Throughout the Clean Air Act's history, economists have criticized the use of command-and-control regulation
as inefficient (see Kneese and Schultze, 1975). As an alternative, they proposed that incentive structures be used to encourage industries to control
pollution where it was cheapest to control. Such proposals as effluent taxes,
pollution permits, and markets in emissions rights have been suggested (see
further on).

The Carter administration EPA head, Douglas Costle, permitted several
innovations in air pollution control that generally pleased economists and
were accepted by environmentalists; these included offsets, bubbles, and
banks. Offsets are used when a new plant wants to open in an air quality
region that fails to meet national standards. In such cases, the new plant can

open if its emissions are offset by a reduction in emissions from other plants. A General Motors plant, for example, was permitted in Oklahoma City after offsets were made to prevent hydrocarbon emissions from oil tanks. In some cases, new plants have actually purchased polluting plants and closed them to gain the offsets necessary to open. EPA requires that offsets exceed total emissions from the new plant so that a net gain in pollution control is realized. In the first 18 months, EPA documented 650 offsets (Harrington and Kruprick, 1981: 556). Ethically, offsets create some problems because dirty plants are given a valuable property right that they can sell.

Bubbles are an effort to eliminate the requirement that every emissions source in a plant be subjected to the same standard. Under the bubble concept, a theoretical bubble is placed over an entire plant, and the success of reducing pollution is measured by overall emissions from the bubble. Industry is given the freedom to reduce emissions wherever it is cheapest to reduce them. Estimates of savings from use of bubbles run as high as 80 percent (if the bubbles cover more than one plant); the first bubble was created in December 1979 (Crandall, 1983a: 84). A subsequent court decision prohibited bubbles in regions not meeting national ambient air quality standards but allowed them in regions that do (*National Journal,* 1982: 1528).

Banks are a way to facilitate trading emissions savings. If a plant reduces emissions more than required, that plant can save these reductions. The reductions can either be used for future expansions or sold to other industries as offsets. Under EPA sponsorship, three banks for trading emissions savings were set up in 1981 in Houston, Louisville, and San Francisco. The success of banks has been limited because most firms prefer to retain their savings for future expansion.

Evaluation.   How successful has the Clean Air Act been? Given the difficulties in implementing the law, major improvements in air quality may be expecting too much. Evaluations of the success of the Clean Air Act are hampered by data problems. Data on air quality and emissions prior to 1970 are virtually nonexistent. In additon, data gathered after 1970 have serious measurement problems (see Lave and Omenn, 1982).

In terms of ambient air quality standards, progress has been made since 1970. There have been substantial reductions in sulfur dioxide and carbon monoxide since 1974 and a modest improvement in ozone. Particulates have not improved since 1974 although major improvements occurred before 1974. Nitrogen dioxide levels, on the other hand, have increased (see Crandall, 1983a: 17–18).

In terms of emissions, the record is more positive. From 1970 to 1980 emissions of particles fell by 56 percent, sulfur dioxide fell by 15 percent, carbon monoxide fell by 23 pecent, and hydrocarbons fell by 20 percent. Nitrogen oxides, on the other hand, rose by 12 percent. Although these figures are based on EPA estimates, clearly some improvements were made, especially when one considers that industrial production increased by 35 percent during this time period (Crandall 1983a: 23). Emissions have been reduced, therefore, even at higher levels of production.

One major success story of air pollution regulation has been the case of lead. Lead in the air builds up in children and is associated with declines in

IQ levels (EPA Mulls, 1984: 1). In 1971, 450 million pounds of lead were discharged annually into the air. By 1983 these emissions were reduced to 120 million pounds. The results for lead were easier to achieve than for other pollutants because the prime source is automobiles burning leaded gasoline. Cars with catalytic converters were designed to make use of leaded gasoline difficult. When a survey showed many car owners used leaded gasoline in cars with catalytic converters, EPA began considering rules to ban leaded gasoline in 1984 (EPA Mulls, 1984: 2).

The Environmental Protection Agency also claims a 20 percent reduction in the number of unhealthy days due to air pollution (unhealthy days are days when certain pollution standards are exceeded; see Lave and Omenn, 1982: 20). Such a decline is misleading, however, because an unhealthy day is defined as one when any one of the standards is not met. A modest decline in one pollutant, therefore, can result in a day's being classified as healthy rather than unhealthy. The results are, however, consistent with other findings that show air quality improving.

Water Pollution

Although the Clean Water Act has many of the characteristics of the Clean Air Act with specific goals and rigid timetables, it has not been as controversial. The Federal Water Pollution Control Act Amendments of 1972 established a national goal of fishable and swimmable waters by 1983 and zero discharges by 1985. To meet these goals, sources were required by the 1972 amendments to install the best practicable technology (BPT) by 1977 and the best available technology (BAT) by 1983.

Implementation.   Under the Federal Water Pollution Control Act and later the Clean Water Act, states are responsible for establishing plans to meet the national goals and implementing these plans via permit systems. In general the EPA has encouraged stringent regulation in state plans; the first plan approved, that for California, involved the EPA heavily in the plan's administration. All evidence of waste discharges, waste discharge applications, waste discharge requirements, and monitoring data were to be forwarded to the EPA regional office. The program was designed to retain EPA control over state water pollution control plans (Lieber, 1975: 98).

Water pollution regulation is based on standards for pollution control technology, not on standards for discharged water. Such an approach has the advantage that it is easy to enforce; one checks to see that the correct equipment is installed. Technology standards also have disadvantages. They treat some wastes that the stream could handle and permit contamination by pollutants unrelated to those controlled by BPT (Ingram and Mann, 1984: 254).

EPA was charged with issuing nationwide pollution guidelines; that is, What is the best practicable technology for effluent control in a tuna-processing plant? To protect the states from industry demands for lax regulation, guidelines were to be uniform nationwide for specific types of plants (Ingram and Mann, 1984: 260). The guidelines were delayed a significant period of time because individual industries vary a great deal in the waste discharges they have. EPA finally established 642 industry subcategories, each with separate guidelines. The subcategories are highly specialized, with one set of guidelines for mechanical, blue crab-processing plants and another for conventional, blue crab-processing plants (Ruff, 1981: 254). Despite the numerous categories, the regulations warn that within categories some variation will exist.

After the establishment of standards, the next step in implementation was the effluent permit system. Point sources of pollution must receive a permit (via state implementing agencies or the EPA) to discharge wastes. By 1982, 67,000 permits were in force. The regulation of water pollution via the permit process than proceeded on a slow case-by-case effort to improve the pollution controls in individual plants. Success was far from universal; a survey of 3,798 plans in 1977 revealed that 724 of them did not meet the best practicable technology standard (Ruff, 1981: 256).

Sewage Treatment Grants.   Sewage treatment grants were easier to implement than the industrial controls aspects of the Clean Water Act because the grants provided an incentive for local governments to clean up their sewage. An EPA grant covering 75 percent (the percentage has changed several times) of construction costs is a sizable incentive for most local governments. Over $30 billion has been dispersed in the program (Ingram and Mann, 1984: 255). The politics of sewage treatment grants has been one of continual expansion; the program is viewed as being as much a pork barrel program as a regulatory program.

The major controversy involving the program has been cost; sewage treatment grants were among those caught in the mid-1970s crisis over presidential impoundment of funds (Lieber, 1975). Future costs may be even higher; one study estimated $120 billion would be needed for all plants to meet EPA standards (Ingram and Mann, 1984: 255). Some people have also criticized the program because it encourages building excess capacity and because plants do not always perform as expected (American Enterprise Institute [AEI], 1983: 20). A GAO survey of 242 treatment plants found that 87 percent had violated standards at least once in a 12-month period (GAO, 1980a: 9). Major causes of problems were inadequate staffing and lack of operating funds.

The 1977 Changes.   The FWPCA Amendments were amended in the same process as the Clean Air Act in 1977. Industries basically lobbied for relaxation of the 1972 standards, arguing that they were impossible to meet and that the 1985 "zero discharge" goal could never be met. Congress responded to these interests. Sources that acted in "good faith" to meet the 1977 policy of best practicable technology but failed to do so were given until 1979 to meet BPT. The 1983 best available technology goal was weakened to best conventional pollution control technology and was effective for 1984. Although the "zero discharge" goal remained in the legislation, the 1977 amendments placed its attainment far into the future (see Marcus, 1980: 297). The 1977 Act, however, did place a priority on regulating toxic discharges into the water system.

Following the 1977 amendments, new issues arose in the implementation process that promised to keep implementation controversial. First, industry pressed for changes in pretreatment requirements. Pretreatment rules require industry to remove or pretreat 129 toxic substances before wastes are released into local sewer lines. Industry including the Business Roundtable claimed such rules were prohibitively expensive (AEI, 1983). Environmentalists support pretreatment because normal sewage treatment procedures are not designed to eliminate many toxics (Ingram and Mann, 1984: 264).

Second, proposals have been made to lengthen the effective duration of permits, for example, to extend NPDES permits from five to ten years. Such an extension would freeze control requirements for a longer period of time, giving more stability to industry actions, but it would also delay new technologies (Ingram and Mann, 1984: 265). Large backlogs in permit renewals suggested that some lengthening of permits might be necessary to ease work loads.

Third, regulations on thermal discharges threatened to limit utility construction. Utilities use large quantities of water for cooling purposes and then return this warmer water to streams. Thermal discharges are regulated because raising water temperatures adversely affects aquatic life and contributes to some pollution problems (AEI, 1983).

Evaluation. How successful has the Clean Water Act been in improving the quality of the nation's waters? Although the data on water quality have limitations (see Feenberg and Mills, 1980: 170), some information is available. The Council on Environmental Quality (CEQ) in 1978 found that water quality had improved from 1963 to 1972 but that the findings from 1975 to 1977 were mixed (CEQ, 1978). Some stations showed improvements in water quality over these two years, some showed deterioration, and most showed no significant changes. In terms of individual pollutants and effect of pollutants, fecal coliform, dissolved oxygen, and zinc showed slight improvements; but nitrogen, phosphorus, fecal streptococci, and dissolved solids showed slight declines (CEQ, 1978: 96).

In 1980 the Council on Environmental Quality's report was more positive. Using median concentration levels, CEQ found that from 1975 to 1979 most pollutants were either declining or holding steady; the only pollutant showing an increase over this time period was mercury (CEQ, 1980: 102 ff). In addition, anecdotal evidence of fish being caught in places where they had not been sighted in years suggested some improvements in water quality (Mosher, 1983e: 1498; Schwartz, 1983: 67). The general consensus, therefore, is that improvements in water quality have been made. These improvements are even more significant given the increases in population that would normally generate greater water wastes.

The absence of greater improvements in water quality can be linked to the failure of individual sources to meet standards. Only 81 percent of industrial sources and 58 percent of municipal dischargers met the 1977 goals of best practicable technology (CEQ, 1978: 108). Among individual industries, steel again was the worst polluter, with only 54 percent of plants in compliance; other industries with mediocre records were electric power plants (66 percent), pulp and paper mills (77 percent), and primary metal industries (79 percent; see CEQ, 1979: 138). The steel industry was rewarded for its lack of compliance in 1981, when eased standards were issued for the industry (Ingram and Mann, 1984: 267).

The second reason why progress was not better is that industries and municipal treatment plants account for only a portion of water pollution. What are called nonpoint sources (urban runoff, agricultural runoff) contribute a significant portion of the nation's pollution. Nonpoint sources account for 92 percent of suspended solids, 98 percent of fecal coliforms, 79 percent of nitrates, 53 percent of phosphates, and 37 percent of biochemical oxygen demand (Freeman, 1978: 52). Nonpoint sources of pollution are essentially unregulated even though states must develop plans to deal with nonpoint source pollution. Resistance to nonpoint source regulation has been high because such pollution is related to land use, an area that has long been a local concern (Ingram and Mann, 1984: 258).

The third reason limiting improvement is that effluent standards are frequently violated. A 1983 General Accounting Office study found that 82 percent of dischargers violated their permits for at least one month in an 18-month time period (GAO, 1983a: 7). In addition, 31 percent of sources were estimated to be significant violators (e.g., violated one or more pollution limits by 50 percent for four consecutive months). Two-thirds of the significant violators were municipal treatment plants. GAO attributed this noncompliance to understaffed treatment plants, poor monitoring that stressed voluntary compliance, lack of EPA authority to levy fines without court action, and a decline in the level of enforcement efforts.

Pesticides

After the Environmental Protection Agency was created in 1970, jurisdiction over pesticides was transferred to it. Legislative authority to regulate pesticides comes from the Federal Insecticide, Fungicide, and Rodenticide Act (FIFRA) of 1947 as amended. Pesticide control was perhaps the first environmental issue to become salient in the 1960s. Rachel Carson in *Silent Spring* raised public awareness and argued that pesticides were not unmitigated blessings as she documented the concentration of pesticides in the food chain and their harmful effects on fish and wildlife.

The EPA regulates pesticides much as the Food and Drug Administration regulates drugs. All pesticides must be registered with the EPA. After studying the pesticide, EPA can place limitations on the pesticide's use or refuse to register it. The EPA can cancel a pesticide registration and remove the product from the market (Dorfman, 1982: 14). In all EPA actions, the burden of proof is on the pesticide marketer not on the EPA (Koren, 1980: 171). EPA also trains pesticide applicators and does research on the impact of pesticides. Pesticides in agriculture and industry can only be applied by trained applicators; homeowners face no such restrictions.

Pesticides are widely dispersed in use; 55 percent of all pesticides are used in agriculture; 30 percent, in industry; and 15 percent, for home and garden use (Maney and Hadwiger, 1980: 201). Americans use approximately one billion pounds of pesticides annually (Koren, 1980: 150). Among the most long-lasting and environmentally harmful pesticides are the chlorinated hydrocarbons, which include DDT, aldrin, dieldrin, chlordane, heptachlor, and mirex. In 1972, EPA banned the use of DDT; since that time some 15 pesticides have been banned, including most of the chlorinated hydrocarbons (occasionally the use of banned pesticides is permitted; DDT was used in the Northwest in 1974).

In 1972, FIFRA was amended to require that EPA evaluate all pesticides currently on the market. Over 50,000 pesticides are currently used, with another 5,000 introduced every year. (The effective life span of a pesticide is approximately ten years because pests gradually develop resistance to pesticides.) EPA's situation is analogous to that of the Food and Drug Administration in 1962, when it was charged with reexamining all drugs on the market.

Few of the 50,000 pesticides have been evaluated by the EPA for three reasons. First, there is tremendous pressure to keep pesticides in use and little organized pressure to withdraw pesticides. Maney and Hadwiger (1980: 210) estimated that pesticides increase the profit from farming by approximately $20.00 per acre; the economic incentive to continue use, therefore, is strong.

Second, the analysis of pesticides is exceedingly complex. The positive and negative aspects of pesticide A must be balanced off against pesticide B. No data on the impact of most pesticides on human beings exists before the pesticides are used, and information on harmful effects often takes years to gather (Dorfman, 1982: 19). Generalization of human responses from animal experiments is difficult owing to differences in metabolism rates, body size, and exposure rates.

Third, the pesticide program is constantly distracted from any long-term regulatory efforts by a series of crises. Kepone in Virginia, 2,4,5-T in Oregon, mirex and fire ants, DDT and fruit flies, and EDB in cereal are just five of numerous crises. The media attention on the "pesticide of the month" followed by congressional hearings requires the agency to drop long-run programs and respond to immediate pressures. The EPA desperately needs to sponsor an outside review of current pesticides as the FDA did with drugs. Only with freedom from the press of day-to-day administration will the backlog of 50,000 pesticides be examined.

Under the Reagan administration, the EPA has relaxed restrictions on pesticides. Justification for this change in policy has been the epigenetic versus genotoxic theory of pesticide impacts. A genotoxic pesticide causes direct changes in the structure of a cell's DNA that lead to the development of cancer. An epigenetic pesticide does not make changes in the DNA, but exposure also correlates with increases in cancer. In theory, genotoxic chemicals are more dangerous because most experts believe that cancer begins with some changes in the genetic nature of the cells (Wines, 1983i: 1268).

By relying heavily on industry data, EPA from 1981 to 1983 increased the pace of pesticide registration (Davies, 1984: 152). Under the genotoxic-epigenetic distinction, the EPA authorized the use of permethrin, EBDC, and ferriamicide. Permethrin is a pesticide used on tomatoes; laboratory tests associate it with cancer in animals. EBDC is a fungicide shown by EPA analysis to pose a risk of as many as 50 additional cancers per 100,000 people. Ferriamicide is an insecticide used on fire ants and is associated with an increased risk of 6.65 cancers per 100,000 people. In addition, the EPA declined to issue regulations on formaldehyde, a commonly used chemical that causes cancer in laboratory animals at levels of exposure common to humans.

The short-run prospects for pesticide regulation are not promising. The monumental nature of the task coupled with the small resources allocated to the program means that, even without outside intervention, progress on evaluating pesticides would be slow. Given the salient nature of pesticides, the strong pressures for their use, and the fact that some of the 50,000 pesticides in use are probably harmful to human beings, EPA will not have the luxury of a program without outside intervention (Andrews, 1984: 169).

Hazardous Waste

Hazardous waste is waste that poses a special threat to human beings and their environment. The EPA classifies eight different types of waste as hazardous, including those that are toxic, inflammable, corrosive, and reactive. The Resource Conservation and Recovery Act of 1976 provided for the regulation of hazardous waste in an environmentally sound manner. EPA was to issue cradle-to-grave regulations to govern hazardous waste from its creation to its disposal (Carnes, 1982: 36). The law itself lists two and one-half pages of substances that are considered hazardous.

The Resource Conservation and Recovery Act of 1976 was designed to be preventative, to solve problems before they occurred. The pattern of administration was the most common one in environmental protection, federal regulations and state enforcement. As EPA was writing the hazardous waste regulations, the Love Canal incident suddenly raised the salience of hazardous waste regulation (see Gibbs, 1983). Love Canal, located in Niagara Falls, New York, was an uncompleted canal that was used as a dump site by the Hooker Chemical and Plastics Company. Hooker used the dump for drums of toxic chemical waste. In 1953, Hooker covered the dump site and sold the land to the Niagara Falls Board of Education. Eventually, an elementary school and a playground were built on the site as well as several hundred homes in the area around the site. After heavy rains in 1976, chemicals leaked from the site into basements; eventually, the canal itself overflowed, and toxic waste entered the environment. Complaints about a wide variety of illnesses prompted an investigation, and 11 different carcinogenic substances were found. Some substances were found in concentrations 5,000 times the "safe" level. The Love Canal area was declared a disaster area by the federal government, and evacuation of the area began.

The Love Canal incident immediately raised the salience of hazardous waste regulation. Congress held a series of hearings; EPA was urged to work with greater dispatch. The hearings revealed a weakness in the 1976 law; it applied to current waste sites only and did not affect abandoned waste sites such as Love Canal. Because the Love Canal problems were not noticed until 23 years after the site had been closed, some process was needed to find hazardous waste sites and clean them up.

The congressional response to Love Canal was the Comprehensive Environmental Response, Compensation, and Liability Act of 1980. Designed to clean up hazardous waste sites, the bill was initially opposed by the Chemical Manufacturers Association because the law provided for a system of compensating those injured by exposure to hazardous waste; the Chemical Manufacturers preferred that court suits be used to assess damages against individual firms (an understandable position because many firms owning abandoned dumps were no longer in business). To save the legislation, the injury provisions were deleted (Mosher, 1983a: 121). The law authorized a $1.6 billion "superfund" to clean up hazardous waste sites. The fund would be funded by taxes on industry (86 percent) and contributions by the federal government (14 percent).

The EPA's effort to issue hazardous waste rules also received a push from the Love Canal incident. Lobbying on the rules was intense; the Chemical Manufacturers Association and the Soap and Detergent Association urged the EPA to go slow and to avoid making rules on the basis of the worst case (e.g., Love Canal). Environmental groups, on the other hand, pressed for stringent regulation of hazardous waste (Carnes, 1982: 39). During the process EPA estimated that industry produced 56 million metric tons of hazardous waste a year with 90 percent inadequately disposed of; EPA estimated that 1.2 million persons were exposed to hazardous waste (Mosher, 1983a: 120). EPA's view might be conservative; the Office of Technology Assessment estimated hazardous waste at 255 to 277 million metric tons a year (Cohen, 1984: 275).

Regulations governing hazardous waste were issued in three sets. On January 12, 1981, EPA issued regulations for storage and treatment facilities. On June 24, 1982, regulations governing hazardous waste incineration were issued; and on January 26, 1983, landfill regulations were issued. Industry was highly critical of the hazardous waste regulations, calling them overprotective. Many states, on the other hand, felt the process was moving too slow (Lieber, 1983). Especially bothersome to industry was the requirement that all landfills be fitted with protective liners and the ban on dumping liquid hazardous wastes (Mosher, 1983c: 797).

The Environmental Protection Agency then began the case-by-case evaluation of the 14,000 hazardous waste sites to issue permits. The permit process was initiated for 1,671 sites, but actual permits were granted to only three sites by April 16, 1983. The initial permit process indicated that the entire procedure would take a long time. One estimate was that the EPA would be able to complete the permit process by 1990 (Mosher, 1983c: 797).

Implementation of the hazardous waste regulations revealed some major loopholes in the law. Disposal sites that handled less than one ton of hazardous waste a month were exempt from the regulations despite the fact that these sites were the least likely to be safe. In February 1982 a major hazardous waste controversy exploded that would eventually result in the resignation of the EPA administrator Anne Burford. For 18 days in February the EPA ban on dumping liquid wastes in landfills was allowed to expire (Andrews, 1984: 169). Dumping liquid hazardous waste was banned because liquids are likely to corrode the drums and leach into ground water. Subsequent congressional hearings revealed that EPA consultant James Sanderson alerted the chemical industry to this loophole, and thousands of drums of liquid hazardous waste were dumped.

Hazardous waste regulation was also affected by variation in state implementation. Programs in New York (Worthley and Torkelson, 1983) and California (Morrel, 1983) are far more active than the federal effort. Other states such as Oklahoma and Arizona have done very little (Lester et al., 1983: 221). More stringent state hazardous waste regulation was found in states with serious waste problems, states with a developed environmental bureaucracy, and states with a professional legislature (Lester et al., 1983: 227). Some state regulation was creative; five states, for example, partially exempt hazardous waste generators from regulation if the waste is recycled (Stubbs and Cole, 1982: 601).

As the hazardous waste permit process continued, the EPA also began action under "superfund." Based on information from states, EPA listed

115 sites for priority cleanup. By February 1984, 546 more sites were on this list. In 1984, EPA had reported that only 16 sites had been cleaned; the average time necessary to clean a site was estimated at 44 months. EPA's administration of the superfund cleanup was criticized as too slow. In 1983, EPA had spent $124 million to clean sites, had obligated $246 more, but had not spent an additional $327 million in the superfund (Lammers, 1983: 124). In addition, the administration of the superfund became involved in a major political scandal that eventually resulted in the resignation of the superfund director Rita Lavelle and the EPA administrator Anne Burford (see following section).

The controversy surrounding the hazardous waste program escalated further when dioxin was found in oil used to control street dust in Times Beach, Missouri. Major health problems occurred, and EPA eventually purchased the entire town and relocated residents. The salience of hazardous waste regulation means that Congress and other political actors will intervene in the regulatory process. The likelihood that hazardous waste regulation will become part of the normal administrative process without continual intervention from the political system appears increasingly remote.

THE EPA AND ANNE BURFORD

No discussion of environmental policy would be complete without some mention of the administration of Anne Burford. After his election as president, Ronald Reagan redeemed his election pledge to reduce the burden of regulation on industry by appointing regulators who were committed to less regulation. James Miller III at the FTC, Thorne Auchter at OSHA, Raymond Peck at NHTSA, and Mark Fowler at the FCC are but four examples. Anne McGill Burford (or Anne Gorsuch as she was known then) was appointed to head the Environmental Protection Agency. Burford was the first nonenvironmentalist to head the EPA; her views on appropriate environmental protection differed dramatically from those nurtured by the EPA's organizational ideology. Since 1970 the bureaucrats in EPA had developed a series of beliefs that included (1) support for vigorous regulation of pollutants, (2) a belief that engineering standards were the most effective way to control pollution, (3) a healthy skepticism of the value industry placed on environmental protection, (4) a belief that pollution control costs were not excessive and were far outweighed by the benefits of regulation, and (5) a belief that regulation was an adversarial process. Burford would challenge all these beliefs.

Anne Burford's first major impact was on the agency's budget. As president, Ronald Reagan stressed major cuts in domestic programs to fund increases in defense expenditures and a tax cut. Burford's budgets reflected this priority. From 1981 to 1983 the EPA's operating budget (exclusive of sewer grants) was cut by 29 percent. During the same two-year period, the number of full-time employees at the EPA was reduced by 2,762 (Gottron, 1982: 115). The EPA research budget, long recognized as a mechanism to avoid reliance on industry for information, was cut by 46 percent from 1981 to 1983 (Kirschten, 1983: 659). Key positions such as that of assistant administrator for research and development were not filled on a permanent basis.

The enforcement process also changed. Burford initially abolished the enforcement office and reallocated the duties to other units; then she re-created the enforcement office as a separate but smaller unit. Enforcement efforts were reorganized four times in a ten-month period in 1981 and 1982 (Kirschten, 1983: 659). In addition to constant restructuring, Burford stressed voluntary compliance with pollution laws; the emphasis on voluntary compliance contrasted vividly with Ruckelshaus's tactic of filing suit against the most visible polluters as a lesson for the others. The number of cases referred to the Justice Department for suit dropped from 252 in 1980 (the last year of the Carter Administration) to 78 in 1981. Other indicators of enforcement activity such as administrative enforcement orders showed a similar decline (Davies, 1984; 153).

Under Burford the EPA made a concerted effort to shift responsibility for program implementation to state agencies. Although states played a major role in environmental implementation, they did so under close supervision by the EPA. Beginning in 1981, that supervision relaxed perceptably. From 1981 to 1983 the number of states authorized to administer air quality deterioration prevention increased by ten, six more states were authorized to take over hazardous waste programs, and three more did so for water quality permitting (Andrews, 1984: 173). With these increased responsibilities, federal grants to states for environmental protection were reduced with proposals made to eliminate them.

The reaction of the EPA bureaucracy was twofold. First, morale dropped precipitously. One indicator of morale was the turnover rate at EPA, which soared to 2.7 percent per month (Gottron, 1982: 115). *Automotive News,* a source not known for its environmental bias, noted the results at the EPA: "What was once a robust, dynamic entity has shriveled to a gray shadow of its former self, wracked by internal dissension, run by people with little expertise in environmental issues, and dogged by a paranoia that has virtually brought it to a standstill" (cited in Crandall, 1982: 29). The bureaucracy's second reaction was to fight back. Internal documents were leaked to friendly members of Congress and the press to counter Burford's actions (Davies, 1984: 155). EPA efforts to propose a comprehensive revision of the Clean Air Act were abandoned after leaks concerning the direction of the drafts were made public. The resulting criticism caused EPA leadership to abandon the project and simply present a list of general principles to Congress (Crandall, 1982: 30; Tobin, 1984: 233).

Responding to these leaks, Congress conducted a series of critical hearings. Between October 1981 and July 1982, EPA officials were called to testify before Congress some 70 times. These hearings provided an opportunity for environmental groups to criticize Burford's performance; criticism covered a wide variety of topics, including hazardous waste regulation, budget adequacy, scientific competence, enforcement credibility, management effectiveness, support for state agencies, openness to public scrutiny, and relationships with industry (Gottron, 1982; 114). During these hearings a number of senior staff resigned over policy conflicts with Burford (see *National Journal,* May 1, 1982).

Congressional-EPA conflict focused on the administration of the superfund and the hazardous waste program. Leaked EPA documents suggested that contact between high level EPA administrators and the industry was frequent. When Congress requested documents relating to five toxic waste sites where questionable practices were alleged, Burford refused to turn over the documents. She cited executive privilege. Congress, in turn, cited Burford for contempt of Congress. Among the more damaging incidents for EPA's credibility was the assignment of two paper shredders to the hazardous waste office shortly after the congressional request for documents.

Superfund improprieties focused on the superfund administrator Rita Lavelle. Lavelle was accused of regular off-the-record contact with industry and harassment of an EPA whistleblower, Hugh Kaufman. After Lavelle's draft memo referring to business as the primary constituent of the agency was leaked, Lavelle and four of her assistants were fired by Burford February 7, 1983. (Lavelle was later convicted of lying to a congressional committee.)

Lavelle's resignation did not quiet critics, and pressure was maintained on Burford. By March 1983, Burford was seen as a major liability to the reelection of Ronald Reagan. White House staff members pressured Burford into resigning; Reagan accepted the resignation and ordered the documents requested by Congress to be released. The housecleaning did not stop with Burford; in the next several months 20 top EPA officials were dismissed (Vig and Kraft, 1984: 3).

Subsequent hearings revealed that congressional suspicions concerning the hazardous waste program were well founded. Cases of lax enforcement and decisions made for political reasons were discovered. Funding for the Stringtown site in California was delayed to avoid helping the Senate election campaign of Democrat Jerry Brown. Two sites in New Jersey were funded to help the campaign of Republican Millicent Fenwick. Documents also showed that a fine imposed on a Texas company for emitting PCBs was reduced for political reasons, that staff members were instructed to look for loopholes in the laws to assist specific industries, and that Burford held 30 meetings with gasoline refiners while considering regulations to relax lead emissions (Tobin, 1984: 237).

President Reagan was able to recoup some of his losses in the Burford affair by appointing William Ruckelshaus to head the agency. Ruckelshaus, the first EPA administrator, was widely respected as a competent administrator and was credited with initially establishing EPA's strong emphasis on enforcement. Ruckelshaus was able to get a $165.5 million increase in the EPA's appropriation; some of these funds were appropriated to be spent at Ruckelshaus' discretion, a rare sign of trust by Congress (Mosher, 1983d: 1344). Within months, Ruckelshaus was credited with operating an open management process and restoring morale to the agency (Mosher, 1983e: 1497).

The Burford affair illustrates the power of the federal bureaucracy when the bureaucracy has political allies in Congress. Agency leadership that fails to consider the cohesion and values of career bureaucrats in an agency is leadership that is taking a major risk. Such action is especially risky if it is in opposition to the policy values held by key members of Congress. Despite the outcome of the crisis, EPA was not undamaged by the process. As of 1984, EPA's budgets were still significantly below their peak in terms of purchasing power, and numerous programs were seriously underfunded.

ENVIRONMENTAL POLITICS IN THE 1980s

Implementation of any law always reveals new issues that were not considered in the original legislation. Environmental policy is no exception in that regard. Much of the legislation passed in the 1970s has expired and has been continued by temporary legislation. A stalemate on rewriting this legislation exists, with the House favoring only modest changes whereas the Reagan administration favors more dramatic changes. Environmental and industry groups take more extreme positions than either the House or the White House. The result has been a legislative deadlock. Eventually, numerous environmental issues must be addressed.

Renewal of CAA and CWA

Among the more important issues are the renewal of the Clean Air Act and the Clean Water Act; both laws have expired. Numerous industry groups, including the American Petroleum Institute, the Chemical Manufacturers Association, the Iron and Steel Institute, the American Paper Institute, the American Automobile Association, the Business Roundtable, the Chamber of Commerce, and the National Association of Manufacturers have lobbied for specific provisions to weaken this legislation. They are opposed by an environmental coalition that includes the Sierra Club, the League of Women Voters, the National Parks and Conservation Association, Friends of the Earth, the Natural Resources Defense Council, and the Environmental Defense Fund (see Gottron, 1982: 124). Initially, with the election of Ronald Reagan and the Republican control of the Senate, the environmental coalition merely hoped that their losses would not be excessive. As the superfund scandal and the administration of Anne Burford developed, however, environmental groups became more aggressive and pressed for some gains. Environmental groups have public opinion on their side; a 1981 Harris poll showed that 80 percent of the American people opposed any relaxation of air pollution laws; 29 percent actually favored stronger laws. Reauthorization of the Clean Air Act, the Clean Water Act, and the numerous other environmental protection laws is likely to be an extremely slow process unless electoral results change the current stalemate.

Cost-Benefit Analysis

Among academics studying regulation, a major issue is the use of cost-benefit analysis in environmental regulation. Economists, in general, advocate that regulations should be issued only if the benefits from regulation exceed costs. More precisely, they argue that if the marginal cost of a regulation exceeds the marginal benefits of the regulation, it should not be issued (e.g., see Crandall, 1983a). After all, what could be more rational than the idea that regulation should create more benefits than costs?

Others seriously criticize the use of cost-benefit analysis (see Kelman, 1981a; Meier, 1983b; 1984). Cost-benefit analysis, the critics claim, is not precise enough to measure the marginal costs and benefits of environmental regulation. The estimation of regulation's benefits is especially difficult because the benefits of better health, fewer cancers, a clean environment, fishable waters, and the like, are incommensurable; and attempts to measure these benefits have little precision. Other criticisms of cost-benefit analysis include a bias toward short-term payoffs, a bias toward consumption rather than conservation, an inability to handle equity and distributional issues, an ability to be manipulated to produce the desired results, and the reliance on a series of assumptions with little grounding in reality (see Meier, 1983b; 1984).

Although cost-benefit analysis does have serious limitations, several attempts to measure the costs and benefits of environmental protection have been attempted. Crandall (1983a), in a review of the literature, estimates that compliance costs for the Clean Air Act range from $8.6 billion to $12.6 billion whereas the benefits range from $7.7 billion to $20.2 billion. The National Commission on Air Quality, on the other hand, estimated that the Clean Air Act cost $16.6 billion in 1978 and returned benefits of $4.6 to $51.2 billion (Gottron, 1982: 123). The Council on Environmental Quality estimated the costs of all pollution regulation in 1979 at $36.9 billion (CEQ, 1980), and Greer (1983: 480), using estimates from several sources, finds benefits of between $10.1 billion and $67.1 billion. Given the amount of error in the estimates of benefits and costs, no reputable scholar has presented a single cost-benefit ratio for environmental protection regulation, nor is one likely to.

One interesting aspect about the debate over cost-benefit analysis is that policymakers have generally ignored it. Neither the proposed revisions of the Clean Air Act nor the revisions of the Clean Water Act include a requirement for cost-benefit analysis. Cost-benefit analysis may provide a general framework for thinking about pollution (and many bureaucrats may implicitly consider the costs of their proposals), but it is far too primitive a technique to be used as the sole basis for decision making.

Effluent Charges

Another academic controversy that has spilled over into the politics of environmental regulation is the economists' proposal to eliminate engineering standards to control pollution and instead to create incentive systems. One incentives proposal is to use effluent charges. Under such a system, a polluter would be charged a predetermined fee for every unit of pollution he or she discharged. In theory, effluent fees would be set above the marginal costs of reducing pollution. This would create an incentive for industry to reduce its pollution and avoid the penalties of the effluent fee (see Kneese and Schultze, 1975). In theory, effluent fees offer the possibility that industries will clean their discharges to such an extent that air and water quality will be better than the current EPA standards.

Effluent fees are not popular among noneconomists. Although the specter of paying for a license to pollute is often raised (see Kelman, 1981a), the true barriers to effluent fees are administrative. An effective effluent fee would require that an accurate pollution monitor be located at every pollution source in every plant. The technology for measuring effluents this precisely simply does not exist. Second, how high effluent fees should be set is unclear. Economics is not precise enough to tell us the marginal cost of pollution control. In a theoretical model, this is no problem because effluent fees could simply be raised until the desired reduction in emissions is achieved (the politics of raising effluent fees once they are in place would be an interesting phenomenon).

Third, even the advocates of effluent fees acknowledge that we will not know for sure if effluent fees will work until the fees are tried.

Related to effluent fees is a proposal to use marketable permits to control pollution (see Hahn and Noll, 1982). Under a permit system, the government would decide how much pollution would be permitted in a given area (e.g., 100 million tons of sulfur dioxide). The government would then auction off permits to emit sulfur dioxide. Those industries that would find it difficult to control sulfur dioxide would pay more for permits than those companies that would find it easier. A market in these permits would then efficiently allocate the pollution permits to firms that need them most.

Pollution permits are no more popular among noneconomists than are effluent fees. The Environmental Protection Agency has taken some small steps in the direction of pollution permits by using its offsets and banking concepts. Offsets permit a new plant to purchase the "pollution rights" of an old plant. Under offsets, current polluters gain a property right in their past emissions. Banking is the process of buying and selling permits.

The New Source Bias

Current environmental laws have a bias against new construction. New sources of pollution are required to have the most stringent form of pollution controls available. The initial justification for greater controls on new sources than on existing sources was the belief that incorporating pollution controls in plant design would be cheaper than retrofitting old plants. The impact of such a policy, however, is to discourage firms from replacing current equipment with new equipment. The policy increases the cost of new investment and causes current plants to be retained longer (see Crandall, 1983a: 43; Harrington and Krupnick, 1981: 544). Such a bias may have ramifications for air and water quality if the old plant is a dirtier plant than the new one (a likely proposition). If clean air and water are the goals, the regulations should create incentives to replace old plants, vehicles, and so on, with new ones.[4]

In addition to the new plant bias, pollution laws do not affect all plants equally. Pashigian (1983: 23) has shown that pollution control is relatively more expensive for small plants than it is for large plants. One distributional impact of pollution laws, therefore, is an increased concentration of industry. Why such a bias operates is reasonably easy to understand; pollution control equipment involves both fixed and variable costs. The larger a plant is, the more production across which to spread the fixed costs (e.g., the research costs for auto pollution cost General Motors less per car than they cost American Motors). Such a regulatory impact is not without historical precedent. The regulation of meat-packing plants allowed large plants to achieve a competitive advantage over small plants (see chapter 4).

The Frostbelt Bias

Recently, the economist Robert Crandall (1983a) has argued that environmental regulation, especially the Clean Air Act, is biased in favor of

---

4. The incentives to replace plants and other investments work at the margin because pollution control costs are not a large part of new plant investment. Other factors that encourage new investment are likely to overwhelm the influence of pollution control costs.

frostbelt states at the expense of sunbelt states. In general, the frostbelt states of the Northeast are more industrially developed than the sunbelt states; accordingly, the frostbelt states are more polluted. With uniform national air quality standards, such a situation would normally create an incentive for industries to close plants in polluted areas, where stringent controls would be required, and to move them to unpolluted areas, where fewer controls would be necessary.

Limiting a sunbelt flight is the prevention of significant deterioration (PSD) policy whereby areas with air quality better than NAAQS are permitted new industry only if those industries meet the stringent standards for new plants. Another policy with some frostbelt bias is the provision that all coal, regardless of sulfur content (see earlier) must be scrubbed. Crandall (1983a) estimates that this policy raises utility rates in the West approximately 11 to 12 percent whereas the rates in the East were raised by only 0.3 to 2.0 percent. Crandall (1983a: 115) further argues that this bias was a conscious effort; he shows a statistical relationship between congressional voting on pollution regulation and the region of the country.

Despite the potential for a regional bias in pollution regulation, Lave and Omenn (1982) argue that these potential biases have no real impact in practice. The PSD policy has not been strongly implemented by all state governments, and the incremental amounts of deterioration allowed have not been exhausted. The net impact is that, in practice, PSD policy has not created incentives to favor the frostbelt (see Lave and Omenn, 1982: 26). In addition, the Crandall hypothesis ignores all the other variables that industry considers in deciding where to locate a plant. Trained labor needs, the quality of the community, local tax laws, transportation demands, and numerous other variables collectively dwarf the impact of pollution controls.

Which Pollutants Should Be Controlled?

As additional research is done on the health implications of pollution (e.g., see Crandall and Lave, 1981; Stewart, 1979), more pollution-related threats to health are identified. Although substantial consensus exists concerning the need to regulate the seven criteria air pollutants, issues about what ambient level to accept and whether or not to add additional standards exist (see also Lave and Omenn, 1982: 16).

One controversy concerns the NAAQS for total suspended particulates. Studies by the Environmental Protection Agency have shown that all particles are not equally dangerous. Small particles, those less than 2.5 microns in diameter, are inhaled deeply into the lungs and are more likely to cause respiratory problems than are large particles. In March 1984, EPA announced it was revising its NAAQS to be more concerned with smaller particles (EPA Changes, 1984: 1).

Similar problems exist in regulating water pollution. The decision as to what pollutants to regulate is illustrated best by drinking water regulations. Drinking water regulations seek to regulate waterborne carcinogens. One major concern has been trihalomethanes, compounds that form when chlorine interacts with organic materials in water (see Hoel and Crump, 1981; Kimm, Kuzmack, and Schnare, 1981). The problem concerns which organic compounds to regulate. Some 500 organic compounds have been identified in drinking water (up from 100 in 1970); unfortunately, only 10 percent of the organic material in water has been identified. If the contaminants in water are not identified, setting standards based on the dangers of contaminants is exceedingly difficult.

Questions about which pollutants to regulate will continue as environmental sciences continue to develop. Given the long period of time necessary to pass laws or develop regulations, regulation will consistently lag behind science. An easy solution to the problem is not likely.

Acid Rain

The relationship between air pollution and environmental quality has proven to be more complex than originally thought. Increased acidity of rainfall has resulted in serious problems for plant and animal life (Howard and Perley, 1980; Weller, 1980; Ostmann, 1982). According to recent research by the National Academy of Science (see Gottron, 1982: 118), acid deposition results when air pollutants—primarily sulfur dioxide, nitrogen oxides, and hydrocarbons or their reaction products—return to the earth either as rain or dry deposition. Some constituents of these pollutants are acidic, or they become acidic when they reach the earth and interact with water, soil, and plant life. Although rain is slightly acidic by itself (pH measures of 5.6), rainfall in Canada and the Northeastern United States has been measured as acidic as 2.0 (a pH about the level of bottled lemon juice).

Acid rain has been recorded in virtually the entire region east of the Mississippi River as well as in Western states such as New Mexico and Idaho (National Research Council, 1983). It is especially hazardous to plants and wildlife; 200 lakes in New York no longer support fish as a result of decreased pH levels; some 1,200 lakes in Ontario are in a similar state (Boyle and Boyle, 1983: 14). Acid rain may also pose a threat to human health because the corrosive nature of the rain can interact with toxic metals in bedrock and soils and release them into drinking water (Boyle and Boyle, 1983: 16).

Acid rain is one way that pollution is exported from one region to another. Some firms met air quality standards by building tall smokestacks so that pollutants would be released high in the air and the wind would disperse them. Over 400 stacks that exceeded 200 feet in height were built in the United States before they were outlawed in 1977 (Lave and Omenn, 1982: 43). Tall stacks essentially export local pollution to other regions in the form of acid deposition.

At the present time, little is being done about acid rain despite strong pressures from Canada to control the problem (Canada is concerned because much of U.S. pollution is carried by prevailing winds to Canada, where it falls as acid rain). The Reagan administration has taken the position that acid rain is an issue that needs to be studied further and has budgeted additional funds for research but little money for control. The belief in the need for further study is in conflict with studies by the EPA, the President's Science Advisor, and the National Research Council (but see Krug and Frink, 1983).

Integrated Enforcement

Pollution regulation in the United States is based on identifying individual pollutants and then attempting to control that individual pollutant. Such a strategy fails to recognize that many forms of pollution are interrelated and that different types of pollution interact. Graves and Krumm (1981), for example, in a review of the literature on the health effects of pollution, found that pollutants interact with each other. Exposure to X parts per million of carbon monoxide by itself, for example, might be perfectly safe; but exposure to X parts per million of carbon monoxide while being exposed to Y parts per million of ozone might be dangerous. The impact of a polluted environment on an individual is a function of not only the impact of individual pollutants but also of the interaction of the pollutants with each other. Regulatory policy has not addressed this issue.

Until recently, regulatory policy failed to recognize that many forms of pollution were interrelated. Programs for air pollution were administered separately from programs for water pollution. Such an administrative approach can result in decreasing one pollutant while increasing another. For example, in an effort to control water pollution from a U.S. Steel plant near Pittsburgh (the production of coke resulted in toxic impurities that were dumped into the river), the EPA required the use of waste water to cool the coke and vaporize the impurities. As a result, no pollutants were released into the nearby river, but major pollutants were released into the air (Mosher, 1983b: 322). Unlike the interaction problem, EPA has begun to address this problem. Several pilot projects are being established to provide an integrated approach to pollution control.

The Impact of Regulation on the Economy

During the early years of pollution control regulation, fears were often expressed that environmental protection was a drag on the economy. Environmental regulations were blamed for everything from the sorry state of the steel industry to the rampant inflation of the 1970s. Although this issue is still raised in the press and in legislative debates, the research on this issue shows that it has little substance.

To be sure, some workers have lost jobs because plants closed rather than comply with pollution laws, but the numbers have been small. The Environmental Protection Agency estimated in 1978 that approximately 96,000 person lost jobs in plant closings linked to pollution regulation (CEQ, 1978: 433). What these figures do not reveal is that many plants that closed were marginal operations in the first place; whether they could have survived the economic disruptions of the 1970s without pollution control regulation is an open question. The 96,000 lost jobs in industry must also be contrasted with the rise in the number of jobs in pollution control; the Council on Environmental Quality estimated that pollution control created an additional 680,000 jobs. Estimates on the impact that pollution control expenditures had on inflation have been low, in the neighborhood of 0.3 to 0.5 percent (Marcus, 1980: 280; see also Peskin, Portney and Kneese, 1981). In sum, the net impact of pollution regulation on the U.S. economy is probably positive.

Enforcement

The key issue in environmental protection in the 1980s should be enforcement. An in-depth examination of environmental protection enforcement (there has not been one) would reveal that enforcement is fairly weak. Several reasons for inadequate enforcement of the law exist.

First, the process by which pollution standards are set for individual firms relies heavily on a bargaining process between the regulator and the industry. In a study in Virginia, Downing and Kimball (1982: 57) found that 83 percent of all firms negotiated with the EPA on how much effluent they were permitted. In general, firms negotiated a standard that was heavily padded; that is, it was greater than the amount of pollution they were currently emitting. Second, violations of the standards are rarely detected. The United States has literally hundreds of thousands of pollution sources; EPA has only 10,000 employees, and many of those employees are engaged in activities other than compliance. One study found that a firm would be likely to see a pollution inspector once a year (Downing and Kimball, 1982: 58). When an inspector does visit, citing violations is difficult because measurement devices have substantial variation. Few violations are found by inspections; most violations are found when third parties complain.

Third, if a source is caught violating a pollution regulation, usually an extended period of negotiation ensues whereby the industry and the regulator negotiate a response to the violation. Rarely are sources taken to court and fined. From 1977 to 1980 the total fines collected by the EPA nationwide totaled $69.3 million. Of these fines, $41.9 million were Clean Air Act violations, $26.2 million were Clean Water Act violations, and the rest were minor fines for violating other laws (Crandall, 1983a: 107). Crandall (1983a) estimates that these fines totaled no more than 0.1 percent of compliance costs.

Enforcement of environmental protection statutes is lenient, to say the least (see the earlier discussion on the Clean Water Act). On the basis of the information given before, gathered during the Carter administration (an administration with the reputation of being proenvironment), the total deterrent effect of enforcement could have been only minor. Under an administration less committed to enforcement, the situation must be significantly worse. The improvements in environmental quality since the adoption of the Clean Air Act Amendments of 1970 and the Federal Water Pollution Control Act Amendments of 1972 have been limited as much by weak enforcement as by any weaknesses in the laws.

CONCLUSION

Who benefits from environmental protection? At first glance, environmental regulation appears to be an issue that seeks to redistribute benefits from polluters to the general public. Pollution control does impose costs on business, and it does provide benefits for individuals who live nearby (Downing, 1984: 230 ff). On closer examination, however, the relationship might not be so simple. As long as pollution controls are uniformly imposed on all plants within an industry and the industry can effectively compete with imports, pollution controls are probably translated into higher prices. Because the general public pays these prices, environmental regulation both benefits and costs the same group of people in the abstract. The general support for such policies illustrates that benefits are perceived to exceed the costs.

If we leave the macrolevel, pollution regulation has some redistributive effects within and between industries. Heavy polluting, noncompetitive in-

Table 6.1 Summary of Environmental Protection

Economics	
Firms	Vary
Entry	Varies
Profits	Vary
Technology	
Complexity	Varies
Stability	Varies
Substitutes	Vary
The Subsystem	
Bureaucratic control	Moderate
Industry coalition	Strong
Nonindustry coalition	Moderate
Bureaucratic resources	
Expertise	Strong
Cohesion	Strong
Leadership	Strong
Legislative authority	
Goals	Specific
Coverage	All
Sanctions	Good
Procedures	Good
Involvement of Macropolitical Actors	
Congress	Strong
President	Strong
Courts	Moderate

See Appendix.

dustries such as steel and automobiles probably absorb some pollution control costs rather than pass them to consumers. Given the level of compliance with the law in these industries, however, the amount of absorbed costs is unlikely to be significant. Notwithstanding the amount of costs, pollution control imposes greater costs on dirtier industries, thus raising their prices and reducing demand. Such sanctions are economically rational, therefore, because pollution regulation does nothing more than reimpose externalities on the firms producing them.

A second distributional impact is on smaller firms. Pashigian (1983) found that pollution control imposed a greater cost on small firms than it did on large firms. To some extent, pollution control has economies of scale. If such a bias is deemed significant, subsidies for pollution control could be granted to small business. On the other hand, the liberal tax provisions for investments in pollution control probably make such incentives unnecessary (see Downing, 1984).

In sum, then, environmental protection places restrictions on the regulated for the benefit of the nonregulated. This policy orientation reflects some of the variables discussed in chapter 2 such as high issue salience, a well-organized nonindustry advocacy coalition, and a bureaucracy equipped with ample resources (Table 6.1). At times, short-term political forces can alter the direction of policy somewhat, but such occurrences are fluctuations from the overall trend.

The politics of pollution regulation is influenced greatly by the issue's salience. Since environmental protection burst on the scene in the 1960s, it has consistently remained important to most Americans. Public opinion polls generally show strong support for environmental protection and significant support for stronger action. Such a level of salience explains the heavy participation in environmental policy by political elites.

Congressional activism and salience go hand in hand. Although Congress generally perceives regulation as its area (versus the president), no regulatory area is as close to Congress as environmental protection. The major initiatives in environmental protection in the 1970s came from Congress. One measure of the interest and activity of Congress is the length of environmental laws. With the exception of the tax code, few other statutes have the detail of the Clean Air Act.

As a counterweight to Congress stands the president. Environmental policy is too important for even presidents not to take an active role. Although presidents have exerted significant influence via appointments and budget controls, in general, presidential impact has been less than that of Congress.

Frequently, the courts have also played a role in environmental policy by forcing administrative action or providing an alternative forum for disputes (Melnick, 1983). The D.C. Circuit Court has been especially receptive to suits by environmentalists; the Supreme Court has been less hospitable (Wenner, 1984: 194).

Within the subsystem, three actors with ample resources operate. Because environmental regulation is complex, the Environmental Protection Agency plays a major role. EPA's major resource in building a power base, however, has been the cohesion of its employees. EPA employees, even though they are recruited from numerous professions, have developed a commitment to the organization and environmental protection. With allies in Congress, they were able to resist the initiatives of Anne Burford in the 1980s. This cohesion coupled with unusual expertise for a regulatory agency and generally positive leadership has made the agency a factor that must be considered in environmental protection. Legislative authority assists the EPA in its battles. Goals are specific, coverage is universal, and sanctions are good even though they are not used frequently. In such circumstances, regulation favoring the regulated is not likely.

Within the subsystem, EPA faces competing advocacy coalitions. Groups representing the industry are well organized and well funded. In the other advocacy coalition, environmental groups have used the salience of environmental protection to build fairly strong public interest groups. Although environmental groups cannot match the industry groups in terms of size and resources, in practice they do not have to do so. Because environmental groups advocate policies with a fair amount of diffuse public support, they need fewer resources to accomplish their ends than does industry.

7

Regulating Occupations

Regulating occupations, that is, determining if a person is qualified to practice law, medicine, carpentry, or naturopathy, is a function that has been left to the states and sometimes to local governments. The federal government does not sponsor national electricians' exams or national barbers' exams; and for lawyers, a federal law even prohibits the development of a federal government bar exam.

The scope of occupational regulation is fairly broad. Every state in the union regulates accountants, architects, attorneys, barbers, chiropractors, cosmetologists, dental hygienists, dentists, insurance agents, practical nurses, registered nurses, optometrists, osteopaths, pharmacists, physical therapists, physicians and surgeons, podiatrists, real estate agents, and elementary and secondary schoolteachers. These 20 occupations are only the tip of the iceberg. Twelve states regulate abstractors, 32 regulate ambulance attendants, 34 regulate chauffeurs, 15 regulate electricians, 48 regulate psychologists, and 11 regulate tree surgeons. A list of some 64 occupations and the number of states that regulate them can be found in table 7.1 (Berry, 1982). An estimated 800 different occupations are regulated somewhere in the United States (Rottenberg, 1980).

WHY REGULATE OCCUPATIONS?

The normal justification for regulating various occupations has been termed "public interest theory" by economists (see Stigler, 1971). To avoid confusing it with the public interest theory of political scientists, we will call it economic public interest theory. This theory holds that government regulation is justified only when markets fail. In the practice of occupations, markets can fail for two reasons—consumer ignorance (asymmetrical information is the polite term) and negative externalities.

Consumer ignorance is a market failure because a perfectly competitive market requires that both the buyer and the seller have perfect information about the product or service being sold. In the case of medicine, for example, the consumer lacks this information. The consumer cannot evaluate beforehand whether or not Dr. X is a competent physician; in fact, the consumer may not be able to evaluate the abilities of Dr. X after treatment because numerous factors other than the treatment may contribute to the consumer's health. In addition, the consumer is in a poor position to evaluate how much of Dr. X's services that he or she needs. Is the chest X ray necessary? Is surgery required, or are there other less radical alternatives?

Table 7.1 Number of States That Regulate Certain Occupations

Abstractor	12	Acupuncturist	12
Aerial duster	8	Ambulance attendant	32
Auctioneer	24	Audiologist	30
Boiler inspector	26	Chauffeur	34
Collection agent	22	General contractor	20
Speciality contractor	5	Well driller	31
Driving instructor	40	Electrician	15
Elevator inspector	12	Funeral director	29
Employment agency	49	Engineer	49
Forester	12	Geologist	9
Guide	24	Hearing aid dealer	41
Landscape architect	35	Librarian	23
Marriage counselor	6	Masseur	15
Medical lab technician	8	Medical lab director	15
Midwife	28	Milk sampler	30
Mine foreman	19	Projectionist	6
Naturopath	11	Nursing home administrator	49
Occupational therapist	10	Occupational therapy assistant	6
Optician	19	Outfitter	4
Pest control applicator	23	Pesticide applicator	18
Pharmacist's assistant	17	Physical therapy assistant	21
Physician's assistant	25	Plumber	30
Polygraph examiners	21	Private detective	35
Private patrol agent	17	Psychologist	48
TV technician	4	Radiologic technician	10
Sanitarian	33	School bus driver	12
Securities agent	49	Harbor pilot	25
Shorthand reporter	13	Social worker	20
Soil tester	7	Surveyor	49
Tree surgeon	11	Veterinarian	16
Watchmaker	10	Watchman/guard	9
Weather modifier	21	Weighmaster	21

Source: Berry, 1982.

Faced with this lack of information, a consumer would normally engage in an agency relationship with a third party. Faced with purchase of stocks, for example, the consumer hires a broker for advice. In the present example, the only agent available is Dr. X. The consumer trusts Dr. X to tell him or her how much medical treatment is needed (Evans, 1980: 250).

The agent then is supposed to act in the interest of the consumer by suggesting how much of a service the consumer should buy from the agent. This creates a potential problem. Dr. X, as agent, has an incentive to recommend more services than the consumer needs because these services will be purchased from Dr. X, the seller. Regulation, in economic interest theory, is therefore needed, to prevent an excessive demand for the product.

Closely related to the problem of overdemand for a service is the problem of poor quality service. Because the consumer normally does not have the skills to prejudge the quality of a service, the consumer risks the possibility that an unscrupulous person will sell him or her a poor or even a dangerous service. A dentist might do actual long-run damage to a patient's teeth, or an abstractor may miss a lien on property sold to a consumer. This problem is less serious when the value of the service is small and when the consumer engages in repeat purchases (e.g., haircuts). Poor quality service, however, is another reason why economic public interest theory suggests that regulation of occupations might be needed.

Negative externalities that can occur from the consumption of a service are one factor accepted by almost all economists as a justification for regulation (see Friedman, 1962). A negative externality results if, by consuming some service, the consumer creates a danger or a threat of danger to third parties. A person who hires an incompetent architect, for example, endangers the lives of those persons who will use the building. A person who employs an incompetent plumber risks the health of others in the community through the spread of disease. In cases where negative externalities are a high probability, the state should step into the market and regulate it to protect the health, welfare, and interests of the public.

THE ENVIRONMENT OF OCCUPATIONAL REGULATION

Most state-regulated occupations have characteristics conducive to competitive markets. The number of practitioners is large, and economic barriers to entry are small (profits vary by occupation). The technology of these occupations varies, but generally the technology is complex (barbers are an exception), the technology is changing (for white-collar professions but not blue-collar ones), and substitutes almost always exist.

THE PROCESS OF REGULATION

Although generalizing from 800 different occupations is difficult, some patterns in occupational regulation are fairly consistent. Usually, the initial demand for regulation comes not from the consumer but from the occupation. Even though the occupation seeks regulation, the terminology of economic public interest theory is prevalent in their claims. The state needs to regulate doctors, for example, to protect the citizens from the harmful effects of incompetent doctors and quacks. Its sole goal is to protect the public's interest.

Responding to these demands, the legislature creates a regulatory commission. In many cases, the commission is composed of practitioners from the regulated occupation. After all, the occupational members claim, who can judge the competence of a doctor (or nurse, plumber, electrician, polygraph examiner, and so on) but another doctor? The problem initially occurs, they claim, because citizens are not competent to judge the skills of a practitioner in the first place. Gellhorn (1956) estimates that 75 percent of regulatory board members are practitioners of the occupation that they regulate.

Sometimes the law goes even further in delegating the power of the state to the occupation. In three states, the state medical association and the state dental association actually appoint the regulatory board for their respective professions (Akers, 1968: 472). In over half the states the governor appoints regulators from a list of nominees provided by the state association (for dentists, physicians, and pharmacists). The occupation, therefore, not only demands regulation but tries to select who the regulators will be. Nonmedical occupations are usually not as successful in restricting how regulators are selected, but state law often requires that a regulator be a member in good standing of the profession that he or she will regulate.

State occupational regulatory commissions are generally small agencies with a great deal of autonomy. As a means of preventing political forces from affecting the agency, often the major control over an agency, the budget, is taken away from the legislature. Many state regulatory commissions are funded solely from the licensing fees that the agency collects from the occupation's practitioners. Sometimes these agencies are so small that they share office space with the occupational association whose members they regulate (Akers, 1968).

Not all state regulation of occupations is done in small commissions controlled exclusively by the regulated occupation. Several states such as Florida and California have a large Department of Occupational Licensing (the name varies) that consolidates the licensing functions for several occupations. New York regulates the occupations with career civil servants. California requires that some members of the regulatory board be public members who do not practice the occupation (see Shimberg et al., 1973).

The choice between numerous small regulatory commissions and a single large regulatory agency has political implications. Occupations prefer to be regulated by a small commission (see Sprecher, 1967; Carey and Doherty, 1967; Connors, 1967). A small commission composed of practitioners and funded by license fees is more likely to be controlled by the occupation and run in its own self-interest. A large consolidated agency is more likely to engage in vigorous regulation for several reasons. First, no single occupation can control the agency; every occupation must compete with all others for attention. In such an agency, for example, physicians will be less likely to use the powers of the regulatory agency to make life miserable for chiropractors. The claims of one occupation will be challenged by the claims of other occupations. Second, political elites are more likely to pay attention to the activities of such an agency because they pass on the agency's budget. Exposing the agency to political interests provides an avenue for nonoccupational interests to affect the agency. Third, the consolidated agency is likely to attract a higher-quality employee. A regulatory commission, being small (some have one or two employees), provides no opportunities for advancement if a good job is done. In fact, if the employee is not a member of the regulated profession, he or she may be prevented from holding several posts in a small agency. A consolidated agency, on the other hand, will attract individuals with a general interest in regulation. Individuals who perform well will have promotion opportunities within the agency. With rewards for good performance, performance should improve (if our economic brethren are correct). The end result is the potential for a more consumer-oriented regulation. No wonder, then, that regulated professions prefer the small commission (Meier and Plumlee, 1979).

THE REGULATORY SUBSYSTEM

At the risk of overgeneralizing, a typical regulatory subsystem for state occupational regulation can be described in terms of the key variables in chapter 2. Because occupational regulation is usually not a salient issue, regulatory issues are normally resolved within the subsystem (see Gormley,

1983a). The subsystem is fairly unusual, however; in most cases it is composed of only the agency and the regulated interest.

The agency is usually a multimember board composed of members of the regulated occupation and employs not more than a few full-time employees. Although the boards may possess some expertise, they cannot be characterized as cohesive, nor do they develop aggressive leadership. In terms of legislative authority, these agencies usually have vague goals, cover the entire profession, have weak or rarely used sanctions, and have elaborate procedures to protect the rights of the practitioners.

For all intents and purposes the subsystem usually has only one advocacy coalition, the coalition dominated by the occupation. A second advocacy coalition is possible when one occupation conflicts with another, when a member of the macropolitical system seeks to intervene, or when a well-organized consumer movement exists. In general, however, the regulated and the regulator operate in isolation.

REGULATORY OPTIONS

In general, a state regulatory agency has three options in regulating an occupation—registration, certification, and licensing. In actuality, the agency does not face these options because law usually specifies the type of regulation. An occupation that seeks regulation in its own self-interest will likely prefer licensing over the other two options.

Registration

Under registration, everyone who practices an occupation must register that fact with the agency. Registration occurs without restriction. Anyone who wishes to register may; there are no barriers to entry. The agency may place restrictions on the type and quality of service that is offered or on any other aspect of practicing the occupation. In general, however, agencies that only register occupations rarely ever restrict them to a significant degree. This need not be the case; even under a registration system, the regulatory agency can receive complaints about the providers of service. It could hold hearings on complaints and suspend registration if circumstances merit. An example of regulation by registration is California's regulation of television repair personnel.

Certification

Under certification, a regulatory agency gives an exam or examines the credentials of individuals wishing to practice an occupation. If the individual passes the exam and meets other necessary criteria, that individual is certified as a practitioner of X occupation. In many states, accountants are certified as are registered nurses in those states that practice "permissive licensing" (Connors, 1967).

Any individual wanting to practice a certified occupation can still do so without certification; that person, however, cannot hold himself or herself out as a "certified" member of the profession. For example, anyone who wishes can prepare tax returns and do other work that is normally done by a certified public accountant (CPA). The practice of accounting is not restricted to CPAs. The only restriction on those accountants who are not CPAs is that they may not represent themselves to the public as such (some states place additional restrictions on noncertified accountants).

Certification has some advantages for consumers if done correctly. A consumer has the option of purchasing services from an individual who is certified as competent by the regulatory agency. If a consumer feels the price of such service is too expensive, he or she still has the option of bearing a greater risk and purchasing the service from a noncertified practitioner. This procedure allows those who wish to purchase lower-quality services to do so. Although few people seek low-quality brain surgery, many do want low-quality legal and accounting services (as evidenced by the demand for divorce-yourself kits and tax preparation services).

Licensing

Licensing is the most restrictive form of regulation. Under licensing, an individual wishing to practice an occupation sits for an examination or has his or her credentials evaluated. If the person meets all the qualifications, he or she is licensed to practice. Individuals who are not licensed to practice are prohibited from doing so. For some occupations, practicing without a license may rate as a felony. Most current regulation is done through licensing. Physicians, attorneys, barbers, cosmetologists, and dry cleaners are only a few of the occupations that are licensed.

The categories of registration, certification, and licensing are not mutually exclusive. A regulator can combine elements of the three. For example, in all states, lawyers are licensed; in some states, they also may be certified. An attorney may be certified as an expert in tax law. Although this does not prevent other attorneys from practicing tax law, they may not represent themselves as certified tax experts. Similarly, physicians are both licensed to the general practice of medicine and certified as specialists.

No discussion of occupational regulation would be complete without a discussion of the infamous "grandfather clause." Whenever regulation is established for an occupation, the current practitioners are not brought in and examined as to their competence. Any effort to do this would probably eliminate the occupation's support for regulation. Rather, all existing practitioners are licensed ("grandfathered in"), and new entry requirements are imposed only on new applicants (see L. Friedman, 1965). The grandfather clause is important because it calls into question the public interest justification of regulation. If regulation is necessary because incompetent practitioners may harm the public, there must be some incompetent practitioners currently practicing. Applying standards to new practitioners and not the current ones, therefore, does little to protect the public from the dangers of malpractice. Only with time (as much as 40 years) will all these "incompetent" practitioners be eliminated.

POTENTIAL HARMS OF REGULATION

Whenever any group of individuals is given the coercive power of the state and asked to regulate themselves, potential for abuse exists. Adam Smith (1937) best summarized this position over 200 years ago: "People of the same trade seldom meet together, even for merriment or diversion, but the conversation ends in a conspiracy against the public or in some contrivance to raise prices." Smith was concerned with guilds, private associations that performed functions similar to state regulatory agencies. Allowing individuals to regulate themselves exposes them to the temptations of greed, the major motivating force that Smith held dear. If they did not seek to enrich themselves, then Smith and the economists he begot would be greatly disappointed.

Adam Smith's viewpoint has been adopted by Milton Friedman and the Chicago school of economics. Friedman (1962) and others (Rottenberg, 1980) charge that occupational regulation results in a multitude of evils. First, it restricts the free flow of labor from one occupation to another. By creating barriers to entry such as examinations, education, apprentice programs, and so on, regulation prevents labor from flowing freely to those occupations with the greatest returns. Second, as supply is restricted or even reduced and demand remains static or increases, prices for the occupational service must rise. Consumers will pay more for a service than they would in a free market. Third, as a result of restricted entry and high prices, members of the regulated occupation will receive economic rents, that is, returns that are not justified in terms of skills, experience, or true scarcity. Finally, regulation will have little impact on the quality of service provide. Members of an occupation that already receive high incomes from provision of services have no incentive to offer greater-quality service and, thus, invest more resources in producing the same income.

The charges raised by Friedman merit closer investigation. If he is correct, little justification exists for regulating occupations in the current manner. His proposed reform, complete deregulation, would then be a reasonable policy option. Before we examine the systematic research on Friedman's charges, one contemporary example, American medicine, needs to be examined in depth.

REGULATING MEDICINE

At the time that the American Medical Association was founded (1847), medical doctors (MDs) were only one of a variety of medical practitioners using the designation "doctor." Medical practice at the time was primitive by modern standards. Amputation and bleeding were common cures for a variety of ailments. Surgery was done by barbers.

Within this context, the AMA had some laudable goals. It sought (1) to require a uniform course of study for premedical students and (2) to elevate and standardize the requirements of medical education (see Kessel, 1959; 1970). The first step in this process was a political effort to convince state legislatures to license physicians. From 1847 to 1900 this effort was fought successfully, and medical examining boards were created in all the states. These medical boards were, of course, manned by physicians.

With control over the practice of medicine established through state regulation, the medical profession pursued its education goals. Although the attempt to raise the educational standards of medical schools was portrayed as an effort to protect the public's health, historians (Shryock, 1967) have discovered that the AMA's concern was the number of physicians. The AMA tied standards to the health issue by arguing that many physicians were poorly educated and that the nation only had resources to produce a limited number of quality physicians. The public would be better off with fewer, better-trained physicians.

In 1904 the United States had 160 medical schools. Many were proprietary schools. Because a proprietary school increased its income by accepting more students, it had an incentive to increase the size of its student body and to produce physicians as fast as possible. This, according to the AMA, led to the evils that they wished to eradicate.

In 1906 the AMA Council on Medical Education examined the medical schools of the United States and found that only 80 met their idea of what a medical school should be (see Kessel, 1959; 1970). Furthermore, 32 schools were completely unacceptable. Using such information to restrict the supply of doctors was not feasible because the AMA might be perceived as seeking economic gain for physicians at the expense of the public.

To solve this credibility problem, the AMA convinced the Carnegie Foundation for the Advancement of Teaching to examine medical schools. The Carnegie Foundation agreed and hired Abraham Flexner to do so. Flexner was assisted in this effort by the staff of the AMA and access to the AMA's 1906 data. The Flexner report on medical education came to conclusions that could have been written by the AMA. Flexner concluded that too many doctors diluted the quality of medical care. The public would be better served by fewer, better-trained doctors. Accordingly, many of the current medical schools should be closed. Those that remained open should restrict their admissions and adopt the uniform curriculum recommended by the AMA.

Armed with the Flexner report and control over state medical examining boards, the American Medical Association proceeded to restrict entry to the medical profession (Kessel, 1970). State medical boards required that a person graduate from a Class A medical school before he or she would be allowed to take the state medical exam. A Class A medical school was one approved by the American Medical Association or the American Association of Medical Colleges. The schools on both lists were identical.

Moving one step backward in the licensing process, the AMA asserted control over the internship process. Serving an internship with a hospital was a prerequisite to licensing. Hospitals, at least those controlled by physicians, required that a student graduate from a Class A medical school to receive an internship.

In combination, these two factors restricted entry to the medical profession. A graduate of a nonaccredited medical school would have difficulty finding an internship at an approved hospital. Without an internship, the student could not sit for the medical exam. Even with an internship at another hospital, the student might not be allowed to take the state exam because he or she failed to graduate from a Class A medical school.

The impact of these policies on medical education was striking. Faced with a system that refused to accept their graduates, proprietary medical schools closed. From 164 U.S. medical schools in 1904, the number dropped to 85 in 1920 and 76 in 1930 (Frech, 1974: 124). Schools with AMA approval restricted admissions dramatically. In 1905, 26,000 students were enrolled in medical schools, and 4,606 students graduated. By 1920 enrollments had been cut to 14,000 with 3,047 graduates, all at a time when the war in Europe should have increased demand for medical services.

The impact of these cutbacks was so effective that 1905 levels for students were not reached again until 1955 (Frech, 1974: 124). Major increases in medical enrollments did not occur until the health care explosion of the 1960s that was inspired by the federal government.

As interesting as the restriction on entry was the process by which medical schools restricted entry—discrimination. Medical schools limited enrollments to white Christian males. The seeds of this policy were found in the Flexner report; Flexner (1910: 180) concluded "an essentially untrained negro wearing an MD degree is dangerous . . . the practice of the negro doctor will be limited to his own race."

The impact of the Flexner "reforms" on black medical education was devastating. Five of the seven black medical schools were closed (Kessel, 1970: 270). In 1920 the 3,409 black doctors represented 2.7 percent of the total. The year 1920 was the high water mark for black physicians; their percentage of total physicians would never be that high again. In 1970 after a decade of affirmative action, only 1.4 percent of the nation's doctors were black (Frech, 1974: 125). In 1948, one-third of all medical schools refused to admit black students, and as late as 1965, five schools were still segregated (Strelnick and Younge, 1980: 2).

Discrimination was also practiced against women wanting to study medicine. In 1910, 8,810 women were practicing physicians, 6.5 percent of the total (Kessel, 1970: 270). The proportion of women dropped dramatically with the implementation of the Flexner report and did not reach this proportion again until the 1970s (Strelnick, 1983: 7). Similarly, Jews were systematically excluded from medical school. Admissions to City College of New York, for example, were 58 percent Jewish in 1925 but dropped to 16 percent by 1936 (Frech, 1974: 126). Discrimination against Jews perhaps also explains the flurry of AMA requirements for citizenship in the 1930s as large numbers of Jewish doctors fled Nazi Germany (Gellhorn, 1976).

The economic impact of this restriction on entry was as dramatic as the racial impacts. Physicians engaged in price discrimination (Kessel, 1959) by adjusting their fees to the income level of the patient. As part of this desire to set prices arbitrarily without outside intervention, the medical community opposed innovations in health care delivery that were not based on individual-fee-for-service medicine. Prepaid health care plans were opposed by local medical societies, and doctors who participated in them were ostracized and denied hospital privileges (see Kessel, 1959: 33–41). This opposition to innovation extended to national policy as well. The AMA opposed free medical care for veterans in Veterans Administration (VA) hospitals as well as medicare and medicaid (Kessel, 1959: 39). They engaged in a series of state level battles with chiropractors, podiatrists, osteopaths, and midwives to restrict and even eliminate these professions (Akers, 1968).

Medicine, in effect, became a closed society as far as consumers were concerned. It was not unknown, for example, that a doctor testifying for a patient in a malpractice suit would have future difficulties in using hospital facilities (Kessel, 1970). All this restriction did not result in health care superior to that of other, less restrictive nations. U.S. infant mortality rates and average life spans, although crude measures of health, fall far below the figures for several European countries. Perhaps one reason why quality did not improve faster was the notorious grandfather clause. By not examining current doctors, any impact of improvements on quality could only be incremental. As Kessel (1970: 275) notes, it is incongruent that we require drivers to take periodic reexaminations but do not impose the same require- ment on physicians. Milton Friedman (1962) feels that AMA-imposed re- strictions on entry have such deleterious consequences that the nation would be better served if medicine were deregulated and the licensing of physicians were abandoned.

The example of medicine illustrates how a profession uses regulation that was proposed in the public interest for its own benefit. The situation in medicine was dramatically altered in the 1960s, when the federal govern- ment became active in health policy. With the implementation of medicare and medicaid as well as federal programs to expand health care, health resources, and health planning, control of the profession by the AMA was weakened. Health policy became too important to be left solely in the hands of doctors (although they still retain the preponderant influence). Three indicators of the federal effort were the increase in medical schools to 127 and the increase in the number of medical students to a number in excess of 66,000 in 1983 (*National Journal,* 1983: 2136), as well as the growing number of women and minorities in medicine.

THE IMPACT OF OCCUPATIONAL REGULATION

Although the case study of the medical profession illustrates the poten- tial ill effects of occupational regulation, it remains a single case. The study of occupational regulation has gone far beyond the study of physicians and has examined the impact of such regulation in a variety of contexts. Five major impacts of occupational regulation have been examined—barriers to entry, the existence of economic rents, impact on price, impact on quality, and the general impact of regulation. Each will be discussed in turn.

Barriers to Entry

Occupational regulation has been charged with creating barriers to entry (Friedman, 1962) that restrict the free flow of labor, thus reducing supply and leading to increases in price. Without a doubt, regulation does create barriers to entry by limiting the number of persons who practice an occupation. A barrier to entry, however, is not by definition bad. If a barrier to entry prevents an incompetent person from selling a service and, thus, raises the overall quality of services to the consumer, it constitutes a reasonable barrier to entry. Barriers to entry that lack any redeeming benefits for consumers, however, must be considered unreasonable barriers to entry that benefit only the producers. Three potential barriers to entry are associated with regula- tion—nonsense requirements, examinations, and lack of reciprocity.

Nonsense Requirements.   State regulatory laws often establish licensing requirements that are unrelated to effective performance. Gellhorn (1976) takes great relish in listing a variety of such requirements. In some states, for example, photographers must pass a venereal disease test, boxers are re- quired to take loyalty oaths, and barbers in California must present evi- dence of knowledge in basic anatomy. During the big Red scare of the 1950s, several professions required oaths that individuals were not Communists. All these requirements plus the general requirements that a person be of good moral character and a citizen of the United States (or the state of registration) are unreasonable barriers to entry. To be sure, some people may be concerned about a horde of Communist plumbers taking over the country, but any requirements that are unrelated to the effective performance of the service being licensed are unreasonable.

Examinations.   Examinations are, of course, by definition barriers to entry. Even a completely valid exam restricts entry because the applicant must invest time and money to travel to where the exam is being given. Such a restriction, however, is reasonable when the exam is valid. Examination validity is a question that should be raised about all occupational exams. Registered nurses, a profession that requires judgment based on a variety of situational variables, somehow reduce their exam to a series of multiple choice questions (Connors, 1967). Cosmetology exams in California allocate a portion of the credit on the exam to the applicant's personality. Plumbing exams in Oklahoma grade plumbers on their ability to join two pieces of iron pipe despite the fact that copper and plastic pipe have eliminated any need for this skill (Shimberg et al., 1973). Only 5 percent of electricians pass the Oklahoma exam on the first try, primarily because the exam covers topics not normally part of an electrician's job. In each of these cases, the validity of the exam is open to question.

   Some research on occupational licensing has directly addressed exam validity. Dorsey (1980), in a study of cosmetologists exams, found that scores on the written portion of the exam were related to formal education and race. The correlation between the skills portion of the exam and the written portion was only 0.25; because a great many applicants failed the written portion of the exam, Dorsey concluded that it was used as a barrier to entry. Other studies have shown that the failure rate on exams is positively related to the per capita income of the profession (Holen, 1965; Leffler, 1978; Pfeffer, 1974). In states where the income for lawyers, dentists, doctors, accountants, pharmacists, and barbers was higher, more applicants failed entry exams. Maurizi (1974) discovered that the failure rate on exams was higher when the number of applicants taking the exam was large. If exams are used as an unreasonable barrier to entry, one would expect to find this sort of impact. By failing larger numbers of applicants, the occupation restricts supply and generates a higher income for current practitioners.

Reciprocity.   Occupations limit entry not only by restrictive examinations but also by limiting reciprocity between states. A barber licensed in Alabama, for example, cannot simply move to Oklahoma and expect to cut hair. For the most part, this barber is expected to meet all the requirements of licensing in Oklahoma and must pass the Oklahoma barber's exam. Although the U.S. Constitution's full faith and credit clause requires states to recognize the acts of other states, this does not apply to occupational licensing. In some cases, such as attorneys, where the practice of law varies from state to state, a state has an interest in limiting practice to individuals licensed by that particular state. For most occupations, including dentists, nurses, barbers, electricians, and so on, the lack of reciprocity is absurd. Good dental practice should be the same in Ohio as it is in Colorado.

Discrimination against nonstate residents usually starts with the examination procedure. Boulier (1980), for example, found that out-of-state students were four times as likely to fail bar exams as in-state students. A consistent finding of the research literature is that reciprocity restrictions limit the interstate mobility of licensed occupations. Doctors, for example, face fewer restrictions on reciprocity than dentists and lawyers and are more likely to move to another state to practice (Holen, 1965; Pashigian, 1979; 1980).

Despite the impact of reciprocity on mobility, it does not appear that restrictive practices have a consistent impact on income. The restrictiveness of state reciprocity standards is unrelated to the income of professionals (e.g., attorneys), but does have some impact in raising the income of nonprofessionals (e.g., barbers, electricians; see Kleiner et al., 1982).

Overall, regulation appears to erect barriers to entry, and some of these barriers are unreasonable restrictions on the free flow of labor. In 1973, for example, all 2,149 applicants for contractor licenses in Florida failed the exam (Elzinga, 1980: 119). Despite the barriers to entry, however, some question exists as to whether or not these barriers are successful in restricting the number of persons licensed in a given occupation. Despite the massive and well-documented effort of the AMA to restrict the number of physicians, the federal government was able to override these restrictions in the 1970s. The number of doctors increased by 116,000 from 1970 to 1979, a growth rate 37 percent faster than the population. Even though many state bar exams are clear attempts to limit the number of attorneys, the number of lawyers practicing in the United States doubled between 1970 and 1980 and is expected to double again to 800,000 by 1990 (Julin, 1980). Arguing that the nation currently faces a critical shortage of lawyers would be difficult. For all their efforts, then, occupations have been less than completely successful in restricting supply.

The entire area of barriers to entry is further complicated by a perverse argument presented by economist Hayne Leland (1979; 1980). Leland argues that all efforts to restrict supply are beneficial to the consumer. He reasons that any effort to increase barriers to entry will limit the quantity of an occupational service that is supplied. Any decline in supply will result in a corresponding increase in the price of a service. An increase in price for a service will rationally attract the attention of more individuals who will want to enter the occupation. If the price rises high enough, the quality as well as the quantity of applicants will increase because individuals with opportunities for high incomes elsewhere will be attracted to the restricted occupation. Even if applicants are licensed on a random basis, according to Leland, the overall quality of service will rise because the market will attract better-quality applicants. Although Leland's argument fits well in economic theory, the process he describes is clearly not efficient. More effective ways exist to improve the quality of services offered to consumers. But he is correct in noting that restrictive licensing may have as one of its by-products a gradual improvement in quality.

The Existence of Rents

According to economic theory, monopoly will produce a return on investment in excess of the return that could be expected in a competitive market. In terms of occupations, restricting entry should produce incomes higher than can be justified by the education, skills, hours, and so on, of the practitioners. Economists call these excess returns rents. Economic rents must be distinguished from income. The existence of rents, for example, does not imply higher incomes because individuals may have preferences for leisure that exceed their preferences for higher incomes. Similarly, high incomes can exist without economic rents if the members of an occupation are willing to work longer hours or invest more in capital.

Milton Friedman (Friedman and Kuznets, 1945), in some of his original work, found that medical doctors earned economic rents that he attributed to the restrictive practices of the AMA. The existence of rents from occupational regulation has generally been assumed (see Rottenberg, 1980: 8) even though many self-regulated occupations take actions that dissipate economic rents. For example, many occupations, when they achieve self-regulation, immediately increase the educational requirements or the apprenticeship requirements to gain entry. Similarly, many occupations require continuing education. Such actions require practitioners to invest more heavily in human capital. Thus, economic rents disappear, to be replaced by a return on investment in education (see Weingast, 1980: 83).

Because economic rents are difficult to determine empirically, only a few studies have examined economic rents and occupational regulation. Keith Leffler (1978) reexamined Friedman's work on doctors and found that Friedman was able to find economic rents because he used an unrealistically low discount rate (4 percent) in his calculations. When more realistic discount rates (i.e., rates consistent with recent economic theory) were used, Leffler found that physicians received no rents at all until the passage of medicare and medicaid. In 1973, Leffler estimated the economic rents to physicians at $15,000. An extrapolation of this trend to 1983 would place current rents in the neighborhood of $25,000 to $30,000. Again, however, these rents were created by federal government actions, not by the economic regulation of physicians. In addition, the rapid increase in physicians since 1973 may have dissipated these rents.

For the important questions of regulation, the existence of rents may be irrelevant. For example, an occupation could receive rents from regulation at the same time that regulation results in improvements in the quality of service. Similarly, an absence of rents says nothing about the quality of service to consumers. An occupation can dissipate the rents due from restricted entry by poor administration, bad luck, or technological change. Oklahoma dry cleaners, for example, were unable to sustain high prices despite price-fixing powers when wash-and-wear fabrics were introduced. The massive drop in demand rendered any regulatory actions to correct the situation meaningless (see Plott, 1965; Meier and Plumlee, 1979). Other examples abound. Barbers, for example, do not appear to be getting excessively wealthy despite the major restrictions on entry and the power to set prices in some states. Perhaps the decline in the demand for their skills as surgeons and a rise in preference for new wave hair styles (neither factor under their control) have dissipated any rents they could expect to earn.

Impact on Price

The heart of the economic argument against occupational regulation is that it raises the price of the services provided. Four aspects of regulation are assumed to decrease supply and, therefore, to increase prices—restrictions on reciprocity, restrictions on advertising, restrictions on input substitution, and the general overall restrictive nature of regulation. Each of these will be discussed in turn.

Reciprocity.   By restricting the free flow of labor within an occupation, lack of reciprocity allows state-to-state variations in supply and demand to persist. Unfortunately, economic theory is not at all that clear about what happens in a specific area when geographic restrictions are created. In states with inadequate supply, allowing full reciprocity will reduce the price of a service. Concomitant with the decrease will be an increase in price in that state that loses occupational members. In actuality, very little research has been done on the effect of reciprocity restrictions on price, and that research conflicts. Shepard (1978), for example, presents evidence that geographic restrictions on dentists increase the price of dental services by 12 to 15 percent. Boulier (1980: 92), on the other hand, found that lack of reciprocity increased the price of dental services by only 1 percent. Further research in this area is necessary, but the difficulty in gathering comparable price data for occupational services makes such research difficult.

Restrictions on Advertising.   Advertising's impact on prices is subject to some dispute. If the services being sold are fairly similar, then if a firm advertises lower prices, demand for that firm's services will increase. Other firms will then have to match the lower prices to retain their share of the market. The market for retail gasoline in a community follows this pattern. A more political theory of advertising, however, argues that advertising stimulates the consumer to purchase more services, perhaps even more than are needed. This greater demand will raise prices if supply is held constant, and the consumer pays for the passed-through costs of advertising. The prescription drug industry with its high advertising costs is cited as an example (Leffler, 1981).

Advertising is one area of occupational regulation that has interested the federal government. The Federal Trade Commission issued more competitive rules for optometrists, including advertising, and pressured other professional groups to eliminate such restrictions. The U.S. Supreme Court in *Bates* v. *Arizona* (1977) struck down provisions that prevented attorneys from advertising. The Supreme Court has also dealt harshly with a symptom of nonadvertising, the collusive setting of fees (*Goldfarb* v. *Virginia,* 1975).

The initial evidence on advertising and price was very positive. In a classic study of the eyeglasses industry, Benham (1972) found that states that permitted advertising price information had prices 25 to 40 percent lower than states that did not. The price of routine legal work dropped as much as 50 percent after advertising was permitted and legal clinics began to advertise prices (Muris and McChesney, 1979). More recent evidence, however, found negative consequences for advertising. Leffler (1981) discovered that large quantities of advertising speeded the use of prescription drugs but that it also retarded the substitution of identical, but cheaper drugs.

Advertising is an area of occupational regulation that is currently undergoing a great deal of change. Barriers to advertising occupational services are dropping rapidly. As more occupations advertise, more data will accumulate on the relationship between advertising and price.

Input Substitution.   Input substitution occurs when a practitioner of an occupation substitutes a cheaper input for a more expensive one. For example, a dentist who uses a hygienist to clean teeth rather than do it himself or herself is engaging in input substitution. If restrictions are placed on input substitution, then the most efficient use of resources will be prevented. In theory, a producer should substitute one input for another until each input generates a marginal return equal to its marginal cost. Restrictions on input substitution, therefore, should result in price increases.

Much occupational regulation concerns input substitution. For example, most states restrict the number of hygienists that any single dentist can hire (DeVany et al., 1982: 378). Bar association rules against joint practice prohibit lawyers from combining forces with accountants or from working under the direction of a nonattorney manager. Input substitution restriction often goes beyond the organization of the occupation in question to prevent other occupations from serving as substitutes. Every state in the United States, for example, places restrictions on nurse practitioners and physician's assistants that prevent them from engaging in the practice of medicine independently of a physician (Dolan, 1980: 229).

The empirical research on input substitution is meager, but it does underscore the theoretical problem. One study found that restrictions on the use of dental assistants and hygienists resulted in an overuse of dental time on routine matters (DeVany et al., 1982). Another study revealed that states not restricting the practice of opticians (the cheapest input in dispensing glasses) had lower eyeglasses prices (Benham and Benham, 1975). Similarly, states with commercial eyeglass dispensers also had lower prices (Maurizi et al., 1981). Although the volume of empirical evidence is small, it is all consistent with the conclusion that restrictions on input substitution result in higher prices.

General Restrictions of Licensing.   Several studies have examined the general impact of occupational regulation on prices. A study of the price of title opinions in Northern Virginia after the *Goldfarb* decision revealed that the price had fallen by 50 percent (Wood, 1978). A study of wages in the construction industry found that licensing increased the wages of electricians and plumbers (Perloff, 1980); but because this study used laborers (an occupation that has a much lower skill level) as the base of comparison, the findings are subject to question. W. D. White (1980) found no impact of licensing on the level of nurses salaries for 1960 and 1970, but in another study he found that requiring a college degree for registered nurses increased wages by 16 percent (W. D. White, 1978). The Federal Trade Commission, in its study of the TV repair industry, discovered that prices were higher in a state that regulated the repair industry (Louisiana) than in a state that used registration (California) or an area with no regulation (Washington D.C., see Phelan, 1974). Plott (1965) found no differences in dry cleaning prices between Oklahoma (a regulation state) and Kansas (a nonregulation state). Pfeffer (1979) could not find any income differences attributable to regulation for plumbers, insurance agents, and real estate agents.

The general impact of licensing on price is an area that does not reveal consistent findings. Several studies claim to show an increase in prices, and several other studies find no price impact. In addition, many studies have serious methodological flaws resulting from an inappropriate research design and inappropriate statistical techniques. The only supportable conclusion in this area is that the general impact of licensing on prices is indeterminate.

In sum, the impact of occupational regulation on price is fairly complex. Restrictions on advertising appear to result in increased prices (with the exception of prescription drugs). Similar impact is found for input substitution limitations although the volume of evidence is small. Restrictions on reciprocity, however, limit the interstate flow of occupational members, but have not shown a consistent impact on price. Licensing, in general, often does not appear to affect the price of a service. The evidence indicates that prices for a service are probably affected only when restrictions on advertising underscore collusive price agreements and when one occupation (optometrists, dentists) restricts the use of another occupation (opticians, hygienists). As these are the areas that have received the greatest federal attention, we should expect that price impacts of occupational regulation will be lessened in the future.

Impact on Quality

Occupational regulation is often justified as a quality control mechanism; it should protect consumers from harmful services. If the quality of service increases under regulation, some of the ill-effects of regulation such as price increases may well be justified.

Poor quality of service can result from two different sources (Blair and Kasserman, 1980: 189). First, some poor quality of service might exist because occupational members vary in the skills that they possess. Such variation is addressed by licensing exams. Second, poor quality of service might exist because some practitioners are tempted to increase their incomes by delivering a larger volume of lower-quality service. If greed is a motivating factor in reducing service quality, then the elements of regulation that restrict entry and, theoretically, raise prices will eliminate much of this motivation by raising the incomes of all practitioners (see also Beales, 1980).

Assessing the impact of regulation on service quality is a difficult undertaking. Quality is an elusive concept to measure. One cannot simply rely on outputs because the quality of service may not be reflected in the outputs. A lawyer, for example, can provide an exceptional defense and still have his or her client convicted. A doctor may perform brilliant surgery and lose the patient (Haug, 1980: 63). In fact, a reputation for skill may well attract the most difficult cases so that the best surgeons or the best lawyers may not have the best overall results (Elzinga, 1980). Similarly, good outputs can be achieved in spite of some occupational treatment; many medical patients of the nineteenth century recovered despite being bled.

Another problem with studying quality under regulation is that little quality-oriented regulation appears to take place. From 1967 to 1973, for example, the average state disciplined 1.6 physicians (Pertschuk, 1980: 345). California, in a recent year, received 3,407 complaints about lawyers but acted in only 1 percent of the cases (Haug, 1980: 72). To be sure, occasionally some vigorous regulation appears; the California contractors board in a recent year suspended 729 licenses and revoked 447 others (Shimberg et al, 1973). In general, however, quality control may be a symbolic goal of occupational regulation rather than an actual goal.

A few studies on quality have been conducted. After the deregulation of advertising for attorneys, a California study showed that the quality of routine legal services did not decline, even with large reductions in price (Muris and McChesney, 1979). Also in California, the number of complaints against contractors increased after the industry became regulated. Although complaint increases might indicate a decline in service, in fact, the increase in complaints simply reflected an easier process for filing complaints (Maurizi, 1980). The Federal Trade Commission's television repair study found that the amount of unnecessary repairs declined when the state of California engaged in output monitoring. California used the well-known device of taking television sets to various repair shops and reporting the costs and the amount of unnecessary repairs (Phelan, 1974). States that have stringent requirements for the practice of dentistry (i.e., as shown by high examination failure rates) also receive better dental care (lower dental malpractice rates and better dental health, Holen; 1977).

The relationship between regulation and quality is difficult to discern. No evidence exists that quality actually declines under regulation, and some regulatory efforts appear to improve the quality of service. Many of these results, however, may be a function of measurement error. A study of medical malpractice (an indicator of poor quality of service) found that the practice of doctors who lost malpractice cases did not drop in volume (Haug, 1980: 63). Until more precise measures of quality are available, therefore, the relationship between quality and regulation must be viewed as indeterminant.

Miscellaneous Impacts

Regulation of occupations has two other impacts that are relatively important. First, occupational regulation restricts consumer choice. A consumer is not allowed to seek out an independent practicing paramedic, for example, to treat a routine illness. Neither is a consumer allowed to find an independent dental hygienist to clean teeth. Both these examples indicate a market for "lower-quality" occupational services. To be sure, a patient would be irrational to seek out an incompetent brain surgeon, but in many cases of health care a high level of skills is not necessary and not justified in terms of cost. If low-quality health care were available, then perhaps more health care services would be purchased and the overall quality of health care would improve. Similarly, low-cost/low-quality legal services would encourage more consumers to draft wills and other routine legal actions.

Much occupational regulation is designed to limit consumer choice. Every state prohibits paramedics from establishing practices independently from physicians (Dolan, 1980). The American Medical Association has conducted campaigns against midwives (also chiropractors, podiatrists, osteopaths, naturopaths, and so on) despite the evidence from European countries that the use of midwives is associated with a lower number of infant deaths (Kessel, 1970). The full-time care of a less trained midwife may be more healthy than the sporadic inattention of a highly trained obstetrician.

Second, occupational regulation is associated with discrimination against women and minorities. Freeman (1980) found that occupational regulation was associated with limiting black access to jobs in the South. The AMA and its post-Flexner discrimination against women, blacks, and

Jews is well documented (Kessel, 1959; 1970; Frech, 1974). Blacks are twice as likely to fail bar exams as white applicants (Freeman, 1980: 72–73). Exam scores for cosmetologists in Missouri and Illinois were found to be correlated with race (Dorsey, 1980). In 1967 the state of Florida did not have a single black optician, and Montgomery County, Alabama, had only one black plumber (who was licensed through a loophole in the law). As recently as 1967, the state of Oklahoma restricted the practice of dental hygiene to females only (Shimberg et al, 1973).

The evidence of discrimination in the regulation of occupations is overwhelming. Minorities are less able to overcome the barriers to entry that are erected by state regulation. This lack of access is clearly not a function of variables other than race because many of the occupations regulated are trades that do not require a great deal of formal education. Clearly, discrimination is one of the consequences of occupational self-regulation.

Several impacts of occupational regulation, therefore, have been identified. First, occupational regulation does create barriers to entry, but there is some question as to how successful those barriers are in limiting the number of practitioners. Second, the evidence indicates that occupational regulation does have some role in increasing the price of regulated services. Third, regulation does not create economic rents for the occupation regulated; or if it does, the actual regulatory process and its actions dissipate these rents. Fourth, the relationship between regulation of occupations and service quality is not clear. Fifth, occupational regulation unnecessarily limits consumer choice. Sixth, the process of regulating occupations results in discrimination against minorities and discrimination on the basis of sex and religion.

THE POLITICS OF OCCUPATIONAL REGULATION

Although occupational regulation has been condemned as nothing but regulation in the economic interest of the regulated (Rottenberg, 1980; Friedman, 1962), this is clearly not the case. Too many examples of regulation that does not benefit the occupation regulated exist for this conclusion to be tenable. For example, funeral directors have been forced by recent Trade Commission regulations to disclose prices and avoid other questionable business practices. The American Bar Association is demanding that Congress exempt it from FTC regulation, not the sort of request one would expect if lawyers benefited from regulation. The California regulation of contractors created a complaint process that made the filing of complaints easier (Maurizi, 1980), and punitive actions are taken against contractors who engage in unfair business practices (Shimberg et al., 1973). Generic drug laws have been enacted by several states over the opposition of the pharmacists (Meyer, 1982). Prohibitions against advertising in the health and legal professions have been struck down, and competition has been encouraged. Numerous state agencies have required midcareer education courses for a variety of professionals (Berry, 1982).

Although no systematic evidence exists, sufficient cases suggest that not all occupational regulation is in the interests of the regulated. Such a situation could occur in one of two ways. Either the regulatory agency seeks to regulate in the self-interest of the occupation but makes major mistakes in the process, or consumers have been able to exert sufficient political pressure to attain some of their objectives. With the rise in organized consumer groups in the 1970s and 1980s, this latter hypothesis is tenable.

Without our being overly cynical, the possibility also exists that an occupational group might seek regulation that is in the consumer's interest as well as in the occupation's interest. In an occupation with an unfavorable public image (used-car sales, medicine in the nineteenth century, chiropractic), vigorous regulation might improve the profession's public image. Such regulation may well serve the needs of individual practitioners because self-regulation may be undertaken for status reasons as well as economic reasons. The ability to regulate one's own practice is often seen as the first step to becoming a "profession" (Benham, 1980).

Before we take up the political forces in occupational regulation, some discussion of what is meant by a "consumer orientation in state regulation" is necessary. Consumer interests are more likely to be served if the regulatory agency is concerned with service quality than it is if the agency focuses its efforts on entry restrictions, legal actions against individuals who practice without a license, advertising restrictions, and price-fixing. Several aspects of regulation might indicate that consumer interests are considered in occupational regulation. Continuing education requirements for professionals are an attempt to keep practitioners current with new skills in the profession and reflect a concern for consumers (a regulated profession has no real interest in keeping current because this entails opportunity costs and dissipates economic rents). Other indicators of a consumer orientation might be consumer representation on the regulatory board, a large consolidated agency where civil servants do the regulating, a large percentage of disciplinary actions for quality reasons, and the use of experimental output monitoring (e.g., TV repair).

A study of state occupational regulation revealed that the direction of regulation (consumer vs. occupational interests) was a function of four variables (Meier, 1983a). First, the size of the occupation in question plays a role in whether or not the occupation is regulated and in the content of the regulation. Size means votes, and votes mean political resources (see Stigler, 1971; Rourke, 1984). Because occupations are likely to form associations, occupational groups tend to be fairly cohesive. Mobilization is not a problem; the group needs only to turn numbers into public policy. The larger the occupation, the more likely that the occupation will be regulated by a state, and the more likely that regulation will be in the interests of the regulated occupation.

With the advent of the consumer movement, occupational interest groups no longer have the political field all to themselves. One restraint on occupational groups is consumer sophistication. As a consumer becomes better educated, he or she becomes more aware of the potential ills in the marketplace. In addition, with education comes an increase in political skills and an increased willingness to use them (Verba and Nie, 1972). States with higher education levels, therefore, have more potent consumer groups, and these groups are more likely to achieve some degree of consumer orientation in occupational regulation.

Sophistication is not the only factor that facilitates or limits the mobilization of consumer interests in this area. The other important factor is contact. Without contact with others who have suffered similar problems, the consumer may believe that the poor service he or she received was only a rare occurrence. As contact between consumers increases, consumer consciousness is raised; and consumers can be mobilized as a political force. One variable that indicates this increased contact is urbanization. In fact, states that are more highly urbanized are more likely to regulate with consumer interests in mind. Urbanization does not affect producer mobilization because contact among producer groups is likely to be high, regardless of the degree of urbanization.

Finally, a competitive party system is essential to consumer-oriented regulation. In a state dominated by one party, legislators of the majority party face a political environment where they can choose between consumer and producer interests. Because producers are likely to have far greater resources and be much better organized, the dominant party legislators will rationally seek an alliance with the producers (in this case, the occupation). Consumers will be ignored by the majority party, and any links between the minority party and consumers will produce no impact on public policy.

In a competitive party state, where both the Democratic and the Republican party have a good chance of winning elections, the occupational interest groups cannot forge an alliance with one party for risk of serious defeat. The rational occupational group, therefore, plays both sides of the fence, making contributions and offering political support to both Democrats and Republicans (just as major economic interest groups contribute to both parties at the national level). Producer resources to both parties, therefore, are in a relative balance. Competitive elections and a balance of political resources mean that the rational politician looks elsewhere for an electoral edge. A marginal contribution that would be of little value in a noncompetitive state could well provide the margin of victory in a competitive state. The rational politician, therefore, will make appeals to consumers to gain their votes to win the election. This does not mean that the politician will become a consumer advocate, but rather that his or her producer orientation will be tempered with some effort to accommodate consumer interests. The result is a balancing of these interests.

This balancing of interests occurs in numerous legislative districts simultaneously. In some districts, producer interests will be overwhelmingly dominant, and the candidates in these districts will temper their pro-producer orientation only slightly. In other districts, there will be few or no producer interests, and candidates in these districts will side with consumer interests. The end result in a competitive state is a legislature that considers consumer interests in regulation (see also Weingast, 1980). Consumer interests do not necessarily win, but they are considered.

REFORMING OCCUPATIONAL REGULATION

Benjamin Shimberg (1973), a perceptive student of occupational regulation, has noted that there are no simple solutions to the evils of occupational regulation because the status quo is a reflection of the political power of the groups involved. The ability to advocate a reasonable solution to a public problem, however, is one step toward changing the political distribution of power. In a state with a competitive political system, this may be sufficient to get consideration of reform.

Similar to regulation in general, the reforms proposed for occupational regulation are a function of what the reformer perceives the problem to be. Those who believe the ills of occupational regulation stem from barriers to entry and restrictions on competition generally favor less regulation. Those who believe that insufficient concern is paid to service quality advocate more regulation or procedures to change the direction of current regulation.

Complete Deregulation

Milton Friedman (1962) has argued that the solution to the evils of occupational regulation is complete deregulation. This position corresponds to his view that barriers to entry and increased prices are the problems to be solved. Friedman, in fact, disputes the public interest reasons for regulation. He does not feel that consumer ignorance is a major problem because ways exist to gather information about the quality of a particular service. When a consumer purchases a service numerous times, experience provides a pool of information on quality. For one-time purchases, the suggestions of friends and relatives often provide some information. Although the consumer may not know as much about the service as the seller, Friedman contends that it is paternalistic to assume the state is a better judge than the individual. Friedman also discounts the impact of externalities. For many occupations (barbers, cosmetologists, abstractors), few externalities exist. In occupations where potential externalities exist (e.g., health care, engineering), peer judgments on referrals and legal remedies if harm occurs limit their impact. Friedman is so convinced that the harmful effects of regulation outweigh any gains that could be made that he advocates complete deregulation even for the medical profession.

Certification

A less radical free market approach to reforming occupational regulation is to replace licensing with certification. Although licensing restricts the practice of an occupation to only those individuals who are licensed, certification allows noncertified persons to practice. The advantage of certification over licensing is that the two processes are theoretically equal in terms of quality control. Just as a licensed professional is deemed competent, so is a certified one. In terms of consumer choice, however, certification is a far superior option. The consumer who wishes to purchase a low-quality service is allowed to make such purchases from uncertified practitioners. The consumer in this case assumes a greater risk that the service will not be satisfactory, but this risk is compensated by a lower price. Consumers who desire high-quality services still have that option.

All-Comers Examinations

An all-comers examination system simply opens up licensing exams or certification exams to any individual who wishes to take them. Often experience or educational requirements are barriers to entry. Under an all-comers system, any individual who wanted to take a state bar exam to practice law would be allowed to sit for the exam; and if the individual passed the exam, he or she would be allowed to practice law. Two benefits are attributed to all-comers exams. First, they eliminate rigidity in a learning process that usually specifies the exact training a person must have and recognize that on-the-job experience may be as valuable as classroom experience and vice versa. Second, such a system places a great deal of pressure on examiners to design valid exams. Without a doubt, the current set of occupational exams leaves much to be desired (see Shimberg et al., 1973). Often covering techniques no longer used, examining over areas of little use to the practitioner, or giving credit for personality and appearance, the current exams are unlikely to pass any validity tests. Allowing all-comers exams would force an occupation to address the question of exam validity; and either changes would be made, or the occupation's reputation would plummet.

Legal Remedies

The lawyers' approach to deregulation couples elimination of regulation with a greater reliance on the legal system. Any damages imposed on a consumer by a practitioner can be pursued under tort law. Jurisdictions with small claims courts permit even minor disputes to be decided in court. Such a system could even be turned into an administrative process with reduced restrictions on evidence and testimony before expert hearing examiners.

To the extent that increased use of legal remedies constitutes an improvement over the current system of regulation, it must be coupled with deregulation and reforms of the legal system. Deregulation is necessary to eliminate many costs of regulation. Without freedom to enter and exit an occupation, increased use of legal remedies offers no improvement over the current system. In addition, without restructuring the legal process to avoid the problems of high cost, slow process, and uncertain remedies, this reform also offers little improvement. Without these changes, increased use of the legal system merely contributes to the well-being of the legal profession.

Institutional Licensure

One option presented in the health field is institutional licensure (Hershey, 1969). Licensing restrictions often prevent a hospital from allocating its personnel to their most effective role. Unlike an individual consumer, a hospital is not subject to the two major ills of an unregulated labor force—consumer ignorance and externalities. A hospital staff is highly trained and, as a unit, is competent to judge the skills and qualifications of its personnel. Even if mistakes are made initially, observation over time will reveal errors in the personnel process.

The proposed reform, therefore, is to license hospitals, clinics, health maintenance organizations, and other systems to deliver health care. A licensed institution is then freed from conforming to any other state laws on occupational licensing. If such a hospital felt that licensed practical nurses could perform a function normally done by registered nurses, then it could act accordingly. Paramedics could be substituted for physicians in a variety of routine medical situations, thus freeing the more expensive resource for more difficult tasks.

The equivalent of institutional licensure occurs in some large legal firms. Legal research is often done by paralegals rather than attorneys; in many cases, legal secretaries fill out the routine legal forms involved in divorces, wills, and similar matters. Management functions may be turned over to a professional manager. Attorneys still retain some functions for themselves exclusively (appearing in court), but such restrictions protect the status of the professional rather than serve the consumer interest.

Sunset Legislation

Sunset legislation is a favorite tool of reformers, so its advocacy for occupational regulation comes as no surprise. Under a sunset law, a regulatory agency is authorized for a set period of time, say, ten years. Once every ten years, if the legislature does not pass a law reauthorizing the agency, it will cease to exist; that is, the sun will "set" on it. Sunset legislation recognizes that many agencies continue to exist because the governmental process is incremental. Agencies exist from year to year without any assessment of whether or not they are still needed. Sunset merely reverses the incremental process so that it works against continuing the agency.

Several states have tried sunset legislation and have applied it to agencies engaged in occupational regulation. One study examined the impact of sunset legislation on occupational regulators in 15 states for 1977 to 1978 (Martin, 1980). In these states, 182 regulatory agencies were reviewed by legislative staff. Of these agencies, 54 were recommended for termination. That over 30 percent of the agencies were recommended for termination illustrates that numerous regulatory agencies exist for which little justification can be made. Unfortunately, the record of legislatures is less admirable. Of these 54 agencies, only 21 were terminated. Still, eliminating 11 percent of the occupational regulatory commissions should be deemed a success given the general practice of not evaluating their performance.

Public Representation

If a major problem with occupational regulation is that consumer interests are rarely considered, then one possible solution is to require consumer or public representatives on the regulatory boards. California, for example, requires public members on many of its regulatory boards, including a voting majority on 15 boards (Schutz, 1983: 506). Where public representation is used in states other than California, however, it is generally only used halfheartedly. Rarely are consumers given a majority on the board—usually one or at most two seats. This voting disadvantage means that, on serious disagreements, the regulated occupation usually has access to a voting majority. Second, public members on a regulatory board may be no different from general consumers; they can probably be snowed by professional expertise. As one regulator said, after we spend some time educating a public member, he or she votes correctly (Shimberg et al., 1973). Schutz (1983) found no significant changes in policy outputs two years after California increased public representation on its licensing boards.

Despite the weaknesses of public members as a way to ensure responsiveness to consumer interests, the reform does have some advantages. The simple presence of public members widens the scope of the conflict by including nonoccupational members in the decision-making process. Such a member should have greater access to news media so that the most self-serving policies would not be considered by the board. A small check, to be sure, but still a check.

A Department of Consumer Affairs

A major structural reform of occupational regulation is to consolidate all regulatory commissions into a single regulatory department, called a Department of Consumer Affairs or Department of Occupational Licensing. If regulation is then done by career civil servants rather than by autonomous occupational boards, greater pressure for consumer interests will be present. Regulated occupations will have to compete with each other for the attention of the regulator, thus expanding the scope of the conflict so that regulatory decisions are made in the open. An open process in a department with sufficient resources means that consumer interests will be given more weight.

One cannot overemphasize the role that bureaucratic ambition can play in this process. In a small, occupation-dominated regulatory commission, positions are unattractive to talented individuals. There is little hope for promotion into a position of authority, and salaries are likely to be low (not even considering the psychological costs of regulating barbers for their own self-interest). In a large regulatory department, however, good performace is likely to be rewarded with promotions and increases in pay. Good performance, that is, performance recognized by others in the department, is not likely to be proproducer performance. The head of a major multioccupational regulatory agency is unlikely to care that X was able to please the polygraph examiners because the agency head does not identify with polygraph examiners. The agency head identifies with regulation and, therefore, is far more likely to notice that X has battled entrenched interests for the consumer's well-being.

A Composite Reform

In actuality, the most effective reform of occupational regulation, political feasibility aside, may well be a combination of the preceding reforms. First, a state should eliminate any state-sanctioned licensing; quite clearly, certification is a process that is superior to licensing in that the quality controls of licensing are present but consumer choice is not restricted.

Second, any occupation that is primarily employed by members of another occupation should not be certified. Certifying or licensing dental hygienists, occupational therapy assistants, physician's assistants, and other similar occupations is a perversion of the governmental process. The employer of all these professionals is in all cases competent to judge the skills of these personnel. If the employing person is not competent to judge these skills, then that person is not competent to practice the occupation he or she is engaged in. Licensing employees only creates barriers to entry that are unrelated to quality performance. This does not mean that some states might not wish to certify health or legal paraprofessionals; such an action is rational if the state also permits an independent practice by these paraprofessionals. A state with the consumer interest foremost in mind will indeed permit such practices. In combination, then, this creates a policy of institutional certification. Any certified practitioner who employs paraprofessionals is free to hire any individuals that he or she desires (bearing in mind liability for malpractice). Any paraprofessional who wishes an independent practice may sit for examinations and be certified to so do.

Third, exams for certification in all fields should be open to all comers. If the exams are valid measures of the skills needed to provide competent service, then unqualified individuals will not pass the exams. If the exams are not valid indicators of occupational skills, then they should not have been given in the first place.

In combination, the preceding three reforms seek to increase consumer choice. Should not the consumer be free to seek occupational services that are tailored to his or her needs? An individual with a routine will does not need the services of Edward Bennett Williams. That individual is better off with a competent paraprofessional who can devote some time to such a matter.

This freedom of market choices should be supplemented with an integrated Department of Consumer Affairs that is responsible for all occupational regulation. Such a department would be staffed with career civil servants who administer all regulations and exams. If occupational advisory boards are necessary, they should be part-time and advisory only. This department should be given regulatory authority to receive consumer complaints about all regulated occupations. It should have a separate administrative hearing unit where complaints, once investigated, can be adjudicated. The department should have the authority to issue subpoenas, to issue cease-and-desist orders, to enforce such orders without court action, and to suspend certification of individuals who violate state regulations.

Such a department also needs broad investigatory powers. The use of output monitoring where services are surreptitiously purchased by the department and evaluated for quality, unnecessary work, and unnecessary cost should be encouraged. Frequent use of such techniques will have an inhibiting effect on unethical actions (see Pelhan, 1974, on TV repair).

Finally, the department must be funded to perform its information functions. The problem with most occupational services is that consumers have less information than the producers. The department's role is to equalize this information gap. The most important element of this information function is educating consumers as to what certification means. Armed with such information, consumers can then decide whether or not they want to purchase services from uncertified practitioners. Concomitant with this role is publicity about how to complain about poor quality service.

In combination, the greater reliance on the market plus an enhanced consumer affairs agency focusing on product quality should result in more concern for consumer interests. To be sure, the political feasibility of these reforms is questionable given that they attack entrenched interests. Given the current status of occupational regulation in most states, however, even small parts of this proposed reform cannot help but improve the situation.

CONCLUSION

Although the large number of regulatory agencies has prevented the detailed analysis of specific policies found in other chapters, an effort to tie the chapter back to the regulatory process described in chapter 2 is still

Table 7-2 A Summary of Occupational Regulation

Economics	
Firms	Many
Entry	Easy
Profits	Vary
Technology	
Complexity	High
Stability	Low/High
Substitutes	High
Subsystem	
Bureaucratic control	Weak
Industry coalition	Strong
Nonindustry coalition	Weak
Bureaucratic Resources	
Expertise	Moderate/High
Cohesion	Low
Leadership	Low
Legislative authority	
Goals	General
Coverage	All
Sanctions	Poor
Procedures	Poor
Involvement of Macropolitical Actors	
Legislature	Weak
Governor	Weak
Courts	Weak

See Appendix.

beneficial. The literature consistently finds that occupational regulation is intended to benefit the regulated. Although the nonregulated can indirectly benefit from educational barriers to entry and other regulations, the prime beneficiary is the regulated.

The key variables in chapter 2 explain why the regulated benefit (Table 7.2). Occupational regulation is not salient; the public is little concerned about this issue. In addition, judging the qualifications of podiatrists, electricians, or morticians can be fairly complex. These factors suggest that occupational regulation will be determined within the subsystem.

The regulatory bureaucracies are not able to dominate this subsystem because they have few resources. The agency might have developed moderate-to-strong expertise because the regulators are drawn from the regulated occupation, but that is the only agency resource. Cohesion is rare; and leadership, unlikely. Goals tend to be vague, sanctions are weak or not used, and selection procedures usually force the governor to select regulators from the regulated profession.

This weak regulatory agency operates in a subsystem with a well-organized advocacy coalition representing the regulated. In fact, the agency was probably created at its request. A nonregulated advocacy coalition is unlikely to be found. Consumer groups are likely to be pressing far more salient issues at the state level. The subsystem's policy outputs, therefore, should favor the regulated.

Neither the macropolitical actors nor the environment is likely to counter proregulated policies. Macroactors, in general, will see no incentives to intervene. Even though most professions have many practitioners, few economic barriers to entry, some degree of instability, and many substitutes, the design of the subsystem will normally prevent these environmental forces from being transformed into proconsumer regulation. The situation is not predetermined, however. Where agency norms encourage a consumer orientation, a consumer-oriented policy is possible. In most state regulatory commissions, however, small agencies with close ties to the regulated occupation prevent the development of such an organizational ideology. In large consolidated regulatory agencies, consumers are more likely to be heard.

The political process also plays an important role in opening these subsystems. In states with competitive party systems that must be responsive to a wide range of interests and a well-organized consumer movement, occupational regulation is less producer-oriented. The political resources of a regulatory agency (as opposed to the regulated occupation) are fairly small and, therefore, sensitive to political pressures. The low salience of occupational regulation in most states, however, means that political actors will generally ignore occupational regulation, thus permitting the occupation and the agency to form a symbiotic relationship that is mutually beneficial.

8

Workplace Safety and Health

Occupational safety and health regulation is probably the best-known and most controversial federal regulatory enterprise. The Occupational Safety and Health Administration (OSHA), the principal federal agency involved, has been condemned for imposing large costs on business for little safety gain. In just 14 years it has become the favorite whipping boy of politicians running for office. Despite the controversy, occupational safety and health regulation is a fairly traditional form of regulation. OSHA, through the rule-making process, establishes standards for safety (e.g., specifications regarding the strength of ladders) and health (e.g., workers shall be exposed to no more than x parts per million of a chemical). OSHA then inspects workplaces for compliance with these standards and levies fines for failure to comply. The basic form of regulation is similar to that of the Environmental Protection Agency.

THE SUBSYSTEM

The Agencies

The regulation of occupational safety and health is handled through a three-agency system. The most visible agency, OSHA, is located in the Department of Labor and is headed by an assistant secretary of labor, who reports directly to the secretary of labor. OSHA issues health and safety standards, inspects firms for compliance, and fines firms for violations. The agency is decentralized, with most activities conducted by 89 field offices. In fiscal year 1985, OSHA had 2,354 employees and a budget of $217 million (a 22 percent increase over the FY 1980 budget). OSHA shares some safety regulation tasks with other federal regulatory agencies such as the Nuclear Regulatory Commission and the Mine Safety and Health Administration, which have jurisdiction over specific industries.

OSHA is not a research agency. Research that forms the basis for regulation is done in the National Institute of Occupational Safety and Health (NIOSH), a small agency in the Department of Health and Human Services. In addition, if businesses wish to contest OSHA decisions, they can appeal to the Occupational Safety and Health Review Commission (OSHRC). OSHRC is an independent agency that exists to adjudicate contested OSHA fines, provisions of corrective action orders, and the adequacy of inspections.

Because OSHA is the major action agency in this area, it will be the focus of our discussion. OSHA has generally not developed the resources to become a powerful political actor. Because NIOSH is the prime research agency, OSHA does not have a reputation for expertise. By cultivating the professional values of industrial hygienists and safety engineers, however, it has become somewhat cohesive. Limiting the use of cohesion and other resources has been OSHA's lack of good leadership; leadership can normally be characterized as poor to average.

Two other political resources are worthy of note—salience and legislative authority (see chapter 2). Occupational safety and health is a salient issue. To be sure, it does not have the salience of environmental protection, but it maintains its salience at a consistent level year after year. The reason for this persistent salience is that occupational safety and health is a labor-management issue with two highly organized advocacy coalitions taking opposite views on the issue.

High salience means that political actors have been motivated to intervene in the regulatory subsystem with great frequency. Such intervention is often highly partisan because labor and management usually have links to different political parties. Congress has continually been involved in the administration of occupational safety and health policy since its inception. Policy implementation at times has been so controversial that since 1978 presidents have addressed OSHA issues and established elaborate review procedures for OSHA initiatives.

Salience in worker safety and health is such that advocacy coalitions rarely accept defeat without exhausting all avenues of influence. Interest groups that fail to convince OSHA of their position usually then sue the agency to have the regulation set aside. Every OSHA health rule issued since 1972 except one has been involved in a court battle. After the court rules (generally in favor of OSHA), the losing party usually presses Congress or the president to intervene in the process and change the outcome. High salience determines that there will be no such thing as a final decision.

OSHA's legislative authority differs little from that of other regulatory agencies. The legislative goals are vague, encouraging OSHA to protect the health and safety of workers so far as is possible. Little specific guidance is given in the 30-page Occupational Safety and Health Act (note the brevity compared to 200-page laws for regulating agriculture and the equally detailed Clean Air Act). Initially, OSHA covered most businesses involved in interstate commerce. In 1977, however, Congress exempted small farms, and in 1981 with a targeting policy the agency exempted a large number of firms from inspections (see later). The sanctions available to OSHA rate in the middle in terms of severity. OSHA has the power to fine businesses administratively and the power to seek injunctions to compel compliance, but the size of fines is severely limited, thus reducing their impact. Agency procedures (discussed later) are not unique and do not limit the actions of the agency.

Advocacy Coalitions

OSHA faces two well-organized advocacy coalitions. Overall business viewpoints are represented via the Business Roundtable or the National

Association of Manufacturers. Individual industries are almost always represented by trade associations such as the Chemical Manufacturers Association. In addition, individual companies often represent themselves. In general, industry groups are large campaign contributors, especially since the election laws were rewritten to permit corporations to establish political action committees. Industry groups often have the support of academic economists who study safety and health issues. The industry coalition has many of the advantages Rourke (1984) details for effective interest group articulation, including resources, prestige, status, and knowledge about the system. Industry groups generally press for no regulation or weak regulation of occupational safety and health.

Industry is opposed in its anti-OSHA lobbying by an advocacy coalition headed by organized labor. One labor spokesman characterized the Occupational Safety and Health Act as "the single most important piece of labor legislation since the National Labor Relations Act of 1935" (quoted in Pettus, 1982: 611). Because the National Labor Relations Act is often referred to as the Magna Charta of organized labor, the high priority of workplace safety and health is evident. Although the AFL-CIO often presses for stronger regulation, the key union is the Oil, Chemical, and Atomic Workers Union because they have developed the scientific expertise on safety issues that is used to counter the arguments of industry (Viscusi, 1983: 54). Unions can often count on various safety and health professionals as allies.

THE ENVIRONMENT

The reach of OSHA is economywide. All industries are subject to OSHA's general regulations, and some industries such as lumbering are subjected to specific regulations. Because the reach of OSHA is so broad, the normal economic and technological environmental variables considered in other chapters have less relevance for explaining the general direction of OSHA regulation. Such economic factors as the number of firms, the ease of entry, and the industry profits vary from industry to industry as do such technological variables as complexity, stability, and substitutes. But when a rule applies specifically to a single industry, these variables are important. For example, the OSHA effort to limit cotton dust exposure (see later on) was strongly resisted by the textile industry because the industry's economic status was fairly marginal. The textile industry suffered from low profits and heavy competition from imports; resistance to health standards that would require large investments was predictable.

One technological factor that is important, however, is that of availability. Occupational safety and health regulations are subject to the same problems that environmental regulations face—often standards are set that cannot be met with the current technology. Under such circumstances, the rule-making process becomes a highly technical debate over the scientific feasibility of meeting the standards.

OCCUPATIONAL SAFETY BEFORE OSHA

Workplace dangers were not suddenly discovered in 1970, when OSHA was created. Injuries, deaths, and illnesses related to specific occupations had been documented for years. The National Safety Council estimated that, in

1970, 14,000 persons were killed in work-related accidents and 2.2 million persons were physically disabled; in addition, some 5.7 million accidents resulted in 1.7 million lost workdays annually (Kelman, 1980: 236). Although these figures showed large decreases from the 1920s (Shaffer, 1977: 198), from 1966 to 1970 injury rates increased rapidly (Smith, 1976: 8).

Data on workplace safety were all based on estimates taken from business and hospital records; many criticized these estimates as far too low (see Ashford, 1976: 3). Compared to statistics on occupational disease, however, accident data were fairly reliable. Ashford (1976: 93), a highly respected expert in this field, estimated that 100,000 persons died from occupationally related diseases and that 400,000 new cases of occupationally related illnesses occurred annually.

Before 1970 the regulation of worker health and safety was left to the states.[1] In fact, most states had adopted a law regulating workplace safety by 1900, following the lead of Massachusetts (Kelman, 1980: 238). In addition, two methods of compensating injured workers were tried. The first option was to treat an occupational injury as a tort and use the legal system to determine damages. A worker injured on the job could sue his or her employer. The effectiveness of lawsuits was limited by court interpretation. To collect damages from an employer, an employee usually had to prove that (1) the employer was negligent, (2) that the employee was not negligent (had not contributed to the danger), and (3) that no fellow workers were at fault (see Buchholz, 1982: 304). Consequently the legal system rarely worked to compensate injured workers.

Option two for the states was the enactment of workers' compensation laws. Workers' compensation laws are essentially no-fault insurance laws; employers are required to carry insurance or pay directly to compensate workers injured on the job. The system is administered by quasi-judicial agencies usually called Workmen's Compensation Courts.

Workers' compensation laws had a shaky start. Many laws were declared unconstitutional before the courts accepted this form of regulation. By 1948 every state had adopted some form of workers' compensation law (Shaffer, 1977: 197), and 85 percent of all workers were covered (Nichols and Zeckhauser, 1981: 213). Under the workers' compensation system, large firms had some incentive to improve safety on the job because their insurance premiums were based on their accident records; small firms' insurance rates were based on industrywide averages, so they had little incentive to incur additional costs to improve safety.

Although workers' compensation programs varied from state to state, in general, they had several weaknesses as a method of protecting workers from unsafe conditions. First, the benefits paid by the system were fairly low; in 1940 state systems paid an average of 66 percent of before-accident wages for a total disability; by 1970 this had fallen to 50 percent in some states (L. White, 1983: 117).[2] Second, the system was slow, often taking

1. There were a few notable exceptions to this policy. Coal mine safety and working conditions for longshoremen were federal concerns. In addition, federal contractors had to have safety plans. For an excellent analysis of coal mine safety, see Lewis-Beck and Alford (1980).

2. A person disabled will generally need less income to maintain the same standard of living as a person working, in theory. Because the disabled worker does not have work-related expenses, benefits were set at a percentage of predisabilty wages. The exact percentage necessary to restore full purchasing power is open to question.

several years to provide benefits; in fact, businesses had an incentive to slow down the process because benefits did not have to be paid (and thus be reflected in insurance rates) until final disposition. Third, the system was compensatory but not preventative. The system provided only weak incentives for businesses to improve the safety of their plants and, as a result, appeared to have no impact on the incidence of industrial accidents (Shaffer, 1977: 197). Fourth, workers' compensation generally ignored occupational diseases. Unlike an injury that could be traced to an on-the-job accident, an occupational disease might be attributable to any one of the worker's employers (if the disease had a long latency period) or even to off-the-job exposure. One indicator of the system's inability to handle occupational diseases is that 13 percent of the Social Security system's disability funds are devoted to individuals with disabilities resulting from occupational diseases (L. White, 1983: 118). Fifth, the workers' compensation system was inefficient. On the average, only 65 percent of insurance premiums were paid out in worker claims; in some states the figures were as low as 50 percent (L. White, 1983: 113). Because premiums are invested and draw interest until needed, benefits as a percentage of earnings were even lower.

ESTABLISHING FEDERAL REGULATION

The Politics of Creation

Despite the weaknesses of the workers' compensation system and the large number of individuals killed and injured on the job, the 1960s saw no great push for federal regulation. Unlike other areas of social regulation, no political entrepreneur seized on occupational safety as an issue. Even the Nader organization came to occupational safety late; the Nader exposé of workplace dangers was not published, for example, until three years after OSHA legislation was passed (Page and O'Brien, 1973). Instead, occupational safety and health reached the political agenda via a series of idiosyncratic events (see Kelman, 1980).

A speech writer for President Lyndon Johnson, Robert Hardesty, had a brother who worked in the Bureau of Occupational Safety and Health, a research unit in the Department of Health, Education, and Welfare. As the result of his brother's urging, Hardesty occasionally slipped references to occupational safety and health in some of Johnson's speeches (Kelman, 1980: 239). At the same time, Assistant Secretary of Labor Esther Peterson became concerned with health conditions in mining and raised the issue with the secretary of labor.

In late 1967, Secretary of Labor Willard Wirtz was looking for new legislative proposals to suggest to the president. After the interest expressed in the issue by Peterson, Department of Labor executives discovered the references to occupational safety and health in the president's speeches (Kelman, 1980: 239). A proposal on occupational safety and health, therefore, appeared to be one that would gain the president's approval. The White House accepted the proposal and included it in the president's legislative program even though the Department of Labor did little to lobby for its inclusion (Kelman, 1980: 239).

Occupational safety and health, therefore, was not placed on the agenda via such normal mechanisms as interest group pressure, political entrepreneurship, or external crisis. Rather, Kelman (1980: 240) attributed its placement on the agenda to bureaucrats looking to push good causes as well as some highly idiosyncratic events.

With an administration proposal, Congress scheduled hearings in 1968. During the hearings, the controversial nature of workplace safety was established. Labor organizations testified in favor of strict regulation of the workplace to enhance safety. The National Association of Manufacturers and other business organizations argued that the record on occupational safety was not so bad and that most accidents were the fault of workers not of business. Business generally opposed any federal efforts. Neither house passed legislation in 1968.

In 1969 three events created an environment conducive to passage of occupational safety and health legislation (see Kelman, 1980: 241). First, a late 1968 mine disaster in Farmington, West Virginia, killed 78 miners, thus increasing the issue's salience. Second, the AFL-CIO made the issue a legislative priority. Third and perhaps most important, Richard Nixon presented his own legislation as part of his strategy to woo the blue-collar workers in the silent majority.

President Nixon's bill, however, was significantly different from the one proposed by the Johnson administration. Nixon proposed that safety regulation rely primarily on voluntary industry compliance; in addition, Nixon's proposal did not authorize rule making but would have relied on case-by-case corrections. Fines were permitted only if the firm engaged in willful violations of the law (Kelman, 1980: 255). Nixon's law would have been administered by a new independent agency, the National Occupational Safety and Health Board.

The nearly unanimous votes by which the Occupational Safety and Health Act pased both houses of Congress masked the highly partisan legislative struggle. The legislation was reported out of committee in the House despite a Republican boycott of committee meetings. Floor amendments to change the legislation resulted in a series of party-line votes. In general, the Democrats won most of the floor fights, but in one concession to conservatives the law permitted states to enforce the federal law (see L. White, 1983: 136). In December 1970, President Nixon signed the Occupational Safety and Health Act into law.

In an excellent summary of the politics of passage, Kelman (1980: 242) notes three key features that would influence the law's implementation. First, the legislation was sought by organized labor and opposed by business. Second, the impact of public interest groups such as those led by Ralph Nader was small to nonexistent. Third, the concern was occupational safety (preventing on-the-job injuries and deaths) not occupational health (preventing diseases).

The Occupational Safety and Health Act

The goal of the Occupational Safety and Health Act is "to assure so far as possible every working man and woman in the Nation safe and healthy work conditions." The act made two significant changes in occupational safety and health regulation policy. First, the policy was nationalized, with the federal government established as the dominant regulator in place of the states. To be sure, states could continue to operate programs if they were "at least as effective" as the federal program, but to operate a state program, the state had to provide one-half of the funds. Approximately half the states operate their own programs. Second, the emphasis changed from compensation of the injured and ill to prevention of injury and illness. The workers' compensation system remained in place for compensating injuries.

The details of how injuries and illnesses would be prevented were left to the bureaucracy (F. J. Thompson, 1982: 203). The task facing the bureaucracy was enormous. The legislation covered all firms in interstate commerce, some 4.1 million establishments with 57 million employees. Only federal, state, and local governments were exempted (Smith, 1976: 7). Although the regulatory agency was faced with a task as impossible as that facing the Environmental Protection Agency, it had one advantage: the act did not require completely safe and healthy workplaces by a specified time.

The act created two new bureaucracies and changed the name of a third. The basic operation of the act was entrusted to the Occupational Safety and Health Administration. OSHA was given the power to issue rules and enforce the rules it issued. OSHA was delegated quasi-legislative (adopting rules), quasi-executive (conducting inspections), and quasi-judicial functions (determining whether an employer was in violation of the rules and, if so, the amount of the fine for violations). The agency's rule-making power was broader than that of most other regulatory agencies. In addition to the authority to adopt rules under rule-making procedures similar to those set out in the Administrative Procedures Act (APA), OSHA could also adopt temporary emergency rules without following APA procedures if a "grave danger" existed. In addition, OSHA was given the authority to promulgate any "consensus" industry standards as rules in the first 28 months of the agency's life.

OSHA's location in the Department of Labor is significant. The Department of Labor employs individuals with sympathies for organized labor (see Seidman, 1980). In Democratic administrations, the political appointees as well as the career bureaucrats see organized labor as their clientele. Within such an organizational environment, OSHA could be expected to give greater attention to labor union concerns than to those of private industry.

The second agency created by the 1970 Act was the Occupational Safety and Health Review Commission. OSHRC is an appeals commission established to adjudicate contested OSHA decisions. OSHRC has always operated independently from OSHA; it has used different criteria for enforcing the law and usually reduces OSHA fines. OSHRC went so far as to hold that businesses need not comply with safety regulations if compliance would be unduly costly (compared to OSHA's view that costs should not be considered, see Harter, 1977: 36).

The Occupational Safety and Health Act also changed the name of the Bureau of Occupational Safety and Health to the National Institute of Occupational Safety and Health (NIOSH). The act left the agency in the Department of Health, Education, and Welfare (now Health and Human Services). NIOSH continued with its research on occupational safety and health issues and was given the authority to suggest new regulations to OSHA.

Of these agencies, OSHA was clearly the most important. The tone for the agency was established with the initial recruitment of personnel. Individuals hired to work for OSHA were generally safety and health professionals such as safety engineers and industrial hygienists (Kelman, 198ʋ. 250). According to Kelman (1980: 250), these professions shared commonly held values that indicated the future direction of regulation. Both professions are concerned with preventing accidents and health hazards; the question of cost is not usually asked. OSHA, therefore, was populated by employees whose professional values consisted of "doing good" (Kelman, 1980; F. J. Thompson, 1982).

Unlike other agencies such as the Federal Aviation Administration or the Environmental Protection Agency, where agency leadership played a strong role in creating an organizational ideology, in OSHA the ideology grew out of professional norms. This ideology was reflected in the agency's regulations. The ideology had a preference for engineering standards, that is, specifying a standard and also specifying how that standard should be met. Included as part of engineering standards was the belief that personal protective gear would not solve any problems. When faced with controlling exposure to an occupational hazard (e.g., cotton dust), OSHA regulators, therefore, would require the air in the workplace to be cleaned rather than require individual workers to wear respirators (Kelman, 1980: 252).

In addition, OSHA employees distrusted the goodwill of employers. Almost four of five OSHA inspectors responded in a survey that many employers would ignore standards (Kelman, 1980: 255). One illustration of the strength of professional values in determining regulatory outcomes in this area is Kelman's finding that occupational safety and health policies are similar in Sweden and the United States despite the vastly different degrees of influence of business and labor. The similarity, he argues, can be attributed to the values of health and safety professionals (see Kelman, 1981b).

Rule-making Procedures

The general rule-making procedure for OSHA is somewhat different from that for other regulatory agencies. Normally, the process begins with NIOSH conducting a literature review of the hazards involved in exposure to substances or dangerous conditions and proposing that OSHA author a regulation in the area. OSHA may also undertake the rule-making process on its own initiative or in response to an individual petition.

OSHA then assigns the problem to an advisory committee; OSHA has both permanent advisory committees and can appoint temporary ones. The advisory committee, composed of scientists and professionals, then proposes the text of a regulation to OSHA. At this point OSHA begins the normal rule-making process: notice of a rule-making procedure is published in the *Federal Register,* and public hearings are held. OSHA hearings are often long and controversial because both labor and management groups (as well as public health people) can be expected to present evidence and dispute the evidence of others. OSHA is also required to do some cost analysis on its proposed regulations. As a nonindependent agency, OSHA was required to file inflationary impact statements under President Ford, was challenged by the economic analysis of the Council on Wage and Price Stability under Carter, and must clear its regulations with the Office of Management and Budget under Reagan. Despite the pressures for cost-benefit analysis, until recently OSHA had successfully avoided doing such analysis before issuing rules. The final rule must then be published in the *Federal Register* before it takes effect.

OSHA also has the authority to issue temporary rules when an emergency exists and when going through the full rule-making process would delay correction of the problem. Under such circumstances, OSHA can issue a temporary emergency rule, but must then begin normal rule-making procedures to issue a permanent rule. In addition, OSHA had authority to bypass normal rule-making procedures in its first 28 months (see the following section).

Experience has shown that the OSHA rule-making process is cumbersome and slow. By an optimistic count, OSHA has issued no more than 40 rules using this procedure (see Wines, 1983k). Many of these rules deal with minor matters, however; the number of major health-oriented rules is less than a dozen.

IMPLEMENTING THE LAW

The Inspection Process

OSHA rules and regulations are enforced by on-site inspections conducted by OSHA personnel. A firm might be selected for inspection for a variety of reasons. First, OSHA engages in targeted inspections. Because OSHA does not have the personnel to inspect the millions of U.S. workplaces, it sets priorities for inspections. In general, targeted inspections focus on more hazardous occupations such as lumbering, meat-packing, longshoring, and so on. Second, OSHA conducts inspections as part of accident investigations. Third, inspections are scheduled if the agency receives complaints about unsafe work conditions. Initially, a large portion of OSHA inspections resulted from worker complaints. Experience showed, however, that complaint-inspired inspections found few safety violations. Such a record suggests that workers probably used the OSHA process to harass employers. Finally, OSHA conducts follow-up inspections to determine if previous violations have been corrected (see Buchholz, 1982: 311).

An OSHA inspection usually begins with a walk-around; that is, the inspector walks through the plant with a management representative (and usually with a union representative in unionized plants) to observe general working conditions and take photographs of potential hazards. The inspector then reviews the plant's health and accident records and follows the review with a conference with management to discuss general findings and potential violations.

An OSHA inspector can find five different types of violations. *De minimis* violations are those that have no direct relation to job safety; the remedy is to give notice of such a violation but not to issue citations or levy fines. Nonserious violations are those with a direct relationship to safety but unlikely to cause death or serious harm. Such violations are subject to a penalty of up to $1,000 at OSHA's discretion. Serious violations are violations that might probably lead to death or serious harm; serious violations are subject to a nondiscretionary $1,000 fine. Willful or repeat violations are serious violations that have not been corrected since a previous inspection; the fine for a willful or repeat violation is $10,000. Finally, OSHA inspectors can find that a situation presents an imminent danger to employees; under such circumstances, the employer is required to correct the situation immediately. OSHA can seek court injunctions to correct imminent dangers.

The OSHA inspector does not levy fines on employers. After completion of the inspection, the inspector presents his or her findings to the OSHA area director, who determines the fine. Any employer who wishes to appeal either the size of the fines or the citation can file an appeal with the Occupational Safety and Health Review Commission.

Implementing Safety Regulation

Safety regulation rather than health regulation was the first priority of the early OSHA. This priority reflected the interests of the advocacy coalition supporting the legislation, and the actions of OSHA in this area created a controversy that engulfed the agency. Many of OSHA's political problems can be attributed to a single major mistake made by the agency in 1971.

The Occupational Safety and Health Act permitted OSHA to adopt any consensus national safety and health standards within two years and 120 days without going through the normal rule-making procedure (Smith, 1976: 9). Rather than carefully examining the consensus standards before adopting them, OSHA after only five months issued some 4,400 standards. In part, the issuance of these standards reflected the agency's desire to take dramatic action even though it had a small budget and few trained staff (see Shaffer, 1977: 203; F. J. Thompson, 1982: 203).

The adopted standards came from two sources. First, 45 percent of the standards came from two private standards-setting organizations, the American National Standards Institute and the National Fire Prevention Association. These standards were generally recommendations to business on accepted procedures in industry such as the number and location of fire extinguishers, construction of ladders, guarding of equipment, and the like. Second, the remaining standards were federal government safety standards for those firms with federal contracts in excess of $10,000; these standards were issued under the Walsh-Healy Act. The 4,400 standards covered 250 pages in the *Federal Register* and referred to numerous other documents that contained thousands of pages. The total volume of rules in practice, therefore, was overwhelming.

A careful review of the consensus standards would have revealed that wholesale adoption was a serious mistake. The standards were dated, were highly technical, and had serious gaps. The dated aspect of the standards was the most amusing. One regulation prohibited the use of ice in drinking water for employees; this standard survived from the days when ice was cut from the top of polluted lakes. The highly technical nature of the standards also created some problems. The standard for ladders was difficult to read without a degree in industrial engineering; 140 standards for ladders were included covering such topics as the types of wood that could be used and the thickness of each of the parts. Despite the volume and the technical detail, the consensus standards had some serious gaps. Almost all the standards dealt with workplace safety, with little attention paid to worker health (Harter, 1977: 35).

In an effort to establish a reputation as a stringent regulator, OSHA gave its inspectors little discretion in citing violations. A combination of silly rules and rigid enforcement was bound to generate controversy. Story after story surfaced about OSHA's citing business for broken toilet seats, failure to hang fire extinguishers an exact distance from the floor, and other violations that only remotely related to safety (see Nichols and Zeckhauser, 1981). In the process, OSHA's reputation was irreparably damaged.

As OSHA discovered its error of acting in haste, it also discovered that issuing rules was easier than repealing rules. To withdraw a rule, OSHA had to go through the elaborate rule-making process established by the Occupational Safety and Health Act even though the rules were issued without using this procedure. A few rules were corrected via this process in the early years of the agency, but little overall progress was made.

Under President Carter, Dr. Eula Bingham, a respected professor of occupational health, was appointed to head the agency. In December 1977, Bingham proposed to eliminate 1,100 consensus-standards rules (F. J. Thompson, 1982: 205). During the rule-making hearings, OSHA discovered that even ineffective rules gather supporters; organized labor strongly opposed the withdrawal process. The repeal hearings drew over 200 witnesses and filled three volumes. In October 1978, OSHA repealed 928 of the initial consensus standards and rewrote several others. The fire prevention standards, for example, were reduced from 400 pages (including those incorporated by reference) to 10 pages.

Although the Bingham-sponsored process corrected many problems with OSHA regulations, the agency received little credit. Critics continued to cite the old regulations as examples of abuse (see Nichols and Zeckhauser, 1981); both business and congressional critics intensified efforts to restrict OSHA. OSHA became in myth something far greater and more disruptive than it was in practice; the agency represented the symbol of overregulation to many businesses and the symbol of protection from occupational hazards to many unions. Neither view was especially accurate.

The record shows that OSHA can learn from its mistakes, however. An examination of early enforcement data showed that OSHA generally deserved its nit-picking image; from 1973 to 1976 over 98 percent of all OSHA citations were for nonserious violations. Only 2 percent of the citations were for serious, willful, and repeat violations. After 1977, however, the OSHA record improved. Although the agency issued fewer citations, more citations were for serious hazards. The number of citations for serious, willful, and repeat violations increased from 9,420 in 1976 to 31,245 in 1979 (Pettus, 1982: 600). The data show a clear reorientation in the priorities of OSHA safety inspection.

The Shift to Health Regulation

Stress on Safety.   In its early years, OSHA focused primarily on safety regulation to prevent accidents and on-the-job deaths. The initial consensus standards were almost exclusively safety standards. With few health standards on the books when the agency emphasized enforcement, it meant safety enforcement. Pettus (1982: 599) found that from 1973 to 1979, 95.4 percent of OSHA citations were issued for safety violations, and only 4.6 percent were for health violations. From 1972 to 1979 the proportion of the agency's budget devoted to the development of health standards ranged between three and seven percent (F. J. Thompson, 1982: 209).

The concentration on safety rather than health reflected the priorities of the individuals who supported the Occupational Safety and Health Act and OSHA's implementation of it. Other than for such problems as black lung, organized labor showed little concern for health issues. Occupational health, however, is a far more important concern. Ashford (1976), for example, estimated that 100,000 persons die annually from occupation-related diseases. This estimate is seven to ten times larger than the number of persons who die in industrial accidents.

Early Health Efforts.   Because OSHA's initial consensus standards contained few health-related rules and because the rule-making process was fairly cumbersome, progress on health regulation was slow. In 1972, OSHA issued its first health regulation, on exposure to asbestos. The year 1974 saw two rules, one governing several carcinogens and one governing vinyl chloride (see Doniger, 1978). A rule for coke was issued in 1976; and in 1978 six rules were issued covering arsenic, benzene, cotton dust, lead, acrylonitrile, and DBCP (Kelman, 1980: 246). Since 1978 no additional new health rules have been issued even though the National Institute of Occupational Safety and Health has identified 2,000 suspected carcinogens.

Rule making in the health area was gradual for two reasons other than the inherent slowness of the process. First, the scientific base needed to write rules was weak. OSHA rule making, similar to that of the EPA, is based on the theory that a dose-response curve exists that shows a relationship between exposure to a substance and subsequent development of a disease. Often the regulations established a threshold below which exposure to a substance is considered safe. Establishing thresholds and dose-response curves are difficult. Scientists are not permitted to experiment on human beings (with some exceptions), and ecological studies (e.g., nonexperimental field research) do not control for all the other causes of disease. As a result, information on toxicity is generalized from animal studies, and such generalizations are limited by differences between animals and human beings in both response and toxicity. In addition, little scientific evidence supports the view that thresholds exist below which exposure to a substance is safe.

Second, rule-making hearings were turned into an adversarial process by the coalitions representing business and labor. Business organizations generally pushed for weak standards or no standards, stressing the costs of compliance. Unions, on the other hand, argued that exposure standards should be set as low as possible. Both sides documented their position with scientific and economic data. OSHA generally followed a policy of trying to please both groups; the rule usually established a fairly stringent standard but allowed business a period of time to phase in compliance. The end result frequently pleased neither group; often both business and labor challenged the rule in court for different reasons.

A Change in Priorities.   The OSHA administrator Eula Bingham on May 19, 1977, announced that OSHA would change its policies to focus on health issues; in the same announcement, she noted that the original consensus safety standards would be reviewed (Harter, 1977: 39). Bingham's new priorities were reflected in both inspections and rule making. She increased the number of inspections focusing on health from 8 percent in 1976 to 19 percent in 1979 (Pettus, 1982: 601). The number of citations for serious, willful, and repeat health violations in the same time period quadrupled. In the rule-making area, Bingham initiated or hurried several rule-making procedures. As noted earlier, in 1978 six major health-related rules were issued, more than had been issued in OSHA's entire previous history.

The change in priorities, although welcomed by most observers of OSHA, was not without difficulties. Business and labor were no more in agreement on health standards than they were on safety standards. Both parties sought court intervention in the process; the success of one suit involving benzene (see later) called into question the entire decision-making process used by OSHA. Until this issue was resolved (in 1981), new health rules were held up; after resolution, priorities changed again with the Reagan administration. As an illustration of the difficulties in issuing health standards, the effort to establish a cotton dust standard will be briefly discussed.

Cotton Dust.   Exposure to cotton dust, an occupational hazard in the textile industry, has been linked to byssinosis, a lung disease. Evidence that cotton dust was related to disease was not new; as early as 1707 at least one observer noted a link (Yandle, 1982: 60). As part of OSHA's early rule making, a standard limiting exposure to no more than five milligrams per cubic meter was adopted (L. White, 1983). In 1974 new hearings began on cotton dust exposure; in 1976, OSHA gave formal notice of rule making.

During the rule-making hearings, over 105,000 pages of evidence were presented. The record showed that OSHA had a variety of regulatory options in dealing with cotton dust. Because early identification of the symptoms of byssinosis permits the disease to be reversed, policies such as medical screening and worker rotation were feasible. Businesses in general pressed for permission to limit exposure via respirators and personal safety gear (see Yandle, 1982: 61). Reflecting the professional values of OSHA employees (see earlier), the final rule opted for engineering standards to limit the total quantity of dust in the workplace.

During the hearings, the Clothing and Textile Workers Union argued for exposure to be limited as much as possible without considering costs. The textile industry was much concerned with the costs, however, because textiles were a declining industry able to survive only with protection from foreign imports (see Corn, 1981: 112). OSHA's review of medical evidence concluded that there was no threshold level below which exposure to cotton dust was safe.

OSHA issued its final rule in June 1978 with a stringent standard of 200 micrograms per cubic meter for yarn manufacturing and 750 micrograms for fabric manufacturing (L. White, 1983: 142) but permitted industry four years to comply. Before the standard was issued, Charles Schultze, chairman of the Council of Economic Advisors, attempted to delay the regulation via the regulatory review process. Appeals were made to get President Carter to intervene. After counterpressure from the Department of Labor and organized labor, President Carter permitted OSHA to issue the rule (Yandle, 1982).

The rule was immediately challenged in court by the Textile Manufacturers Association. In October 1978 the Court of Appeals stayed implementation of the rule. Evidence presented showed wide variance in estimates of the dangers. OSHA estimated the rule would affect 314,000 workers, prevent 35,000 cases of byssinosis, and cost $656 million; business claimed that the rule would affect 535,000 workers, prevent 3,000 cases of byssinosis, and cost $2.7 billion (Yandle, 1982: 63). The issue was whether or not OSHA had to consider costs in relation to benefits as an earlier decision (*Industrial Union Department* v. *American Petroleum Institute*) had implied; the Court of Appeals' stay was appealed to the Supreme Court.

The Supreme Court heard arguments on January 21, 1981. Because President Reagan had been inaugurated the previous day, the OSHA case was presented by holdovers from the Carter administration. The new administration (including the eventual OSHA head, Thorne Auchter) was a strong advocate of cost-benefit analysis and thus found itself in opposition to OSHA's position. The Reagan administration asked the Court to permit it to withdraw the case so that the cotton dust rule could be subjected to cost-benefit analysis. The Court declined the president's offer and ruled on the case in July 1981. The Court held that, when Congress wanted agencies to consider costs and benefits, Congress usually included such provisions in the enabling legislation. Because the law included no such requirement in this case, OSHA need not consider costs when issuing its regulations (see *American Textile Workers* v. *Donavan*, 1981).

The cotton dust issue was not settled with the Supreme Court decision. If we assume that the Reagan administration does not undertake a revision of the standard, industries still have four years from the time of the decision to comply. In addition, compliance with the standard can be determined only by inspections, an activity that was de-emphasized after 1981 (see further on).

A Comprehensive Health Policy.   Not only is the case-by-case approach to regulating health hazards slow; too many carcinogenic substances exist to regulate them effectively in this manner. If NIOSH's estimate of over 2,000 workplace carcinogens is correct, at the rate of 11 rules in the first decade of OSHA, total coverage would take centuries.

In 1980 to provide a more comprehensive approach, OSHA announced its cancer policy. The agency, based on scientific research, would classify suspected carcinogens into two groups. If conclusive evidence exists that a substance causes cancer, that substance would be placed in category I. Conclusive evidence consists of either one study linking the substance to cancer in human beings or one study revealing cancer in mammals if the mammalian study meets certain research design criteria. For any substance placed in category I, one of two actions will be taken. If a substitute for the substance exists, the use of the suspected substance will be banned. If no substitutes exist, exposure to the substance must be reduced to the lowest feasible level.

Category II includes all those substances for which tests show a suggestion of carcinogenicity. Substances in category II are subject to less restrictive standards to be determined on a case-by-case basis. In 1980, OSHA announced a list of 207 substances that would be evaluated for inclusion in category I or category II (AEI, 1981: 30).

Before the cancer policy could be implemented, the 1980 election changed presidents and, therefore, OSHA administrators. With an agency leadership more concerned about the burdens that regulation places on industry, a policy change in the cancer policy was announced in 1981. The clause requiring that category I carcinogens be reduced to the lowest feasible level was deleted. Such a deletion implied that cost factors would be considered in setting individual standards for category I substances. Actions implementing the cancer policy since 1981 have not been numerous.

THE POLITICS OF OSHA

Because the actions of OSHA are salient, political actors frequently intervene in the regulatory process to influence decisions. As both labor and business have strong ties to the political parties, when either one loses a regulatory battle, appeals to political officials are almost automatic. The actions of OSHA have been the subject of influence efforts by Congress, the president, and the courts.

Congress

Congress has served as the focal point for criticism of OSHA. When OSHA adopted rules or conducted inspections, it imposed costs on business. The heads of small and large businesses are often active in politics at the local level and are heavy contributors to election campaigns. As a general rule, such persons have access to members of Congress when they wish to complain about a regulatory agency.

Congress has been responsive to these complaints, both by providing a forum for criticism via hearings and by occasionally taking action. In 1977, Congress added a rider to the OSHA appropriations bill, exempting farms employing fewer than ten persons from OSHA regulations. The rider has been continued in subsequent years.

Numerous other proposals to limit OSHA's powers have also been considered. In the first six years of the agency, one hundred bills a year were introduced that would have restricted OSHA (Shaffer, 1977: 192). Generally, the bills proposed exemptions for small business or a legislative veto for OSHA rules. Although none of these bills passed, they did suggest to OSHA that policies needed to be changed. In a 1979 effort to respond to these demands, OSHA exempted small businesses with good safety records from some record-keeping requirements. OSHA estimated that 1.5 million businesses with 5 million employees were exempted by this policy.

Presidents

Presidents have been involved in OSHA policy only in a general sense. Every president since Gerald Ford has attempted to create a review system that would subject OSHA decisions to outside analysis. President Ford required inflationary impact analysis. President Carter required economic analysis of costs through his Regulatory Analysis Review Group and the Council on Wage and Price Stability. President Reagan required cost-benefit analysis by the Office of Management and Budget. In addition, incumbent presidents found OSHA useful during election campaigns; both Nixon in 1972 and Ford in 1976 denounced OSHA's "unjustified harassment of citizens" (Singer, 1976: 973).

In terms of actual personal involvement in the OSHA process, however, the record is less clear. Kelman (1980: 254) could find no evidence of direct presidential involvement in OSHA decision making prior to 1978.[3] In 1978 the Council of Economic Advisors chairman Charles Schultze, attempted to persuade Jimmy Carter to intervene on the cotton dust regulation. After lobbying by organized labor and Department of Labor political appointees, however, Carter supported the OSHA rule (Kelman, 1980: 262; see earlier).

The president's major impact on OSHA policies has been through the appointment process. Carter's appointment of Eula Bingham resulted in a reorientation of agency priorities from regulating safety to regulating health hazards. President Reagan's appointment of Thorne Auchter dramatically improved the relationship between OSHA and business (see further on). Kelman (1980: 263) recognized the president's ability to influence OSHA when he stated, "The most dramatic step a president could take to make OSHA responsive to his political views would be to appoint a head of the agency (say, an economist) who is strongly committed to changing agency decisions on regulations."

The Courts

To a degree rivaled only in environmental protection, losers in administrative battles on occupational safety and health seek court intervention. Every major health regulation except the first one (on asbestos) has been challenged in court—often by both business and labor. Although all the major health regulations except the benzene regulation were subsequently upheld by the courts, the actions of the court system have resulted in changed policies and procedures.

The Supreme Court served notice early that it would be involved. In 1974 an emergency rule regulating exposure of agricultural workers to pesticides was disallowed because OSHA failed to demonstrate an emergency existed (*Wall Street Journal*, August 20, 1974: 1). In *Atlas Roofing Company* v. *OSHRC* (1977), the method of assessing fines by OSHA was challenged as a violation of the constitutional requirement of trial by jury. The Supreme Court ruled that this constitutional provision did not apply to administrative fines. In *Marshall* v. *Barlow's* (1978), the Supreme Court held that OSHA inspectors could not inspect a plant without a warrant. Although this decision initially appeared devastating (because the law prohibited notice of inspections), in practice its impact was minor. Warrants were required only if businesses refused to admit inspectors, and only 1.5 percent of employers did so after the ruling (Job Safety, 1978: 13). In addition, warrants were easy to obtain because OSHA did not have to prove probable cause but only had to state that the inspection was part of its systematic inspection process.

More disrupting for the agency was the Supreme Court's decision on benzene (*Industrial Union Department* v. *American Petroleum Institute*). Medical studies showed that exposure to benzene in concentrations greater than 100 parts per million (ppm) was linked to leukemia. Although few valid data exist on lower levels of exposure, in 1978 OSHA reduced its benzene standard from 10 parts per million to 1 part per million. A federal

---

3. Intervention by other executive branch personnel, however, did occur. In 1977 the Department of Labor's Office of Policy, Evaluation, and Research blocked a noise exposure rule. The office argued that only rules with more benefits than costs could be approved.

Court of Appeals set aside the benzene regulation in 1978, holding that OSHA could not legally regulate benzene exposure without determining whether "the benefits expected from the standard bear a reasonable relationship to the costs imposed." The court's decision implied that OSHA regulations must yield benefits in excess of costs. The decision had a chilling effect on rule-making activity. No new health rules were issued after 1978, reflecting the uncertainty about their validity.

When the Supreme Court reviewed the benzene case, it failed to clarify the issue. The Supreme Court accepted the Circuit Court's decision but rejected its reasoning. Four of the five majority judges held that the rule was invalid because OSHA did not demonstrate that a one ppm standard was more beneficial than a ten ppm standard. Only one justice unambiguously supported cost-benefit analysis. The issue of cost-benefit analysis was resolved one year later in *American Textile Manufacturers* v. *Donavan* (1981), when the Court held that cost-benefit analysis was not required by the Occupational Safety and Health Act (see earlier). In combination, the benzene case and the cotton dust case established that OSHA must justify its regulations in terms of benefits but need not use cost-benefit analysis; the decisions do not prevent OSHA from using cost-benefit analysis if it so desires.

The OSHA situation clearly shows the advantage of delay in appealing to the courts. As the legal process unfolds, implementation of a regulation is delayed. Industry gains by delay alone because it gives the industry more time to conduct business without the additional costs imposed by the regulation. The cotton dust standard is a good example. Issued in 1978, it was delayed by the court suit until 1981; with a four-year phase-in period, the regulation would not become effective until 1985. Even without winning court cases, benefits can be gained.

Political Leadership

OSHA leadership has played a key role in the politics affecting the agency. The first OSHA administrator, George Guenther, recognized the political value of OSHA during the 1972 campaign. Guenther drafted a memo to the under secretary of labor, stating that OSHA would issue no controversial rules during the campaign and suggesting that OSHA was a good sales point for fund raising (*National Journal*, December 7, 1974: 1837). Guenther's lack of management caution in promulgating the early consensus standards was one reason why OSHA became a point for potential fund raising.

Guenther was not the only politically involved person to head OSHA. Morton Corn, the first OSHA head with professional qualifications, eventually resigned over the lack of political support for the agency. Both Eula Bingham and Thorne Auchter, although they disagree as to who OSHA's constituency is, have been more receptive to what they see as the political constituency of OSHA. By using this political support, both Bingham and Auchter were able to redirect OSHA policies.

THE REAGAN INITIATIVES

One of Ronald Reagan's issues in his quest for the presidency was the overregulation of American business. His transition teams were highly critical of the Carter administration's regulatory fervor and had several suggestions about limiting regulation. In general, Reagan appointed regulatory critics to head the regulatory agencies. OSHA was no exception; Thorne Auchter was named assistant secretary of labor for occupational safety and health.

In 1980, Auchter coordinated Florida political events for Reagan. His experience with OSHA was as an executive with his family-owned construction firm; one of his areas of responsibility was safety and health. In the early 1970s he had served on the committee that authored a Florida state OSHA implementation plan. Auchter's firm had been cited by OSHA 48 times for safety violations and fined $1,200.

Auchter's tenure affected both agency rule making and enforcement. First, in rule making, OSHA has not engaged in major innovations. Rules have been issued; some rules were strengthened; some were weakened; but the agency did not develop a reputation for aggressive rule making. Second, enforcement activities of OSHA were dramatically altered; Auchter wanted to eliminate OSHA's police officer image. Each of these efforts merits further discussion.

Rule Making

As discussed earlier, the rule-making process is fairly complex. Reducing the amount of regulation via withdrawing rules is a slow process that, given the inevitable court challenges, would provide few immediate benefits. Auchter's rule-making policy, therefore, has not been a wholesale elimination but rather an unhurried look at minor rules.

Initially, the Auchter OSHA appeared to favor weaker standards than the Bingham agency. In 1981, OSHA changed its cancer policy (see earlier); category I carcinogens (those that were confirmed causes of cancer) would not automatically have to be reduced to the lowest feasible level (Kosters, 1982). Levels would be established on a case-by-case basis. Also in 1982, OSHA withdrew the walk-around rule that required firms to pay for the time of union representatives who accompanied OSHA inspectors during walk-around inspections. In July 1982 the agency restricted workers' access to medical and safety records. In March 1983, OSHA issued its rule on worker exposure to noise, a rule held over from the Carter administration. Essentially, the noise rule reduced the amount of testing and the number of warning signs required in order to lower the costs imposed on business.

Although these actions were praised by business and condemned by labor, the record of the Auchter OSHA was not so clear-cut. In 1981 the lead exposure level was reduced by 75 percent (Kosters, 1982). Auchter also took an active role in pressing OMB to release an OSHA regulation on the labeling of hazardous chemicals (Wines, 1983k: 2012). In 1983 a newly revised asbestos rule surprised many people when it established a stricter exposure standard (Wines, 1983k: 2008). In April, OSHA announced it would reissue the benzene rule with a lower exposure limit than currently on the books.

Auchter's mixed record on rule making has been attributed to two factors. First, Auchter is conceded to be a good manager and a fairly good political infighter. One White House official attributed Auchter's occasional willingness to press for stronger rules to his management background: "[H]e was a construction executive in a family-owned firm. In that sort of situation, when you're the boss, you're the boss" (cited in Wines, 1983k: 2012). Second, others attribute Auchter's actions to congressional criticism and the example of Anne Burford. The asbestos rule was issued shortly after a critical congressional hearing. Congressman David Obey has been especially critical of OSHA; he condemned the agency for failing to issue emergency regulations on EDB and ethylene oxide even though both substances met the criteria for emergency regulations and the courts had ordered OSHA to issue an ethylene oxide regulation (Wines, 1983k: 2011).

Enforcement

Thorne Auchter's greatest impact has been in enforcement. First, OSHA changed its policies for determining which firms to inspect. OSHA exempted all industries with a lost workday rate due to injuries below the national average. Individual firms in high-risk industries were also exempted if they had a low lost workday rate. This policy exempts some three-fourths of the businesses in the United States from OSHA inspection (Wines, 1983k: 2009; Viscusi, 1982: 34). The remaining fourth accounts for nearly 75 percent of all worker injuries.

The priority system was widely criticized. By using average workdays lost for an entire industry, an unsafe firm within a safe industry would avoid inspection. In addition, injury data collected by industry is highly suspect; many injuries are not reported, or injured workers are required to report to work even though no work is assigned (L. White, 1983). Injury data calculations are also based on total employment, so that firms with large white-collar employment often can have unsafe manufacturing plants and a low injury rate. Perhaps most important, using injuries as the criterion for inspection downplays those industries with health problems because injury rates reflect safety problems only. Economist W. Kip Viscusi (1983: 23) argued that the injury rate criterion was misguided; a frequent critic of OSHA, Viscusi argued that inspections should be targeted on the basis of the risks involved and the degree of hazard. Injury rates do not reflect either of these phenomena.

Second, the emphasis was changed to rely on voluntary industry cooperation (Wines, 1983k: 2009). An increase in consulting visits reflected this policy. Consulting visits are designed to advise firms on how to comply with the law; citations are not issued during such a visit. The number of consulting visits increased from 22,000 in 1980 to 28,000 in 1982. OSHA regional directors were instructed to make inspections less confrontational and were told that they would be evaluated negatively if the number of contested violations was large. Contested violations dropped from 22 percent in Bingham's last year to 5 percent in 1982. Clearly, inspections were less confrontational than in previous years (according to critics, this indicated less vigorous regulation).

Third, the level of enforcement was reduced. In two years the number of OSHA inspectors dropped 26 percent from 1,328 to 981 (Wines, 1983k). In 1982 (compared to 1980, the last year of the Carter administration), the number of citations for violations dropped 22 percent, citations for serious violations dropped 47 percent, citations for willful violations dropped 90 percent, and citations for repeat offenses dropped 64 percent. Total fines levied dropped 69 percent to $5.8 million (Wines, 1983k: 2013). In health areas, the record was even less active. Regarding testing for compliance with the asbestos standard, the number of tests dropped from 8,606 to 2,636. Citations in the area dropped by 60 percent and fines by 76 percent.

Similar to some other regulatory areas, then, the area of occupational safety and health has seen significant efforts to deregulate. The deregulation, however, has not eliminated regulations; to the extent that OSHA regulations have been pruned, that process occurred under Bingham. Deregulation for the Auchter OSHA has been a deregulation of enforcement, a reduction in the amount of enforcement activity, and a reliance on voluntary compliance.

Although OSHA's enforcement policy was widely criticized, Thorne Auchter argued that the policy had a major impact on worker safety. As evidence, Auchter cited a decline in workdays lost due to injury; the figure dropped from 5.9 days per 100 workers in 1979 to 4.7 in 1983 (Glen and Shearer, 1984: 9). These raw figures, however, also reflect the decline in injuries normally associated with economic recession (see Viscusi, 1983).

EVALUATING OSHA POLICY

OSHA's activities have frequently been denounced as both costly and ineffective by critics. Given organized labor's support for the agency, this view is hardly unanimous. In the decade and one-half since the creation of OSHA, several scholars have examined the effectiveness of OSHA regulations. These studies can be divided into studies of enforcement and studies of impact.

Enforcement

Even before the Reagan administration, the enforcement of OSHA standards was considered weak. The criticisms of the enforcement efforts included these: (1) Few firms are ever inspected, (2) firms that are inspected are cited for minor violations, (3) inspectors do not find major health problems, and (4) the size of the fines is trivial.

Few Inspections.   With at most 1,500 federal inspectors (at OSHA's peak) supplemented by a similar number of state inspectors, many firms will avoid inspection. According to Robert Stewart Smith (1976: 62), "Only 1.3 percent of all covered plants were inspected in fiscal year 1973, implying the typical establishment will see an OSHA inspector once every seventy-seven years, about as often as we see Halley's Comet." OSHA recognized that the agency would not be given sufficient resources to inspect all workplaces, so it established a system of inspection priorities from the beginning. In May 1971, OSHA targeted the longshoring, roofing and sheet metal, meat, lumbering, and miscellaneous transportation equipment industries for closer inspection because the accident rates in these industries were high (Smith, 1976: 67). Within these industries, larger firms were inspected before smaller firms (Pettus, 1982: 599). Despite targeting, resources were still inadequate; only 23 percent of firms found in violation of the regulations were reinspected later.

Trivial Violations.   The violations found in the rare inspections of industry were often viewed as trivial. Initially, OSHA inspectors were given little discretion and were required to cite every violation. From 1973 to 1976, for example, the number of serious, willful, or repeat violations never exceeded 3 percent in any one year. In other words, 97 percent of OSHA citations were for violations that posed little danger to workers.

This focus on minor matters gave rise to the view that OSHA was citing industries for "Mickey Mouse" violations such as broken toilet seats. Some progress was made to correct this focus under the administration of Eula Bingham. By reducing the number of trivial citations, Bingham increased the proportion of citations for serious, willful, and repeat violations to 37 percent by 1980; the total number of citations issued for such violations increased by a factor of five (F. J. Thompson, 1982: 204). Unfortunately, the proportion of citations for serious, willful, or repeat violations dropped back to 22 percent in 1982 (Wines, 1983k: 2013).

Safety Emphasis.   Inspectors were initially drawn from the ranks of safety engineers and, as a result, were better trained to detect safety violations than health violations. Smith (1976: 33) estimated that the agency spent four to five times more on safety regulation than on health regulation; in 1974 the agency inspected 100 percent of the targeted industries for safety violations but only 5 percent for health violations.

Again, this emphasis changed in 1977 with the arrival of Eula Bingham. The proportion of inspections devoted to health increased from 8 percent in 1976 to 15 percent in 1977 and 19 percent in 1979 (Viscusi, 1983: 18). Although the safety program still dwarfs the health program, some progress was made in changing the priorities.

Minor Penalties.   Although the record on inspections is not positive, OSHA's record on penalties is even worse. In the agency's first three years, the average fine for a serious violation was $600, and the average fine for a nonserious violation was $25 (Harter, 1977: 37). By 1979 the average fine for serious violations had dropped to $495; and the fine for nonserious violation to $2.84 (reflecting the de-emphasis on trivial violations).

Such minor fines can hardly be an incentive to business to correct problems. Rather, after an OSHA inspector raises the level of anxiety of management and disrupts the operation of the plant for a day, a small fine is more likely to anger businesspeople than motivate them to change. Even when serious violations are found, fines can be trivial. OSHA fined a West Virginia firm $108,000 when a cooling tower collapsed, killing 51 workers, approximately $2,000 per death. Even the largest fine levied to date, $786,190 against Newport News Shipbuilding and Dry Dock Company, amounts to only $34 per worker (Viscusi, 1983: 24). The trivial nature of these fines to a large corporation, however, is not totally OSHA's fault. The size of fines per violation is limited by law, and OSHRC often reduces the fines.

In combination, all these factors indicate that OSHA enforcement can be characterized as weak. Viscusi (1983: 24) estimates that the average firm today has 1 chance in 100 of being inspected (down from Smith's Halley's Comet estimate). The average inspection finds 2.1 violations. The fine is approximately $193 for each. The total expected cost of an OSHA inspection, then, is about 34 cents per worker—not an amount large enough to encourage businesses to change behavior.

Impact

Given the weak enforcement level of the Occupational Safety and Health Act, the impact of OSHA on occupational safety and health cannot be great. Although several scholars have attempted to estimate the OSHA's impact, any efforts to evaluate the program comprehensively are limited by three data problems. First, data on the impact of health regulations are nonexistent because occupational diseases have long latency periods. It may be decades before the impact of health regulations is reflected in occupational death rates; in addition, death rates are a poor indicator of occupational health impact because several other factors also affect the rates. Nichols and Zeckhauser (1981: 216) note that the impact of health regulations may never be resolved. Second, plant-by-plant data are not available (Viscusi, 1983: 85); as a result, industrywide data that lump safe plants together with dangerous plants must be used. Third, in 1971 the Bureau of Labor Statistics changed the definitions of workplace injuries and accidents; data before 1970, therefore, are not comparable to data after 1971. Unfortunately, the change in definition occurred at the same time as the creation of OSHA, thus confounding any evaluation with measurement error.

Two widely cited studies of OSHA show little impact of occupational safety regulation. Mendeloff (1979) compared pre- and post-OSHA injury rates and found no difference between them. Viscusi (1982) found no relationship between the amount of inspection, the size of penalties levied, and the injury rate for 61 industries. Both these studies have serious data flaws. Mendeloff is essentially comparing data under two different definitions, and Viscusi has eliminated any firm-specific as opposed to industry-specific impacts of OSHA and does not recognize that firms might be inspected because they have high injury rates. In a simpler study, Nichols and Zeckhauser (1981) examined post-OSHA data only; they found that from 1972 to 1978 injuries declined by 13.8 percent but that workdays lost rose by 24.2 percent. Because both injuries and workdays are affected by numerous other variables such as the state of the economy and the experience of the workers, simple comparisons such as these have little value.

A few other studies have attempted to disaggregate accident data, and these studies showed positive, but modest impacts. By examining the types of accidents most likely to be affected by OSHA regulations such as accidents involving people caught in machinery, Mendeloff (1979: 117) found a 30 percent reduction. This translates into an overall reduction of from 2 to 3 percent in all accidents. Smith (1979) found a 16 percent reduction in injury rates in plants that had been inspected in 1973 and a 5 percent reduction for those inspected in 1974. The impact was greater in smaller plants. Even though these studies found small, but positive results, they have many of the same data problems that plague the other studies.

At a theoretical level with perfect enforcement, the amount of reduction in accidents and injuries that occupational safety and health regulation could reduce is open to question. The National Safety Council (cited in Nichols and Zeckhauser, 1981: 115) found that 19 percent of industrial accidents were the result of human causes, 18 percent were the result of environmental causes (such as unsafe working conditions), and 63 percent were the result of both human and environmental causes. They estimated that perhaps only 25 percent of all industrial accidents were preventable. Bailey (1980: 7), in fact, argues that little more can be done to eliminate on-the-job accidents.

Both the potential impact of OSHA and the actual impact of OSHA are still empirical questions. The data problems in the area are so severe that we may never know if regulation improves safety. In occupational health, both the nature of occupational diseases and limitations of data have prevented any studies to date. To conclude that OSHA has been ineffective or effective would be premature.

CURRENT POLITICAL ISSUES

Similar to many other areas of regulation, new issues in occupational safety and health develop faster than old issues are resolved. Five current issues in addition to those discussed earlier are shaping the debate over ocupational safety and health regulation. These issues are the effectiveness of state-run programs, the impact of OSHA on small business, the use of higher wages to compensate workers for risky jobs, the possibility of an injury tax, and the overall benefits and costs of OSHA. Each will be discussed in turn.

State-Run Programs

Under the Occupational Safety and Health Act, states may opt to administer the law if the state program is "at least as effective" as the federal program. States wanting to operate their own programs must have plans for doing so approved by OSHA; OSHA then provides a grant equivalent to 50 percent of the operating costs. Although the exact number of states operating mini-OSHAs varies somewhat, approximately half the states chose to implement their own programs.

A potential problem with state-operated programs is that states have incentives to engage in limited regulation of occupational safety and health. Such regulations impose costs on business and in extreme cases might eliminate the marginal revenues necessary to operate the firm. Because states want to attract and keep industry, Rowland and Marz (1982) argue that a process they call Gresham's law of regulation will occur. States with lax regulation will attract industry from states with stringent regulation; as a result, states will compete to have lax regulation and attract business. Because the federal government has no incentive to regulate one state differently from the others, the Gresham's law analogy implies that federal regulation will be more stringent than state regulation.[4]

In an analysis comparing 22 state OSHA programs with the federal program operated in 28 states, Marvel (1982: 21) found that the federal

---

4. There are exceptions to Gresham's law in terms of the hypothesis that state regulation will be less stringent than federal regulation. Air pollution programs operated by the state of California have always been more stringent than the federal program; in fact, the law is written to permit California to do this.

program held more inspections, found more violations, issued more citations, and levied greater penalties. The differences were major; in 1978 the penalties were 10 times larger in federally regulated states. These statistically significant findings hold even when the industrialization of the state is controlled.

As another indicator that state regulation is more accommodating to industry than federal regulation, Marvel (1982: 26) found that more federal citations are contested than are state citations. In addition, in states where a larger proportion of the state population is employed in manufacturing (i.e., the businesses regulated by OSHA), states generally conduct fewer inspections. The federal government, on the other hand, conducts more inspections in states where manufacturing is a larger part of the economy.

Such behavior on the part of states has some impact. Later research (Marvel, 1983) showed that states operating their own programs were able to attract new investment. These states had faster industrial growth rates than those states with federal programs; they also had slightly higher industrial accident rates. Such differences are likely to increase; under Thorne Auchter, OSHA removed federal inspectors completely from 21 states that operated their own occupational safety and health programs, thus eliminating any federal check on state administration (Wines, 1983k: 2009).

Impact on Small Business

Small business has been especially critical of OSHA; legislation to grant small firms relief from OSHA regulation has been introduced in every session of Congress since 1970. Small business claims that OSHA regulations are especially burdensome to plants with limited capital. One reason for this apparent bias, however, may well be the safety record of larger business. Larger firms are generally unionized and as a result are pressed by their unions to improve on-the-job safety. Consequently, large firms are safer places to work than are small firms (Butler, 1983: 73). In addition, the fixed costs of safety or health investment can be spread over more output in a large business than in a small one. OSHA regulations, therefore, may appear more burdensome to small business because large businesses have already made some safety investments and because the relative investment is larger for a smaller firm.

Although systematic data on impact is limited, a study by Pettus (1982: 601) showed that OSHA imposed larger costs on large businesses than on small ones. Establishments with ten or fewer employees had 37 percent of the inspections in 1976, but only 29 percent in 1979. In 1979 less than 0.8 percent of small businesses were inspected by OSHA. Of the far more costly health inspections, more than seven times as many large businesses were inspected as small businesses (reflecting the agency's priority system that inspected larger firms first). In no year did more than 1,330 of the nation's 2.2 million small businesses receive a health inspection visit from OSHA. Although an inspected small business may feel persecuted by OSHA, overall, small business has had little contact with OSHA.

Risk-Based Wages

Some economists argue that government safety regulation duplicates a process that is handled by the free market. Recognizing that some hazardous occupations such as stunt performers are paid fairly well, these economists propose that hazardous jobs in general have to pay more to attract workers. The solution to workplace hazards, therefore, is to provide information concerning the hazards associated with various occupations and let individual workers make the trade-off between higher wages and safety. In theory, employers will make safety improvements if the marginal costs of safety measures are less than the marginal costs of risk-based wages.

The topic of risk-based wages has received some empirical analysis. Bailey (1980: 36) noted that workers in hazardous jobs were paid less than workers in safe jobs, but that this was a function of the low skill levels of workers in hazardous jobs. To control for such variables as skills, age, education, and union membership, elaborate multiple regression models are used to estimate the additional wages paid for high-risk occupations. Using such techniques, Smith (1976: 30) found that wages were 1.5 percent higher in occupations where the risk of on-the-job death was doubled. Leigh (1981: 776), in two separate estimates, found wage premiums of 2.2 percent and 0.8 percent for a doubling of risk (see also Leigh, 1984). Leigh found no impact for occupational disease. Occupational disease impacts are difficult to find because mortality rates for various occupations are affected by numerous variables other than exposure to health hazards; one of the occupations with a high mortality rate, for example, is short-order cooks, not one of the more hazardous occupations.

Other studies have attempted to measure risk premiums in other ways; Viscusi (1983: 44) compared wages of persons who perceived that their job was dangerous with those who did not and found that the former were paid $925 more per year. Although this amount is small at the individual level (45 cents per hour), when aggregated, it totals $2 million per industrial death or about $69 billion economywide.

These findings on risk-based premiums are statistically significant but substantively trivial. If we take the Smith estimate, a worker earning $15,000 per year in an occupation with the mean death rate of 24 per 100,000 would earn $225 more a year than a person working in an occupation with 12 deaths per 100,000 (about the national average). This risk-based premium translates to approximately 11 cents an hour, hardly an incentive to increase risk to life. Smith (1976: 31) argues that differentials need not be large because the incentive operates for the marginal worker only. This assumes that a worker can rationally assess risk probabilities of 0.00012 versus 0.00024, however; and studies show that most individuals have difficulty making decisions based on low probability events (see Nichols and Zeckhauser, 1981: 207). As Viscusi (1983: 107) notes, "a typical worker in a hazardous occupation does not receive enough additional remuneration to be obvious to the casual observer."

These studies show that a worker in a hazardous occupation would be far better off unionizing the plant than seeking direct compensation for on-the-job hazards. Viscusi (1983: 55) found that the presence of a union in a plant doubled the rise in salary associated with risk. In fact, unions per se have a far greater impact on wages than any risk premium; Leigh (1981: 776) found that unions had from 10 times to 300 times greater impact on wages than did job hazard premiums.

One reason for skepticism concerning the use of risk-based wages to compensate for safety dangers (other than the trivial amount of the increase) is that these studies have methodological problems so serious that the findings may not be valid. In general, these studies use survey data that cut across a variety of industries. Because industry-specific factors are difficult to control, a more valid study would focus on a single industry to determine if unsafe plants pay higher wages than safe plants. In addition, the entire concept of controlling for age, education, unionization, and other factors may be inappropriate. These studies tell the worker in a hazardous job that he or she is paid more than other persons with similar skills in similar plants; they do not tell the worker that he or she is actually paid less than workers in safer plants (such plants tend to be unionized, have more experienced workers, have better educated workers, and so on). *In an artificial statistical sense, therefore, a worker in an unsafe plant is paid better, but in terms of money in the pay envelope that worker is paid less.*

Finally, whether or not labor would respond to such small incentives to undertake risky jobs is open to question. In a theoretical world, incentives would create a response because moves between jobs are assumed to be costless. In the real world, changing jobs is never costless; a move might reduce seniority and its wage incentives; and if relocation is required, additional costs must be incurred. In addition, in a small town with a textile mill, the choice might not be between working in a safe plant and an unsafe plant but between working in an unsafe plant and not working at all.

The Injury Tax

Another incentives-based reform of occupational safety is Robert Stewart Smith's (1974) proposal for an injury tax. Because OSHA fines are so small that they create no incentives to correct workplace dangers, Smith proposes a direct tax on workplace injuries. Whenever a worker in plant A is injured, plant A would have to pay a fine directly to the government. Smith estimated that a tax of $4,000 per injury would end up reducing injuries by 16.3 percent.

Smith's proposal is interesting and might be part of an overall program to combat occupational health and safety problems (see further on). Two administrative obstacles, however, would need to be corrected before such a system could be used. First, injury rates are conceded to be fairly inaccurate; plants have incentives to underreport injuries to avoid increases in workers' compensation insurance. A fairly large bureaucracy would be needed to monitor injuries, or some reliable system of reporting would be needed. Second, unless the tax would be placed fairly high, it would not create any incentives to improve plant safety. Only if injury taxes exceeded the needed investment in safety would a plant choose to correct safety problems. A low tax would reverse current policy that is designed to be preventative rather than compensatory.[5]

Costs and Benefits

Whether or not OSHA generates greater benefits than costs has been an issue just as it has in environmental regulation and consumer protection. Although OSHA itself does not do cost-benefit analysis and it is not re-

---

5. The political problems of adopting an injury tax merit some discussion. Passing such a law would be close to impossible. Even minor incentives-based pollution policies such as bubbles have been heavily criticized. Getting unions to accept what they would term "licenses to maim" and getting businesses to accept the stiff penalties necessary to provide any incentives would be a difficult political task.

quired to do so (see the cotton dust case earlier), its regulations have not been free from such analysis. OSHA is located in the Department of Labor. Because it is not an independent agency, its actions are subject to review at the presidential level and are governed by the numerous executive orders issued concerning regulation. Outside organizations have subjected OSHA regulations to analysis since at least 1974 under President Ford's inflation impact program. Currently, OSHA regulations must be cleared through the Office of Management and Budget, an organization that performs some limted cost-benefit analysis.

Cost-benefit analysis in regard to OSHA has been controversial and difficult to do because all the benefits of OSHA policies are incommensurable. That is, the benefits of OSHA, injuries prevented and lives saved, are benefits that cannot be purchased in the market; none of the attempts to place a value on human life or human health has been satisfactory (see M. S. Thompson, 1980). To circumvent this problem, Thorne Auchter advocated cost-effectiveness analysis whereby different standards are contrasted in terms of the costs required to save an individual life.

Even the cost side of OSHA is subject to dispute. The best cost data belong to industry, but industry has an incentive to overestimate OSHA compliance costs. For example, when OSHA reduced the exposure standard for vinyl chloride in 1974 from 500 ppm to 1 ppm, industry estimated that the standard would shut down the polyvinyl chloride industry and severely damage the plastics industry. The loss to gross national product was estimated at between $65 and $90 billion with 1.7 to 2.2 million jobs lost. The actual total costs were $250 million (a price increase of 6 percent), and few jobs were lost (Greer, 1983: 451).

With questionable cost estimates and no accepted technique to estimate benefits, cost-benefit ratios for OSHA regulations have varied greatly. Mendeloff (1979: 188) found that the 1972 asbestos standard produced 72 different cost-benefit ratios, some with more benefits than costs and others with more costs than benefits.

Estimates of the total costs imposed by OSHA have not been large. Mendeloff (1979) found that the total annual costs that OSHA imposed on industry ranged between $.5 billion and $2.5 billion. According to Pettus (1982: 612), "In the first decade, inspection costs and costs of compliance with OSHA regulations, even in health, apparently have not been heavy, despite the body of rhetoric to the contrary." Good cost-benefit analysis might prevent some of the more extreme claims made about OSHA regulations; unfortunately, quality studies are limited by both biased cost estimates and inability to estimate benefits.

A COMBINATION REFORM

Given OSHA's limited impact and the problems with such alternatives as risk-based wages and cost-benefit analysis, is it possible to design an occupational safety and health system that will produce greater protection for workers? If elements proposed by a variety of others are combined, a reform can be designed that encompasses two major changes—eliminating the responsibility for occupational safety from OSHA jurisdiction and refocusing the agency on occupational health.

From an economic standpoint, when occupational hazards exist, the price of goods does not reflect their true social cost because the costs of injuries and deaths on the job are not included. OSHA's impact on overall worker safety in the United States has been at best modest because the agency lacks sufficient inspectors, the fines for violations are trivial, and regulations do not cover all safety hazards. In addition, OSHA itself has become an issue; the mere mention of the name generates resistance. The prospects for improving worker safety would be better if a new agency and a new policy approach were established.

A policy on worker safety must both compensate workers for injuries and at the same time generate efforts to prevent workplace accidents. Workers' compensation (see earlier) has several limitations as a compensation device, including delays, high administrative costs, and inadequate benefits. The workers' compensation system should be taken over by a federal government corporation. State-operated systems, in general, have lower premiums and pay higher benefits to workers than insurance systems privately operated. To guarantee uniformity in the application of the system, a federal program is a necessity. Included in the changes from the current system would be making benefits retroactive with interest to the claim date to avoid court appeals that serve only to delay benefits and also making the administrative determination in terms of benefits and facts final, limiting judicial appeals to questions of law only. Preferably, decisions on individual cases would be made by arbitration rather than by adjudication.

The federal workers' compensation system would be funded by an insurance premium based on the safety record of the individual firm. The agency would require some nonarbitrators on the staff to insure that publicity about the program is widespread and to monitor the plants to guarantee that all injuries are reported. State occupational safety agencies could continue doing what most of them do now, offering consulting services to industries on how to improve their plant safety.

If some incentive for preventing injuries other than just low insurance premiums is to be provided, Robert Smith's injury tax should be implemented. Clearly, such a tax needs to be fairly high to work. If 25 percent of workplace accidents are preventable, extrapolating Smith's data suggests a tax in the neighborhood of $6,000 to $8,000 per injury (in 1974 dollars). Actually, a scale based on the severity of the injury and the preventability of the injury should be established; the economics profession could easily figure out a system such that prevention is always preferable to paying injury taxes. Taxes should be mandatory with no appeal; the taxes would be paid into the workers' compensation fund. Although using both insurance and taxes penalizes firms doubly for accidents, a large incentive is necessary so that businesses both alter workplace environments and offer incentives to employees to improve their own safety records.

OSHA should be merged with the National Institute of Occupational Safety and Health, and the new agency should be called something like the Workplace Health Agency. The major problem in occupational health is the lack of data on the effects of hazards. The new agency would operate under general standards such as the 1980 Cancer Policy adopted by OSHA, but the research component needs to be expanded dramatically; increasing the NIOSH budget by a factor of ten would be a start. In addition, the new agency should take responsibility for its own regulations by also sponsoring research on alternative methods of complying with health exposure standards, including new equipment designs. Occupational health problems are responsible for far more deaths annually than are safety problems; the regulatory efforts of the federal government should be focused there. Such an emphasis implies a larger budget commitment, but even increasing the OSHA budget by a factor of ten results in a budget of less than $3 billion.

CONCLUSION

Who benefits from occupational safety and health regulation? If an effective program of regulation existed in the United States, workers would benefit greatly, and industry would absorb some of the costs. The impact on industry would not be all negative, however, for effective regulation would reduce workers' compensation insurance premiums and possibly even avoid situations like that of the Manville Corporation, where suits for asbestos exposure will exceed the net worth of the company. Because the current policy is far from effective (limited by minor penalties and a lack of funding), an assessment of who benefits is more difficult. The safest conclusion is that workers benefit a small amount (especially workers in nonunion plants who lack bargaining power over safety issues) and industry bears a small cost.

The reasons why occupational safety and health regulation benefits labor rather than industry can be directly tied to two variables, the environment of the agency and the values of the agency employees (see Table 8.1).

Table 8.1 A Summary of Occupational Safety and Health Regulation

Economy	
Ease of entry	Varies
Number of firms	Varies
Profits	Vary
Technology	
Complexity	Varies
Stability	Varies
Substitutes	Vary
Subsystem	
Bureaucratic control	Weak
Industry coalition	Strong
Nonindustry coalition	Strong
Bureaucratic resources	
Expertise	Weak
Cohesion	Moderate
Leadership	Weak/Moderate
Legislative authority	
Goals	General
Coverage	Universal
Sanctions	Poor
Procedures	Fair
Involvement of Macropolitical Actors	
Congress	Strong
President	Moderate
Courts	Moderate

See Appendix.

Located in the Department of Labor, OSHA is in an environment that supports policies favorable to organized labor. Although this support is greatest in Democratic administrations, it remains in Republican administrations. If the agency were located in the Department of Commerce, OSHA would probably be a far different regulator. In addition, agency employees have incorporated the values of the safety engineering and industrial hygienist professions. Their orientation is to protect workers even if protection requires that industry spend large amounts of money to do so.

Even though OSHA may be predisposed to favor labor, it lacks the resources to impose its policies on the regulatory subsystem. OSHA has failed to develop a high level of expertise; it lacks sufficient resources for its assigned duties and has few effective sanctions. Although recent agency leadership has been fair, generally an absense of strong leadership has hurt the agency.

The actions of OSHA are highly salient; for any proposal, highly organized advocacy coalitions will both support and oppose it. Consequently, OSHA cannot dominate politics even within the subsystem. OSHA politics has become institutionalized as labor-management politics. As a result of the high salience, outside political elites have frequently intervened in the regulatory subsystem. The past three presidents have designed systems to monitor OSHA rules. President Carter and President Reagan both appointed individuals who fundamentally changed OSHA policies. Congress, in turn, has stressed continual oversight; hearings before 1980 were forums to criticize agency actions; some hearings after 1981 were used to criticize the enforcement policies of Thorne Auchter. Finally, courts are as active in this area as they are in any regulatory area other than those where courts serve as the decisionmaker (e.g., antitrust). Agency decisions will be subjected to court scrutiny via appeals from the coalition that loses in front of the agency.

Although the salience of occupational safety and health is generally high, the salience will vary with variations in the economy. Both for the entire economy and for individual industries, salience will increase as the economy slows down. A sluggish economy means that firms will have fewer discretionary funds and will likely resist any regulatory attempts to impose greater costs. When the economy is robust, however, safety and health costs are easier to absorb.

9

Antitrust Policy

Antitrust policy is fairly unique to the United States and its market economy. Antitrust is both a regulatory policy and an alternative to regulation. One portion of antitrust law provides the rules for "fair competition" and, thus, is similar to other regulatory policies that restrict individual choice. Another portion of antitrust is directed at monopolies and, therefore, is proposed by some as an alternative to regulation (e.g., Kohlmeier, 1969).

Because antitrust is a hybrid policy covering most of the economy rather than specific industries, this chapter will be organized differently from the others. Commonly used variables such as technology, profits, number of firms, and so on, vary by industry and are used in judicial determinations of antitrust decisions. Because many industries are involved, an extended discussion of these specific environmental variables will not be included. Rather, this chapter will briefly introduce the regulatory subsystem, note the economic underpinnings of antitrust, and discuss the laws and political goals of antitrust. With this introductory base, the five major areas of antitrust policy—monopoly, collusion, mergers, price discrimination, and exclusionary practices will be discussed. Finally, an extended discussion of the merits of antitrust will conclude the chapter.

THE SUBSYSTEM

The Agencies

Antitrust regulation is handled in a variety of different ways. The Antitrust Division of the Department of Justice has authority over both the civil and criminal aspects of antitrust law. Under the criminal provisions of the law, the Antitrust Division has grand jury powers to investigate possible violations of antitrust laws. If violations are found, the division files suit in a federal district court. Federal district court tries the case on its merits with appeals on questions of law to the Circuit Court and the Supreme Court. In most criminal cases, the Antitrust Division negotiates a plea rather than going through the lengthy process of a trial. Some 87 percent of all cases won by the division result from nolo contendere pleas or no contest pleas by the industry. Nolo pleas are often attractive to the defendant because private parties can file civil suits under the law (see later).

Under its civil authority, the Antitrust Division can sue a firm for the damages that it caused by violating the antitrust laws. Often the government files both civil and criminal suits because the government can appeal a civil suit lost in district court but cannot appeal a criminal case it has lost. Again, civil suits are usually negotiated by a consent decree whereby the company does not admit any guilt but agrees to avoid certain behavior in the future. Some 90 percent of all civil cases are resolved through consent decrees (Posner, 1970: 375). In 1985 the Antitrust Division had a budget of $44.5 million (a 9 percent decrease from 1980) and 740 employees.

The Antitrust Division shares its civil authority with the Federal Trade Commission. Unlike the Antitrust Division's procedures, the FTC's procedures are administrative. Antitrust cases are tried before an administrative law judge. If a violation is found, the administrative law judge can issue a cease and desist order (the administrative equivalent of an injunction). The decision of the administrative law judge can be appealed to the full Federal Trade Commission and from there to the courts on questions of law. The FTC can also negotiate consent orders whereby a company does not admit guilt but agrees not to commit certain acts in the future.

A major advantage of the FTC over the Antitrust Division is that the FTC has the authority to issue rules. These trade regulation rules have the force of law and can be issued by the FTC by following the rule-making procedures of the Magnuson-Moss Act. In theory, this permits the FTC to be preventative rather than waiting for violations to occur. In FY 1985 the FTC's budget was $67 million (a 2 percent increase from 1980) with 1,300 employees.

Both the Antitrust Division and the FTC have some resources at their disposal. Neither agency has developed a reputation for expertise because antitrust lawyers do not make government a career. The normal career pattern for an antitrust lawyer is a few years in government and then a private practice in antitrust law (Weaver, 1977; Katzman, 1980). Recently, the agencies have developed some economic expertise so that overall expertise must be rated as moderate. With the exception of a few aggressive antitrust heads such as Thurman Arnold and William Baxter, leadership has been average. Consistent with these variables, cohesion in the Antitrust Division is low; in the FTC, cohesion is higher, but this is a function of its consumer protection functions.

A potential agency resource is the salience of antitrust. Antitrust is a sporadically salient issue. The merger of large corporations, for example, is highly salient, often making headlines for weeks. At other times, antitrust policy is rarely noticed. Legislative authority, on the other hand, is weak for a regulatory agency. Legislative goals are vague and in conflict (see later). Coverage is limited because the agencies share antitrust authority with several other regulators. Mergers in banking, for example, are handled by the national bank regulators; the Interstate Commerce Commission oversees mergers in transportation; the Federal Communications Commission has some antitrust powers in broadcasting. Sanctions are strong but rarely used. Procedures are a key weakness; both agencies must ultimately rely on the courts to enforce their policy decisions; such a reliance makes enforcement slow and uncertain.

The government provisions for antitrust enforcement are buttressed by the ability of individuals to file private antitrust suits against corporations. If, for example, firm A contends that firm B has engaged in unfair competitive practices that are prohibited by the antitrust laws, A may sue B. If illegal activity is found, the court determines damages and orders B to pay A three times the amount of the damages. Criminal guilt established by a Justice Department suit is prima facie evidence in all private antitrust suits.

Advocacy Coalitions

Because a business is interested in antitrust law only when the law is applied to it, the advocacy coalitions do not break down into the normal regulated-nonregulated coalitions. Two broad shifting advocacy coalitions do exist, however. One advocacy coalition might be termed the proantitrust coalition. This coalition favors the vigorous prosecution of all antitrust laws. Members of this coalition often share populist roots with the early advocates of trustbusting. Among the recent individuals active in this coalition are Ralph Nader, Senator Howard Metzenbaum, former Senator Phillip Hart, and the small business community. The members of the antitrust bar might also be included in this coalition because they directly benefit from vigorous antitrust activity.

A second advocacy coalition might be termed the antitrust critics. This coalition is supported by a large scholarship that argues antitrust enforcement is counterproductive. Individuals such as Robert Bork and Richard Posner (now both judges) are prominent critics as was former Assistant Attorney General William Baxter. Although large business supports this advocacy coalition, the support is usually sporadic.

ECONOMIC PREMISES OF ANTITRUST

Economists' support for antitrust policy is based on their models of pure competition (Posner, 1976: 8–22). In a purely competitive situation, a market is made up of numerous sellers and numerous buyers so that no single buyer or seller can affect the price of a good by his or her actions. In addition, each seller offers identical products so that no buyer prefers the product of one seller over that of another. Producers and sellers have perfect information, and entry and exit from the market are costless. Under such conditions, price is set by supply and demand, and production is adjusted until marginal cost is equal to marginal revenue. Sellers do not make economic profits (as opposed to return on capital), and buyers benefit from low prices.

According to neoclassical economics (see Armentano, 1982: 19), deviations from perfect competition allow sellers to exploit buyers. In the most obvious case, monopoly, the one seller can limit the production of a good and, thus, raise the price that buyers pay. Consumers are injured because they pay more for a good than they would under conditions of pure competition.

In situations where the number of sellers are limited (i.e., oligopoly) monopolylike ill-effects are possible through collusion of the sellers or restrictive marketing practices. The assumptions of neoclassical economics, therefore, imply that the market failures resulting from lack of competition can be remedied by introducing more competition. If monopolies and oligopolies are broken up, the benefits of competition can accrue to the consumer. Antitrust, therefore, can be an alternative to economic regulation (instead of regulation to hold monopoly prices down, use competition to achieve this) and at the same time be regulation in that the policies are designed to limit behavior detrimental to competition.

A LEGAL HISTORY OF ANTITRUST

The origins of antitrust are grounded in the Populist movement of the nineteenth century. Following the withdrawal of greenbacks from circulation after the Civil War (see chapter 3), the nation experienced a major period of deflation. Deflation contributed to the economic woes of debtors, especially farmers who were hurt by low prices and the chronic recession following the Civil War. Faced with expensive loan payments, low agricultural prices, and high transportation costs, farmers manifested this discontent in the agrarian politics of the day. Farmers were joined by small businessmen and other individuals dislocated by the growth of large corporations. The unfavorable economic conditions of many stood in vivid contrast to the flaunting of wealth by the rich (Johnson, 1965: 302). As a result, part of the blame for the situation was laid at the feet of the large industrial corporations of the day—the railroads and the new trusts such as Standard Oil.

The discontent was translated into political action by the disadvantaged groups. By 1890, 17 states had passed legislation against trusts. Both the Democratic and the Republican parties included planks in their 1888 platforms calling for federal antitrust legislation (Kintner, 1964: 12). In Congress, Senator John Sherman articulated this distrust in the legislation that bears his name. Sherman sought to prohibit business practices that tended to "advance the cost to the consumer" (in the original bill, see Thorelli, 1955: 164 ff). The intent of the act was clearly to redistribute some of the benefits of the marketplace from producers to consumers; productive efficiency is little discussed in the legislative debates over the act.[1] As Sherman was quoted on the Senate floor, "If we will not endure a King as a political power, we should not endure a King over the production, transporation, and sale of the necessaries of life."

Specifically, the Sherman Act was aimed at industrial trusts, an invention of John D. Rockefeller's Standard Oil. In an industrial trust, the stock of individual companies was transferred to the directors of a trust, who then operated the companies. If enough companies joined the trust, control over the market could be established.

The Sherman Antitrust Act of 1890 did two things. First, it prohibited contracts, combinations, and conspiracies in restraint of trade; and, second, it declared that acts of monopolizing were illegal (Van Cise, 1982: 11–12). To its ardent supporters, the Sherman Act must have been a disappointment. First, the act was technically obsolete because it was aimed at trusts that had been replaced by a more efficient method of controlling an industry, the holding company. Second, in the first major court case, the Supreme Court (see later) held that manufacturing was not commerce and, therefore,

---

1. The Sherman Act passed both Houses of Congress with only one dissenting vote. The vagueness of the law plus the unanimity may indicate the Sherman Act was intended to be an exercise in symbolic politics.

exempted much of industry from the Sherman Act. Third, perhaps the most effective use of the Sherman Act was by business against labor unions as courts determined that unions were combinations in restraint of trade.

As a result, the Sherman Act did not prevent the cartelization of major portions of American industry from 1897 to 1904. Some 70 major industries merged into monopolies or near monopolies. Between 1897 and 1904, 4,227 firms merged into 257 combinations that established "trusts" in over 300 different industries. "Trusts" were created in oil (Standard Oil), cigarettes (American Tobacco), steel (U.S. Steel), farm machinery (International Harvester), biscuits (Nabisco), and other areas (Markham, 1965: 157). Obscured in history is the fact that many trusts such as those in leather, rope, buttons, glue, wallpaper, starch, and salt failed to survive (McCraw, 1981: 33).

In response to the problems of the Sherman Act, almost everyone proposed changes in the antitrust laws. The platforms of Taft, Roosevelt, and Wilson in 1912 were all committed to changes in the law. Labor unions opposed the Sherman Act because it was used to break up unions; in fact, the Supreme Court held that unions could be sued for treble damages as the result of strikes (*Loewe* v. *Lawler,* 1908). Small business opposed the Sherman Act because it questioned their own efforts to work out cooperative arrangements. Big business opposed the act because the "rule of reason" guidelines for court action were so vague that what constituted illegal behavior was unclear (Johnson, 1965: 315).

The House of Representatives under the leadership of Representative Clayton listed several business practices that were to be considered illegal while the Senate pursued the idea of creating an agency with general powers to regulate antitrust. The debates over the reforms illustrated that reformers had multiple goals. Louis Brandeis, an economic adviser to Wilson, testified before Congress that antitrust should be used to protect small business from the evil practices of the large businessperson (McCraw, 1981: 44). Business organizations, on the other hand, favored the creation of a federal agency to make government antitrust policy predictable; an agency could then advise business as to the legality of their proposed actions (see Kolko, 1963: 262). Congress eventually followed both strategies. The Clayton Antitrust Act listed a series of behaviors that would be illegal while the Federal Trade Commission Act created the Federal Trade Commission to regulate "unfair competition."

Two major amendments to the antitrust laws were enacted in 1938 and 1950 in response to political pressures to control big business. In 1938 the Robinson-Patman Act was passed to prohibit price discrimination in response to demands for legislative action against the large chain stores. By purchasing in bulk, large chain stores could undercut the prices of local stores and drive them out of business. The Robinson-Patman Act prohibited price discrimination by sellers that might lead to monopoly (Kintner, 1964: 59).

In 1950 the Celler-Kefauver Act was passed to close some loopholes in the Clayton Act with respect to mergers. Section 7 of the Clayton Act dealt with mergers but had three weaknesses. First, it prohibited monopolizing mergers only via the purchase of stock and not by the purchase of assets. Second, courts had interpreted Clayton as applying only to horizontal mergers (see later). Third, the government had to prove that the effect of the merger would be to injure the public by lessening competition (Audretsch, 1983: 4–5). The result of these weaknesses was little prosecution; the FTC filed 58 merger suits from 1914 to 1950 but lost 48 of them; the Justice Department in the same time period lost 10 of 20 (Markham, 1965: 167–168). The Celler-Kefauver Act essentially applied the law to acquisitions of assets and stated that mergers were illegal if they *might* lead to monopoly or a lessening of competition.

In several other legislative actions, Congress has from time to time exempted portions of the economy from the antitrust laws. The Capper-Volstead Act exempts agricultural cooperatives and federal marketing orders from antitrust. The Webb-Pomerene Act of 1918 exempts export trade associations from antitrust although very few such associations exist. The Clayton Act exempts labor unions from the provisions of the law. Government enterprises such as the post office have not been subjected to antitrust. Several price-setting functions of private organizations that are federally regulated have traditionally been exempt from antitrust by law, but these exemptions are slowly being reexamined as part of the deregulation movement of the 1980s. Finally, in a 1922 court case that would probably be overruled if challenged, professional baseball holds an exemption as a "sport."

MONOPOLY

The most visible portion of antitrust law and the most important initially was the Sherman Act's consideration of monopolies. Section 2 of the Sherman Act provides that every "person who shall monopolize, or attempt to monopolize, or combine or conspire with any other person or persons, to monopolize any part of the trade or commerce among the several States, or with foreign nations, shall be deemed guilty of a misdemeanor" (now a felony). Before discussing the judicial interpretation of section 2, we should note that the act prohibits "monopolizing," not the possession of a monopoly. In other words, the mere possession of a monopoly was not declared illegal, only the process of attempting to or intending to monopolize. In addition, the statute does not discuss the size of the market that must be subject to monopolization. Whether the market to be monopolized is defined as a national market, a regional market, or a local market may determine guilt or innocence in an antitrust case.

The Initial Failures

The first monopoly case to arrive at the Supreme Court, *U.S. v. E. C. Knight* (1895), involved the sugar trust. The American Sugar Refining Company acquired E. C. Knight and several other sugar refining companies to gain control over 98 percent of the market. In a decision that virtually destroyed the Sherman Act, the Supreme Court held that American Sugar was in manufacturing, not commerce, and that the act prevented monopolizing in commerce, not in manufacturing. Because the law did not apply to the Sugar Trust, a decision on the merits, therefore, was not necessary.

The E. C. Knight case was devastating for any attempt to use antitrust powers against the "trusts" of the day. If commerce did not include manufacturing, then most of the great industrial trusts of the day were exempt.

The period following the *E. C. Knight* case saw thousands of mergers and the creation of monopolies in some 70 industries.[2]

Not until 1904 did the U.S. government win its first monopoly case, *Northern Securities* v. *U.S.* (1904). Northern Securities was a holding company formed as the result of a business rivalry between three major railroads, James J. Hill's Great Northern, J. P. Morgan's Northern Pacific, and E. H. Harriman's Union Pacific. Although all three railroads covered the Northwest from St. Paul to Seattle, they had not vigorously competed against each other for at least 20 years (Meyer, 1906: 227). Hill and Morgan jointly purchased the Burlington line, which linked St. Paul with Chicago. Perceiving that he was being squeezed out of an important market, Harriman began purchasing Northern Pacific stock in an effort to gain control of Morgan's railroad.

Northern Securities was designed as an effort to prevent Harriman's control over the the lines. Incorporated in New Jersey, it served as a holding company to control the stock of the Great Northern and the Northern Pacific. The Supreme Court found that railroads were clearly in commerce and under the Sherman Act. Because the holding company "combined" two previously independent and "competitive" railroads, it was declared illegal.

Busting the Trusts

Encouraged by the victory in *Northern Securities,* the government filed numerous antitrust suits under both Roosevelt and Taft.[3] Two of these cases against the oil trust and the tobacco trust became the cornerstone of American antitrust policy. Significantly, these cases were the last major cases that the government won in court and that empowered it to break up large companies into their component parts.

Standard Oil. In the 1860s, John D. Rockefeller, with several partners, entered the oil refining business in Cleveland, Ohio. In 1870, Rockefeller interests controlled no more than 4 percent of the oil refining market. The oil refining industry at the time was intensely competitive; prices for kerosene fell from 30 cents a gallon in 1869 to 10 cents in 1880 (see Tarbell, 1950). Standard Oil survived and prospered in this environment because the company invented many of the improvements in oil refining and was able to take advantage of the large economies of scale in oil refining (see McCraw, 1981: 8). By 1874, Rockefeller interests controlled 25 percent of refining, and by 1880 they controlled in excess of 80 percent.

To ensure long-run profits and environmental stability, Standard Oil began a vertical integration effort. To ensure a market for the product, Standard Oil integrated forward into transportation and wholesaling. To assure itself of plentiful supplies of crude oil, the company integrated backward into transportation of crude and exploration. Fully integrated,

2. There is some question as to whether the government could have won the *E. C. Knight* case on the merits. Armentano (1982: 51) presents evidence that the sugar trust never did wield monopoly power. During the history of the trust, the trust did not reduce output or increase prices. In fact, the evidence shows that prices fell from 9 cents a pound in 1880 to 5.3 cents in 1895. Because the sugar trust had no efficiencies of scale, the trust eventually collapsed by itself. By 1927, American Sugar held only 25 percent of the U.S. market.

3. Although Roosevelt has the reputation as the great trustbuster, historians agree that Taft was far more aggressive in this area, filing approximately twice as many antitrust suits as Roosevelt (see Kolko, 1963).

Standard Oil was a formidable and ruthless competitor. It was able to extract rebates from railroads because of its huge volume (such rebates were probably rational for the railroads because the rates exceeded their variable costs and could be justified for volume reasons). In addition, Standard charged prices lower than other firms, which resulted in numerous bankruptcies.[4]

In an effort to manage the far-flung Rockefeller interests, a legal trust was created with the assets of 39 companies assigned to the trust. When the Ohio courts declared the trust arrangement illegal, a holding company, Standard Oil of New Jersey, was created to manage the companies. This holding company was challenged by the government.

In *Standard Oil* v. *U.S.* (1911), the Supreme Court stated that the important question was not the monopoly position of Standard but whether Standard had attained that position by other than normal business practices; that is, was Standard Oil guilty of monopolization? The Court held that Standard's practices of local price wars, dummy corporations, preferential railroad rates, and coercion of suppliers did not constitute normal business practices. Standard Oil, therefore, was found guilty of monopolizing, and the remedy was to break Standard Oil into 33 separate companies (most organized on a geographic basis).

In weighing the methods of attaining a monopoly, the Court enunciated a "rule of reason" approach to determine whether or not monopolies were legal under antitrust law. Under the rule of reason, monopolies were legal if they resulted from efficiency or government grants. Monopolies that resulted from the control of scarce inputs or from business combinations may or may not be legal depending on the methods used (see Strickland, 1980).

American Tobacco.   The American Tobacco Company was the result of a merger instigated by James Duke, who pioneered aggressive advertising in the cigarette industry. By both advertising and the use of new tobacco-rolling machines, American Tobacco controlled 93 percent of the cigarette market by 1899. Duke then used this market power to move into the smoking tobacco, chewing tobacco, snuff, and cigar industries, gaining sizable market shares in all except cigars (which had few economies of scale in manufacturing; see McCraw, 1981).

Using the rule of reason, the Supreme court found American Tobacco guilty of monopolizing (*U.S.* v. *American Tobacco,* 1911). Specifically mentioned in terms of "unreasonable tactics" were mergers to avoid competition, use of monopoly power in cigarettes to monopolize other tobacco markets, vertical integration to create barriers to entry, purchasing tobacco plants for the sole purpose of closing them, and agreement with independent tobacco producers not to compete against each other. Like Standard Oil, American Tobacco was found guilty as the result of the tactics it used to gain a dominant position rather than for any monopolistic behavior after a

---

4. There is some question about the legality of the competitive methods of John D. Rockefeller. Traditionally, Standard Oil is portrayed as a massive giant that used rebates and predatory pricing to drive others from the market. Armentano (1982: 61–64), however, argues that Standard Oil was simply an aggressive competitor and that because it was more efficient, less efficient firms were driven out of business. Regardless of the economic merits of Standard Oil's actions, such actions are bound to make numerous enemies and result in numerous petitions for government intervention.

dominant position was achieved. American Tobacco was split into three companies.[5]

The End of Trustbusting

For all practical purposes, the *Standard Oil* and the *American Tobacco* cases marked the end of what objective observers would term effective antitrust. Effective antitrust, if the goal of antitrust policy is the introduction of efficiency by increasing the number of competitors in a market, requires that the government both win antitrust cases and achieve some breakup of the monopoly upon victory. Since 1911, the government has generally failed to do so. Other ordered breakups (either by court order or consent decree) such as International Harvester (1918), Corn Products (1919), Kodak (1920), Pullman (1947), Grinnel (1968), IBM (1956), United Fruit (1958), and MCI (1962), resulted in trivial spin-offs from the losing company (see Posner, 1976: 86–87) or in spin-offs that actually helped the company (e.g., AT&T, 1984). In addition, the government often wins monopoly cases (see further on) and fails to get a remedy that includes any breakup.

The end of trustbusting did not result from a rationally established policy but rather from a series of court decisions that showed that "intent to monopolize" under section 2 was difficult to demonstrate. In addition, the large cost of major antitrust suits (see later) in quest of uncertain remedies meant that few major antitrust suits were filed. As two students of the antitrust bureaucracy have concluded (Weaver, 1977; Katzman, 1980), ambitious antitrust lawyers are unlikely to file suits with uncertain outcomes that require major investments in time and energy.

U.S. Steel.   In 1920 the Supreme Court decided the antitrust suit against U.S. Steel (*U.S.* v. *U.S. Steel,* 1920). At one time in its history, U.S. Steel was clearly guilty under the Sherman Antitrust Act of monopolizing and engaging in monopolistic behavior. U.S. Steel was formed in 1901 by merging ten independent steel producers and one ore and transportation company. One requirement of the U.S. Steel merger was that Andrew Carnegie, the head of Carnegie Steel, would retire from the industry. Carnegie Steel was one of the more innovative and competitive steel producers of the nineteenth century and was the reason why previous attempts at forming a steel cartel failed (see Kolko, 1963).

With Carnegie out of the way, J.P. Morgan and others involved in U.S. Steel engaged in monopolistic behavior. Using its 66 percent of the market, U.S. Steel was able to increase steel prices by 50 percent in 1901 (Parsons and Ray, 1975: 186). In addition, U.S. Steel sponsored a series of "Gary Dinners," meeting with other steel producers in an effort to restrain price competition.

By 1920, however, the threat of U.S. Steel was less imposing. The monopolizing behavior had occurred years earlier. In addition, U.S. Steel had become a conservative, uninnovative firm; its market share dropped to 50 percent by 1920. The Supreme Court held that U.S. Steel's share of the market was insufficient for monopoly power and that even that share was

---

5. The remedy did not solve the problem of collusion, for the three firms continued to collude and restrict competition in the cigarette industry, eventually being convicted for such behavior in 1930 (see Posner, 1976: 86)

achieved through normal business practices. (Given the long-run performance of U.S. Steel's dropping to less than 20 percent of the market, the Court was clearly correct on the first point; it was probably in error on the second point; see Armentano, 1982: 98–99 for an alternative view.)

Alcoa.   The next major opportunity to establish antitrust policy came in *U.S.* v. *Aluminum Company of America* (1945). Alcoa first established dominance over the aluminum market by government-granted patents. Charles Hall developed the first practical method of reducing alumina into aluminum via electrolytic reduction. With a patent monopoly until 1909, Alcoa integrated backward into ownership of bauxite, conversion of bauxite into alumina, and ownership of the large electrical plants necessary for converting alumina into aluminum. It also integrated forward into the fabrication of aluminum goods. In fact, Alcoa through market development created most of the demand for aluminum.

Aluminum reduction is subject to large economies of scale, and Alcoa used these economies of scale to control 90 percent of the market (10 percent came from imports). Economies of scale were so great that Alcoa supplied the entire nation's demand from a single alumina plant as late as 1938 (Greer, 1983: 152). Because four of the Supreme Court justices had participated in the suit before appeal to the Supreme Court was made, the Alcoa case was decided by a special panel of appeals court judges.

The establishment of monopoly rested with the market definition. If the market for aluminum consisted of all aluminum sold to companies other than Alcoa, then Alcoa had only 33 percent of the market. If the market was defined as the amount sold to Alcoa and everyone else, then Alcoa had 64 percent of the market. If only the market for virgin aluminum was considered (omitting scrap), then Alcoa held 90 percent of the market. The court accepted the 90 percent definition and examined Alcoa for monopolizing behavior.

Essentially, the monopolistic behavior that Alcoa was found guilty of was continued expansion of output to meet demand. The court reasoned that by expanding, Alcoa preempted other companies from entering the market. Although this was monopolizing in the court's terms, it was very unmonopolylike behavior. The identifying characteristic of monopolies is restriction of output to raise prices. Alcoa increased output and cut prices.

The remedy in Alcoa was more bizarre than the decision. Alcoa was not broken up. Rather, Alcoa was prohibited from purchasing the surplus aluminum plants that the government planned to sell after World War II. Eventually, these plants were sold to Reynolds and Kaiser, which left a market of Alcoa with 50 percent, Reynolds with 30 percent, and Kaiser with 20 percent. In the 1950s the government also assisted the entry of Anaconda, Harvey, and Ormet with loans, cheap government electricity, and access to government supplies of raw materials (Greer, 1983: 153).

From the completion of the Alcoa case until 1969, the monopoly area of antitrust was fairly quiet. To be sure, cases involving United Shoe, Du Pont, and Grinnel were tried; but no new law was established; and the total impact of these cases was minimal. Not until antitrust became advocated by individuals with such disparate views as conservative economists and Ralph Nader did the U.S. government take new action in the area.

The New Attack and the Surrender

On the last day of the Johnson administration, an antitrust suit was filed against International Business Machines. When the market was defined as mainframe computer systems, IBM controlled 70 percent of the U.S. market, with Control Data the only other major manufacturer with more than a few percent. IBM was charged with bundling (selling computers, software, and support for one price), price cutting, and selling paper machines (e.g., computers that they had not produced yet).

IBM's share of the market, in fact, could be explained by IBM's aggressive marketing. IBM clearly was not the leader in computer technology; that title went to Remington Rand, RCA, Philco, Data General, Honeywell, Burroughs, General Electric, and countless other companies. What IBM did especially well was produce machines similar to the breakthroughs very quickly and sell service and reliability (Fisher, McKie, and Mancke, 1983: 95–96). Its market position was based on marketing skill and little else (in its earlier days IBM dominated the punch card tabulating market the same way).

The IBM case set records for futility. Filed in 1969, the case went to trial in 1975. In 1978 the government ended its case, and IBM began its defense. In 1982, Assistant Attorney General William Baxter dropped the case because it lacked "merit."

The other major case involved the 1974 suit against American Telephone and Telegraph (AT&T). AT&T controlled 83 percent of the telephone market. Unlike IBM, AT&T was clearly guilty of monopolizing behavior in originally establishing its monopoly. AT&T aggressively protected its patents and extended their life with additional patents based on trivial changes. Refusing to connect its lines with other phone company lines, AT&T also discriminated against non-Bell equipment. The early history of AT&T has substantial evidence of monopolizing behavior.

Charges of decades-old violations of the Sherman Act, however, are not likely to be upheld in 1980. The government charged 83 instances of monopolizing behavior (MacAvoy and Robinson, 1983). In essence, these boiled down to two charges that (1) AT&T used long-distance profits to subsidize local service and (2) AT&T refused access to its lines by long-distance competitors. In both cases, the charges were weak because the cross subsidization was ordered by the Federal Communications Commission and state regulatory commissions and the connecting problem had been resolved in favor of the other competitors.

As the case progressed, AT&T discovered that it would be better off losing than winning (see MacAvoy and Robinson, 1983). AT&T agreed to a consent decree dissolving the company. The 22 local telephone monopolies would be consolidated into 7 regional companies, and the long lines division (long distance), Bell Labs, and Western Electric would form the new AT&T. Although the regional monopolies would remain regulated, AT&T would be free to enter any new nonregulated fields that it wished. Containing the most profitable portions of the system, the new AT&T accounted for over half of the telephone system's revenues (MacAvoy and Robinson, 1983: 21). The projected result was a rapid rise in local telephone costs and large profits for the new AT&T. Final breakup of the system occurred January 1, 1984, and AT&T achieved by "losing" an antitrust suit something that it would never have been allowed to do on its own.

An Evaluation of Monopoly Antitrust

The status of monopoly antitrust law under section 2 of the Sherman Act is unclear. The courts have not clearly defined what monopoly power is. They have stated that 90 percent of the market is a monopoly but that 50 percent of the market is not. Exactly where the line is, is unclear. In addition, possession of monopoly power by itself is not illegal; rather, to be found guilty the company must have commited acts of monopolization. Monopoly that results from superior products, business acumen, or historical accident is acceptable.

From both political and economic perspectives, monopoly antitrust law has serious failings. First, the existence of section 2 and the threat of monopoly prosecution may lead to inefficiencies. Corporations may become passive and fail to exploit new developments and new markets. IBM, for example, ignored the microcomputer market until after its antitrust suit was dropped. Within one year after the suit was dropped, the IBM personal computer was the largest-selling microcomputer in the United States. Similar arguments have been made about Bell Labs, reputed to be one of the best research labs in the world. With the threat of antitrust over the heads of such corporations, they have little incentive to innovate; and the end loser is the consumer.

Similar criticisms can be heard from historians and economists. McCraw (1981), for example, argues that monopolies occur naturally in what he calls center firms where some part of the production process is subject to large economies of scale. In industries without such economies, attempts at monopolization inevitably fail. Breaking up monopolies, according to McCraw, results in losses of productive efficiency and higher prices to consumers. Dominick Armentano (1982) presents similar arguments from an economic perspective. Armentano argues that most major "trusts" got to be monopolies because they were aggressive competitors and that they continued to compete by cutting prices and expanding output after market control was established. When they failed to compete (e.g., U.S. Steel), these firms lost market shares to more aggressive competitors. Armentano argues that antitrust law with its emphasis on intent actually punishes firms that are aggressive competitors.

Second, antitrust law really has not had any impact on economic concentration. Rational firms today diversify into conglomerates rather than seek monopoly control of a single market. Such action is outside the scope of antitrust, and, as a result, aggregrate concentration has increased. In 1929 the 100 largest firms (less than one-tenth of 1 percent of the total number of firms) controlled 39.7 percent of the nation's assets. In 1978 the 100 largest firms controlled 45.5 percent of the nation's assets. For the 200 largest firms, the figures are 47.7 percent and 58.3 percent respectively.

Even within industries, monopolies continue to exist. Western Electric controls 98 percent of its market; Kellogg, 45 percent; Kodak, 80 percent; IBM, 70 percent; Campbell Soup, 85 percent; Caterpillar, 50 percent; Gillette, 77 percent; Hershey, 70 percent; and Coca-Cola, 50 percent (Shepherd, 1975: 309). If the goal of section 2 is to prevent economic concentration, it has failed dismally.

Why antitrust policy has had little impact on economic concentration is fairly clear—poor remedies and difficulty proving intent. Failure to achieve competitive remedies is the major administrative failure of antitrust policy. As Posner (1976: 82–83) argues, the government has shown a great deal of ability in winning cases but losing remedies; that is, firms were found guilty but not punished. Of the 118 monopoly cases from 1890 to 1974, the government either won in litigation or signed a consent decree in 81 percent of the cases. The government was able to get a substantial divestiture, however, in only 23 percent of the cases. Since 1940 the government's winning percentage has increased (84 percent), but the proportion of substantial divestitures has decreased (15 percent). Antitrust cannot have much impact on economic concentration if monopolizing companies are left intact.

In addition, under the rule of reason, the government must prove intent to monopolize; and such proof is fairly difficult. The case law is vague about what specific conduct is prohibited, and proving conspiracy is a difficult undertaking.

Third, antitrust law is slow and expensive. Antitrust cases drag on for years. Filed in 1938, *Alcoa* was resolved in 1945; *U.S. Steel* was filed in 1911 and resolved in 1920. Filed in 1969, the *IBM* case covered some 8,000 exhibits, 104,400 pages of transcript, 473 court days, and then was dropped without a decision in 1982 (Fisher, McKie, and Mancke, 1983: x). Carried to completion, the *IBM* case may well have continued to 1990 with appeals. The massive investment of resources in monopolization cases with little to show in results clearly indicates that allocating resources to monopoly antitrust is inefficient.

Several proposals for reforming monopoly antitrust law exist and deserve brief mention. First, the individuals who believe in the goals of monopoly antitrust law advocate procedural reforms to avoid long court proceedings. Specifically, they advocate administratively narrowing the issues so that only the disputed core is taken to court (see Posner, 1976), and they advocate time limits on trials. Second, liberals who favor antitrust law (such as former Senator Phillip Hart) have proposed that the law be rewritten to outlaw monopoly per se and to require divestiture when the government wins. Third, still others feel that monopoly antitrust should be abolished (see further on) and other forms of regulation or policy substituted.

COLLUSION

Section 1 of the Sherman Antitrust Act states: "Every contract, combination in the form of trust or otherwise, or conspiracy, in restraint of trade or commerce . ... is hereby declared to be illegal." Clearly, Congress did not intend section 1 to be taken literally, for almost every contract restrains trade or commerce in some way. Even simple partnerships restrain trade because two persons join forces as partners instead of competing.

Under section 1, two things must be demonstrated. First, an agreement exists (e.g., a contract, combination, or conspiracy); and second, the agreement restrains trade. Under court-interpreted law, some agreements such as agreements to fix prices are illegal per se; and the government or the filing party need only prove an agreement exists. In other types of agreements such as trade associations, a "rule of reason" applies.

The courts have characterized restraints of trade as of two types— ancillary and nonancillary. An ancillary restraint of trade is one that serves a legitimate business function. For example, if A sells his or her business to B, B might stipulate that A cannot engage in the same business for a period of years. Because B buys both the business and the goodwill of A's business, such a restraint has a legitimate business function and, therefore, is an ancillary restraint. A nonancillary restraint has no legitimate business function except to limit competition (e.g., deciding to divide up the market into regions and not compete with each other) and is illegal.

Price-Fixing

The Supreme Court enunciated the basic principles of collusion in *Addyston Pipe* v. *U.S.* (1899). Six iron pipe manufacturers, including Addyston, divided a portion of the United States into regions and agreed not to compete with each other in the regions. Establishing a system of prearranged bids, manufacturers did not bid competitively against each other. The winning bidder paid a bonus, which was then split among the other firms.

The pipe manufacturers defended their conspiracy, contending that the prices charged were reasonable, and some evidence indicates that they were (see Armentano, 1982: 140). The Court refused to apply the rule of reason to price-fixing and held that price-fixing was an ancillary restraint and was illegal per se.

The Court has been fairly consistent in the area of price-fixing. In *U.S.* v. *Trenton Potteries* (1927), 23 bathroom fixtures companies were found guilty of price-fixing, and their defense of reasonable prices was disallowed. In *U.S.* v. *Socony-Vacuum* (1940), indirect price-fixing was declared illegal. The major gasoline companies in the Midwest, including Socony-Vacuum (now Mobil), agreed to purchase any surplus gasoline refined by independent refineries so that prices would not fall. The Court found that this was merely an indirect form of price-fixing and, therefore, illegal.

The classic price-fixing case of all time was the Electrical Equipment Case (*Philadelphia* v. *Westinghouse* [1961]). Sometime in the 1920s or 1930s, the electrical equipment manufacturers as part of their trade association began to share price and bid information. By the 1950s the conspiracy included almost the entire $7-billion-a-year market, covering equipment ranging from turbine generators to electrical meters. The conspiracy was elaborate with code names, calls from pay phones, information passed in plain envelopes, clandestine meetings, and secret agreements (see Walton and Cleveland, 1964).

Some 29 companies and 44 individuals were indicted, with 7 executives actually serving jail terms and a total of nearly $2 million in fines. Despite conclusive evidence of conspiracy (even though corporate chief executives denied they knew about the conspiracy), the conspiracy might not have been successful. Cheating by members of the conspiracy was common, and some competition still existed.

More important in terms of law is *Illinois Brick* v. *Illinois* (1977). The case involved companies fixing prices on materials sold to another set of companies, which then passed along the costs of the price-fixing to downstream purchasers. The Supreme Court held that downstream purchasers did not have standing to sue. What *Illinois Brick* means is that consumers cannot use antitrust law to combat price-fixing unless they are the direct (first) purchasers of the price-fixed product.

Although empirical data is difficult to find, the Sherman Act does not seem to have deterred price-fixing among major corporations. In the 1970s alone, the following corporations were either found guilty of price-fixing, pleaded no contest, or signed consent decrees: Allied Chemical, Bethlehem Steel, Combustion Engineering, Dean Foods, Du Pont, FMC, Flintkote, Gulf Oil, ITT, International Paper, Purolator, R. J. Reynolds, and Rockwell International. Both the Carter and Reagan Antitrust Divisions made price-fixing a major priority. Focusing on highway construction and electrical equipment, this effort resulted in 147 jail terms and $47 million in fines by 1984 (Anderson, Thomas, and Ma, 1983: 52).

Information Agreements

Trade information among corporations is a gray area of Sherman law. In *American Column and Lumber* v. *U.S.* (1921), known as the Hardwoods Case, the hardwood flooring trade association gathered information from its members on the prices they charged for various products as well as on production and stock estimates. These figures were then sent to all association members, who adjusted their prices to conform with other prices in the industry. The Supreme Court held that such behavior was illegal.

Similar findings were presented in *U.S.* v. *Container Corporation of America* (1969), when cardboard box manufacturers exchanged price and cost information. Trade associations are not illegal per se, however; they may gather and disseminate information. They may share data on past transactions if those data are aggregated, they can set up rules for ethical behavior in the trade, and they can promote the industry (Van Cise, 1982: 31).

Innovations in the 1970s

As part of its revitalization, the Federal Trade Commission in the 1970s established or tried to establish new legal precedents in this area of law. Its first battle, against professional associations, was successful; its second, against the cereal manufacturers' "shared monopoly," was not; its third, against gasoline additive makers, is currently in court.

Professional associations (see chapter 7) such as bar associations, medical associations, and optometry associations have traditionally been exempt from antitrust law as "learned professions." The courts in a series of cases and the FTC by administrative procedures have gradually eliminated this exemption. In *Goldfarb* v. *Virginia Bar Association* (1975), the Supreme Court held that the establishment of minimum fees by bar associations was price-fixing. Using *Goldfarb,* the FTC and the Justice Department signed agreements or convinced medical associations, accounting associations, architects, civil engineers, and mechanical engineers to drop their fee schedules. The FTC issued a rule banning the practice by optometrists.

In another new area of law, the FTC addressed the problem of conscious parallelism, whereby firms raise or lower prices following an industry price leader. In such cases, no agreement exists, but the result is similar to price-fixing. The FTC filed suit against the three largest cereal manufacturers, Kellogg, General Foods and General Mills, alleging that they were a "shared monopoly." Specifically, the cereal manufacturers were charged with controlling supermarket shelf space, not competing on the basis of price, and proliferating cereals to keep other cereals off the shelves. In 1982 this attempt to set precedent was abandoned when the FTC, under James Miller III, dropped the case.

In 1983 the FTC found manufacturers of lead-based gasoline additives guilty of conscious parallelism. From 1974 to 1979, the four firms controlling this market raised the price of lead additives by 100 percent despite a declining demand for the product. Twenty of the 24 price increases occurred for all 4 firms on the same day with the exact same price increase. Du Pont and the other firms found guilty appealed this case to the courts.

Summary and Evaluation

The law on collusion is divisible into two parts. Certain activities are illegal per se such as price-fixing or market divisions, and a demonstration of an agreement is sufficient to establish guilt. Other activities such as information sharing or trade associations are illegal only if they serve no legitimate business function and restrain trade.

Antitrust law on collusion is probably the least controversial part of antitrust law. Posner (1976), for example, is willing to repeal all antitrust legislation except section 1 of the Sherman Act. Strickland (1980: 123) feels the law has been a success and has prevented the formation of the formal cartels that are so dominant in European markets (see also Posner, 1976: 39).

Whether or not the lack of formal cartels in the United States is a function of the Sherman Act, however, is open to question. European cartels have one crucial ingredient that U.S. cartel attempts have lacked, government support. Without clear government support, Armentano (1982) argues that price-collusion cartels are inherently unstable. For a successful cartel, Armentano (1982: 134) argues that eight conditions must be met. First, demand for the good must be inelastic so that consumers are forced to absorb higher prices (there are no substitute goods). Second, demand must be stable; declines in demand, as demonstrated by OPEC, will cause conspirators to cheat and undercut prices. Third, the cartel must agree on output quotas as well as prices. Fourth, each firm must have relatively equal costs, or the high cost firms will realize lower profits and be tempted to cheat on the cartel. Fifth, importation of the cartelized good must be limited. Sixth, the conspirators must trust each other. Seventh, the product must be fairly homogeneous so that the agreement can be enforced. Eighth, if the goods must be transported, the price of transportation must be factored into the cartel price.

Armentano's conditions suggest that price-fixing cartels will rarely succeed. In fact, he argues that all the price-fixing cartels in the United States eventually failed to work on their own without any assist from the antitrust laws. Only where the cartel had the support of government (e.g., bar associations with the powers of the state) did the cartels successfully fix prices. The lack of cartels in the United States, therefore, may be less a function of the Sherman Act than a lack of explicit government support for cartels.[6]

6. The United States does have cartels that operate. Agricultural cooperatives are classic cartels that set output quotas and prices (see chapter 5). In this case, however, the government sanctions the cartels, exempts them from antitrust law, and enforces the cartel agreements in court. Similar cartels were found among professional occupations such as doctors, lawyers, and optometrists and among state-regulated, blue-collar professions such as electricians, plumbers, and so on. Recent FTC efforts have limited some, but not all, of these occupational cartels.

Even among those who consider section 1 a success, the law comes in for some criticism. First, section 1 of the Sherman Act is a weak deterrent to collusion. Whether they are successful or not, a great many attempts at price-fixing take place. Posner (1970) documented 365 such cases before 1969, and several more have been filed since then. The law fails to deter price-fixing because the penalties for violating the law are trivial compared to the potential profits. Posner (1976: 32) found that the average price-fixing fine in the 1960s was 0.21 percent of the sales involved in the conspiracy. As low as this figure is, it represents a 150 percent increase from the 1950s, when the average fine was 0.08 percent. Prison sentences are even less of a deterrent. Of the 33 cases that resulted in prison sentences from 1890 to 1974, the average sentence was only a few months. Although the number of jail sentences has increased dramatically under recent prosecution of individuals for rigging bids in highway construction, the average sentence is still only 3.7 months. A rational businessperson could conclude that the gains from price-fixing far exceed the penalities if caught (for a theoretical view of compliance with the law, see Meier and Morgan, 1982).

Private antitrust suits with the threat of treble damages, in fact, may be a greater deterrent to collusion than government prosecution. Whether private antitrust suits have a deterrent effort or whether they just add to the already overcrowded courts by encouraging suits is not clear. Many observers of antitrust law have suggested that the treble damages portion of antitrust law encourages too many private suits (Schwartz, 1981).

Second, the reliance on conspiracy and combination places a difficult burden of proof on the individual charging price-fixing. Posner (1976) advocates going to a behavior-based standard; suits would be filed if the pricing behavior in an industry followed a pattern that would be expected if price-fixing were occurring. Posner essentially argues that one should not have to prove intent and agreement, only result.

Third, the absence of standing for most consumers is a fundamental weakness. If the intent of antitrust laws is to protect consumer welfare (e.g., Bork, 1978), then preventing consumers from filing suits when they are not the direct purchaser of a good makes little sense. If the law only permits one business to sue another over collusion, then the intent of the law must be to protect businesses from collusion rather than to protect consumers. Although many argue that one goal of antitrust is to protect small business (see Van Cise, 1982), the protection and encouragement of small business can be done in far more effective ways than antitrust law.

MERGERS

A merger is the consolidation of two or more independent firms into a single unit. Mergers were basically outside antitrust law until the passage of the Celler-Kefauver Act of 1950. Celler-Kefauver, which amended the Clayton Act, prohibited the acquisition of stock of one firm by another firm or the merger of two firms where "the effect of such acquisition may be substantially to lessen competition or to tend to create a monopoly."

Three types of mergers are possible—horizontal, vertical, and conglomerate. A horizontal merger is a merger between two competitors in the same market; a merger of Mobil Oil with Exxon, for example, would be a horizontal merger. A vertical merger is a merger between a company and either a supplier or a distributor; a merger of a textile manufacturer with a garment manufacturer would be a vertical merger. A conglomerate merger is a merger between two firms that do not compete in the same markets and do not buy or sell to each other. If Getty Oil purchased the Texas Rangers baseball team, for example, that would be a conglomerate merger.

Mergers in History

American business has witnessed three eras of great merger activity. The first period from 1897 to 1904 was a period of horizontal mergers and the creation of "trusts." Some 2,864 mergers involving over 4,000 firms took place, resulting in the creation of near monopolies in 70 different industries (Nelson, 1959). The era of horizontal mergers ended with the recession of 1904 and the government victory in the *Northern Securities* case.

The second era of mergers from 1916 to 1929 might be termed the oligopoly mergers. Essentially, small firms merged into larger firms so that they could compete with the major firms in the industry. Bethlehem Steel, for example, merged out of several smaller firms to compete with U.S. Steel. From 1925 through 1929, 5,382 firms merged (Markham, 1955: 180). This era of mergers was effectively ended by the Great Depression.

The final merger period began in 1945 and continues to the present day. The contemporary merger period, however, differs from earlier ones in that most mergers are conglomerate mergers. Conglomerate mergers are essentially a way for corporations to grow and to spread their risks by engaging in a variety of different industries. From 1960 to 1970 the Federal Trade Commission recorded an average of 2,500 mergers a year. From 1970 to 1980 the merger pace tapered off but did not cease (Greer, 1983: 169); by 1981 the annual merger rate again exceeded 2,400 (Brownstein, 1983d: 1538).

Horizontal Mergers

The Celler-Kefauver Act most directly addressed horizontal mergers because mergers are illegal only if the merger substantially lessens competition or tends to create a monopoly. When two competitors merge, competition by definition decreases. As a result, the courts have dealt harshly with horizontal mergers.

Bethlehem Steel.   Bethlehem Steel's purchase of Youngstown Sheet and Tube was the first horizontal merger challenged under the Celler-Kefauver Act. Bethlehem and Youngstown together controlled 21 percent of the market and would have been the number two steel producer after U.S. Steel with 30 percent. Bethlehem defended the purchase, arguing that it did not have any plants in the center of the country and, therefore, did not compete in Youngstown's market area. The district court held that Bethlehem could have entered the Chicago market by building a plant there and ruled, thereford, that the merger would lessen competition and could not take place (*U.S.* v. *Bethlehem Steel Corp.*, 1958). Later Bethlehem vindicated the court's reasoning by opening a plant in the Chicago area.

Brown Shoe.   Because Bethlehem Steel did not appeal its case, the first case to reach the Supreme Court was *Brown Shoe Company* v. *U.S.* (1962). The *Brown Shoe* case involved both horizontal and vertical merger aspects. Brown Shoe Company was the fourth largest shoe manufacturer with 4 percent of the market and, in addition, had some 1,200 retail shoe stores (6 percent of the market). Brown purchased Kinney, the eighth largest shoe retailer with 1.2 percent of the market.

Clearly, the shoe manufacturing and retailing market at this time was not concentrated. The Supreme Court ruled that one need only show that a merger would *probably* lessen competition. Although 1.2 percent of the market nationwide was not much, the Court found that in some cities these two firms would control over 20 percent of the retail market in women's shoes. In rejecting the Brown-Kinney merger, the Court suggested two defenses under the Celler-Kefauver Act. First, one of the firms was failing, and, therefore, a merger would not lessen competition. Second, the merger combined two small firms into a larger, more effective competitor.

Banks and Grocery Stores.   Because the *Brown Shoe* case contained both horizontal and vertical merger elements, its impact on horizontal mergers was not totally clear. In *U.S.* v. *Philadelphia National Bank* (1963), the Court rejected the merger of two Philadelphia banks that would have given the new bank 30 percent of the Philadelphia market. The banks argued that they merged to compete more effectively with the financial center banks in New York.

In *U.S.* v. *Von's Grocery* (1966), the Court held illegal a merger between two reasonably small firms. Von's Grocery with 4.3 percent of the Los Angeles market merged with Shopping Bag Food Stores with 3.2 percent of the market. After the merger only Safeway with 8 percent had a larger market share. Even though Von's and Shopping Bag were rarely in the same neighborhoods, the Supreme Court prevented this merger under the Celler-Kefauver Act.

Under the Court rulings in *Brown Shoe* and *Von's Grocery,* most mergers except for the very smallest are subject to challenge under the antitrust laws. The Justice Department and the FTC have used informal guidelines to determine whether or not to challenge horizontal mergers. Before 1981 the four-firm concentration figure was used. If a merger increased the concentration of the industry to over 60 percent, it was closely examined for a potential challenge. In 1981 the antitrust bureaucrats adopted the Herfindahl index (the sum of the squares of the market shares of the firms). If the merger increased the Herfindahl index above 1000, the merger was studied more closely.

Under Assistant Attorney General William Baxter and the FTC antitrust head Timothy Muris, the application of the Herfindahl index resulted in a series of megamergers in the oil industry. Because the oil industry is relatively unconcentrated (no company has more than 8.1 percent of U.S. reserves), mergers do not raise the Herfindahl index above 1000. The oil industry consolidation began when Mobil attempted to buy Marathon Oil, which avoided the merger by combining with U.S. Steel. The proposed Mobil takeover received no objection from the FTC in 1981. The oil industry responded with a series of record-setting mergers: Du Pont purchased Conoco (a vertical merger) for $7.4 billion, Kuwait Petroleum Corp. acquired Santa Fe International ($2.5 billion), the French oil company Elf Aquitaine bought Texasgulf ($2.8 billion), Occidental Petroleum merged with Cities Service ($4 billion), Texaco took over Getty Oil ($10.1 billion), Mobil grabbed Superior Oil ($5.7 billion) and Socal acquired Gulf ($13.2 billion). Although some of these mergers required minor divestitures to gain FTC approval, FTC antitrust head Timothy J. Muris told Congress that "no merger between competing oil companies is likely to be challenged based on its effect on the overall crude oil market" (Corrigan, 1984: 602).

Although the Reagan antitrust bureaucracy has been consistent in using the Herfindahl index, the results of their policy have not been consistent in terms of competition. Heilmann, the brewing company, was prevented from acquiring additional beer companies that would enable it to compete with the two giants, Miller and Budweiser. In the steel industry, an industry with low profits and excess capacity, a merger between the number three and number four producers was accepted (LTV and Republic) but not a merger between numbers one and seven (U.S. Steel and National Steel). Many analysts felt that the steel mergers would improve productive efficiency and the oil mergers would not (Wines, 1984: 605–606).

In both cases, oil and steel, policy was set by the bureaucracy when it exercised discretion to not challenge the mergers. Using the *Von's Grocery* case as a precedent, the courts would probably have found all these mergers illegal under the Celler-Kefauver Act. The policy also generated some congressional hearings and legislative proposals to limit mergers in the oil industry.

Vertical Mergers

The status of vertical mergers under antitrust law is less clear. A vertical merger is illegal if the merger closes substantial markets to competitors. For example, if Ford Motor Company purchased Firestone Tires, Ford probably would purchase its tires from Firestone. Thus, a large portion of the tire market would be foreclosed to other tire manufacturers. Under such circumstances, a vertical merger would lessen competition.

In general, however, a vertical merger lessens competition only if the market share of one of the firms is substantial (*Brown Shoe Company* v. *U.S.*, 1962). A vertical merger is unlikely to be challenged, therefore, unless the market for one firm or the other is concentrated or one firm holds a dominant market share. Without such horizontal aspects, most vertical mergers will not be challenged, and the number of vertical merger challenges have been very few (Greer, 1983: 182).

Conglomerate Mergers

In a pure conglomerate merger where the companies do not compete with each other in any markets, showing a lessening of competition is extremely difficult. In general, the merger laws have had little effect on conglomerate mergers. Only those mergers that can somehow be linked to competing markets, even in an obscure way, are subject to challenge.

In *FTC* v. *Consolidated Foods* (1965), the Courts used the logic of vertical mergers to void a conglomerate merger. Consolidated Foods, a large food wholesaler and retailer, purchased Gentry, a manufacturer of dehydrated onion and garlic. Consolidated Foods asked firms from which it purchased who used dehydrated onion and garlic to purchase from Gentry. Gentry's market share increased from 32 to 35 percent. The Court held that this merger foreclosed markets (via reciprocal buying) and was, therefore, illegal.

The precedent-setting "potential competitor" doctrine was established by the FTC in FTC v. Procter & Gamble (1967). Procter & Gamble, a major producer of household products, purchased Clorox, which controlled approximately 50 percent of the liquid bleach market. Although Procter & Gamble did not market any liquid bleaches, they did account for 54 percent of packaged detergent sales and did market dry bleaches. The FTC argued that the merger was anticompetitive because Procter & Gamble was a potential liquid bleach manufacturer. The Supreme Court agreed with the FTC.

In an attempt to challenge a pure conglomerate merger, the Justice Department filed suit when ITT acquired Grinnel, the major manufacturer of automatic sprinkler devices. The Justice Department contended that aggregate concentration alone lessened competition given the trend toward aggregate concentration in the economy. The federal district court refused to set new law by condemning a merger on the ground of aggregate concentration alone (U.S. v. ITT, 1970). The case was settled by consent decree after the district court decision, and the Supreme Court was denied a chance to rule on this issue.

Summary and Evaluation

The Celler-Kefauver Act prohibits mergers if the "effect of such acquisition may be substantially to lessen competition or tend to create a monopoly." Under the act, all but the very smallest horizontal mergers are illegal. Vertical mergers are legal unless they foreclose markets, which usually means that one of the firms competes in a market that is somewhat concentrated. Conglomerate mergers are generally legal unless the government can prove that one firm is a potential competitor of the other.

Allyn Strickland (1980: 152) feels that the Celler-Kefauver Act can be termed a success because it has eliminated the horizontal mergers to monopoly that once plagued the country. Strickland, however, is overly optimistic. The period of horizontal mergers to monopoly ended in 1904 and may well have ended for economic reasons rather than antitrust reasons. Armentano (1982) presents evidence that large, near-monopoly firms have consistently lost market shares to smaller, more aggressive competitors. Only when government has protected the monopoly or the monopoly firm has remained an innovator has market power been maintained. Armentano would not credit antitrust policy for any of the reduction in horizontal mergers. The reduction occurred because horizontal mergers are an inefficient use of capital.

Success or not, antitrust merger policy has serious shortcomings. First, the policy has been ineffective in slowing down the number of mergers in the economy. Aggregate concentration in U.S. industry has increased by 10 percentage points for the 200 largest firms from 1928 to the present. In 1981 a record $81 billion in mergers occurred. What the policy did was shift the focus of mergers from horizontal mergers to conglomerate mergers. Eis (1969: 294) found that 60 percent of pre-1950 mergers were horizontal whereas only 25 percent were horizontal during the 1950s and 12 percent in the early 1960s. If aggregate concentration is a concern, therefore, antitrust has been ineffective in preventing such concentration.

Second, antitrust policy is subject to bureaucratic inertia. A merger is acceptable unless challenged by the FTC or the Justice Department. Before passage of the Hart-Scott-Rodino Act of 1976, this meant a delay of several months after a merger before a legal suit was filed. The 1976 act requires premerger notification for larger mergers, but one of the agencies must still object in order to prevent a merger. One problem with bureaucratic discretion in this area is that sometimes the discretion is abused (the ITT and Hartford Insurance merger during the Nixon administration) and sometimes mergers that clearly would not pass court scrutiny are accepted by the agencies (the FTC did not object to the Texaco-Getty or the Socal-Gulf mergers in 1984). From 1950 to 1977 only 27.6 percent of all horizontal mergers were challenged (Mueller, 1979). Under the Reagan administration's antitrust leaders William Baxter (now J. Paul McGrath) and Timothy Muris, vertical and conglomerate mergers were not challenged, and only those horizontal mergers in highly concentrated industries were opposed (Wines, 1982e: 1204).

Third, the law is unpredictable and inconsistent. How large (in terms of market size) a horizontal merger can be is not clear, and this uncertainty is heightened by variation in the agencies' willingness to challenge mergers (variation that appears to correlate with presidential administrations). In vertical and conglomerate mergers, the law is even more unpredictable. What constitutes a "potential competitor" is not clear because almost every business is the potential competitor of every other business. The proportion of a market that must be foreclosed by a vertical merger is also not clear.

Fourth, as is true of the monopoly area, the merger area is another one where the government frequently loses the remedy when it wins the case. Elzinga (1969) found that in 39 cases won by the government, the government was able to get the merger disallowed in only 10 cases. Even court victories, therefore, do not contribute to more competitors.

Fifth, some economists feel that merger policy is not efficient. In a major study of costs and benefits of the Celler-Kefauver Act, Audretsch (1983) found that horizontal merger suits often cost more than the benefits that were gained (especially when the remedy failed). The only positive benefit was that these cases often had a redistributive effect within the industry.

PRICE DISCRIMINATION

Price discrimination occurs when a firm charges more than one price for a good sold to other firms. The Clayton Act prevents price discrimination but only predatory price discrimination. The Robinson-Patman Act prohibits price discrimination where the effect may be "to lessen competition or tend to create a monopoly" or "to injure, destroy or prevent competition." Price discrimination is an area of the law that pits small business against large business. The pressure for the Robinson-Patman Act was from small businesses that found themselves at a competitive disadvantage with big business. Congress in 1936 in essence modified the Clayton Act to protect competitors as well as competition. The conflict between the two business sectors can be seen from the issues that evolved in price discrimination.

Retail Price Maintenance

If one business, say, a large retail chain, can sell goods at a price less than another business, say, a locally owned store, then competitive pressures suggest that the second business will fail. To prevent large businesses from undercutting the prices of small business, the first policy mechanism was fair-trade pricing. Under fair-trade pricing or resale price maintenance, the manufacturer set a suggested retail price for a good and expected that all firms would sell at that price.

The Supreme Court held that fair-trade pricing was illegal as early as 1911 (*Miles Medical Co. v. John Park*). The same pressure that resulted in the Robinson-Patman Act also produced the Miller-Tydings Act of 1937, which exempted fair-trade pricing from antitrust. Unfortunately, for small business, fair-trade pricing is impossible to enforce. Manufacturer M probably does not care what price chain store C sells M's goods for at retail. In fact, the lower the price C charges for the goods, the greater the demand, and the more goods C will buy from M. M is unlikely to alienate a good customer like C over a minor matter, particularly one that does not affect the profits of M such as fair-trade pricing. Fair-trade pricing's exemption from the antitrust laws was eventually repealed by the Consumer Goods Pricing Act of 1975.

In recent days, resale price maintenance has been the subject of some debate. Both the FTC and the Antitrust Division have proposed that resale price maintenance be subjected to a "rule of reason" test rather than be illegal per se. Several arguments for a change in policy have been presented. First, a rule of reason approach would make resale price maintenance consistent with the law on exclusionary practices (see later; Areeda, 1984: 20; Easterbrook, 1984: 23). Second, because resale price maintenance will be effective only in rare circumstances (i.e., when there are few manufacturers, few dealers, homogeneous products, and a way to enforce it), resale price maintenance is not worth worrying about (Easterbrook, 1984: 25). Third, restricted dealing via resale price maintenance can be competitive behavior if it permits a manufacturer to sell a different mix of goods or services (Easterbrook, 1984: 26). Fourth, the manufacturer might have an essential interest in the resale price to protect the "status" of a good (Pitofsky, 1984: 28). Fifth, without resale price maintenance, a store that provides services as well as sales (e.g., advice about computers, repairs, and so on) is exploited by discounters who merely sell the good (Miller, 1984: 31).

Both antitrust agencies have accepted these arguments and de-emphasized cases involving retail price maintenance. Such cases averaged about ten a year prior to 1981. From 1981 to 1983 neither the Antitrust Division nor the FTC filed a single resale price maintenance case.

Price Discrimination

The classic price discrimination case is *FTC v. Morton Salt* (1948). Morton Salt priced its salt on the volume ordered. The basic price for less than carload lots was $1.60 per case; for carload lots, $1.50; for more than 5,000 cases per year, $1.40; and for more than 50,000 cases per year, $1.35. Only four major chains qualified for the lowest prices, but almost every store through group purchases paid less than the $1.60 price. The

Supreme Court recognized Congress' intent to protect small business and noted that the higher prices paid by small business might lead to monopoly. Morton Salt, therefore, was guilty of price discrimination.

The Robinson-Patman Act has actually been used to limit competition. A good example is *Utah Pie* v. *Continental Baking* (1967). Utah Pie had a monopoly in the frozen pie market in Utah. Moving into this market from California, Continental Baking charged lower prices than Utah and lower prices than it charged in California. The judicial question is, Was Utah Pie injured? In general, the courts find injury whenever a competitor must significantly drop prices to meet competition. The court found that Utah Pie was injured despite the fact that Utah Pie had a monopoly (and, therefore, may have charged monopoly prices) before Continental moved in.

The courts have generally permitted three defenses in price discrimination suits. First, one can underprice competitors if the prices are justified by lower costs. This defense is rare because businesses hesitate to reveal this amount of financial information to competitors and because cost accounting lacks the precision to handle such concepts as marginal cost. Second, an acceptable defense is changing conditions such as a going-out-of-business sale. Third, dropping prices in order to meet the prices of a competitor is also acceptable.

Evaluation

Robinson-Patman law is a complex, involved field. Legal textbooks are written about the area, and individuals spend their entire lives practicing Robinson-Patman law. Although the law is complex from a legal perspective, it is not so from a policy perspective. Robinson-Patman, by outlawing price discrimination and making the defenses for price discrimination difficult, is essentially anticompetitive. Consumers benefit from competitive markets where price competition is vigorous. Prices fall, inefficient businesses fail, and efficient businesses survive. The goal of protecting small business is inconsistent with the goal of benefiting individual consumers. How are consumers injured if a large department store sells goods at prices lower than a local store? How were the people of Utah injured when Continental Baking sold frozen pies at less than their prices in California?

If one policy goal is to protect small business, clearly, more effective ways exist to do so without having consumers bear the cost. Tax incentives, loan programs, and preferential awarding of contracts are three possible ways. Price cutting is an essential element of a market system that works. Rather than establish barriers that increase costs to consumers without compensating benefits, the government should be advocating the interests of consumers. The general public would be better served if the Robinson-Patman Act were repealed.

EXCLUSIONARY PRACTICES

Exclusionary practices are practices that attempt to exclude individuals from a market. Section 3 of the Clayton Act prohibits selling goods or charging prices "on the condition . . . that . . . purchaser thereof shall not use or deal in the goods . . . of a competitor . . . where the effect of such . . .

may be to substantially lessen competition or tend to create a monopoly in any line of commerce." As in the Robinson-Patman area, exclusionary practices are a grievance that one business files against another. Consumer interests are only indirectly involved. Three common exclusionary practices will be discussed in this section—tying agreements, exclusive dealing agreements, and exclusive distributorships. Other types of "exclusionary practices," including boycotts, predatory price cutting, and vertical mergers (see Posner, 1976: 171), will not be discussed in this section because they were included elsewhere in the chapter or are of minor importance.

Tying Agreements

A tying agreement is an agreement that requires an individual who purchases one good from a company to purchase a second good. If a copy machine corporation refused to rent or sell copy machines to a business unless the business also purchased paper from the company, this would be a tying agreement. In actual practice, thousands of goods are tied because common sense requires tying. When a consumer purchases a new automobile, the purchase of tires is tied to the automobile (rationally because the automobile does not work without them). Shirts come with buttons, shoes come with shoelaces, tennis rackets usually come with strings, and so forth.

Tying agreements become a problem when one of the goods involved is monopolized or the company exerts some monopoly power. When the selling firm lacks monopoly power, the buyer can simply go elsewhere for a nontied good. Butterball Turkeys, for example, has recently tied some of its turkeys to a premixed stuffing. Because Butterball lacks market power, individuals who wish turkeys without premade stuffing can simply buy other turkeys. Only if Butterball had a monopoly on the frozen turkey market would this form of tying be a problem to the consumer.

Unfortunately, the law on tying agreements is not so simple. Complexity results because the law is intended to protect businesses from each other rather than to protect consumers. *International Salt* v. *U.S.* (1947) established that a tying agreement was illegal if the seller possessed sufficient market power and presented no reasonable justification for the tying. International Salt had a patent on salt-dispensing machines used in food processing. Companies that used International Salt machines had to purchase their salt from International Salt. The Supreme Court held that International Salt had market power in the salt machines business and that tying the sale of salt to the use of machines served no purpose other than to foreclose the market.

The Court has also rejected tying the rental of good movies to bad ones when selling them to television (*U.S.* v. *Loew's Inc*, 1962), but accepted tying morning and afternoon newspaper advertisements (*Times-Picayune Publishing Co.* v. *U.S.*). The Court has suggested two defenses to tying agreements when the state of the market indicates tying is harmful. First, tying might be justified if the tied goods are inputs and certain quality inputs are required to maintain the quality of the tied good. Although the Supreme Court suggested the quality inputs defense, the Circuit Court rejected such a defense when Chicken Delight required franchises to purchase both chicken and cooking equipment from Chicken Delight (*Siegel* v. *Chicken Delight, Inc.*, 1971).

Second, the Court has accepted tying as a method of protecting the quality of service in a new industry. In *U.S.* v. *Jerrold Electronics* (1961), the Court upheld Jerrold's practices in the cable TV industry. Jerrold only sold cable systems that included the equipment, installation, layout, and maintenance. The Court accepted tying in this case to protect a new industry but hinted that the acceptance was temporary until the industry reached maturity.

Exclusive Dealing Agreements

Exclusive dealing agreements are agreements between a supplier and a distributor whereby the distributor agrees not to handle products of the supplier's competitors. Justifications for exclusive dealing agreements include a guarantee of a steady supply of a good, the ability to reduce inventory by stocking fewer brands, and the pledge of advertising or other services. Exclusive dealing agreements are illegal if they foreclose a significant market and, thus, lessen competition.

In the Standard Stations case (*Standard Oil of California* v. *U.S.*, 1949), Standard Oil of California required that its dealers purchase all their gasoline from Standard and in some instances purchase their batteries, tires, and other parts as well. (The case concerned the independent dealers marketing Standard products, not the stations owned by Standard.) The Supreme Court held that Standard's share of the market (6.7 percent) effectively foreclosed a $58 million market from competitors and, therefore, was illegal. If the size of the market was substantial, no evidence of market power was necessary in exclusive dealing.

Exclusive dealing is not a concise area of the law. Exclusive dealing is allowed if the market share is small or the dollar value of the market is small. In *Tampa Electric Co.* v. *Nashville Coal Co.* (1961), the Court accepted exclusive dealing when the market share was only 1 percent and the seller provided additional services to the dealer.

Exclusive Distributorships

An exclusive distributorship is a grant by a supplier to a distributor that the distributor will be the sole distributor in a geographic area. Beverage companies, for example, usually only use a single distributor in any geographic area. The distributor, in practice, is granted a local monopoly in the distribution of goods from the supplier.

The Supreme Court addressed the issue of exclusive distributorships in *Packard Motor Car Co.* v. *Webster* (1957). In an effort to protect the largest Packard dealer in Baltimore, Packard did not renew two other Baltimore dealerships, including Webster. The Circuit Court (affirmed by the Supreme Court) held that this was a reasonable restraint of trade. Exclusive dealerships could be used to promote the brand or to protect individual dealers.

Although the Packard case upheld the right of companies to select their distributors, it did not address the issue of whether or not the company could place restrictions on the resale of the product (e.g., limit it to a geographic area or to specific customers). This issue was addressed twice. In *U.S.* v. *Arnold, Schwinn & Co.* (1969), the Supreme Court held that product resale restrictions on an independent dealer were illegal per se. Eight years later, the Court modified this position in *Continental TV* v. *GTE Sylvania* (1977). GTE marketed television sets through independent dealers who were limited to specified geographic areas (but could also sell other brands). Continental opened another store outside its geographic area, and GTE canceled its dealership. Adopting a "rule of reason" standard, the Court held that such restrictions were permissible to increase brand promotion and, thus, interbrand competition.

Evaluation

From a public policy perspective, exclusionary agreements law is relatively unimportant. The law basically deals with relationships between businesses and has little direct impact on the consumer. Tying agreements are illegal if the seller exerts substantial market power in a tied good. Exclusive dealing agreements are illegal except when the dollar value of the market is small. Exclusive distributorships are legal, and restrictions on distributors are governed by a rule of reason.

The most interesting question of all in this area is, Why should there be any laws at all? Buyers do not lack information; tying agreements, exclusive dealing agreements, and exclusive distributorships are contracts that one business voluntarily enters into with another. If terms are unfavorable, the business may terminate the relationship. If the selling company makes unreasonable demands or ties goods unreasonably, then that company will lose business to others. Exclusionary practices law is an attempt to address the power differences between larger businesses (suppliers) and small ones (distributors).

From the perspective of consumers, exclusionary agreements are irrelevant. Whether goods are offered to consumers via exclusive dealerships or not probably has little impact on price or variety of goods as long as the market for the goods was not concentrated beforehand. If problems exist, they are problems of market concentration rather than problems of exclusionary agreements. Policies designed to limit concentration will be more likely to benefit the consumer in this regard than exclusionary practices law.

ANTITRUST LAW AS PUBLIC POLICY

Antitrust law is frequently discussed in legal terms; that is, What is the law? Is the law consistent? What should the law be? Antitrust law has been subjected to a fair amount of economic analysis by people like Posner, Armentano, Elzinga, Bork, and Audretsch. What is generally lacking from the literature is any analysis of antitrust law from a political perspective. This final section will add to the political analysis in the preceding sections and examine antitrust as a public policy from a political perspective.

The Goals of Antitrust

One major problem with antitrust policy is that it attempts to attain several goals simultaneously. Multiple goals are a characteristic of many public policies, but rarely are the policy goals as inherently contradictory as they are in antitrust policy. An examination of legislative debates and subsequent implementation reveals at least five proposed goals for antitrust policy.

First, one antitrust goal is clearly economic deconcentration. The problem addressed by the Fifty-first Congress was the problem of trusts, which, by nature of their size, stifled competition. According to Senator Sherman, "The popular mind is agitated with . . . the inequality of condition, of wealth, and opportunity that has grown within a single generation out of the concentration of capital into vast combinations" (cited in Van Cise, 1982: 23). Again, Sherman stated, "If we will not endure a King as a political power, we should not endure a King over the production, transportation and sale of the necessaries of life." Conspiracies alone were not sufficient to pass the Sherman Act, but conspiracies to set prices along with economic concentration were.

The economic deconcentration goal is as much a political goal as an economic goal. By deciding where to locate rail lines and the rates to charge, railroads could decide if cities were to flourish or to disappear. Trusts were seen by the muckrakers and cartoonists of the day as exacting political concessions from politicians. Deconcentration is linked, therefore, to arguments for political democracy as well as for economic democracy (see Van Cise, 1982). Large business, according to the argument, undermines the competitive marketplace and perverts the political process. This suggests a second goal for antitrust, political democracy.

A third proposed goal for antitrust is economic efficiency. Monopolies, according to traditional microeconomic theory (see Armentano, 1982), restrict output and set prices higher than the competitive market price. Such a process is inefficient. This antitrust goal is embraced by most economists. Posner (1976: 20), for example, states that for the Sherman Act "the dominant legislative intent has been to promote some approximation to the economist's ideal of competition, viewed as a means toward the end of maximizing efficiency." Efficiency was the goal, and competition was the means.

Efficiency as a goal of antitrust policy is clearly correct; when individuals argue, as Bork (1978) does, that efficiency is the *only* goal, they are clearly incorrect. Efficiency as an economic concept was hardly developed at the time of the Sherman Act (see Brozen, 1982). The debates over the Sherman Act (or over the Robinson-Patman Act or the Celler-Kefauver Act for that matter) do not reveal a solid grasp of microeconomics and an understanding of the economic concept of efficiency. To argue that efficiency is the *sole* goal of antitrust, therefore, is to argue that the goal of antitrust policy *should* be efficiency.

Fourth, consumer welfare has been proposed as an antitrust goal. The most persuasive arguments on this point are made by Bork (1978: 20): "[D]elegation [of legislative authority to the judiciary in the Sherman Act] was confined by the policy of advancing consumer welfare." Bork argues that only consumer welfare can be justified as a goal of antitrust policy from the legislative intent of the Sherman Act. Bork then, however, makes an economic leap of analysis to equate "consumer welfare" with efficiency.

To be sure, consumer welfare does increase from the results of allocative and productive efficiency. As prices drop as the result of efficiency, consumers benefit. Consumer welfare, however, should not be defined in such narrow economic terms. Consumers have interests in things other than

Figure 9.1. The relationship between the goals of antitrust policy.

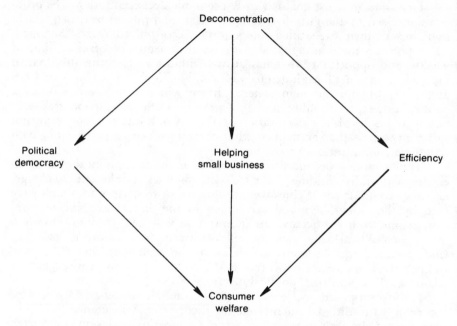

low prices. Consumer welfare is enhanced by expanding consumer choice, a prospect not likely if monopoly production of a homogeneous good is the end result of efficiency. Consumer welfare is also enhanced by the responsiveness of the market to individual consumer demands—again, something less likely in a concentrated, yet efficient market because large firms produce efficiencies often by eliminating service (e.g., chain supermarkets). Consumer welfare is clearly a goal of antitrust policy, and it encompasses more than mere efficiency.

Fifth, antitrust policy has the goal of assisting small business (Van Cise, 1982). The arguments of Brandeis for the Clayton Act refer to the necessities of protecting small business from the evils of large business (McCraw, 1981). The Robinson-Patman Act was passed in response to pressures of small businesses that sought to limit the national chain stores. Interpreting the law under exclusionary practices and price discrimination as anything other than an effort to protect small business is difficult.

Are the Goals Consistent?

Is it possible to treat the five antitrust goals as consistent? In the eyes of various persons, the goals of antitrust policy can be seen as complementary.[7] The goals can be linked together in a "model of goals" as seen in figure 9.1. According to this view, the base problem is that industry is concentrated (either by trusts, monopolies, or collusion). The economic side of this argu-

---

7. By making this argument, using a model of goals, I do not mean to imply that any one person holds all the views expressed here. What is presented is a combination of views from a variety of different individuals and should not be attributed an any single individual.

ment holds that concentration results in inefficiency because it violates the assumptions of neoclassical microeconomic theory. Inefficiency, in turn, results in a drop in consumer welfare (broadly defined).

The political side of the argument holds that economic concentration is easily translated into political power and that the political power is used for abusive purposes. Securing preferential treatment from legislators, influencing court decisions by determining appointments (e.g., the number of railroad lawyers serving on the Supreme Court from 1880 to 1930 far exceeds the number one would expect by chance alone), or buying Senate seats are three possibilities. Political abuses, in turn, result in a decline in consumer welfare as the political process is used to protect large business.

The small business branch of the argument holds that concentration tends to drive small businesspeople out of business. With the decline in the number of small businesses, consumers lose some of the benefits they were receiving in terms of special service, responsiveness, and even price competition. Brandeis' arguments about the inherent goodness of small business are relevant here.

All the antitrust goals, therefore, could be compatible in a theoretical ideal. In the real world, however, they are not. The relationship between concentration and efficiency has been directly and competently challenged by Armentano (1982). In many cases, concentrated industries with large, almost monopolistic firms are more efficient than a series of small firms (see McCraw, 1981).[8] If efficiency is unrelated to concentration, then efficiency conflicts with the goal of helping small business. Exclusionary practices and price discrimination are competitive devices, yet they are harmful to small business. Efficiency and protection of small business may not be consistent. Similar logic contrasts the goals of political democracy with those of efficiency and small business. If efficiency leads to concentration, then efficiency can contribute to political abuses by concentrated industries. Posner, Brozen, Bork, and others rejected this conflict; and this rejection will be discussed later on. What Posner and the others argue is that small business is far more likely to abuse the political system with truckers fixing prices, agricultural co-ops getting preferential price supports, and textile makers gaining import tariffs. Although Posner's argument that small business has far more influence on government than big business is open to question, he does show how the goal of protecting small business might conflict with the political abuse goal. With little effort, all the goals in figure 9.1 can be shown to conflict with each other.

Has Antitrust Attained Its Goals?

Comparing antitrust policy to its goals reveals a policy that must be considered a failure. First, if the goal of antitrust policy is to prevent economic concentration, it has clearly failed. As noted earlier, the aggregate

8. What Armentano (1982) argues is that the microeconomic ideal of perfect competition never exists in the real world. As a result, seeking such an ideal often diverts us from realizing that efficient structures can exist that do not follow the ideal. By rejecting the model of perfect competition as an ideal against which public policy is to be measured, Armentano implicitly calls into question much of the economic arguments in other areas of regulation. A single phone company, for example, might be more efficient than a series of competing phone systems. A system of government regulation might provide more consumer benefits than the market might ever hope to attain. The implications of Armentano's arguments are important for the study of regulation; unfortunately he does not pursue them.

concentration of American industry has increased since 1929 even though the increase is not dramatic. The concentration ratios within individual industries have varied. Some industries have become more concentrated whereas other industries have become less concentrated (see Brozen, 1982: 24). Between 1935 and 1972, for example, the top four firms in the beer industry increased their market share from 11 percent to 50 percent (with substantial increases since 1972 to at least 70 percent). The top four firms in meat-packing, on the other hand, dropped from 56 percent of the market to 20 percent. One result that is clear, however, is that antitrust policy has not led to a significant deconcentration of industry.

Second, has antitrust policy resulted in improvements in efficiency? Armentano (1982) marshals convincing evidence that the large industrial firms of the early twentieth century achieved and held large market shares because they were more efficient than other firms. Breaking up such efficient firms resulted in smaller, less efficient firms. In addition, the antitrust actions under the Robinson-Patman Act and the Clayton Act's provisions on exclusionary practices are designed to limit competition and the resulting efficiencies. The conclusion of recent economic analysis (e.g., Armentano, 1982; Brozen, 1982; Posner, 1976; Bork, 1978) is that antitrust law has not led to greater efficiency.

Third, has antitrust law contributed to greater political and economic democracy? Is our government less subject to the abuses of big business than it was in the nineteenth century? This is a fairly complex question, and an answer will be attempted later. The weight of the scholarly literature in political science, however, does not indicate that government has become any less responsive to the pressures of large business (see Lowi, 1969).

Fourth, has antitrust policy aided small business? No systematic evidence has been gathered on this question, and, therefore, no unequivocal answer is possible. Price discrimination cases clearly benefit small business at the expense of others. Exclusionary practices suits probably do likewise. If antitrust policy meets any goal, it probably meets this one.

Finally, are consumers better off with antitrust policy than they would be without it? Probably not. Some evidence exists that antitrust policy sanctions inefficiencies in the market. Other evidence indicates that it has had no impact on economic concentration, and, as a result, the choices available to consumers are being limited. The brands of beer, the types of American-made automobiles, the variation in grocery stores, and the choices in countless other areas have decreased. Maintaining that consumers have benefited from antitrust policy would be difficult.

Market Concentration Aside, Should We Worry About Bigness?

The economic revisionists (e.g., Bork, Brozen, Armentano, Posner) argue that the goal of antitrust policy ought to be economic efficiency and that we should accept big business for the benefits it yields. They argue that firms grow to large proportions and retain a large market share over time because they serve the needs of the market better than small firms. Firms such as IBM or Campbell's Soup face no lack of potential competitors, but retain their market share because they have achieved superior efficiencies somewhere in the process. Firms that are not competitive, such as U.S. Steel, which dropped from 65 percent of the market to 20 percent, or International Harvester, which dropped from a near monopoly to near bankruptcy, will be punished by the market. Armentano (1982: 121) concludes: "All of the corporations [e.g. Standard Oil, American Tobacco, Alcoa] examined in these classic cases had expanded outputs, reduced prices, and engaged in important technological innovation, entirely consistent with competitive behavior and efficient performance."

Brozen (1982) goes so far as to argue that bigness is a positive good. He presents data that show large businesses are more productive, pay higher wages, and raise prices more slowly than do small businesses. Other evidence not presented by Brozen indicates that large businesses are generally safer places to work (see chapter 8, although this may be a function of visibility to OSHA or to labor union pressure).[9]

As to the political influence of big business, Brozen pooh-poohs it. He correctly notes that definitive studies of the relationship between government influence and the size of business do not exist. To support his argument that large business is not influential, he cites two case studies of political scientists (one from 1961 and one from 1969), argues that big oil companies have not been successful in pressing their demands on government, argues that local drugstores are more protected than large pharmaceutical companies, and then quotes Posner. Powner (1976: 18) states "it is therefore unclear whether on balance concentrated, or monopolistic, industries will obtain greater help from the political process than unconcentrated, or competitive industries. This theoretical indeterminancy is mirrored in the empirical works, where we observe many unconcentrated industries—agriculture, trucking, local broadcasting, banking, medicine, to name a few—enjoying governmental protection against competition."

Both the economic and the political arguments for large business merit some response. First, in terms of economics, to realize that a monopolistic firm will lose its market percentage if it fails to compete effectively is gratifying but not satisfying. A noncompetitive firm will lose its market share in the long run, but that long run is fairly long. U.S. Steel began its existence in 1901 with a market share of 66 percent. In its corporate history, U.S. Steel has been characterized by conservative, risk-avoiding management, has failed to innovate, has sought the protection of import duties, and has clearly not been competitive. Despite all this, U.S. Steel still controls 20 percent of the steel market in the United States and is the largest steel producer in the country. At the same time that it was pressing for import duties against "unfair" foreign competition, rather than modernize to compete, U.S. Steel purchased Marathon Oil. Market punishment for large firms that are not competitive appears to be very slow and somewhat uncertain.

Second, the argument that government is not more responsive to large business is difficult to maintain. Large businesses have inherent advantages in the process of lobbying governments. Among the variables that scholars of interest groups feel are important in affecting the policy process are size, resources, and cohesion (see Zeigler and Peak, 1972; Rourke, 1984; Meier, 1979; and chapter 2). Size in either employment or sales translates into power resources such as votes that are valued in the political process. Resources, especially with the laws that now permit corporations to set up

9. Small business, on the other hand, is more innovative and more likely to create new jobs.

political action committees, are essential in gaining access to policymakers. Cohesion is important because it can be used to argue that there is only one side to the issue. Lack of cohesion is less a problem for businesses in concentrated industries because there are fewer firms to coordinate.

The advantages can be translated into political results. Large corporations can argue that they need protection because if they are allowed to fail, it will have a major disruptive impact on the economy. Both Chrysler and Penn Central Railroad were given loan guarantees after making this argument. Continental of Illinois, the seventh largest bank in the nation, was kept open with an influx of federal money in May 1984, the same week that First Continental Bank of Del City, Oklahoma (a much smaller bank), was allowed to fold. Large businesses inherently make larger demands on government. Surely no small business has ever abused the political system in the manner of ITT in the 1970s. Direct bribes of legislators, a proposed underwriting of the Republican National Convention, and a condemning connection with coups and electoral manipulation in Chile make the local drug stores' efforts at fair trade laws seem pretty mild.

The noncompetitive practices in agriculture that Posner notes are true, but he fails to realize that these practices are also the work of large corporations. Clearly, the most protected and heavily subsidized portion of agriculture is dairy farming; and with the milk scandals of the 1970s, it may also be the most corrupt. The massive campaign contributions and political influence are not the result of small dairy farmers from Wisconsin lobbying their member of Congress but the result of giant agricultural cooperatives committed to noncompetitive public policies. Five dairy cooperatives received more than $100 million in subsidies in 1983 (Wines, 1983h: 2668); each had sales in excess of $1 billion, hardly the size of a small business.

Small business is less worrisome in politics because small business simply lacks the resources or the need to make the same types of demands on government as large business. The domestic shoe industry would love to have "domestic content" legislation for all shoes sold in the United States, but they lack the resources to convert such a demand. Beef import quotas are minor compared to the "Harley-Davidson" import fee. To argue that large businesses are not as effective as small business in politics is to ignore reality. The Business Roundtable and direct business lobbying in recent years have had an impact on the restriction of the powers of the FTC, the failure to establish an Agency for Consumer Advocacy, and the limitation of payments to outside intervenors in the regulatory process (see chapter 4).

In addition to political concerns about the influence of large businesses in politics, their impact on the economy is also worthy of concern. The concern, however, is not as some present it that the *Fortune* 500 companies will eventually own the entire economy; that is clearly not a threat. Large corporations, like all large bureaucracies, are risk-averse and are unlikely to take the economic risks necessary to dominate the entire economic market. In every decade, new product lines develop as the result of risk-taking by entrepreneurs in small and marginal firms. The success of the personal computer market can be attributed to Apple and other small firms, not to the industry giants (IBM's PC is still very much a non-IBM machine with many non-IBM components). The economic arguments against large corporations lie elsewhere.

First, large corporations by definition are more bureaucratic than small corporations. Because they need to oversee the work of more individuals, large corporations will have more levels of control and more levels of supervision (see Downs, 1967). As bureaucratized organizations, they will devote a greater portion of their resources to nonproductive activities and rely on cumbersome committee decision patterns (see Wright, 1978). Such large organizations are slow to respond to changes in the enironment. IBM, for example, would not have entered the computer business at all were it not for a separate unit under Thomas Watson, Jr. (Fisher, McKie, and Mancke, 1983). In sum, theoretical reasons exist why large corporations are likely to be slower to change, to invest more resources in control than production, and to be less innovative.

Second, large corporations can weather mistakes much more easily than can small ones. A small corporation is unlikely to be able to survive a major error in product line innovation as General Motors did with the X-car. Despite introducing a car that performed poorly compared to other models and despite known safety problems, General Motors was able to survive and flourish (GM Knew, 1983). Similarly, Eli Lilly knowingly failed to disclose information about deaths attributed to Oraflex in Europe when applying for distribution of the drug in the United States (Oraflex Linked, 1983: 26). Economic mistakes by small corporations simply do not compare in magnitude to those of large corporations, and small corporations are more likely to bear the penalties of such mistakes.

Third, large conglomerates have the ability to avoid the brutality of a competitive marketplace. Inefficient units in a conglomerate can be subsidized with the profits of other units. ITT, for example, has held onto its less profitable subsidiaries such as Continental Baking and Sheraton Hotels, subsidizing them with profits elsewhere in the firm (Pauly with Ipsen, 1984: 50). Although such a process is not economically rational, such behavior might occur when size rather than profits is the dominant concern of management or when the unit has some other value to top management (Chrysler, for example, sold off a profitable defense unit to funnel money into its money-losing car production).

Fourth, large corporations often have the option of not responding to environmental pressures and may be large enough to force the environment to adapt to them (see Azumi and Hage, 1972). This applies in both economic and political situations. Rather than respond to the competitive pressures of Japanese automakers, a large corporation can seek to change the environment by pressing for import quotas and domestic content (efforts that work even better if labor can be convinced to take the point, a lesson learned from the Clean Air Act Amendments in 1977; see Ornstein and Elder, 1978). With enough skill, political solutions can be substituted for economic solutions as long as governments can be persuaded to impose such solutions.

The arguments against large corporations (which economists confuse with arguments against concentration in specific industries) are not so irrational as economists paint them. Although some of the arguments have an economic base, they are essentially political arguments about the distribution of power in society. Advocating that government avoid action in this area is the same as advocating that the current distribution of power is acceptable. Such arguments, despite their reliance on economic analysis, are essentially political.

Reforming Antitrust Policy

The goal of antitrust policy should be to improve consumer welfare, broadly defined. The policy should permit the consumer the widest choice of goods, at the lowest prices, with the types of quality and supporting services that are desired. Using this as the goal of antitrust policy suggests that several changes should be made.

First, the only area of antitrust policy that clearly leads to gains in consumer welfare is the section 1 Sherman Act prohibition against collusion. Price-fixing is detrimental to consumer interests; and judged by the number of cases prosecuted, substantial price-fixing occurs in our economy (see Bork, 1978). The resources of the antitrust agencies should be committed to this area.

Second, if the political decisions of this country indicate that small business is somehow especially meritorious, then direct policies should be undertaken to encourage small business. Such action should be direct, open, and handled through the Small Business Administration. Antitrust law, when used to protect small business from competition, can be harmful to consumers. The Clayton Act and the Robinson-Patman Act should be repealed.

Third, section 2 of the Sherman Act and all antitrust laws other than section 1 of the Sherman Act should also be repealed. Section 2 has occasionally been used to break up effective, efficient firms and to saddle similar firms with costly antitrust suits. If economic bigness and concentration are major concerns of people, then the United States should adopt a policy on economic concentration. Allowing the courts to guess at what Senators Sherman, Edmunds, or Hoar intended under the Sherman Act is an inefficient method of dealing with the problems of concentration.

An economic concentration policy might take the following form. First, the market will be allowed to determine the optimal size of firms; the government will not file any suits to break up firms in an industry. Second, once an industry becomes concentrated (say, with a Herfindahl index of over 1000 or a four-firm concentration figure of 60 + percent), then all government policies designed to assist that industry will be repealed. A concentrated industry would be denied the protection of any tariffs or import quotas. Competition from foreign manufacturers appears to be a reasonable way of ensuring that large firms remain competitive. If goods can be produced more cheaply in other countries, we should import them and produce goods where the United States maintains a competitive advantage. In addition, once an industry becomes concentrated, all special tax systems or tax expenditures for this industry would be automatically repealed. This process should greatly simplify the tax code in the process. Finally, if such a concentrated firm wishes to acquire another firm, either vertical, horizontal or conglomerate, it should absorb the full costs of such an acquisition, including the full cost of money borrowed (i.e., no tax deductions for interest payments).

The preceding brief outline of a concentration policy is not the only one nor may it even be the best one. The point of the argument is that if economic concentration is a concern, then the issue should be addressed directly. If the consensus of the governmental process is to encourage corporate growth, then corporate growth should be encouraged. If the consensus

Table 9.1 Summary of Antitrust Policy

Economics	
Firms	Vary
Entry	Varies
Profits	Vary
Technology	
Complexity	Varies
Stability	Varies
Substitutes	Vary
The Subsystem	
Bureaucracy	Strong
Industry coalition	Weak
Nonindustry coalition (critics)	Weak
Bureaucratic Resources	
Expertise	Moderate
Cohesion	Low/High
Leadership	Moderate
Legislative authority	
Goals	Vague
Coverage	Limited
Sanctions	Weak
Procedures	Weak
Involvement of MacroPolitical Actors	
Congress	Moderate
President	Moderate
Courts	High

See Appendix.

is to limit corporate growth, then measures to limit corporate growth should be instituted. If the consensus is to do neither, then concentration should be determined by the market. The question of economic concentration is as much a political question as an economic question, and it should be addressed in the political process. This is a far more reasonable way to consider economic concentration than the current system of antitrust laws.

SUMMARY

Who benefits from antitrust policy? The only clear beneficiary of antitrust policy is small business. The total benefit, however, is marginal; antitrust is unable to insulate these firms from the penalties of the marketplace. Antitrust policy imposes some costs on large business and consumers. Costs and benefits are generally minor because antitrust policy has failed to attain its goals.

In terms of the variables discussed in chapter 2, why does antitrust policy benefit no one? (see Table 9.1.) The general environment has had little impact on the direction of antitrust policy. Technology (see McCraw, 1981) should influence antitrust policy if some large firms are more efficient than small firms, but it does not. Economics, especially the number of firms and the profit level in an industry, should be related to antitrust policy. The courts' emphasis on intent, however, has generally removed such structural economic factors from antitrust policy.

The explanation for the state of antitrust policy lies in the political environment and in bureaucratic motivations. Antitrust policy is sometimes salient so that changes in the law have been enacted in response to political demands. The Populists of the 1890s, the labor unions and businesses in 1914, and the small businesses of 1938 all pressed Congress for relief from some type of oppression. Broadening the scope of antitrust can be attributed to Congress. Presidents, in turn, have emphasized and de-emphasized antitrust. The Nixon, Ford, and Carter administrations increased antitrust activity; the Reagan administration dropped many of these suits. Presidential encouragement appears important in stimulating antitrust activities. Through the appointment process, presidents can have a major impact on the direction of antitrust policy.

These political forces are tempered by the bureaucracy. Although antitrust bureaucracies are fairly responsive to presidential initiatives, they also reflect the norms of the legal profession. Trial experience is important to these bureaucrats, especially experience where the attorney can demonstrate his or her talents (Weaver, 1977; Katzman, 1980). As a result, the simpler, easy to win Robinson-Patman cases have been stressed rather than structural monopoly cases.

Bureaucracies have been allowed discretion in antitrust because it is a complex, legalistic area. The bureaucracy, however, has failed to dominate the subsystem because the bureaucracies have only moderate expertise and lack cohesion and often leadership. With vague goals and procedures that require court action for enforcement, the bureaucracy must respond to, rather than resist, the pressures from the political environment. The lack of strong advocacy coalitions, however, means that at times there will be no environmental pressures.

Finally, the courts remain a major policy force in this area. Antitrust policy is implemented through the courts; even the FTC usually ends up in court after its administrative procedures are exhausted. Case-by-case resolution means that application is uneven and policy is inconsistent.

In total, antitrust policy may be a symbolic policy. Antitrust evokes strong images of Teddy Roosevelt busting trusts. Despite the inability of antitrust policy to produce economic deconcentration, antitrust advocates often retain this idealized goal. In practice, however, the policy rarely benefits the general public or anyone other than antitrust lawyers and an occasional small business.

10

Reforming Regulation

Regulatory reform has been continually on the national agenda since the New Deal. Although regulatory reform rarely ever dominates the agenda, several reforms have been enacted. The deregulation efforts of the late 1970s in surface transportation, airline transportation, and banking were all billed as regulatory reforms as were the early 1970s efforts to protect consumers. To propose regulatory reforms, however, implies that regulation has shortcomings. The implication of shortcomings suggests that regulation has failed to meet its goals. This chapter examines regulatory reform within this context. First, the general goals of regulation, both current and proposed, are discussed. Second, regulation's failure to meet these goals is briefly examined. Third, a series of reforms designed to improve regulatory performance is evaluated.

REGULATORY GOALS

Regulation, like all other public policies, is purposive (Anderson, 1984). Regulatory agencies are created and regulations are issued to attain some goal. Although goals might be as vague as "the public interest, convenience, and necessity" or as specific as "fishable and swimmable waters by 1985," all programs have some goals. To integrate this discussion across numerous policy areas, we will treat the goals of regulation in general rather than the specific goals of any single policy. Regulation's goals can be divided at a general level into two clusters—those dealing with efficiency and those dealing with equity.[1]

Efficiency

The dominant goal of regulation as expressed in the literature is efficiency. After an analysis of government regulation's various goals, for example, Thompson and Jones (1982: 232) conclude, "This leaves only one function for regulation to perform: promotion of the more efficient use of society's scarce resources." Efficiency is normally defined as the optimal allocation of resources such that total utility for a society is maximized.

---

1. This discussion assumes that such specific goals as safe workplaces, fishable waters, safe consumer products, national transportation systems, and so on can be generalized for comparison purposes.

In practice, efficiency is a slippery term; knowing when any allocation of resources is optimal is impossible simply because such perfect knowledge does not exist. In a practical situation, efficiency is generally used in a comparative sense; if firm A produces a good more cheaply than firm B, then firm A is more efficient than firm B. The comparative standard usually employed to evaluate regulation's efficiency is the theoretical distribution of goods resulting from perfect competition in microeconomic theory.[2]

In a perfectly competitive market system, all goods are allocated to their optimal use. Perfect competition exists when six conditions are met (see Stokey and Zeckhauser, 1978: 293, or any economics text). First, all participants in the market have perfect information; sellers know the quantity that will be demanded at various prices; buyers know the relevant performance information about the good offered for sale. Second, all exchanges of goods are costless; that is, individuals can buy or sell goods in the marketplace without transaction costs. Third, a market exists for all goods; if markets do not exist, the model does not hold because black markets impose transaction costs. Fourth, the number of buyers and sellers is large so that no buyer can affect price by his or her decision to sell. Fifth, consumption by one individual does not affect the consumption of others; that is, no externalities exist. Sixth, the goods concerned are not common goods such as national defense; a common good is a good that must be provided for everyone if it is provided for anyone. Common goods create a free rider problem whereby individuals can enjoy the benefit of a good without paying for it. In a perfectly competitive market, prices are set by supply and demand, and prices allocate goods and services to their optimal uses.

The market described by the microeconomist is a theoretical ideal to be used for comparison purposes.[3] No one argues that actual markets work like this although some markets approach this ideal more than others. The current market for money, for example, resembles a perfectly competitive market with interest rates set by supply and demand. The market for farm products such as wheat and corn also approaches this ideal. Other markets such as the market for medical care (with restrictions on practice) or the market for local phone service deviate greatly from the ideal.

Economists recognize that real markets do not operate the way the theoretical model works. They argue, however, that the theoretical model is superior to any alternative and failure to attain such an ideal in the real world may be justification for regulation. Four major deviations from the ideal model have been identified—lack of competition, externalities, imper-

2. Although economists often compare the actions of government to this ideal, perfectly competitive market, they rarely compare the actions of individual private firms to the ideal. Such firms are given the benefit of the doubt; either they are efficient or they tolerate inefficiencies because they are maximizing other goals. Just as public organizations generally fail to meet this ideal standard, private organizations would probably also fail.

3. Economists are generally not bothered by the criticism of political scientists that this model does not fit the real world (see Kelman, 1981a). For the most part, few argue that the real world ever meets the requirements of the model; usually, the argument is that the private sector better approaches the model than public sector intervention. A more serious criticism is that offered by Armentano. In his analysis of antitrust policy, Armentano (1982) argues that the model may be less efficient than some instances of monopoly markets in the real world. If the model is inappropriate (either because it produces inefficient outcomes or because efficiency is not a goal), then the prescriptions based on this model have little justification.

fect information, and public goods. Collectively, these deviations are termed market failures, and each provides an efficiency-related goal for regulation. Although market failures can be used to justify regulation, regulation in this view should be undertaken only if regulation is superior to the unregulated market (that is, if the market is more efficient after regulation than before).

Lack of competition.   Regulation may be justified when the market fails because it lacks competition (Daly and Brady, 1976: 172; Thompson and Jones, 1982: 232; Breyer, 1982: 15). Competition is guaranteed in the ideal model by the requirement that the market have numerous sellers and buyers so that no one seller or buyer can determine the market price. In practice, a market may not be large enough to support numerous sellers (e.g., local markets for professional services), or capital investments might create large barriers to entry, thus limiting the number of firms that enter or are likely to enter (e.g., railroads).

The most extreme case of lack of competition is monopoly, dominance of the market by a single firm. If one firm controls 100 percent of the market, that firm can set prices by manipulating supply. Classic monopoly behavior is to restrict output, thus creating shortages that raise prices and allow the monopolist to make economic profits (i.e., profits greater than the normal return to capital). In strictly economic terms, monopoly is inefficient because fewer goods are produced at higher prices than in a perfectly competitive world.

In some cases, natural monopolies exist and may be more practical than a competitive market. Clearly, one would not expect the government to provide land grants so that five railroads would serve the same community, nor would one find value in having several local telephone companies if these companies were not interconnected. In cases of monopoly, regulation is justified in the theoretical model; the purpose of such regulation is efficiency, to set prices such that the monopolist's marginal revenue is equal to marginal cost. An option other than regulation in this situation is government operation of the enterprise; this option, however, is rarely considered in the United States.

In monopoly, the absence of competition is clear-cut; the monopoly firm has no competitors. Monopoly, however, is only a special case; absence of competition can occur anytime the number of firms is small and explicit or implicit collusion is permitted.[4] Oligopoly can create the same problems as monopoly (restricted output and higher prices) if the firms are permitted to meet and set prices such as merchant marine shippers do and as local professionals, trucking firms, and airlines once did. If collusion is evident, regulations can be used either to control prices or to prevent collusion (e.g., vigorous prosecution of antitrust laws).

Regulation in the absence of total monopoly is controversial even within the economics profession. Recent antitrust critics have argued that many of the famous trusts such as Standard Oil and the Sugar Trust never engaged in monopoly behavior and were actually opposed because they were ruthless

---

4. One type of collusion is not addressed here, collusion that is expressly granted by government. Governments from time to time sponsor cartels to eliminate competitive behavior. European industries are often formed into cartels. In recent years, the U.S. government has been hard on cartels opposing such practices by professional groups, truckers, airlines, railroads, and stockbrokers.

competitors. Such large concentrations often resulted from large economies of scale in some facet of production (see chapter 9).

Externalities. When consumption by one person affects consumption by another person, an externality exists. Although externalities can be either positive or negative, we normally are concerned only with negative externalities (when consumption by one person harms the consumption of another; see Breyer, 1982: 23; Daly and Brady, 1976: 172; Thompson and Jones, 1982: 232). Pollution, workplace accidents, and communicable diseases are negative externalities.[5] In economic terms, externalities are inefficient because the cost of a good to an individual is less than the cost of the good to society. For example, if a firm manufacturing steel does not have to worry about air pollution, it will be able to produce steel more cheaply by polluting the air. This pollution affects third parties and imposes a cost on them. Because this cost is not incorporated into the price of steel, more steel than optimal will be demanded (which, of course, aggravates the externality).[6]

The solution to externalities is simple. If regulation is merited, then the regulatory agency's function is to make sure the good's market price is equal to its social price. As the debates over environmental policy illustrate (see chapter 6), such regulation might take more than one form. The regulator could rule that the externality be eliminated (zero discharges in water pollution) or impose a tax on the manufacturer equal to the difference between the market price and the social cost (an effluent tax).

Lack of Information. When buyers lack information about goods or services, they make decisions that misallocate resources (Daly and Brady, 1976: 173; Thompson and Jones, 1982; 232). In a variety of markets, consumers lack information to make rational decisions. In choosing the services of a lawyer or doctor, for example, the layperson usually has little information about the quality of service that individual practitioners provide or about the optimal amount of service to purchase. Because consumers often rely on the seller for advice about such matters, they are likely to purchase more services than needed (a situation that occurs in pesticide use as well).

Lack of information also encompasses those situations when consumers purchase harmful products. Consumers would not normally eat foods that contain carcinogenic additives or purchase automobiles that are unsafe. At the very least, with adequate consumer information, the price of such goods would drop compared to the price of similar goods without the defects.

In a situation with information asymmetry (that is, where the seller's information is superior to the buyer's), two major regulatory options exist. The simplest remedy is to provide information to the consumer. Because

5. A positive externality would exist if one person who appreciated art a great deal collected art in a gallery (and was willing to pay the full price of such a collection) and then opened the gallery to the public. Education is believed to have positive externalties in terms of civic contributions and quality of life.

6. In a strict economic sense, consumption of every good creates some externalities, however small. Resources are not infinite; because they are scarce, the consumption of any good reduces the total supply of that good that can be consumed by others. Such externalities may be small, but they still exist and limit the strict application of the concept to regulatory problems because almost every act of consumption has externalities.

consumers may be unwilling to consider such information (information consumption has costs, and without consuming the information, it is difficult to know what the costs of not consuming it are), a second alternative is to ban unsafe products.

Public Goods.   The final market failure justification for regulation is public goods. A public good is a good that, if provided to one person, must be provided to all persons. Opening a public park in a city creates a public good that is available to all citizens. Because public goods once provided are often free, public goods can be overused, thus diminishing their value. For example, after the invention of radio, the public airways (a public good) were available to all who wished to broadcast. The result was overuse and chaos; the broadcast industry demanded federal regulation so that orderly broadcasting could be undertaken.

Creating a public good, therefore, requires regulation either to limit access to the public good or to guarantee that the public good is paid for by the users. In general, the problem with most public goods is the latter. Citizens have an interest in such public goods as national defense, police protection, and pest control (Daly and Brady, 1976: 172); but they have no interest in paying for them. The mandatory tax system is the normal solution for such situations, however, rather than regulation.[7]

Equity

According to Arthur Okun (1976), the major trade-off in public policy is between efficiency and equality. Market systems are designed to enhance efficiency but are unconcerned with the distribution of benefits in society. A concern with equity or the justice of any distribution of goods falls outside the range of economic analysis based on the microeconomic model. Regulation has never been solely concerned with efficiency; as Schuck (1980: 120) notes, "significant regulatory decisions are ineluctably political." Under a broad interpretation of equity, a variety of regulatory values can be subsumed, including fairness, justice, openness, and equality. Three specific equity goals that combine elements of all these values will be discussed— equalizing the distribution of political and economic power, altering the distribution of income, and reducing uncertainty.

Equalizing Power.   The history of regulation provides numerous examples of regulation designed to neutralize the political or economic power of other individuals (see Daly and Brady, 1976: 174). Legislative battles in collective bargaining followed such a pattern as first unions sought government intervention to support their collective bargaining position (the

---

7. Daly and Brady (1976) list one additional economic justification for regulation, the inefficient extraction of natural resources. As an example they note the practice of flaring gas from oil fields before the invention of the seamless pipe. They argue that government regulation is justified to conserve such resources. Such an argument could be made to defend the federal automobile mileage requirements. This argument is not included here because it is not solely an economic argument. Gas in oil fields actually had no market value until it could be transported; without flaring, it was a hazard. Similarly, gasoline mileage regulation is more likely to be justified for political reasons (e.g., unstable foreign supplies, balance of payment problems, and so on) than for economic reasons.

Wagner Act) and then business made a similar effort to limit the power of unions (the Taft-Hartley Act). The movement to regulate railroads can be attributed as much to efforts by farmers and shippers to limit the economic power of railroads and their ability to decide what towns would survive and prosper (see Kolko, 1965) as to any effort to limit monopoly pricing. In fact, railroad practices such as rebates, long-haul discounts, and volume discounts can be interpreted as competitive behavior.

The argument that regulation was established to alter power distributions can also be made for more recent regulatory efforts. Automobile safety advocates seek to impose the costs of safer vehicles on the manufacturers rather than let the market or a newly designed market determine safety. Support for, and opposition to, OSHA illustrate that OSHA regulation concerns workplace power relationships; organized labor opposed the repeal of the "Mickey Mouse" safety regulations in 1978 and used complaints to trigger inspections even though few violations were found (see chapter 8).

Without a doubt, regulation has been used to alter power relationships in American society. Individuals in unfavorable economic situations often seek the aid of government. Farmers demanded subsidies, Grangers wanted lower railroad rates, and small businesses requested Robinson-Patman protection. Because economic advantages are not difficult to translate into political advantages, seeking political solutions to economic problems is a rational political action.[8]

Unacceptable Income Distributions.   Often regulation is an effort to alter the distribution of income within society. Regulations and market orders that limit farm production and subsidize the incomes of farmers redistribute income from urban to rural residents (see chapter 5). Laws requiring equal pay for equal work were originally proposed to *prevent* a redistribution of income from men to women and later were used to *seek* a redistribution of income from men to women. The meager legislative history of the Sherman Act suggests that the lavish life-styles of the trust owners had as much to do with mobilizing public support for the Sherman Act as anything else (see chapter 9).

Regulation may not be the most efficient way to redistribute income from one group to another; transfer payments such as Social Security can clearly redistribute greater amounts of money with fewer transaction costs. Regulation, however, is traditionally less visible than direct transfers of income and probably has fewer political obstacles to overcome. Efficient or not, some regulation is designed to redistribute income.

Reducing Uncertainty.   Unfettered free markets contain a great deal of uncertainty for both business and consumers. Regulation can be used as a means to reduce this uncertainty. The system of bank regulation and deposit insurance was established to restore the confidence of consumers in the banking system and reduce their uncertainty about the safety of such institutions. Agricultural regulation is often justified in a similar manner; market

8. Thompson and Jones (1982) and others would reject the political and economic power goals as inappropriate for regulatory policy. Such a rejection is based on a normative argument that other mechanisms are better able to address such problems. The empirical reality is that regulation is used to alter the distribution of both economic and political power.

orders were authorized, in part, to assure consumers a stable flow of food to market and, thus, reduce consumer uncertainty. Food and drug safety laws can be supported in a similar fashion.

Businesses also see certainty and regulation to provide it. One member of Congress quoted the pleas of the oil and gas industry in the late 1970s: "We would just like to get Congress to do something—regulate, deregulate, put on a tax—but let us know as soon as you can what it is so we can go out and make our plans" (Brown, 1980: 72). Examples of business seeking protection from marketplace uncertainty include the radio industry requesting the FCC, the airline industry demanding a CAB, and the utility industry seeking state regulation (Anderson, 1980).

A final point about equity goals is in order. Although equity is a value-neutral term in that one could advocate more or less equity, equity arguments are rarely used to advocate greater inequality (and when regulation creates inequity as the Federal Maritime Commission does, the actions are usually wrapped in other values). Democratic nations such as the United States have a general bias favoring equity. Government action, therefore, is more easily justified if it is undertaken on behalf of the politically disadvantaged, the poor, or consumers. In fact, in a democratic society, little justification exists for marketplace interventions that exacerbate political inequality, increase the maldistribution of income, or protect the privileged from uncertainty. Accepting equity as a regulatory goal implies normative preferences about equity in society.

Efficiency, Equity, and Regulation

Three points about the regulatory goals of efficiency and equity merit discussion. First, equity and efficiency are two distinct criteria for regulatory policy. Some equity goals clearly conflict with some efficiency goals. The equity goal of low utility prices conflicts with the efficiency goal of providing utilities with sufficient returns to attract investment; the equity goal of providing farmers with greater incomes conflicts with the efficiency goal of optimal allocation of resources across economic sectors. Equity and efficiency may also coincide; correcting imperfect information in consumer areas is consistent with reducing uncertainty; eliminating the externalities of workplace safety corresponds to adjustments in the political balance between management and labor.

Second, both equity and efficiency are normative goals; they are proposals for what regulatory goals should be. Of the two, equity is far more likely to be the *actual* goal of regulation than efficiency; that is, an analyst is more likely to be able to explain why regulation exists in an area by referring to equity than by referring to efficiency. The creation of the ICC reflected the concerns of farmers and others about the economic power of the railroads; the creation of the FCC was at the request of the radio industry to reduce uncertainty; and the FDA was created to eliminate the dangers of unsanitary food.

The legislative history of regulation, including those areas discussed in this book, demonstrates that the United States regulates for political reasons. Business, consumers, or other groups organize politically and press for regulation. They seek to acquire the benefits of regulation for themselves; they do not seek an efficient allocation of resources. Concerns about efficiency in regulation are fairly recent, dating from the post-World War II economic studies of regulation (Weiss, 1981: 3). When such agencies as the Interstate Commerce Commission, the Food and Drug Administration, the Federal Trade Commission, and the New Deal regulatory agencies were created, efficiency was an underdeveloped concept in economics. Legislative justifications for action accordingly did not rely on efficiency. To argue efficiency is the prime goal of regulatory agencies, therefore, is to argue that the agencies should seek a goal different from the one that policymakers intended (Litan and Nordhaus, 1983: 36).

Third, the goal of a regulatory program is not always clear. Chapter 9 discussed the multiple goals attributed to antitrust policy—protection of small business, reduction of uncertainty for large business, limiting the economic power of trusts, providing for consumer welfare, and so on. By viewing various parts of antitrust policy, one can make an argument for any of these goals. Similarly, economic regulation in agriculture is defended in terms of reducing uncertainty, ensuring adequate supplies, and redistributing incomes. Even at levels more specific than such general goals as equity and efficiency, regulatory agencies' goals are multiple; and often these goals conflict.

REGULATION'S SHORTCOMINGS

Regulatory policy is not perfect; no government policy is. Large-scale bureaucratic organizations, be they public or private, make mistakes and fail to attain goals. Regulatory agencies are no exceptions to this rule. This section details the criticisms of regulation. These shortcomings may be divided into political shortcomings and economic second-order consequences. The first are considered direct failings of regulation; the second are indirect failings that may be unintended.

Political Shortcomings

Lack of Responsiveness. The core political criticism of regulation revolves around the beneficiaries of regulation. Regulation has long been justified as action in some vague public interest, which, in turn, has been interpreted as regulation in the interests of the nonregulated rather than the regulated. The charge that regulatory agencies are more responsive to the individuals that they regulate than to a more general public has a long scholarly tradition. Samuel Huntington (1952) first proposed this as a hypothesis based on a case study of the Interstate Commerce Commission. Marver Bernstein (1955) generalized it in his life cycle theory of regulation when he argued that all regulatory agencies eventually become captives of the industry that they regulate. George Stigler (1971), Richard Posner (1974), and Sam Peltzman (1976) formalized this theory in economic terms. Ralph Nader's early studies of regulation (e.g., Fellmuth, 1970) introduced this theory to the popular press. Regulation that protects the regulated industry is perceived as a perversion of the regulatory process, as the use of regulation to protect the fortunate rather than the unfortunate.

Although some scholars would apply the capture criticism to all regulatory agencies (e.g., Lowi, 1969), it clearly applies to some agencies more than to others. The chapters in this book illustrated that the relationship between the agency and the regulated varied a great deal. In some cases (occupational regulation), capture was an appropriate description; in others (consumer protection), it was not (see Quirk, 1981). Because all public bureaucracies are political institutions, they are responsive to their environments (see Salamon and Wamsley, 1975). When regulatory agencies respond to the regulated portion of the environment, intended or not, such responsiveness is perceived as a failure.

Unresponsiveness to Political Institutions.   In the literature on bureaucratic politics, the unresponsiveness of bureaucratic institutions to elected public officials is seen as a major shortcoming (see Rourke, 1984; Redford, 1969; Meier, 1979). Because policymaking bureaucrats are not elected, the responsiveness of bureaus to democratic political institutions is essential. Only through the electoral process is public policy accorded legitimacy. Bureaucracies, including the regulatory bureaucracies, are criticized for being unresponsive to the president or to Congress. Congress, for example, frequently criticized the Federal Trade Commission in the late 1970s for aggressively regulating funeral directors, optometrists, and a variety of other businesses (Weingast and Moran, 1982). Many proposals to reorganize regulatory agencies and eliminate the commission form (e.g., the Ash Council Report) were designed to make regulatory agencies more responsive to the president (see also Ball, 1984).

Support for responsiveness to political institutions operates at two levels. At the most abstract level, responsiveness is supported for the democratic reasons mentioned earlier. At a more specific level, responsiveness is supported because it affects the regulator's policy orientation. For example, one could advocate that the Environmental Protection Agency be more responsive to the president because such responsiveness today would mean a less active EPA. Similarly, many who advocate that the EPA be more responsive to Congress are individuals who seek such responsiveness because they favor more stringent regulation. *The responsiveness of regulatory agencies to government's political institutions has policy implications.*

Ineffectiveness.   A regulatory agency can be considered ineffective when it fails to attain specific legislative goals. Although a judgment of ineffectiveness under the "public interest" goals normally used before 1970 was difficult, since 1970 regulatory goals have become more specific. OSHA has been criticized as ineffective in improving workplace safety (see chapter 8); EPA has moved toward its goals of clean air and clean water only slowly. Regulatory policy in agriculture has been strikingly unsuccessful in reducing the overproduction of agricultural goods, and antitrust policy has been faulted for failing to reach any of its myriad goals. At a general level, sufficient evidence of ineffectiveness exists to designate it as a serious shortcoming.

A closer look at regulatory policy, however, reveals some difficulties with the term *ineffective.* Crandall (1983a) has criticized EPA's Clean Air Act policies as ineffective because they impose costs on business whereas the Sierra Club criticizes the same policies because they are not strong enough. Disputes over effectiveness may, in fact, be disputes over goals. In addition, some regulatory agencies will never attain their legislative goals and, therefore, will be "ineffective" for two reasons. First, some regulatory goals are impossible to meet. The Clean Water Act still requires "zero discharges" by 1985, an outcome that no analyst defends as feasible. Second, many regulatory agencies are not given the resources to attain the goals established by Congress. Regulation in occupational safety and health or environmental protection is characterized by a lack of resources (both personnel and money), inadequate sanctions, and a lack of political support for vigorous regulation. Many regulatory policies may well be ineffective, but the explanation for such failures can often be found at the political level, not at the bureaucratic level.[9]

Poor Decisions.   Regulatory policy has been criticized for simply making bad decisions (see Daly and Brady, 1976: 181). Recent criticized decisions include the EPA decision to require both clean and dirty coal to be scrubbed, OSHA's wholesale adoption of consensus safety standards in 1971, the anticompetitive aspects of state-level occupational regulation, the impact of FDA procedures on drug innovation, and the failure of antitrust policy to prevent large mergers in the oil industry. The charge of poor decisions, although clearly correct, also is problematic for three reasons.

First, whether or not a decision is a poor one is a function of the critic's perception. The EPA decision to scrub all coal is perceived as an excellent decision from the perspective of Eastern coal producers. Organized labor vigorously defended the OSHA consensus standards in 1978. In the wake of Oraflex, some members of Congress feel that FDA should have tighter procedures, and both oil companies and many critics of antitrust policy (such as former Assistant Attorney General William Baxter) feel current antitrust policies are beneficial. Few regulatory decisions will be universally condemned. If regulatory agencies had only a single goal, criticism might reflect poor decisions only. With multiple goals, however, many poor decisions can be viewed as maximizing one goal rather than another.

Second, some poor decisions can be explained, though not justified, by the limitations placed on the regulatory organization. Only a few regulatory agencies have their own research and information units. For the most part, regulatory agencies rely on industry for data. Because industry is not disinterested in the outcome of regulatory decisions, data from industry are suspect. When complex decisions are made with questionable information, less than optimal decisions will result.

Third, all large bureaucratic organizations make mistakes. To expect that regulatory agencies will be less prone to mistakes is unrealistic. Because the decisions made by public organizations are more visible than those made by private organizations, the general perception will be that public organizations make more mistakes. Given the nature of the problems faced by regulatory agencies and the resources at their disposal, an occasional error by regulators must be expected. If such errors are intolerable, the solution is either more realistic goals or greater resources committed to regulation.

9. Legislative actions to create regulatory agencies always reflect compromises even if the compromise concerns only the level of funding. The creation of the Equal Employment Opportunity Commission (EEOC) illustrates the use of symbolic politics in establishing regulation. By creating the EEOC, the advocates of equal employment achieved some of their ends; by not giving the agency any real power, the opponents of equal employment also achieved some of their ends. The price of passage of any controversial regulatory legislation may be the limitation of agency resources; in such cases, regulatory agencies may be ineffective by design.

Lack of Coordination.   Regulatory policy is charged with a lack of coordination resulting in policies that work at cross-purposes. In part, the absence of coordination results because different regulatory agencies attempt to maximize different goals. OSHA, for example, may require that an industrial firm vent emissions to protect workers from exposure whereas EPA prohibits such venting to protect individuals living nearby. Often regulatory authority overlaps. Exposure to carcinogens is regulated by EPA, OSHA, FDA, and CPSC with little effort to prevent duplication or conflict. Overlapping jurisdictions may result in inconsistent policy. Insurance companies, because they are "regulated" by state insurance commissions, have moved rapidly into other financial services whereas banks regulated at the federal level have been restricted.

Even within agencies a lack of coordination is evident. The Environmental Protection Agency regulates air pollution separately from water pollution; this resulted in one Pittsburgh plant's cleaning its water emissions by increasing its air emissions. OSHA regulates, as many agencies do, on a case-by-case basis, resulting in different levels of enforcement in different parts of the country. The Federal Communications Commission has been strongly criticized for the unplanned development of television because it decided to mix UHF and VHF television stations in the same market (see Krasnow, Longley, and Terry, 1982).

Absence of coordination is a serious problem, not just in regulation but in all policy areas at the national level. Failure to coordinate regulation means that regulation will work at cross-purposes (e.g., requiring greater fuel economy and lower emissions from automobiles). The result will be regulatory policy that is ineffective and confusing.

Delay.   In theory, bureaucracies are organizations capable of making a large number of decisions quickly. Several regulatory procedures, however, result in significant delays. The Magnuson-Moss Act required that the Federal Trade Commission adopt rules via a formal rule-making procedure; the result was that rules took 3 times as long to promulgate as before the act (West, 1982; Breyer, 1982: 347). The application to market a new drug takes the FDA 8 to 9 years to process (Grabowski and Vernon, 1983). The Nuclear Regulatory Commission, back in the days when new licenses to operate nuclear plants were granted, took 10 years to license a new plant (Daly and Brady, 1976: 181). Even on trivial issues, the bureaucracy sometimes takes an inordinate amount of time; the FDA took 12 years, for example, to decide whether peanut butter should contain 87 percent or 90 percent peanuts (Stone, 1982: 212).

Although regulatory bureaucracies can move quickly as the tamper-proof regulations following the Tylenol poisonings illustrated, in many cases it does not. One reason for slowness in regulatory procedures is that laws governing participation encourage processes that are slow and deliberate. In a sense, then, the ill-effects of delay must be traded off against the benefits of procedural fairness (Breyer, 1982: 348).

Unfair Procedures.   Administrative procedures have been the subject of many reform efforts. Under the leadership of the American Bar Association, administrative procedures have come to resemble courtroom procedures to a significant degree. Although most agencies are subject to the requirements of the Administrative Procedure Act, an agency's enabling legislation often specifies additional procedures.

In terms of rule making, one distinction is between formal and informal rule making. Informal rule making is fairly brief, requiring notice and an opportunity to comment; it resembles the legislative process. Formal rule making has far more elaborate procedures, including extensive cross-examination of witnesses by other witnesses. Among the "unfair" administrative procedures are limiting verbal testimony, restricting cross-examination, and limiting who can participate (e.g., the FCC and the United Church of Christ). A more recent charge of unfairness involved the Office of Management and Budget's review of regulations and the off-the-record nature of OMB actions (Eads, 1982).

Adjudicative procedures have also been criticized for denying rights to citizens. Administrative proceedings, for example, have no formal pleadings (the agency can change the subject of the hearing by giving adequate notice), use a lower standard of evidence than courts, have less formal rules of evidence (Cooper, 1983: 147), and usually place the burden of proof on the citizen, not on the agency (Warren, 1982: 294). In addition, regulatory agencies fuse powers that are normally kept separate in the American polity. The same agency often has the authority to establish regulations, inspect to enforce the regulations, try the individual for violations, and levy fines.

The literature normally defines fair procedures as those resembling courtroom procedures (Davis, 1972; but see Warren, 1982: 289). Under such a definition, a clear trade-off exists between fair procedures and delays. More procedural safeguards require slower procedures. To a proponent of regulation, delay may be a greater evil than the lack of courtroom procedures.

Second-Order Failings

Economists have detailed a series of second-order economic consequences to regulation. In essence, these criticisms charge that regulation distorts the efficient operation of the marketplace. According to Stokey and Zeckhauser (1978), government policy (including regulation) should always be evaluated against the standard of doing nothing; that is, Is regulation an improvement over the imperfect operations of the marketplace? Among the distortions attributed to regulation are price-fixing, subsidies, limiting compeition, restricting choice, retarding technology, and acting as a drag on productivity (see Daly and Brady, 1976: 177–179; MacAvoy, 1979; Stone, 1982).

Price-Fixing.   Price-fixing in regulation is not inappropriate per se; after all, one economic justification for price-fixing is monopoly because monopolists set prices too high. Of concern to economic critics is price setting in areas that are not natural monopolies (e.g., agriculture, railroads, trucking, merchant marine shipping). If the regulatory agency sets the price too high, surpluses will result; if the price is set too low, more will be demanded than produced, and shortages will result. Government-determined prices, in general, are less flexible than those set by the market and will not fluctuate fast enough to prevent shortages and surpluses.

The criticism of inappropriate price-fixing was more telling in 1976 than it is today. Beginning with the Ford administration, the federal government has eliminated or partially eliminated regulatory price setting for natural gas, brokerage commissions, airline fares, railroad and truck rates, interest rates, and some long-distance telephone rates. In addition, the federal government has taken a strong stand against price setting by professional associations and state occupational regulators.

Despite the federal government's general withdrawal from the price-setting area, serious problems still exist. By setting high price floors for agricultural products, the U.S. government has encouraged farmers to overproduce and generate large surpluses. Although many crops are not permanently overproduced, such goods as milk and peanuts are chronically in surplus. At the state level, price regulation of utilities has also created problems (Anderson, 1980; Gormley 1983b). Some state regulators set prices too high, thus hurting consumers whereas others set prices too low, thus preventing the utilities from attracting capital to expand.

Subsidies and Cross-subsidies.   A second way that government regulation distorts the marketplace is by the use of regulation to create subsidies or cross-subsidies. With subsidies, the production of a good is partially underwritten by government so that more will be produced than the market demands. Under cross-subsidies, profits in one area of an industry's production are kept high to compensate for low profits in other areas.

In our regulatory history, subsidies have been used to create inefficiencies. By subsidizing shipping rates, the ICC permitted trucking companies to undercut railroads on their more efficient long hauls (see Daly and Brady, 1976: 178). Subsidies as a component of regulation, however, have become less common. Some subsidies still exist in such programs as agriculture regulation, maritime regulation, and the EPA's waste water treatment grants.

Cross-subsidies were often used in regulation to expand service. Airline companies were granted highly profitable routes in exchange for flying unprofitable routes to smaller cities (Brown, 1984). Federal regulation permitted high profits from long-distance service to subsidize local telephone service to maximize the number of telephone users.

From a political-economic perspective, the exact criticism of subsidies and cross-subsidies is difficult to pin down. Economists have consistently urged that incentives (both taxes and subsidies) be used to encourage pollution control. The use of subsidies in the preceding areas reflects or reflected values other than efficiency that the political system wanted to attain. Universal telephone service, a national pattern of air transportation, elimination of food shortages, and a U.S. flag merchant marine fleet are all goals that subsidies were used to obtain. The legitimacy or illegitimacy of subsidies and cross-subsidies must rest on a political judgment about the merits of the programs.

Limiting Competition.   Regulatory agencies are charged with limiting competition, and in many cases they are guilty. Before the federal deregulation movement of the 1970s, several examples of regulation limiting competition were evident—government-sponsored cartels were allowed to set trucking rates, marketing orders limited the amount of fruits and vegetables sent to market, financial institutions were not permitted to compete via interest rates paid to depositors, and the FCC restricted technology to prevent competition in the television industry. At the state level, many professions used occupational regulation to limit competition both from other professions (physicians vs. osteopaths, chiropractors, podiatrists, midwives, and so on) and from within the profession (fee schedules, advertising limits).

As the record in the financial industry illustrates, competitive industries often provide more benefits to consumers. Whether or not limiting competition is an evil, however, should be judged on a case-by-case basis because competition is not always an unmitigated blessing. The highly competitive banking industry of the 1920s, for example, produced far fewer benefits to consumers than the uncompetitive system established in the 1930s.

Price-fixing, subsidies, and limiting competition are the three classic economic criticisms of regulation. These criticisms were developed shortly after World War II in response to perceived problems of economic regulation. As emphasis changed from economic to social regulation, these three classic criticisms were joined by three new ones—restrictions on choice, retarding technological development, and limiting productivity.

Restricting Choice.   The microeconomic model of perfect competition is based on voluntary choices by individuals; restrictions on such choices mean that the overall selection of goods and services will be less than optimal. Regulation, by definition, is governmental action designed to limit the choices of individuals, corporations, or other governments. Regulation, therefore, limits individual choice and correspondingly individual freedom (see Friedman and Friedman, 1980).

As with competition, however, unlimited choice is a mixed blessing. Without perfect information about products, their use, and their hazards, restrictions on choice can often be justified. No one, for example, believes that any valuable freedom is lost because pregnant women are denied thalidomide or because parents are denied the opportunity to purchase baby cribs with slats more than 2.375 inches apart.[10]

Some restrictions on individual choice, however, have little justification. Restrictions on individual practice by nurse practitioners and physicians' assistants deprive many individuals of low-cost, routine health care. Similar restrictions on the practice of law eliminate an individual's choice of low cost–low quality legal assistance. The remnants of financial regulation limit the access of many individuals in small towns to a variety of investments and savings plans, thus limiting return on investments or encouraging the flow of funds out of local communities.

Restricting choice via regulation may have second-order consequences. If the Environmental Protection Agency bans the use of leaded gasoline, the owners of pre-1974 vehicles will suffer engine damage. If NHTSA requires air bags in all vehicles (under review), those who already use seat belts will subsidize those who do not.

Clearly, restrictions on choice must be challenged as deleterious second-

10. Occasionally, one will see passionate defenses of an individual's right to choose dangerous or worthless activities. The Food and Drug Administration was criticized by many for prohibiting the drug laetrile as a cancer treatment. Similarly, Congress responded to criticism of seat belt interlock systems by preventing the Department of Transportation from requiring them. Similar defenses can be found against motorcycle helmet laws and against laws that require medical treatment for severely ill children.

order consequences on a case-by-case basis. Limiting individual choice is necessary for the operation of modern society. Because the nation has not adopted utilitarian political theory as the paramount rationale for society, some balancing of choice with the benefits received is necessary. Although no one should be denied the choice of a wide range of foodstuffs simply because many foods naturally contain small amounts of carcinogenic substances, no one should be free to drive while intoxicated.

Retarding Technology.   In some cases, regulation has restricted the development of new technology. The Federal Communications Commission limited the development of cable technology until recently and did not encourage such new technologies as direct satellite broadcasting, low power television, and multipoint distribution systems until the late 1970s. The Interstate Commerce Commission refused to permit larger boxcars to avoid disturbing the relationship between railroads and trucks (Fellmuth, 1970), and the Food and Drug Administration has been charged with restricting the development of new drugs and creating a drug lag (see chapter 4).

Regulation may have had some success in retarding technology, but it is not omnipotent. Technological changes in financial services overwhelmed the elaborate network of banking regulation in the 1980s. New options in telecommunications forced the FCC to consider new technologies or risk the chance that commercial television would be damaged by nonregulated sources of entertainment. The FDA has recently increased the rate of new drug approval but is more comfortable trading off delays in introducing new drugs for higher guarantees of safety.

Limiting Productivity.   The most persistent economic criticism of regulation is that it limits industrial productivity. The growth in regulation of the 1970s corresponded with a decline in the growth rate of productivity for American industry and a sluggish economy. Productivity grew at the rate of 2.5 percent annually from 1948 to 1973 but only at the rate of 0.5 percent from 1973 to 1982 (Litan and Nordhaus, 1983: 27). Social regulation of worker health and safety and the environment, according to the critics, has required industry to make investments that add little to productivity. With a limited amount of capital to invest, investments in regulation divert capital from productive investments.

Some argue that the decline in productivity is substantial; Weidenbaum (1981: 344) estimated that regulation imposed annual costs of $120 billion on industry (but see Schwartz, 1983: 99–106). Denison (1979) estimated that regulation reduced productivity growth by 0.25 percent. In addition, Litan and Nordhaus (1983: 31) argued that indirect costs of regulation add another 0.15 percent annual decline in productivity. Together direct and indirect regulatory costs reduced productivity growth by 0.4 percent per annum, not an insignificant amount.

Before concluding that regulation is a major factor in the decline of the American economy, we should consider some additional information. First, the rise of regulation and decline in productivity occurred at the same time as three other important trends—the elimination of cheap energy, the rise of an inflation mentality, and the increase in foreign competition. Because the productivity studies rely heavily on correlational methods, accurately discerning the impact of several simultaneous trends is difficult.

Second, much of the data analysis does not find significant results; the analysis of Litan and Nordhaus (1983) clearly shows no impact of regulation when all industries are examined. Only when a few industries with very high regulatory costs are examined does a relationship exist. Basing a conclusion on the steel industry and similar manufacturing industries is tenuous. The steel industry is characterized by poor management, obsolete plants, little concern for costs, and an absence of any willingness to compete. To blame regulation for the sorry state of the steel industry is unfair, and it is equally unfair to use extreme cases such as the steel industry to argue about the impact of regulation on productivity. The productivity of such capital-intensive industries as steel, automobiles, copper, aluminum, cement, and petroleum refining is affected far more by the general state of the economy and foreign competition than by regulation.

Third, precisely how regulation is placing burdens on industry is not clear. Pettus (1982) found that the average firm has a probability of 0.8 of seeing an OSHA inspector and will be fined about $400 for violations; certainly, this could hardly affect productivity. Downing (1984) notes that most environmental standards are negotiated favorably to the industry, and most investment in pollution controls is subject to highly favorable tax write-offs. The only indication that regulation is placing an onerous burden on industry comes from industry estimates of costs, estimates that in past experience demonstrate a strong bias toward overestimation. Even the economic analysis of Litan and Nordhaus (1983: 31) concludes that "there would have been a significant decline in the rate of productivity growth in all industries after 1973, regardless of the intensity with which the federal government pursued its regulatory program."[11]

REGULATORY REFORMS

Within each of the chapters specific substantive reforms were proposed and evaluated. In addition to agency-specific reforms, many analysts propose general reforms that can be undertaken in all areas of regulation. General regulatory reforms can be grouped into two categories. First, among those who perceive that regulation in general is a problem, the solution is usually less regulation. Second, among those who feel regulation is necessary but that the pattern of regulation is ineffective, better control mechanisms are advocated. In the latter case, regulation is perceived as responsive to the wrong groups, and changes need to be made so that regulation responds to different groups. The reforms of these two groups can be divided into those who seek to decentralize decision making, usually to the market, and those who wish to centralize regulation by vesting greater control in the political branches of government.

Market-Oriented Reforms

If correcting market failures is the goal of regulation and regulation often creates greater market distortions via subsidies, price-fixing, increasing costs, and so on, the solution is less regulation. Regulation is seen as a set of

11. In fairness to Litan and Nordhaus, their quote continues, "Nevertheless, the results suggest that intensity of regulation exacerbated the decline in the overall rate of growth of productivity." For reasons noted in the text, the author disagrees with this conclusion.

policies that on balance contributes less in benefits than it imposes in costs. As Stokey and Zeckhauser (1978: 309–310) conclude, "the history of [government] interventions to deal with market failure is a history of disappointments. In a variety of areas, programs have accomplished much less than we had hoped, at a cost far greater than we expected."[12] Five general reforms are proposed by market advocates—more vigorous prosecution of antitrust laws, general deregulation, cost-benefit analysis, tax-based incentive systems, and nontax incentive systems.

Vigorous Antitrust Action.   If the problems facing government regulators stem from lack of competition in the marketplace, the obvious solution is to increase the amount of competition. A lack of competition is perceived as especially harmful when it has the sanction of the government (see Armentano, 1982). One mechanism proposed to increase competition is the vigorous use of the federal government's antitrust powers (see Kohlmeier, 1969).

The advocates of antitrust action might be termed structural competition advocates because they believe that competition is a function of the number of firms in the marketplace. By the use of antitrust laws to break up large firms into numerous smaller firms, the total number of firms increases; and competition should also increase. Advocates estimate that a costless and effective antitrust policy could increase the nation's gross national product by 5 to 12 percent (Schwartzman, 1961; Comanor and Leibenstein, 1969). Such a use of antitrust laws, of course, would require that the law be amended to ban monopoly per se rather than the current ban on monopolizing because the lack of competitors per se is viewed as the problem (see chapter 9).

In classical microeconomic theory, the relationship between the number of firms, the amount of competition, and the basic evils of marketplace failure are well known (see Armentano's [1982] review). If prices are set too high, competition will reduce prices because price-cutters will take market shares away from nonprice-cutters. If imperfect information is the problem, firms will compete to offer information about their products so that greater information is available to consumers. The only major market failure that competition does not address is externalities because firms in a competitive marketplace have even less incentive to consider externalities, for doing so will reduce already limited profits. In addition, structural competition advocates are not concerned with the political failings of regulation.

Vigorous antitrust prosecution as a regulatory reform has three problems that must be addressed before one concludes that antitrust can correct regulatory ills. First, such a strategy is essentially untried. At no time in the nation's history could antitrust enforcement ever be characterized as vigorous. The last time the government won major "monopoly" cases in court and achieved a significant breakup of a monopoly firm was in 1911 (the U.S. Steel and American Tobacco Cases; see chapter 9). Even the market-oriented Reagan administration has shown little interest in vigorous structural antitrust; it dropped the IBM case, granted AT&T a highly favorable settlement, and did not prevent a series of large oil company mergers.

---

12. The advocates of the following reforms show a general bias against all forms of government intervention. To receive a good sampling of opinion in this area, see any issue of *Regulation*. For more academic views on regulation with the same conclusions, see recent issues of the *Journal of Law and Economics*.

Second, antitrust enforcement to date is slow, expensive, and uncertain. The famed IBM case took 13 years before the government dropped the case because it lacked merit. Numerous days of court time, hundreds of lawyers, and millions of dollars were spent for no gain. Except for increasing legal employment opportunities, no net benefits were produced in this process.

Third, even among economists, a large literature criticizing the use of structural antitrust has developed. Brozen (1982) and others have argued that no systematic relationship between the number of firms and the competitiveness of an industry has been found. Armentano (1982) argues that large-scale organizations usually develop because they achieve significant economies of scale. When a large firm loses these advantages, it loses its market share. In general, Armentano and others believe that vigorous antitrust enforcement would be devastating to the American economy and produce no benefits.

General Deregulation.   If regulation results in a net loss to society, then one solution to regulatory problems is to eliminate regulation (Daly and Brady, 1976: 182). As Alan Stone (1982: 252) noted, deregulation and a return to the free market usually are defined as the elimination of restrictions on entry, exit, and prices. A strategy of general deregulation is designed to address the second-order economic consequences of regulation noted earlier. Deregulation should result in increased competition and, therefore, in lower prices and provision of as much product information as is efficient.

Advocates of deregulation have a pattern of successes to illustrate that deregulation works (Weiss, 1981: 7–9). In the mid 1970s, brokerage fees were deregulated, with the result being an increase in competition and a decline in fees. The economic deregulation of airlines was mandated in 1978 and implemented by the early 1980s. Following in rapid succession were the deregulation of cable TV at the federal level, the elimination of economic regulation for trucking with price flexibility for railroads, the deregulation of natural gas, and the easing of economic regulations on depository institutions. Each of these cases resulted in some gains and losses, but in general consumers benefited from deregulation efforts.[13]

All the deregulation successes, however, have been in economic regulation rather than in newer areas of social regulation. The total benefits of deregulation, therefore, might be close to being exhausted because at the federal level only a few industries (e.g., parts of agriculture, the merchant marine, and possibly rail and truck common carriers) are still regulated economically. Most problems amenable to solution via general deregulation have already been addressed. Krier (1982: 156) relates this to the basic difference between economic and social regulation: "[T]he theory underlying deregulation of the airlines, for example—that competition works—simply does not apply to environmental problems—where competition does

---

13. Deregulation usually resulted in some economic shakeouts. The number of brokerage firms dropped by 20 percent following deregulation (Stoll, 1981: 33). Braniff and Continental Airlines were the first bankruptcies among major airlines since the advent of regulation. Failures have increased among financial institutions and trucking firms. Whether these difficulties were the result of deregulation or the result of an unfavorable economy from 1975 to 1983 is unclear. The more important question is whether or not these failures have adversely affected consumers; the evidence on this question is mixed; any generalization would be premature.

not work." Similar statements could be made about hazardous waste, occupational health, pure food and drugs, and other areas of social regulation.

Cost-Benefit Analysis.   Cost-benefit analysis is perhaps the most intuitively attractive reform proposed for regulation. Nothing could make more sense than to issue regulations only if the regulation provided more benefits than costs. Cost-benefit analysis has been the cornerstone of regulatory reform efforts of the last three presidents.[14] Gerald Ford required inflation impact analyses that included cost considerations. Jimmy Carter used the Council of Economic Advisors and other staff to conduct regulatory analysis reviews that included costs and benefits. Ronald Reagan's OMB control mechanism stressed the use of cost-benefit analysis.

Cost-benefit analysis is applicable to both economic and social regulation. In fact, the most prominent use of cost-benefit analysis has been in social regulation areas such as environmental protection, occupational health, and consumer protection. Although cost-benefit analysis seeks to apply the principles of the market to government decision making (both costs and benefits are based either on market values or on hypothetical market values) and, therefore, in theory uses decentralized criteria for decisions in practice, cost-benefit analysis has been used to centralize regulatory decision making (see further on).

Although cost-benefit analysis appears simple (one merely adds up the benefits and costs), in reality cost-benefit analysis is difficult to do well. Thompson and Jones (1982: 153) note this: "Costs and benefits are not easily defined; the relationships between direct and indirect costs often are not easily discernible; the estimate of costs is highly sensitive to assumptions; and the price of good staff work is high, and high-quality analysis typically requires a long time to perform." Discretion in the estimation of benefits and costs is widely recognized, and in the view of some, manipulable. Mark Green (1980: 114) contends that cost-benefit analysis can use widely varying data estimates. To estimate the benefits of banning saccharin, for example, not only did analysts have to place a value human lives, but they also faced mortality estimates for a 50-year period that ranged from less than one to more than 1.4 million. Reporting only a single cost-benefit ratio in such a study would be irresponsible, but the range of values for all cost-benefit ratios would be so large as to render them useless for decision making.

If cost-benefit analysis were not limited by a series of technical problems, it might provide valuable information concerning regulatory programs. Even without valid techniques, the use of cost-benefit analysis often raises questions not considered by regulators. In the best of circumstances, however, cost-benefit analysis can play only a limited role because such analysis proceeds from the assumption that efficiency is the primary goal of regulation. In areas of regulation with other goals (that is, most of them), cost-benefit analysis is of only moderate value.

In operation, cost-benefit analysis has been of less value than its propo-

14. The exact methods used to estimate costs and benefits are not important from a reform perspective. The best example of the procedures used can be found in Stokey and Zeckhauser (1978). A critique of these techniques can be found in Meier (1983b; 1984) and Kelman (1981a).

nents suggest. First, the analysis done on regulatory programs has been of poor quality, especially that analysis done early enough to be an input in the decision-making process (Thompson and Jones, 1982: 154). Second, until recently, the organizations conducting the cost-benefit assessments had little influence. The Council of Wage and Price Stability was not one of the agencies in the Carter administration recognized for clout (Thompson and Jones, 1982: 154). Under the Reagan administration, the Office of Management and Budget has been given the cost-benefit review authority, and this limitation has been avoided. Third, a significant investment in analysis has not been funded. The requirement for analysis has not been matched by the availability of funds to do such studies; as a result, the Reagan administration process has been widely criticized (see Eads, 1982).

Fourth, in some cases the commitment to cost-benefit analysis has been less than the commitment to policy goals. Christopher DeMuth, Reagan's OMB regulation director, rejected the Department of Agriculture's cost-benefit analysis of marketing orders. Because the analysis showed more benefits than costs, Demuth (1984: 29) stated, "we knew the analysis was wrong without reading it."

Cost-benefit analysis has become politicized because it has been used to centralize regulatory power for the president and because it has been used exclusively by advocates of less regulation. Accordingly, its value as an analytical tool has dropped. Cost-benefit analysis was oversold and underfunded. Little evidence exists that the quality of regulation has improved with the introduction of the technique to regulatory analysis.

Incentive Systems.   Creating incentive systems is a reform proposed by those who feel that regulation is inefficient and creates a serious drag on the economy (see Poole, 1982). By using command-and-control systems, they argue, regulation in excess of what consumers would be willing to pay for is introduced. Government, they feel, should limit its role in regulation to creating incentives that eliminate market failures. Rather than specify how a plant should control its pollution emissions, for example, the tax system should be used to tax the firm based on the amount of pollution that it produces. Each plant then can make efficient decisions about how much pollution control equipment to install.

In contrast to command-and-control systems, incentive systems are credited with several advantages (Litan and Nordhaus, 1983: 97). First, incentive systems stress the attainment of regulatory goals in the most efficient manner possible because decisions are made under the constraints of the marketplace. Second, incentive systems are more likely to encourage innovation; firms discovering more effective methods of pollution control may use them without penalty. Third, decisions regarding costs are decentralized so that each firm can decide the mix of controls and penalities that is optimum for it. Fourth, such systems can be used to avoid politically volatile questions about income redistribution. Litan and Nordhaus (1983: 98) argue that "regulation is often accompanied by poorly designed equalitarian baggage that frustrates the regulation's purpose or introduces yet new complications. That markets are heartless is actually a plus, for they can accomplish major structural changes when it is necessary."[15]

Proposals for incentive systems rather than regulation are not new. The English economist A. C. Pigou proposed a smokestack emissions tax in the 1930s. In recent years, a variety of incentive systems has been suggested in social regulation. Robert S. Smith (1974) proposed an injury tax as an alternative to OSHA safety regulation. Dales (1968) suggested that water pollutants be taxed as an incentive for industries to clean up their effluents. Effluent taxes have also been popular in air pollution and have seen some use in the EPA's bubble, offset, and bankable emissions policies (see also Hahn and Noll, 1982).

Although economists, in general, are enthusiastic about incentives as a replacement for regulation, they recognize that incentives might have some problems. First, the use of incentives such as pollution taxes requires monitoring systems that are far advanced over current systems. The advantage of engineering controls is that one can easily tell if such a system is installed and operating. With emissions, monitoring must be continual (see Krier, 1982: 154, Hahn and Noll, 1982: 127). Second, tax incentives in place of regulation might result in even larger federal bureaucracies. One cannot imagine the implementation of an injury tax, which implies a staff of economic analysts to set rates, a group of auditors to guarantee data accuracy, and another agency to compensate victims being operated with a staff as small as that of OSHA.

Third, any attempt to create incentive systems will be hopelessly tied up in debates over moral issues. Environmentalists generally see emissions taxes as licenses to pollute; labor unions see an injury tax as permission to maim (see Kelman, 1981a). Cool, reasoned debate is not likely in this area. Fourth and most important, no one is sure that incentive systems will actually work. As Gamse (1982: 161) says, "If economic approaches in the social regulatory areas are going to gain full acceptance, there must be some successes that demonstrate their feasibility." Incentives may not work. Ignored in the debate over incentives is the one area of federal regulation that relies heavily on incentives to operate—regulation of crop production. Agricultural regulation links benefits (subsidies) to compliance (reducing acreage). Individual farmers decide whether or not to accept regulation and benefits or to forego benefits and operate outside the regulatory system. Decisions on what land to idle are made on a decentralized basis. The record has been one of failure with high-program costs and chronic oversupply.

Nontax Incentive Systems.   Incentive systems have not been limited to proposals that use the federal tax system only. Other proposals seek to strengthen the incentives that already operate in the private sector. The three most often proposed nontax incentive systems are collective bargaining, information, and liability law.

---

15. One need not accept any of Litan and Nordhaus' benefits of incentive-based regulatory systems. The last benefit is especially controversial. Rather than delegate redistributive decisions to a decentralized market, a responsive political system needs to make such decisions openly in its political institutions. It may be efficient to leave such decisions to a structured market, but it is not democratic. The normative objection to Litan and Nordhaus' point does not detract from their empirical claim; eliminating inefficient industries is much easier when the political system does not intervene. The current steel industry is a noteworthy example.

Collective bargaining has been proposed as a private sector alternative to workplace safety regulation (see Bacow, 1982). Rather than impose safety requirements from the outside by a regulatory agency, unions and management can negotiate safety requirements more acceptable to each other (a form of Lindblom's [1965] partisan mutual adjustment). Collective bargaining has some advantages over direct regulation. It can permit greater consideration of local conditions, it can be more flexible because contracts are renegotiated periodically, and it may be more enforceable via grievance procedures and job actions (Bacow, 1982: 204). The United Auto Workers and the Oil, Chemical and Atomic Workers have been especially active in safety negotiations. Some states have encouraged this form of collective bargaining by exempting such firms from normal inspections (Bardach and Kagan, 1982: 237).

Collective bargaining approaches, however, have some major limitations. Because safety benefits are long-term in nature, unions have a greater incentive to stress short-term benefits such as wages rather than use scarce bargaining capital on safety issues (Bacow, 1982: 206). Effective collective bargaining also assumes that unions possess accurate information about job hazards; in cases such as exposure to hazardous substances, this may not be true. Finally, collective bargaining offers no protection to the 72 percent of the workers who do not work in unionized facilities (Bacow, 1982: 218).

Providing the buyer with product information about performance or safety is another alternative to direct regulation. When nutritional information is posted on food products, the consumer can make his or her own trade-offs between quality and price. Included as information are guarantees, warranties, and sometimes insurance (e.g., some bonds are insured). The proposed advantages of information over regulation include lower costs, greater choice given to consumers, and allowing individual flexibility (O'Hare, 1982: 227).

The major problem with information is that most consumers ignore it (see chapter 4). Bardach and Kagan (1982), for example, note that one bank offered ATM customers $10 if they would write the words *Regulation E* on a postcard and send it to the bank. Of 115,000 customers who received this offer via the ATM disclosure statement, none made a claim. On the other hand, lack of use may simply be a rational decision on the part of a consumer that getting additional information has costs in excess of benefits.

The traditional private remedy for injuries is litigation. Lawsuits can be used in worker safety cases, hazardous product cases, defective goods, and environmental damages among others. Sobel (1977) proposed this procedure as a solution to the dangers of exposure to toxic substances. Greater use of private litigation in place of regulation is proposed to have three advantages. First, the legal penalties are larger and, therefore, provide a greater deterrent than regulatory fines (Heffron with McFeeley, 1983: 384). Second, private litigation provides incentives for companies to establish safety departments and quality control (Bardach and Kagan, 1982: 272). The incentives are significant. Although plaintiffs win only 40 percent of product liability cases, total settlements cost $409 million in 1981 (Wines, 1983l: 748). An estimated 60,000 to 140,000 suits are filed a year. Suits over airport noise are credited with creating the incentives for noise regulation (Burke, 1980). Third, litigation punishes firms for actual damages rather than for potential damages.

The use of litigation is often linked to the use of private insurance (Ferreira, 1982). Insurance companies have an incentive to change the behavior of the insured and can often provide cheaper rates in the process. Insurance systems work best when risks are easy to assess, the parties are financially responsible, and sufficient information exists. In such cases, litigation resolves insurance disputes.

Over time, states have made litigation easier by moving to a standard of strict liability (Meiners, 1982: 298). Strict liability holds the maker of a product liable if the product is "unreasonably dangerous" even if the user was negligent. In fact, corporations feel the courts have gone too far and support Senator Robert Kasten's effort to preempt state liability laws with a uniform federal law (Wines, 1983l: 748). The Kasten proposal would limit strict liability and authorize several defenses in liability suits.

Although litigation has some impact, it is clearly not a cure-all. Several limitations exist. The burden of proof rests with the injured party, and courts are notoriously slow and expensive (Bardach and Kagan, 1982: 272). The delays inherent in the legal process are perceived to hurt meritorious claims the most (Ferreira, 1982: 272). Litigation is also difficult to use when damages are remote in time, damages are collective in nature, and damages are hard to quantify (Bardach and Kagan, 1982: 280). The ex post facto nature of litigation is also a problem; liability suits compensate victims or their heirs; they are not preventative.

Because litigation has weaknesses, several states have made efforts to facilitate product liability suits. Among the incentives that encourage the use of courts are laws that permit awarding attorneys' fees, treble damage awards, class actions, and legal assistance. Sobel (1977) proposes the use of administrative tribunals with eased burdens of proof to make litigation a more efficient check.

Responsiveness Reforms

Reforms that stress increased responsiveness must answer this question: responsive to whom? In general, some consensus exists that regulation, as in all government programs, should be responsive to the general public; but the literature also recognizes that defining what being responsive to the general public entails is difficult (Gilbert, 1959). One argument often presented by Ralph Nader and other populists is that regulatory agencies should be directly responsive to consumers. A second argument holds that regulatory agencies should be responsive to the major political institutions and that these institutions, in turn, should be responsive via elections to the general public (see Redford, 1969). As the following discussion will illustrate, arguments about responsiveness have substantive implications concerning who should benefit from regulation.

Responsiveness to Consumers.   Among those who feel regulatory agencies are captured by the industries they regulate, an oft-advocated solution is to redesign agencies so that they are more responsive to consumers than they are to the industry. Such an argument is easy to justify normatively because reconciling democracy with responsiveness to vested interests is not easy. Two formal mechanisms have been proposed to increase the responsiveness of regulatory agencies to consumers—an Agency for Consumer

Advocacy and the use of public funds to support consumer participation in agency procedures. Other proposals sometimes linked to consumer responsiveness are requirements that regulatory meetings be open to the public, requirements that citizens have access to agency information (the Freedom of Information Act), and establishment of agency advisory committees (see Cooper, 1983: 295 ff).

The proposal to create an agency whose function would be to represent the consumer viewpoint before other agencies was at one time an issue on the agenda. In 1976 both houses of Congress passed legislation creating an Agency for Consumer Advocacy. Despite earlier support by President Ford, the legislation was vetoed for political reasons. Ford at the time was locked in a heated battle for the Republican nomination with Ronald Reagan, and the move was seen as an effort to attract conservative votes. A similar bill was defeated by Congress in 1978, marking for some observers the end of the contemporary era of consumer protection (see Pertschuk, 1982). The short-term prospects for a consumer agency are not promising.

A second option for consumer representation is to allow individual consumers to represent themselves and to permit them to do so by providing federal funds to underwrite the costs. Without assistance, participation by regulated groups outnumbers that of public interest groups nine to one (Breyer, 1982: 352). The Federal Trade Commission, for example, funded intervenors for a time during the 1970s. The program was intensely disliked by business, which perceived that the government was funding the other side and, therefore, was somewhat biased. Congress restricted intervenor programs by limiting funds and using riders to prevent spending for this purpose.

Efforts to create mechanisms to increase responsiveness to consumers face two fundamental problems. First, consumers as a group are similar to the general public; they are far too varied a group to be represented by a single viewpoint. Interesting arguments have been presented by individuals such as James Miller that some consumers might actually prefer cheap quality (and possibly unsafe) goods. Representing the diversity of views that consumers have within a single agency might well be impossible.

Second, representation of consumer interests does not necessarily result in responsiveness to consumer viewpoints. At the present time, a wide variety of public interest groups exists on the Washington scene, but regulatory agencies, in general, are not overly responsive to their petitions. Perhaps formal representation of consumer interests is less important than appointing regulators who hold proconsumer values.

Responsiveness to the President.   Proposals for making regulatory agencies more responsive to the president date back to Franklin Roosevelt's attempt to remove William Humphrey from the Federal Trade Commission. In light of recent evidence, however, some questions must be raised about whether or not presidents need additional authority to govern regulation. By using the powers of appointment and budget, both President Carter and President Reagan were able to redirect the activities of many regulatory agencies. Several examples of policy change in response to presidential initiatives can be noted. OSHA changed from a nitpicking enforcer of safety regulations to an organization concerned with health issues under Carter's administrator Eula Bingham; under Reagan's head, Thorne Auchter, the agency de-emphasized its enforcement programs. Under Joan Claybrook (Carter), the National Highway Traffic Safety Administration was a strict regulator of automobile safety whereas under Raymond Peck and Diane Steed (Reagan), many safety rules have been relaxed. Similar changes under Carter and Reagan could be noted for the EEOC, the FTC, the ICC, and other agencies.

Recent presidents have had little trouble in gaining control over the direction of regulation; Carter generally increased the intensity of social regulation while moving toward economic deregulation; Reagan has decreased the intensity of regulation in all areas (except trucking). President Reagan has been able to achieve major budget cuts in regulatory agencies and reduce the size of the *Federal Register* by approximately one-half (Litan and Nordhaus, 1983: 125).[16]

For those seeking to enhance further the president's control over regulatory agencies, three mechanisms are proposed. Advocates favor decreased independence for regulatory commissions, greater formal oversight by the president, or a regulatory budget. Each of these is discussed in turn.

Independent regulatory commissions have always concerned regulatory analysts. Because regulatory commissioners serve long, overlapping terms, commissioners appointed by previous presidents often continue to serve. In such a situation, the regulatory commission can operate independently from the president's wishes. Some independent commissions also have the authority to submit their budgets directly to Congress so that the budget control normally operated through OMB is absent. The most recent advocate for eliminating independent regulatory commissions and replacing them with regulatory agencies headed by one person located within executive departments was Richard Nixon's Ash Council on Government Reorganization.

Advocates of decreased independence fail to realize, however, that independence is a minor obstacle for the president. The president can designate the chairperson of all but three independent commissions (the Federal Reserve, the Nuclear Regulatory Commission, and the Federal Energy Regulatory Commission have chairpersons who serve a fixed term; see Heffron with McFeeley, 1983: 391) and with resignations can often control a majority of the board within a year or two. President Reagan, for example, had little trouble asserting control over the EEOC, the ICC, and the FTC. In the process, he was able to alter the direction of regulatory policy established by President Carter. Given the attachment of Congress to the independent commission structure, proposals to limit independence are likely to generate a great deal of political conflict for little potential gain.

Proposals for increased oversight involve establishing formal mechanisms for reviewing regulations issued by the agencies. As noted earlier, the past three presidents established formal review mechanisms. Gerald Ford had the inflation impact process, Carter had his Regulatory Analysis Review Group, and Ronald Reagen established a Presidential Task Force on Regulatory Relief supplemented by analysis performed by the Office of Management and Budget. The latter mechanism provides a good opportunity to examine the effectiveness of increased presidential oversight.

---

16. The *Federal Register* is a measure of regulatory activity because all rules must be published in the *Federal Register* both before and after adoption. Because a variety of other material also appears in the *Federal Register*, it is only an indirect measure.

President Reagan, on taking office, froze a series of "midnight rules" issued in the last days of the Carter administration. He then issued executive order 12291, subjecting regulations to cost-benefit standards with review based in OMB. Actions on the midnight rules suggested the direction of the new oversight procedure. Of the 172 frozen rules, 100 were eventually approved. Many of these rules were minor or were mandated by emergencies or court orders (Thompson and Jones, 1982: 161). Thirty-five rules were withdrawn, and 37 more were held back for further study. The volume of regulation was clearly on the decline.

After two and one-half years of operation, the president announced that the President's Task Force on Regulatory Relief had achieved its goal and was being disbanded (Presidential Task Force, 1983). According to Vice-President Bush, the actions of the Task Force along with OMB would save the American public $150 billion over a ten-year period. Closer analysis, however, suggests that such savings were exaggerated. The largest saving, for example, was $40 billion in increased interest paid on deposits resulting from the Garn-St Germain Act, an action hardly the result of the Presidential Task Force. In addition, many other gains such as reduced costs to the automobile industry were transfers because they imposed additional costs on insurance companies and consumers.

The review process had examined 6,701 regulations by June of 1983; of these rules, 89 final and 53 proposed rules were reviewed because they were defined as major (imposing costs of $100 million or more). A total of 59 impact analyses were performed (Presidential Task Force, 1983: 56). An overwhelming proportion of the rules was approved. Some 86 percent were accepted as is, another 8 percent were accepted after only minor changes. Only 3 percent of all rules (182) were withdrawn or returned to the agencies. A closer examination of these rules suggests that they were primarily social regulations. The EPA had by far the greatest number of rules rejected (53); the Department of Commerce and the Department of Transportation (NHTSA rules on automobile safety) were the only other agencies in double figures. The reasons for rejecting rules were made fairly clear: "[T]he administration has made little effort to hide the fact that reviews of some rules have been designed primarily to provide relief to a troubled industry" (Litan and Nordhaus, 1983: 122). As the Reagan administration exerted control over the regulatory agencies, the OMB review process became less important because fewer "controversial" rules were submitted by the agencies; accordingly, most of the rules withdrawn or rejected occurred early in the process.

A final reform to increase presidential control favored by a variety of regulatory analysts is the regulatory budget (see Thompson and Jones, 1982: 180 ff; Litan and Nordhaus, 1983: 133 ff). Originally proposed by the economist Robert Crandall, the regulatory budget recognizes that agency budgets are only a small part of the costs of regulation and that a far larger cost is the cost of compliance. Under the regulatory budget, a governmentwide budget for regulatory costs would be adopted, and each agency would be allocated a cost budget. The process would parallel the regular budget process through both the executive and Congress. The idea behind a regulatory budget is not only to limit private sector costs but also to force Congress and the president to make trade-offs between regulatory programs (i.e., should we require air bags at a cost of X or tighten exposure to benzene standards?—see Kosters, 1980: 69). Legislation to establish a regulatory budget has been sponsored by Senator Lloyd Bentsen.

Although the regulatory budget is intuitively attractive, it has four limitations that might prevent its achieving politically efficient trade-offs. First, costs are often extremely difficult to measure (Litan and Nordhaus, 1983: 82; Stone, 1982: 265), and industry estimates are clearly biased. In the classic vinyl chloride case, industry estimated compliance costs at between $60 and $90 billion whereas actual compliance costs were only $250 million (see chapter 8). The CPSC estimated compliance costs for flammable fabrics regulation in the furniture industry at $57 million to $87 million; the textile manufacturers' estimate was $1.3 billion (see Litan and Nordhaus, 1983: 152).

Second, the regulatory budget would overemphasize costs relative to benefits. A high-cost program may well be preferred over a low-cost program if the former program yields greater benefits to society. Focusing on costs only encourages regulatory agencies to suboptimize (Thompson and Jones, 1982: 184).

Third, the regulatory budget might have as a second-order consequence the creation of an even larger federal bureaucracy. To operate successfully, regulatory agencies as well as OMB and Congress would need more staff. Neither industry nor agency estimates could be taken as unbiased without further checks. The process would create numerous jobs for economists and auditors (see Stone, 1982: 264).

Fourth, the regulatory budget does not appear to have any incentives for agency compliance. If the agency incorrectly estimates its costs, a regulatory budget provides no obvious penalty as there is in the regular budget process when the agency runs out of money (Litan and Nordhaus, 1983: 135; L. J. White, 1981: 227). Agency overruns could be deducted from the next year's budget as a penalty; however, such a process does not allow the trade-off that is the heart of the regulatory budget.

Although the regulatory budget may improve the regulatory process, it is no panacea. The likely impact of a regulatory budget would be to delay the regulatory process even more than it is delayed now. Such delays are not policy neutral; they benefit opponents of regulation and discourage regulatory agencies from action. According to Lawrence J. White (1981: 221), the RARG process in the Carter administration actually resulted in no major rules being issued for a six-month period in 1979.

Responsiveness to Congress.   Regulatory agencies have been criticized as unresponsive to the wishes of Congress. Claims of unresponsiveness should not be unexpected given the vague goals established for most regulatory agencies and the passing interest most members of Congress have in regulation. In fact, regulatory agencies do respond to Congress, but they do not respond as fast as Congress would like. In the late 1970s, the FTC was frequently criticized for being unresponsive to Congress when FTC programs vigorously regulated small business (see Pertschuk, 1982). The FTC, however, began these initiatives after urging from Congress in the early 1970s, a Congress more liberal than the one in the late 1970s (see Weingast and Moran, 1982). Regulators respond to Congress; they just do so slowly. The slow response is a function of two factors. First, regulatory agencies are fairly small and, thus, often get lost in the budget and oversight process;

they may go years with little direction from Congress. Second, Congress speaks with many voices so that responsiveness to one member of Congress may result in actions unresponsive to another.

Sunset legislation is often proposed to make regulatory agencies more responsive to Congress. Under sunset legislation, an agency is authorized to operate for a fixed period of years. If Congress fails to reauthorize the agency, it will cease to exist. Sunset legislation forces the agency to justify itself periodically; by requiring formal reauthorization, the sunset concept makes the normal, incremental, decision-making processes work against retaining the agency.

Sunset legislation is fairly popular. Approximately 35 states (Heffron with McFeeley, 1983: 388) and several federal statutes have sunset provisions (Stone, 1982: 272). At the federal level both the Commodity Futures Trading Commission (CFTC) and the Consumer Product Safety Commission have been subjected to sunset reviews. Unfortunately, experience with the sunset concept suggests that it "is unlikely to provide significant deregulatory benefits for the American people" (Avery, 1980: 41). Sunset review motivates an agency to mobilize its supporters, and even the least effective agencies have some supporters. Avery (1980: 41) concluded that both the CFTC and the CPSC emerged from sunset legislation stronger than before.

In addition to sunset review's lack of major successes, the process itself has shortcomings. The sunset process is expensive (Stone, 1982: 273; Avery, 1980: 42). Funds must be spent to analyze agency missions and performance. In Colorado, the first sunset review abolished 3 of the 13 agencies reviewed (agencies that regulated boxing, sanitarians, and shorthand reporters); this saved $11,000, but the process itself cost $212,000 (Stone, 1982: 273).

The minor agencies affected in Colorado suggests that the sunset process's impact may be trivial. At the federal level, this has been true. The Commodity Futures Trading Commission had its law changed to have the chairman serve at the pleasure of the president rather than for a fixed term. The only impact of the CPSC sunset legislation was that the commission chairperson resigned (Avery, 1980: 43). The sunset process appears to have an impact only on minor agencies too weak to defend themselves. It was used, for example, to eliminate 800 advisory commissions during the Carter administration (Clark, Kosters, and Miller, 1980: 46). The example of Colorado has been repeated several times by other states (Heffron with McFeeley, 1983: 388).

Finally, failure to reauthorize an agency does not mean the agency's termination. The Federal Trade Commission has often operated via continuing resolution when its authorizing legislation lapsed. Most of the legislation supporting the Environmental Protection Agency had expired by 1984, but the agency continued to operate.

A second major reform designed to make regulatory agencies more responsive to Congress is the legislative veto. According to former Senator Harrison Schmitt (1980: 53), "The legislative veto is a means to return legislative responsibility to elected representatives while at the same time improving the quality of necessary administrative action." Under the legislative veto, Congress authorizes an agency to act in a certain area, but all rules must be presented to Congress for action before they are finalized. Legislative vetoes were adopted in over 200 pieces of legislation and vary in the exact procedure Congress must use to veto an administrative action.

The legislative veto was declared unconstitutional by the Supreme Court in *INS* v. *Chadha*. The Court objected to the veto because it violated separation of powers and eliminated the president (by preventing a veto) from the legislative process. Several alternative veto methods are being considered by Congress under the leadership of the veto advocate Elliot Levitas, including one that would send the veto to the president for signature. Although the veto was used fairly frequently in the congressional budget process (for recisions and deferments), the only major regulatory case of a veto was the FTC's used-car rule.

The legislative veto is nothing more than a streamlined version of legislation that allows Congress to intervene in the regulatory process. In fact, legislation has resulted in far more interventions than has the legislative veto. The detail of the Clean Air Act illustrates congressional influence in regulatory administration; the automobile emissions standards are set specifically in legislation (agricultural legislation also sets price support levels). Instances of legislation used to change regulatory decisions after the fact also exist; Congress prohibited NHTSA from requiring seat belt interlock ignition systems and restricted the FTC's regulation of cigarette advertising (Fritschler, 1975).

Because Congress via legislation can and has determined the direction of regulation, a new legislative veto offers little improvement over current methods. In addition, the veto suffers from three limitations. First, literally thousands of regulations are proposed and issued every year. Unless some selection device was used (limited to major regulations), the volume of regulations would overwhelm Congress. Second, the veto by definition involves a case-by-case review of regulations. In terms of responsiveness to Congress, the problem is not a matter of individual deviations but rather of control over the general direction of regulatory policy. Litan and Nordhaus (1983: 108) feel that vetoes are nothing more than a symbolic action that ignores the real weaknesses of regulation.

Third, regulation was initially delegated to agencies so that some expertise could be applied to solving regulatory problems. Congress has shown little willingness to develop expertise on complex regulatory issues; the decision to require scrubbing all coal no matter how little sulfur content it contained is an excellent example. Given this lack of expertise, would case-by-case veto actions improve the overall quality of regulation? Arguing that FTC regulation was improved via the used-car veto is difficult. The veto offers little chance of improvement because it does not permit Congress to do anything it could not do via other mechanisms. As Scalia (1980: 60) says, "The real problem is not congressional power to reverse the agencies. Congress has that power and has always had it. The question is congressional will or congressional capacity."

Responsiveness to Courts.   The responsiveness of bureaucratic organizations to the rule of law is a hallowed tradition (Fried, 1976). To foster this responsiveness, regulatory agencies could be made more accountable to the courts. The foremost advocate of this is Senator Dale Bumpers of Arkansas. Although the Bumpers proposal has gone through a variety of forms, it essentially has three parts. First, the standard for an administrative decision on questions of fact would be increased from "supported by the evidence" to "preponderance of the evidence." In theory, this would make regulatory agencies use the stricter standard of the courts. Second, in determining questions of law, courts would no longer defer to agency expertise. Third, in disputes between citizens and agencies, the burden of proof would be on the agency rather than on the citizen.

Bumpers' proposal has been popular. The 1980 Republican party platform had a plank supporting similar reforms. In 1982 the proposal passed the Senate but not the House. The Bumpers proposal is not the only one designed to judicialize the administrative process further. Other proposals suggest lengthening the time period for comments in rule making, expanding notice procedures, and requiring more impact analyses (Litan and Nordhaus, 1983: 225). In essence, all attempts to make regulation more responsive to the courts seek to maximize procedural fairness and are willing to tolerate longer delays.

Suggestions to judicialize the regulatory process further go counter to much of the scholarship on regulation (see Warren, 1982: 287). Regulation is an administrative process because administrative agencies have advantages of speed and expertise. To judicialize administrative procedures robs the administrative process of a major strength. In areas of regulation where decisions are made by the courts (equal employment policy, antitrust policy), the policy process operates at a leisurely pace; and the quality of policy is probably no better.

Recent critics of judicializing the administrative process have also been numerous. The Ash Council argued that judicial review often stressed legal values to the detriment of economic, technical, and social values (see Daly and Brady, 1976: 183). The presidential adviser Lloyd Cutler suggested that the most effective regulatory reform might be to close the law schools; although said in jest, his criticism was overlegalized regulation (Cutler, 1980: 154). A former EPA administrator, Douglas Costle, noted that the delay resulting from judicialized procedures and legal appeals has substantive implications in that "litigation often benefits the polluter more than it does the public. By dragging a suit through the courts as long as possible, a polluter can postpone necessary capital expenditures and delay using pollution controls long enough to gain a substantial financial advantage over complying competitors" (Costle, 1980: 132).

CONCLUSION

Regulatory policy is far too varied for simple solutions to work in all areas of regulation. General reforms such as those discussed in this chapter are unlikely to produce the benefits that substantive reforms of specific regulatory policies can. Deregulation, an effective policy in banking, for example, has little chance of effectively controlling pollution. The regulatory policies of the United States reflect political forces, economic constraints, legal imperatives, bureaucratic routines, and numerous other social forces. The exact combination of forces varies from area to area, limiting generalizations about regulation and making uniform reforms impossible.

Disagreements about the most effective reform proposals are often at heart disagreements about the goals that regulation should serve. Just as those who favor efficiency goals predictably favor deregulation or incentive systems, so those who favor equity goals are likely to call for greater regulation. Disagreements over regulatory reforms reflect disagreements over fundamental political goals.

Despite this variation and conflict, regulatory reform is possible. Breyer (1982) accurately notes that regulatory reform must be conducted on a case-by-case basis, focusing on substantive changes in regulation. The success of reform in the airline industry, trucking, banking, occupational safety and health, and other areas has come as the result of substantive changes in the policies rather than as the result of general changes in the regulatory process. The potential areas of reform are numerous, and they can only be reformed by addressing each problem area one at a time.

Appendix

Hypotheses Concerning Regulatory Policy

All entries in summary Table 3.2 and the summary tables in the other chapters are based solely on the judgment of the author. So that readers can compare regulation in different areas, an effort was made to be consistent in coding the table entries. The coding is as follows:

Ease of entry is coded as *hard* if significant economic barriers to entry exist in the industry; it is coded as *easy* if few do. Profits are coded as *high* if profits are above the average for all manufacturing; otherwise, they are coded as *low*. Complexity is coded as *high, moderate,* or *low,* depending on the complexity of the industry's production technology; these measures indicate how close the industry's technology is to the scientific state of the art. Stability is coded as *high* if the industry's production process changes slowly and predictably; it is coded as *low* if major or abrupt changes in the industry have occurred. Substitutes are coded as *high, moderate,* or *low,* depending on the number of substitutes there are for the industry's product.

Within the subsystem, bureaucratic control, the industry coalition, and the nonindustry coalition are coded as *strong, moderate,* or *weak. Strong* designates a continuous, effective force in making policy. *Moderate* denotes an occasional force in policy, and *weak* indicates a rare force. The macropolitical forces are coded in the same way.

Bureaucratic resources of expertise, cohesion, and leadership are coded as *high* if agencies have a reputation for these characteristics and are coded as *low* if they have poor reputations. Agencies without reputations are coded as *moderate.*

In terms of legislative authority, goals are coded as *general* or *specific.* Coverage (*all* or *limited*) refers to the proportion of the industry covered by the regulator. Sanctions are rated as *good, fair,* or *poor,* depending on the range of effective sanctions available to the agency. Procedures are rated as *good* if they do not restrict the regulatory actions of the agency and as *poor* if they do.

The hypotheses linking these variables to the direction of regulation (that is, whether regulation favors the regulated or the nonregulated) were presented in chapter 2. Because each of the hypotheses was presented with the qualifier "all other things being equal" and because, in any one particular regulatory area, several forces are pushing regulation in different directions, any simple assessment of these hypotheses is difficult. In fact, the impact of some of these variables depends heavily on the interaction between the variable and the other variables in the policy area. To provide a general guide for examining the summary tables, we list the hypotheses as follows:

· H_1 The greater the ease of entry into the industry, the more likely that regulation will favor the nonregulated.

· H_2 The more firms in an industry, the more likely that regulation will benefit the nonregulated.

· H_3 The higher the profits in an industry, the more likely that regulation will benefit the nonregulated.

· H_4 (the qualifying economic hypothesis) Industries with easy entry, a large number of firms, and high profits provide the opportunity for a regulator to regulate in the interests of the nonregulated. To the extent that regulation in such circumstances will benefit the nonregulated is a function of the political forces that favor regulation versus those that oppose it.

· H_5 The less complex the production technology of the regulated industry, the more likely regulation will benefit the nonregulated.

· H_6 The less stable the production technology of the regulated industry, the more likely regulation will benefit the nonregulated.

· H_7 The more substitutes there are available for the industry's product, the more likely that regulation will benefit the nonregulated.

· H_8 (qualifying hypothesis on technology) In industries with simple but changing technologies and many substitutes, regulators will have a greater opportunity to regulate in the interests of the nonregulated.

· H_9 The greater the complexity of regulation, the more likely that regulatory issues will be decided within the subsystem and that the bureaucracy will exercise control over the subsystem.

· H_{10} The greater the salience of regulatory issues, the more likely that the regulatory issue will be resolved in the macropolitical subsystem. The outcome of such issues will depend on the strength of the political forces of the various advocacy coalitions.

· H_{11} Either in a subsystem or the macropolitical system, regulation in the interests of the nonregulated is more likely if the nonregulated have a well-organized advocacy coalition.

· H_{12} In a subsystem dominated by the bureaucracy, the goals of the bureaucracy will determine who benefits from regulation.

· H_{13} The greater the expertise of the bureaucracy, the more likely the bureaucracy will control the subsystem and the more likely that regulation will benefit the nonregulated.

· H_{14} The more cohesive the regulatory bureaucracy, the more likely that the bureaucracy will control the subsystem and the more likely that regulation will benefit the nonregulated.

· H_{15} The stronger the political leadership of the bureaucracy, the more likely that the bureaucracy will control the subsystem.

· H_{16} The more specific the goals of regulatory legislation, the more likely that regulation will benefit the group with greater access to the legislative branch.

· H_{17} The more universal the coverage of the regulatory agency's legislative authority, the more likely that the regulation will benefit the nonregulated.

H_{18} The greater the range of sanctions available to the regulator, the more likely that regulation will benefit the nonregulated.

H_{19} If agency procedures do not limit agency actions, the probability that regulation will benefit the regulated increases.

Although the hypotheses are generally expressed in terms of benefits to the nonregulated, they could each be expressed in terms of benefits to the regulated. The research in this book did not exhaust the potential to test these hypotheses. It did, however, illustrate that theories of regulation need to provide a series of hypotheses that incorporate a wide range of variables in order to be valuable in studying regulation.

References

Abramson, Paul R., John H. Aldrich, and David W. Rohde. 1983. *Continuity and Change in the 1980 Election*. Washington, D.C.: Congressional Quarterly Press.

Ackerman, Bruce A., and William T. Hassler. 1981. *Clean Coal/Dirty Air*. New Haven: Yale University Press.

Akers, Ronald L. 1968. "The Professional Association and the Legal Regulation of Practice." *Law and Society Review* 2 (May) 463–482.

American Enterprise Institute. 1983. *Reauthorization of the Clean Water Act*. Washington, D.C.: American Enterprise Institute.

———. 1981. *Major Regulatory Initiatives During 1980*. Washington, D.C.: American Enterprise Institute.

Anderson, Douglas D. 1980. "State Regulation of Electric Utilities." In James Q. Wilson, ed., *The Politics of Regulation*. New York: Basic Books, pp. 3–41.

Anderson, Harry, Rich Thomas, and Christopher Ma. 1983. "Rewriting Antitrust Rules." *Newsweek* (August 29), 50–52.

Anderson, James E. 1984. *Public Policy-Making*. New York: Holt, Rinehart and Winston.

———. 1982. "Agricultural Marketing Orders and the Process and Politics of Self-Regulation." *Policy Studies Review* 2 (August), 97–111.

———, David W. Brady, and Charles S. Bullock. 1977. *Public Policy and Politics in America*. N. Scituate, Mass.: Duxbury Press.

Andrews, Richard N. L. 1984. "Deregulation: The Failure at EPA." In Norman J. Vig and Michael E. Kraft, eds., *Environmental Policy in the 1980s*. Washington, D.C.: Congressional Quarterly Press, pp. 3–26.

———. 1976. *Environmental Policy and Administrative Change*. Lexington, Mass.: Lexington Books.

Anthan, George. 1980. "The Super Farm Policy." *Des Moines Register* (June 1).

Areeda Phillip. 1984. "The State of the Law." *Regulation* 8 (January–February), 19–23.

Armentano, Dominick T. 1982. *Antitrust and Monopoly*. New York: Wiley.

Ashford, Nicholas A. 1976. *Crisis in the Workplace: Occupational Disease and Injury*. Cambridge, Mass.: MIT Press.

Audretsch, David B. 1983. *The Effectiveness of Antitrust Policy Toward Horizontal Mergers*. Ann Arbor, Mich.: UMI Research Press.

Aug, Stephen M. 1982. "The Financial Revolution." *Nation's Business* 48 (April), 47–50.

Avery, Dennis. 1980. "The Record on Sunset Review of Two Agencies." In Timothy B. Clark, Marvin H. Kosters, and James C. Miller, eds., *Reforming Regulations*. Washington, D.C.: American Enterprise Institute, pp. 41–45.

Azumi, Koya, and Jerald Hage. 1972. *Organizational Systems*. Lexington, Mass.: D. C. Heath.

Bacow, Lawrence S. 1982. "Private Bargaining and Public Regulation." In Eugene Bardach and Robert A. Kagan, eds. *Social Regulation*. San Francisco: ICS Press, pp. 201–220.

Bailey, Martin J. 1980. *Reducing Risks to Life*. Washington, D.C.: American Enterprise Institute.

Baldwin, Sidney. 1968. *Politics and Poverty*. Chapel Hill: University of North Carolina Press.

Ball, Howard. 1984. *Controlling Regulatory Sprawl*. Westport, Conn.: Greenwood Press.

"Bank Failures at Highest Rate in Four Decades." 1984. *Omaha World Herald* (January 4), 26.

Bardach, Eugene, and Robert A. Kagan. 1982. *Going by the Book*. Philadelphia: Temple University Press.

Barton, Weldon V. 1976. "Coalition-Building in the United States House of Representatives." In James E. Anderson, ed., *Cases in Public Policy-making*. New York: Praeger, pp. 141–161.

Beales, J. Howard. 1980. "The Economics of Regulating the Professions." In Roger D. Blair and Stephen Rubin, eds., *Regulating the Professions*. Lexington, Mass.: Lexington Books, pp. 125–142.

Behrman, Bradley. 1980. "Civil Aeronautics Board." In James Q. Wilson, ed., *The Politics of Regulation*. New York: Basic Books, pp. 75–121.

Belonzi, Arthur, Arthur D'Antonio, and Gary Helfand. 1977. *The Weary Watchdogs*. Wayne, N.J.: Avery Publishing Group.

Benham, Lee. 1972. "The Effects of Advertising on the Price of Eyeglasses." *Journal of Law and Economics* 15 (October), 337–351.

———. 1980. "The Demand for Occupational Licensure." In Simon Rottenberg, ed., *Occupational Licensing and Regulation*. Washington, D.C.: American Enterprise Institute, pp. 13–25.

———, and Alexandra Benham. 1975. "Regulating Through the Professions: A Perspective on Information Control." *Journal of Law and Economics* 18 (October), 421–447.

Bequai, August. 1981. *The Cashless Society: EFTs at the Crossroads*. New York: Wiley.

Bernstein, Marver H. 1955. *Regulating Business by Independent Commission*. Princeton: Princeton University Press.

Berry, Frances Stokes. 1982. "The States' Occupational Licensing Debate." *State Government News* 25 (May), 10–14.

Berry, Jeffrey M. 1984. *The Interest Group Society*. Boston: Little, Brown.

———. 1977. *Lobbying for the People*. Princeton: Princeton University Press.

Blair, Roger D., and David L. Kaserman. 1980. "Preservation of Quality and Sanctions Within the Professions." In Roger D. Blair and Stephen Rubin, eds., *Regulating the Professions*. Lexington, Mass.: Lexington Books, pp. 185–198.

———, and Stephen Rubin. 1980. *Regulating the Professions*. Lexington, Mass.: Lexington Books.

Bork, Robert H. 1978. *The Antitrust Paradox*. New York: Basic Books.

Boulier, Bryan D. 1980. "An Empirical Examination of the Influence of Licensure and Licensure Reform on the Geographical Distribution of Dentists." In Simon Rottenberg, ed., *Occupational Licensing and Regulation*. Washington, D.C.: American Enterprise Institute, pp. 73–97.

Boyle, Robert H., and R. Alexander Boyle. 1983. *Acid Rain*. New York: Schocken Books.

Breyer, Stephen. 1982. *Regulation and Its Reform*. Cambridge, Mass.: Harvard University Press.

Brown, Anthony E. 1984. "The CAB Policy Cycle and the Airline Deregulation Movement." Presented at the annual meeting of the Southwest Political Science Association, Ft. Worth.

———. 1981. "The Politics of the Civil Air Transportation Deregulation." Paper presented at the annual meeting of the American Political Science Association, New York, N.Y.

Brown, Clarence J. 1980. "Legislating a Regulatory Budget." In Timothy B. Clark, Marvin H. Kosters, and James C. Miller, eds., *Reforming Regulation*. Washington, D.C.: American Enterprise Institute, pp. 71–75.

Browne, William P. 1983. "Mobilizing and Activating Group Demands: The American Agriculture Movement." *Social Science Quarterly* 64 (March), 19–34.

Brownstein, Ronald. 1984. "In Era of Record Deficits, Farm Price Supports Seem Likely Targets for Cuts." *National Journal* 16 (February 11), 270–273.

———. 1983a. "Congress Hesitant About Moving to End Financial Industry Turmoil." *National Journal* 15 (July 2), 1372–1378.

———. 1983b. "A Wall of Money." *National Journal* 15 (July 30), 1603.

———. 1983c. "Allowed to Play New Instruments, S&Ls Finally Making Sweet Music." *National Journal* 15 (August 13), 1690–1694.

———. 1983d. "Merger Wars—Congress, SEC Take Aim at Hostile Corporate Takeover Moves." *National Journal* 15 (July 23), 1538–1541.

Brozen, Yale. 1982. *Concentration, Mergers and Public Policy*. New York: Macmillan.

Buchholz, Rogene A. 1982. *Business, Environment and Public Policy*. Englewood Cliffs, N.J.: Prentice-Hall.

Bureau of National Affairs. 1973. *The Consumer Product Safety Act*. Washington, D.C.: Bureau of National Affairs.

Burke, Edward J. 1980. "Legal Roar over Jet Noise." *National Law Journal* 3 (December 1), 1 ff.

Butler, Richard J. 1983. "Wage and Injury Rate Response to Shifting Levels of Workers'

Compensation." In John D. Worrall, ed., *Safety and the Workforce*. Ithaca, N.Y.: ILR Press, pp. 61–86.

Caldwell, Lynton. 1982. *Science and the National Environmental Policy Act*. University, Ala.: University of Alabama Press, 1982.

Campbell, Colin, and Rosemary Campbell. 1975. *An Introduction to Money and Banking*. 2d ed. Hinsdale, Ill.: Dryden Press.

Cannon, Bradley, and Micheal Giles. 1972. "Recurring Litigants: Federal Agencies Before the Supreme Court." *Western Political Quarterly* 25, 183–191.

Carey, John L., and William O. Doherty. 1967. "State Regulation of Certified Public Accountants." *State Government* (Winter), 26–30.

Carnes, Sam A. 1982. "Confronting Complexity and Uncertainty: Implementation of Hazardous-Waste-Management Policy." In Dean E. Mann, ed., *Environmental Policy Implementation*. Lexington, Mass.: Lexington Books.

Carron, Andrew S. 1982. *The Plight of the Thrift Institutions*. Washington, D.C.: Brookings.

———. 1983. "The Political Economy of Financial Regulation." In Roger Noll and Bruce M. Owen, eds., *The Political Economy of Deregulation*. Washington, D.C.: American Enterprise Institute, 69–83.

"Child-resistant Caps Saving Lives." 1984. *Norman Transcript* (February 26), 26.

Clark, Timothy B. 1982. "Bailout Bid: Thrifts Call Their Plan Better, Cheaper than More Failures." *National Journal* 14 (April 24), 711–715.

———, Marvin H. Kosters, and James C. Miller, 1980. *Reforming Regulation*. Washington, D.C.: American Enterprise Institute.

Clarkson, Kenneth W., and Timothy J. Muris. 1981. *The Federal Trade Commission Since 1970*. Cambridge: Cambridge University Press.

Cochrane, Willard W., and Mary E. Ryan. 1976. *American Farm Policy, 1948–1973*. Minneapolis: University of Minnesota Press.

Cohen, Richard E. 1983. "Life Without the Legislative Veto—Will Congress Ever Learn to Like It?" *National Journal* 15 (July 2), 1379–1381.

Cohen, Steven. 1984. "Defusing the Toxic Time Bomb: Federal Hazardous Waste Programs." In Norman J. Vig and Michael E. Kraft, eds., *Environmental Policy in the 1980s*. Washington, D.C.: Congressional Quarterly Press, pp. 273–292.

Colton, Kent W., and Kenneth W. Kraemer. 1980. *Computers and Banking*. New York: Plenum Press.

Comanor, W. S., and Harvey Leibenstein. 1969. "Allocative Efficiency, X-Efficiency, and the Measurement of Welfare Losses." *Economica* (August), 304–309.

Connors, Helen V. 1967. "Laws Regulating the Practice of Nursing." *State Government* (Winter), 30–34.

Consumer Reports. 1973. "The Peculiar Success of Chloromycetin." In Ralph Nader, ed., *The Consumer and Corporate Accountability*. New York: Harcourt Brace, pp. 98–105.

Conte, Christopher. 1979. "A Reluctant Congress Faces New Debate on Banking Laws." *Congressional Quarterly Weekly Report* (July 7), 1364–1369.

Cooper, Phillip J. 1983. *Public Law and Public Administration*. Palo Alto, Calif.: Mayfield.

Corn, Morton. 1981. "Cotton Dust: A Regulator's View." In Robert W. Crandall and Lester B. Lave, eds., *The Scientific Basis of Health and Safety Regulation*. Washington, D.C.: Brookings, pp. 109–115.

Corrigan, Richard. 1984. "Oil: Hunting for Bargains." *National Journal* 16 (March 31), 598–602.

Costle, Douglas M. 1980. "The Environmental Protection Agency's Initiatives." In Timothy B. Clark, Marvin H. Kosters, and James C. Miller, eds., *Reforming Regulation*. Washington, D.C.: American Enterprise Institute, pp. 130–133.

Council on Environmental Quality. 1980. *Environmental Quality 1980*. Washington, D.C.: U.S. Government Printing Office.

———. 1979. *Environmental Quality 1979*. Washington, D.C.: U.S. Government Printing Office.

———. 1978. *Environmental Quality 1978*. Washington, D.C.: U.S. Government Printing Office.

Cox, Edward, Robert Fellmeth, and John Schulz. 1969. *The "Nader Report" on the Federal Trade Commission*. New York: Baron.

Crandall, Robert W. 1983a. *Controlling Industrial Pollution*. Washington, D.C.: Brookings.

———. 1983b. "Air Pollution, Environmentalists, and the Coal Lobby." In Roger G. Noll and Bruce M. Owen, eds., *The Political Economy of Deregulation*. Washington, D.C.: American Enterprise Institute.

————. 1982. "The Environment." *Regulation* 6 (January–February), 29–32.

————, and Lester B. Lave. 1981. *The Scientific Basis of Health and Safety Regulation.* Washington, D.C.: Brookings.

Creighton, Lucy Black. 1976. *Pretenders to the Throne.* Lexington, Mass.: Lexington Books.

Cromley, Allan. 1983. "Congressional Investigators Critical of FDA over Zomax." *Daily Oklahoman* (December 12), 1.

Cutler, Lloyd N. 1980. "Reforms in Procedure, Structure, Personnel, and Substance." In Timothy B. Clark, Marvin H. Kosters, and James C. Miller, eds., *Reforming Regulation.* Washington, D.C.: American Enterprise Institute, pp. 153–158.

Dales, J. H. 1968. *Pollution, Property and Prices.* Toronto: University of Toronto Press.

Daly, George, and David W. Brady. 1976. "Federal Regulation of Economic Activity." In James E. Anderson, ed., *Economic Regulatory Policies.* Lexington, Mass., Lexington Books, pp. 171–186.

Davies, J. Clarence. 1984. "Environmental Institutions and the Reagan Administration." In Norman J. Vig and Michael E. Kraft, eds., *Environmental Policy in the 1980s.* Washington, D.C.: Congressional Quarterly Press, 143–160.

————, and Barbara S. Davies. 1975. *The Politics of Pollution.* 2d ed. Indianapolis: Pegasus.

Davis, Kenneth Culp. 1972. *Administrative Law Text.* 3d ed. St. Paul: West.

Demkovich, Linda E. 1984. "Playing the FDA Waiting Game." *National Journal* 16 (March 3), 410–412.

————. 1982. "Critics Fear the FDA Is Going Too Far in Cutting Industry's Regulatory Load." *National Journal* 14 (July 17), 1249–1252.

DeMuth, Christopher C. 1984. "A Strategy for Regulatory Reform." *Regulation* 8 (March–April), 25–29.

Denison, Edward F. 1979. *Accounting for Slower Economic Growth.* Washington, D.C.: Brookings.

DeVany, Arthur S., Wendy L. Gramm, Thomas R. Saving, and Charles W. Smith. 1982. "The Impact of Input Regulation: The Case of the U.S. Dental Industry." *Journal of Law and Economics* 25 (October), 367–381.

Dolan, Andrew K. 1980. "Occupational Licensure and Obstruction of Change in the Health Care Delivery System." In Roger D. Blair and Stephen Rubin, eds., *Regulating the Professions.* Lexington, Mass.: Lexington Books, 223–244.

Doniger, David D. 1978. *The Law and Policy of Toxic Substances Control.* Baltimore: Johns Hopkins University Press.

Dorfman, Robert. 1982. "Lessons of Pesticide Regulation." In Wesley A. Magat, ed., *Reform of Environmental Regulation.* Cambridge, Mass.: Ballinger, pp. 13–30.

Dorsey, Stuart. 1980. "The Occupational Licensing Queue." *Journal of Human Resources* 15 (Summer), 424–434.

Dougall, Herbert E., and Jack E. Gaumnitz. 1980. *Capital Markets and Institutions.* Englewood Cliffs, N.J.: Prentice-Hall.

Downing, Paul B. 1984. *Environmental Economics and Policy.* Boston: Little, Brown.

————, and James N. Kimball. 1982. "Enforcing Pollution Control Laws in the United States." *Policy Studies Journal* 11 (September), 55–65.

Downs, Anthony. 1967. *Inside Bureaucracy.* Boston: Little, Brown.

Eads, George C. 1982. "Testimony Before Congress." Committee on Energy and Commerce, House of Representatives (June 18), 8–26.

Easterbrook, Frank. 1984. "Restricted Dealing is a Way to Compete." *Regulation* 8 (January–February), 23–27.

Eis, Carl. 1969. "The 1919–1930 Merger Movement in American Industry." *Journal of Law and Economics* 12 (October), 267–296.

Elzinga, Kenneth G. 1969. "The Antimerger Law: Pyrrhic Victories?" *Journal of Law and Economics* 12 (April), 43–78.

————. 1980. "The Compass of Competition for Professional Services." In Roger D. Blair and Stephen Rubin, eds., *Regulating the Professions.* Lexington, Mass.: Lexington Books, pp. 107–123.

Enloe, Cynthia H. 1975. *The Politics of Pollution in a Comparative Perspective.* New York: McKay.

Environmental Protection Agency. 1978. *1978 Motor Vehicle Tampering Survey.* Washington, D.C.: Environmental Protection Agency.

"EPA Changes Way It Defines Key Air Pollutant." 1984. *Norman Transcript* (March 9), 1.

"EPA Mulls Ban on Leaded Gas." 1984. *The Daily Oklahoman* (February 29), 1.

Esposito, John C. 1970. *Vanishing Air.* New York: Grossman.

Evans, Robert G. 1980. "Professionals and the Production Function." In Simon Rottenberg, ed., *Occupational Licensing and Regulation*. Washington, D.C.: American Enterprise Institute, 225–264.

Ewalt, Josephine Hedges. 1962. *A Business Reborn: The Savings and Loan Story, 1930–1960*. Chicago: American Savings and Loan Institute Press.

"FDA Completes Review of 700 Drug Ingredients." 1983. *Saturday Oklahoman and Times* (October 8), 12.

Feenberg, Daniel, and Edwin S. Mills. 1980. *Measuring the Benefits of Water Pollution Abatement*. New York: Academic Press.

Feldman, Lawrence P. 1976. *Consumer Protection*. St. Paul: West.

Fellmuth, Robert C. 1970. *The Interstate Commerce Commission*. New York: Grossman.

Ferreira, Joseph. 1982. "Promoting Safety Through Insurance." In Eugene Bardach and Robert A. Kagan, eds., *Social Regulation*. San Francisco: ICS Press, pp. 267–283.

Fisher, Franklin M., James W. McKie, and Richard B. Mancke. 1983. *IBM and the Data Processing Industry*. New York: Praeger.

Flexner, Abraham. 1910. *Medical Education in the United States and Canada*. New York: Carnegie Foundation.

Ford, Gary T. 1977. "State Characteristics Affecting the Passage of Consumer Legislation." *Journal of Consumer Affairs* 11 (Summer), 177–182.

Forste, Robert H., and George E. Frick. 1979. "Dairy." In Lyle P. Schertz and others, eds., *Another Revolution in U.S. Farming?* Washington, D.C.: U.S. Department of Agriculture.

Frank, John N. 1981. "New Competitors Zero in on Savings Market." *Savings and Loan News* 102 (April), 36–41.

Frech, H. E. 1974. "Occupational Licensure and Health Care Productivity." In John Rafferty, ed., *Health Manpower and Productivity*. Lexington, Mass.: Lexington Books, pp. 119–139.

Freeman, A. Myrick. 1978. "Air and Water Pollution Policy." In Paul R. Portney, ed., *Current Issues in U. S. Environmental Policy*. Baltimore: Johns Hopkins University Press.

Freeman, J. Leiper. 1965. *The Political Process*. New York: Random House.

Freeman, Richard B. 1980. "The Effect of Occupational Licensure on Occupational Attainment." In Simon Rottenberg, ed., *Occupational Licensing and Regulation*. Washington, D.C.: American Enterprise Institute, pp. 165–179.

Fried, Robert. 1976. *Performance in American Bureaucracy*. Boston: Little, Brown.

Friedman, Lawrence M. 1965. "Freedom of Contract and Occupational Licensing 1890–1910." *California Law Review* 53, 487–534.

Friedman, Milton. 1962. *Capitalism and Freedom*. Chicago: University of Chicago Press.

——, and Rose Friedman. 1980. *Free to Choose*. New York: Harcourt Brace Jovanovich.

——, and Simon Kuznets. 1945. *Income from Independent Professional Practice*. New York: National Bureau of Economic Research.

Friedrich, Carl J. 1940. "Public Policy and the Nature of Administrative Responsibility." In Carl J. Friedrich and Edward S. Mason, eds., *Public Policy*. Vol. 1. Cambridge, Mass.: Harvard University Press.

Fritschler, A. Lee. 1975. *Smoking and Politics*. Englewood Cliffs, N.J.: Prentice-Hall.

Furlong, Frederick T. 1983. "New Deposit Instruments." *Federal Reserve Bulletin* 69 (May), 319–236.

Gamse, Roy N. 1982. "Economic Incentives." In LeRoy Graymer and Frederick Thompson, eds., *Reforming Social Regulation*. Beverly Hills: Sage, pp. 159–164.

Gardner, Bruce L. 1981a. *The Governing of Agriculture*. Lawrence: Regents Press of Kansas.

Gardner, Bruce L. 1981b. "Consequences of Farm Policies During the 1970s." In D. Gale Johnson, ed., *Food and Agricultural Policy for the 1980s*. Washington, D.C.: American Enterprise Institute, pp. 48–72.

Gellhorn, Walter. 1956. *Individual Freedom and Governmental Restraints*. Baton Rouge: Louisiana State University Press.

——. 1976. "The Abuse of Occupational Licensing." *University of Chicago Law Review* 44 (Fall), 6–27.

General Accounting Office. 1983a. *Wastewater Dischargers Are Not Complying with EPA Pollution Control Permits*. Washington, D.C.: GAO (December 2).

——. 1983b. *USDA's Oversight of State Meat and Poultry Inspection Programs Could be Strengthened*. Washington, D.C.: GAO (October 21).

——. 1983c. *Monitoring and Enforcing Food Safety—An Overview of Past Studies*. Washington, D.C.: GAO (September 9).

——. 1981a. *Emerging Issues from New Product Development in Food Manufacturing Industries*. Washington, D.C.: GAO (August 19).

———. 1981b. *Improving Sanitation and Federal Inspection at Slaughter Plants*. Washington, D.C.: GAO (July 30).

———. 1980a. *Costly Wastewater Treatment Plants Fail to Perform as Expected*. Washington, D.C.: GAO.

———. 1980b. *Need More Effective Regulation of Direct Additives to Food*. Washington, D.C.: GAO (August 14).

———. 1972. *Dimensions of Insanitary Conditions in the Food Marketing Industry*. B-160431 (April 18), Washington, D.C.

Gibbs, Lois Marie. 1983. *Love Canal*. Albany: State University of New York Press.

Gilbert, Charles E. 1959. "The Framework for Administrative Responsibility." *Journal of Politics* 21 (August), 373–407.

Ginsberg, Benjamin, and John Green. 1979. "The Best Congress Money Can Buy." Paper presented at the annual meeting of the American Political Science Association, Washington, D.C.

Glen, Maxwell, and Cody Shearer. 1984. "Workers' Safety: Is It Better?" *Oklahoma Daily* (March 7), 9.

"GM Knew of Brake Problem Before Production?" 1983. *Norman Transcript* (September 25), 3.

Gormley, William T. 1983a. "Regulatory Issue Networks in a Federal System." Paper presented at the annual meeting of the American Political Science Association, Chicago.

———. 1983b. *The Politics of Public Utility Regulation*. Pittsburgh: Pittsburgh University Press.

Gottron, Martha V., ed. 1982. *Regulation: Process and Politics*. Washington, D.C.: Congressional Quarterly Press.

Grabowski, Henry G., and John M. Vernon. 1983. *The Regulation of Pharmaceuticals*. Washington, D.C.: American Enterprise Institute.

Graves, Philip E., and Ronald J. Krumm. 1981. *Health and Air Quality*. Washington, D.C.: American Enterprise Institute.

Green, Mark J. 1980. "Cost-Benefit Analysis as a Mirage." In Timothy B. Clark, Marvin H. Kosters, and James C. Miller, eds., *Reforming Regulation*. Washington, D.C.: American Enterprise Institute, pp. 113–116.

Greenwald, Carol S. 1980. *Banks Are Dangerous to Your Wealth*. Englewood Cliffs, N.J.: Prentice-Hall.

———. 1977. *Group Power*. New York: Praeger.

Greer, Douglas F. 1983. *Business, Government, and Society*. New York: Macmillan.

Gregg, Gail. 1979. "House Attaches Federal Reserve Bill to Sweeping Senate Banking Measure." *Congressional Quarterly Weekly Report* (November 10), 2546–2548.

Guth, James L. 1980. "Federal Dairy Programs." Presented at the Symposium on Farm Structure and Rural Policy, Ames, Iowa, October 20–22.

Guyot, James F. 1979. "The Convergence of Public and Private Sector Bureaucracies." Paper presented at the annual meeting of the American Political Science Association, Washington, D.C.

Hagstrom, Jerry. 1984. "Candidates Woo Farmers as Agricultural PACs Step Up Their Contributions." *National Journal* 16 (March 3), 420–424.

Hahn, Robert W., and Roger G. Noll. 1982. "Implementing Tradable Emissions Permits." In LeRoy Graymer and Frederick Thompson, eds., *Reforming Social Regulation*. Beverly Hills: Sage, pp. 125–150.

Hammond, Bray. 1957. *Banks and Politics in America from the Revolution to the Civil War*. Princeton: Princeton University Press.

Harrington, Winston, and Alan J. Krupnick. 1981. "Stationary Source Pollution Policy and Choices for Reform." *Natural Resources Journal* 21 (July), 539–564.

Harter, Philip J. 1977. "In Search of OSHA." *Regulation* 1 (September–October), 33–39.

Haug, Marie. 1980. "The Sociological Approach to Self-Regulation." In Roger D. Blair and Stephen Rubin, eds., *Regulating the Professions*. Lexington: Lexington Books, pp. 61–80.

Heady, Earl O. 1983. "Economic Policies and Variables." In David Brewster, Wayne Rasmussen, and Garth Youngberg, eds., *Farms in Transition*. Ames, Iowa: Iowa State University Press, 23–26.

Heclo, Hugh. 1978. "Issue Networks and the Executive Establishment." In Anthony King, ed., *The New American Political System*. Washington, D.C.: American Enterprise Institute.

———. 1977. *Government of Strangers*. Washington, D.C.: Brookings.

Heffron, Florence, with Neil McFeeley. 1983. *The Administrative Regulatory Process*. New York: Longman.

Herrmann, Robert O. 1978. "The Consumer Movement in Historical Perspective." In David A. Acker and George S. Day, eds., *Consumerism*. New York: The Free Press, pp. 27–36.

Hershey, Nathan. 1969. "An Alternative to Mandatory Licensure of Health Professionals." *Hospital Progress* 50 (March), 71–74.

Hinich, Melvin J. and Richard Staelin. 1980. *Consumer Protection Legislation and the U.S. Food Industry*. New York: Pergamon Press.

Hoel, David G., and Kenny S. Crump. 1981. "Waterborne Carcinogens: A Scientist's View." In Robert W. Crandall and Lester B. Lave, eds., *The Scientific Basis of Health and Safety Regulation*. Washington, D.C.: Brookings, pp. 173–196.

Holen, Arlene S. 1977. "The Economics of Dental Licensing." Center for Naval Analysis. Mimeographed.

Holen, Arlene S. 1965. "Effects of Professional Licensing Arrangements on Interstate Mobility and Resource Allocation." *Journal of Political Economy* 73 (October), 492–498.

"House Panel Raps FDA's Approval of Now Banned Drug." 1983. *The Daily Oklahoman* (November 3), 15.

Howard, Ross, and Michael Perley. 1980. *Acid Rain: The North American Forecast*. Toronto: Anansi Press.

Huntington, Samuel P. 1952. "The Marasmus of the ICC." *Yale Law Journal* 61 (April), 467–509.

Ingram, Helen, and Dean E. Mann. 1984. "Preserving the Clean Water Act." In Norman J. Vig and Michael E. Kraft, eds., *Environmental Policy in the 1980s*. Washington, D.C.: Congressional Quarterly Press, pp. 251–272.

Jacoby, J., R. Chestnut, and W. Silberman. 1977. "Consumer Use and Comprehension of Nutritional Information." *Journal of Consumer Research* 4:2.

Jessee, Michael A., and Steven A. Seelig. 1977. *Bank Holding Companies and the Public Interest*. Lexington, Mass.: Lexington Books.

"Job Safety Inspectors Seldom Required to Get Warrants Despite Justices' Ruling." 1978. *Wall Street Journal* (July 17), 13.

Johnson, Arthur M. 1965. *Government Business Relations*. Columbus: Charles Merrill.

Johnson, D. Gale. 1981. "Agriculture Policy Alternatives for the 1980s." In D. Gale Johnson, ed., *Food and Agricultural Policy for the 1980s*. Washington, D.C.: American Enterprise Institute, pp. 183–209.

Johnson, Ivan C., and William W. Roberts. 1982. *Money and Banking*. Chicago: Dryden Press.

Jones, Charles O. 1975. *Clean Air*. Pittsburgh: University of Pittsburgh Press.

Julin, Joseph R. 1980. "The Legal Profession: Education and Entry." In Roger D. Blair and Stephen Rubin, eds., *Regulating the Professions*. Lexington, Mass.: Lexington Books, pp. 201–221.

Kalogeras, Gus. 1981. "Examining the Money-Market Funds." *The Bankers Magazine* 164 (January–February), 66–72.

Katzman, Robert A. 1980. *Regulatory Bureaucracy*. Cambridge, Mass.: MIT Press.

Keller, Bill. 1982. "Liberation of Bank Industry This Year May be Thwarted by Fractured Finance Lobbies." *Congressional Quarterly Weekly Report* 40 (February 6), 187–191.

Kelman, Steven. 1981a. *What Price Incentives?* Boston: Auburn House.

———. 1981b. *Regulating Sweden, Regulating America*. Cambridge, Mass.: MIT Press.

———. 1980. "Occupational Safety and Health Administration." In James Q. Wilson, ed., *The Politics of Regulation*. New York: Basic Books, pp. 236–266.

Kemp, Kathleen A. 1983. "The Regulators: Partisanship and Public Policy." *Policy Studies Journal* 11 (March), 386–397.

———. 1982a. "Accidents and Political Support for Regulatory Agencies." Paper presented at the Midwest Political Science Association, Milwaukee.

———. 1982b. "Instability in Budgeting for Federal Regulatory Agencies." *Social Science Quarterly* 63 (December), 643–660.

Kennedy, Susan Estabrook. 1973. *The Banking Crisis of 1933*. Lexington, Ky.: University Press of Kentucky.

Kenski, Henry C., and Margaret Corgan Kenski. 1984. "Congress Against the President: The Struggle over the Environment." In Norman J. Vig and Michael E. Kraft, eds., *Environmental Policy in the 1980s*. Washington, D.C.: Congressional Quarterly Press, pp. 97–120.

Kessel, Reuben A. 1959. "Price Discrimination in Medicine." *Journal of Law and Economics* 1 (October), 20–51.

———. 1970. "The AMA and the Supply of Physicians." *Law and Contemporary Problems*. 35 (Spring), 267–283.

Kessler, David A. 1984. "Food Safety: Revising the Statute." *Science* 223 (March 9), 1034–1044.

Kimm, Victor J., Arnold J. Kuzmack, and David W. Schnare. 1981. "Waterborne Carcinogens:

A Regulator's View." In Robert W. Crandall and Lester B. Lave, eds., *The Scientific Basis of Health and Safety Regulation*. Washington, D.C.: Brookings, 229–251.

Kinter, Earl W. 1964. *An Antitrust Primer*. New York: Macmillan.

Kirkendall, Richard S. 1980. "The New Deal for Agriculture: Recent Writings, 1971–76." In Trudy Huskamp Peterson, ed., *Farmers, Bureaucrats, and Middlemen*. Washington, D.C.: Howard University Press.

Kirschten, Dick. 1983. "Ruckelshaus May Find EPA's Problems Are Budgetary as much as Political." *National Journal* 15 (March 26), 659–660.

Kirst, Michael W. 1969. *Government Without Passing Laws*. Chapel Hill: University of North Carolina Press.

Klebaner, Benjamin L. 1974. *Commercial Banking in the United States: A History*. Hinsdale, Ill.: Dryden Press.

Kleiner, Morris M., Robert S. Gay, and Karen Greene. 1982. "Licensing, Migration, and Earnings: Some Empirical Insights." *Policy Studies Review* 1 (February), 510–522.

Kneese, Allen V., and Charles L. Schultze. 1975. *Pollution, Prices, and Public Policy*. Washington, D.C.: Brookings.

Kohlmeier, Louis M. 1969. *The Regulators*. New York: Harper & Row.

Kolko, Gabriel. 1965. *Railroads and Regulation*. Princeton: Princeton University Press.

———. 1963. *The Triumph of Conservatism*. New York: Free Press.

Koren, Herman. 1980. *Handbook of Environmental Health and Safety*. New York: Pergamon Press.

Kosters, Marvin H. 1982. *Major Regulatory Initiatives During 1981*. Washington, D.C.: American Enterprise Institute.

———. 1980. "Introduction." In Timothy B. Clark, Marvin H. Kosters, and James C. Miller, eds., *Reforming Regulation*. Washington, D.C.: American Enterprise Institute, pp. 69–70.

Krasnow, Erwin G., Lawrence D. Longley, and Herbert A. Terry. 1982. *The Politics of Broadcast Regulation*. 3d ed. New York: St. Martin's Press.

Krier, James E. 1982. "Marketlike Approaches." In LeRoy Gramer and Frederick Thompson, eds., *Reforming Social Regulation*. Beverly Hills: Sage, pp. 151–158.

Krug, Edward C., and Charles R. Frink. 1983. "Acid Rain on Acid Soil." *Science* 221 (August 5), 520–525.

Kurtz, Howie. 1977. "The Consumer Product Safety Commission and Asbestos." *Washington Monthly* (December).

LaBarbera, Priscella. 1977. *Consumers and the Federal Trade Commission*. East Lansing, Mich.: MSU Business Studies.

Lammers, Nancy, ed. 1983. *Congressional Quarterly's Federal Regulatory Directory, 1983–4*. Washington, D.C.: Congressional Quarterly.

Lasswell, Harold D. 1936. *Politics: Who Gets What, When, How*. New York: McGraw-Hill.

Lave, Lester B., and Gilbert S. Omenn. 1982. *Clearing the Air: Reforming the Clean Air Act*. Washington, D.C.: Brookings.

Lee, John E. 1983. "Some Consequences of the New Reality in U.S. Agriculture." In David Brewster, Wayne Rasmussen, and Garth Youngberg, eds., *Farms in Transition*. Ames, Iowa: Iowa State University Press, pp. 3–22.

Leffler, Keith B. 1981. "Persuasion or Information?: The Economics of Prescription Drug Advertising." *Journal of Law and Economics* 24 (April), 45–74.

———. 1978. "Physician Licensure: Competition and Monopoly in American Medicine." *Journal of Law and Economics* 21 (April), 165–186.

Leigh, J. Paul. 1984. "Compensating Wages for Employment in Strike-Prone or Hazardous Industries." *Social Science Quarterly* 65 (March), 89–99.

———. 1981. "Compensating Wages for Occupational Injuries and Diseases." *Social Science Quarterly* 62 (December), 773–778.

Leland, Hayne E. 1979. "Quacks, Lemons, and Licensing: A Theory of Minimum Quality Standards." *Journal of Political Economy* 87 (November–December), 1328–1348.

———. 1980. "Minimum-Quality Standards and Licensing in Markets with Asymmetrical Information." In Simon Rottenberg, ed., *Occupational Licensing and Regulation*. Washington, D.C.: American Enterprise Institute, pp. 265–284.

Lester, James P., James L. Franke, Ann O'M. Bowman, and Kenneth W. Kramer. 1983. "A Comparative Perspective on State Hazardous Waste Regulation." In James P. Lester and Ann O'M. Bowman, eds., *The Politics of Hazardous Waste Management*. Durham, N.C.: Duke University Press, pp. 212–233.

Levine, Michael E. 1982. "Regulating the Auto Industry." In LeRoy Gramer and Frederick Thompson, eds., *Reforming Social Regulation*. Beverly Hills: Sage, pp. 111–124.

Lewis-Beck, Michael S., and John R. Alford, "Can Government Regulate Safety? The Coal Mine Example." *American Political Science Review* 74 (September), 745–756.

Lieber, Harvey. 1983. "Federalism and Hazardous Waste Policy." In James P. Lester and Ann O'M. Bowman, eds., *The Politics of Hazardous Waste Management*. Durham, N.C.: Duke University Press, pp. 60–73.

———. 1975. *Federalism and Clean Waters*. Lexington, Mass.: Lexington Books.

Lin, William, Linda Calvin, and James Johnson. 1980. *Farm Commodity Programs: Who Participates and Who Gets the Benefits?* Washington, D.C.: U.S. Department of Agriculture.

Lindblom, Charles E. 1965. *The Intelligence of Democracy*. New York: Free Press.

Litan, Robert E., and William D. Nordhaus. 1983. *Reforming Federal Regulation*. New Haven: Yale University Press.

Long, Norton. 1962. *The Polity*. Chicago: Rand McNally.

Lordan, James F. 1983. "More Changes Needed to Reach ACH Potential." *ABA Banking Journal* 75 (April), 38–42.

Lowi, Theodore. 1969. *The End of Liberalism*. New York: Norton.

MacAvoy, Paul W. 1979. *The Regulated Industries and the Economy*. New York: Norton.

MacAvoy, Paul W. 1977. *Federal Milk Marketing Orders and Price Supports*. Washington, D.C.: American Enterprise Institute.

MacAvoy, Paul W., and Kenneth Robinson. 1983. "Winning Buy Losing: The AT&T Settlement and Its Impact on Telecommunications." *Yale Journal on Regulation* 1 (No. 1), 1–42.

McConnell, Grant. 1966. *Private Power and American Democracy*. New York: Knopf.

McCraw, Thomas K. 1981. "Rethinking the Trust Question." In Thomas K. McCraw, ed., *Regulation in Perspective*. Cambridge, Mass.: Harvard University Press, 1–55.

McCubbins, Mathew D., and Thomas Schwartz. 1984. "Congressional Oversight Overlooked: Police Patrols Versus Fire Alarms." *American Journal of Political Science* 28 (February), 165–179.

McFarland, Andrew S. 1976. *Public Interest Lobbys*. Washington, D.C.: American Enterprise Institute.

McGregor, Eugene B. 1974. "Politics and Career Mobility of Civil Servants." *American Political Science Review* 68 (March), 18–26.

Maney, Ardith L., and Donald F. Hadwiger. 1980. "Taking 'Cides: The Controversy over Agricultural Chemicals." In Trudy Huscamp Peterson, ed., *Farmers, Bureaucrats, and Middlemen*. Washington, D.C.: Howard University Press.

Marcus, Alfred. 1980. "Environmental Protection Agency." In James Q. Wilson, ed., *The Politics of Regulation*. New York: Basic Books, pp. 267–303.

Markham, Jesse W. 1955. "Survey of the Evidence and Findings on Mergers." In *Business Concentration and Public Policy*. Princeton: Princeton University Press.

———. 1965. "Mergers and the Adequacy of New Section 7." In Almarin Phillips, ed., *Perspectives on Antitrust Policy*. Princeton: Princeton University Press.

Martin, Donald L. 1980. "Will the Sun Set on Occupational Licensing?" In Simon Rottenberg, ed., *Occupational Licensing and Regulation*. Washington, D.C.: American Enterprise Institute, pp. 142–154.

Marvel, Mary K. 1983. "Safety Regulation: Industry Capture or State Competition." Paper presented at the American Political Science Association Meetings, Chicago.

———. 1982. "Implementation and Safety Regulations." *Administration and Society* 14 (May), 5–14.

Maslow, Abraham H. 1970. *Motivation and Personality*. 2d ed. New York: Harper & Row.

Maurizi, Alex R., Ruth L. Moore, and Lawrence Shepard. 1981. "Competing for Professional Control: Professional Mix in the Eyeglasses Industry." *Journal of Law and Economics* 24 (October), 351–364.

———. 1974. "Occupational Licensing and the Public Interest." *Journal of Political Economy* 82 (March–April), 399–413.

———. 1980. "The Impact of Regulation on Quality: The Case of California Contractors." In Simon Rottenberg, ed., *Occupational Licensing and Regulation*. Washington, D.C.: American Enterprise Institute, pp. 26–35.

Mayer, Martin. 1974. *The Bankers*. New York: Ballantine.

Mayer, Robert N. 1981. "Consumerism in the 70s: The Emergence of New Issues." *Journal of Consumer Affairs* 15 (Winter), 375–391.

Mazmanian, Daniel A., and Mordecai Lee. 1975. "Tradition Be Damned: The Army Corps of Engineers is Changing." *Public Administration Review* 35 (March–April), 166–172.

———. and Paul A. Sabatier. 1983. *Implementation and Public Policy*. Glenview, Ill.: Scott, Foresman.

————, and ————. 1980. "A Multivariate Model of Public Policy-Making." *American Journal of Political Science* 24 (August), 439–468.

Meier, Kenneth J. 1984. "The Limits of Cost-Benefit Analysis." In Lloyd G. Nigro, ed., *Decisionmaking in Public Administration.* New York: Marcel Dekker, pp. 43–63.

————. 1983a. "Consumerism or Protectionism: State Regulation of Occupations." Paper presented at the annual meeting of the American Political Science Association, Chicago.

————. 1983b. "Political Economy and Cost-Benefit Analysis." In Alan Stone and Edward J. Harpham, eds., *The Political Economy of Public Policy.* Beverly Hills: Sage, pp. 143–162.

————. 1982. "Technology, Politics, and Public Policy: Deregulating Financial Institutions." Paper presented at the annual meeting of the Midwest Political Science Association, Milwaukee.

————. 1980. "The Impact of Regulatory Agency Structure: IRCs or DRAs." *Southern Review of Public Administration* 3 (March), 427–443.

————. 1979. *Politics and the Bureaucracy.* N. Scituate, Mass.: Duxbury Press.

————, and David R. Morgan. 1981. "Speed Kills: A Longitudinal Analysis of Traffic Fatalities and the 55 MPH Speed Limit." *Policy Studies Review* 1 (August), 157–167.

————, and ————. 1982. "Citizen Compliance with Public Policy." *Western Political Quarterly* 35 (June), 258–273.

————, and John P. Plumlee. 1978. "Regulatory Administration and Organizational Rigidity." *Western Political Quarterly* 31 (March), 80–95.

————, and ————. 1979. "The Impact of Organizational Structure on Regulatory Policy." Paper presented at the Symposium on Strategies for Change in Regulatory Policy, Chicago.

Meiners, Roger E. 1982. "What to Do About Hazardous Products." In Robert W. Poole, ed., *Instead of Regulation.* Lexington, Mass.: Lexington Books, pp. 285–310.

Melnick, R. Shep. 1983. *Regulation and the Courts.* Washington, D.C.: Brookings.

Mendeloff, John. 1979. *Regulating Safety.* Cambridge, Mass.: MIT Press.

Menzel, Donald C., and Irwin Feller. 1977. "Leadership and Interaction Patterns in the Diffusion of Innovations Among the States." *Western Political Quarterly* 30 (December), 528–536.

Meyer, Henry Balthasar. 1906. "A History of the Northern Securities Case." *Wisconsin University Bulletins 1.*

Meyer, Louis S. 1982. "Consumer Protection." *Book of the States, 1982–83.* Lexington, Ky.: Council of State Governments, pp. 540–545.

Milbrath, Lester. 1963. *The Washington Lobbyists.* Chicago: Rand McNally.

Miller, James C. 1984. "An Analytical Framework." *Regulation* 8 (January–February), 31–32.

Miller, John A., David G. Topel, and Robert E. Rust. 1976. "USDA Beef Grading: A Failure in Consumer Information." *Journal of Marketing* 40 (January), 25–31.

Miller, Richard B. 1983. "The Administration, Congress, and Banking." *The Bankers Magazine* 166 (March–April), 54–59.

Mingo, John J. 1981. "The Economic Impact of Deposit Rate Ceilings." In Arnold A. Heggestad, ed., *Regulation of Consumer Financial Services.* Cambridge, Mass.: Abt Books, 124–143.

Mitchell, Robert Cameron. 1984. "Public Opinion and Environmental Politics in the 1970s and 1980s." In Norman J. Vig and Michael E. Kraft, eds., *Environmental Policy in the 1980s.* Washington, D.C.: Congressional Quarterly Press, pp. 51–74.

Mitnick, Barry M. 1980. *The Political Economy of Regulation.* New York: Columbia University Press.

Moe, Terry M. 1982. "Regulatory Performance and Presidential Administration." *American Journal of Political Science* 26 (May), 197–225.

Moody, J. Carroll, and Gilbert C. Fite. 1971. *The Credit Union Movement.* Lincoln: University of Nebraska Press.

Morrell, David R. 1983. "Technological Policies and Hazardous Waste in California." In James P. Lester and Ann O'M. Bowman, eds., *The Politics of Hazardous Waste Management.* Durham, N.C.: Duke University Press, pp. 139–175.

Mosher, Lawrence B. 1983a. " 'A Ticking Time Bomb'—Compensation for Victims of Hazardous Waste Dumps." *National Journal* 15 (January 15), 120–121.

————. 1983b. "Distrust of Gorsuch May Stymie EPA Attempt to Integrate Pollution Wars." *National Journal* 15 (February 12), 322–324.

————. 1983c. "EPA Still Doesn't Know the Dimensions of Nation's Hazardous Waste Problem." *National Journal* 15 (April 16), 796–799.

————. 1983d. "Ruckelshaus' First Mark on EPA—Another $165.5 Million for Its Budget." *National Journal* 15 (June 25), 1344–1345.

————. 1983e. "Ruckelshaus Is Seen as His Own Man in Battle to Renew Clean Water Act." *National Journal* 15 (July 16), 1497–1500.

Mueller, Willard F. 1979. *The Celler-Kefauver Act.* Washington, D.C.: U.S. House of Representatives, Committee on the Judiciary, Subcommittee on Monopolies and Commercial Law. (November 7).

Mulinix, Kim W., and Kenneth J. Meier. 1983. "Economics, Technology and Public Policy: Deregulating the Thrift Industry." Paper presented at the annual meeting of the Southwestern Political Science Association, Houston, Tex.

Muris, Timothy J., and Fred S. McChesney. 1979. "Advertising and the Price and Quality of Legal Services." *American Bar Foundation Research Journal* 1979 (Winter), 179–208.

Nadel, Mark V. 1971. *The Politics of Consumer Protection.* Indianapolis: Bobbs-Merrill.

Natchez, Peter, and Irvin C. Bupp. 1973. "Policy and Priority in the Budgetary Process." *American Political Science Review* 67 (September), 951–963.

National Research Council. 1983. *Acid Deposition: Atmospheric Processes in Eastern North America—A Review of Current Scientific Understanding.* Washington, D.C.: National Academy Press.

Nelson, Ralph L. 1959. *Merger Movements in American Industry, 1895–1956.* Princeton: Princeton University Press.

Nichols, Albert, and Richard Zeckhauser. 1981. "OSHA After a Decade." In Leonard W. Weiss and Michael K. Klass, eds., *Case Studies in Regulation.* Boston: Little, Brown, pp. 202–234.

Niskanen, William. 1971. *Bureaucracy and Representative Government.* Chicago: Aldine.

Noll, Roger G., and Bruce M. Owen. 1983. *The Political Economy of Deregulation.* Washington, D.C.: American Enterprise Institute.

Norton, Clark F. 1976. *Congressional Review, Deferral and Disapproval of Executive Actions.* Washington, D.C.: Congressional Research Service.

O'Hare, Michael. 1982. "Information Strategies as Regulatory Surrogates." In Eugene Bardach and Robert A. Kagan, eds., *Social Regulation.* San Francisco: ICS Press, pp. 221–236.

Okun, Arthur. 1976. *Equality vs. Efficiency: The Big Tradeoff.* Washington, D.C.: Brookings.

Opper, Barbara Negri. 1983. "Profitability of Insured Commercial Banks in 1982." *Federal Reserve Bulletin* 69 (July), 489–507.

"Oraflex Linked to Cancer in Mice, Lilly Tells FDA." 1983. *Saturday Oklahoman and Times* (December 24), 26.

Ornstein, Norman J., and Shirley Elder. 1978. *Interest Groups, Lobbying and Policymaking.* Washington, D.C.: Congressional Quality Press.

Oster, Sharon M. 1980. "An Analysis of Some Causes of Interstate Differences in Consumer Regulations." *Economic Inquiry* 18 (January), 39–54.

Ostmann, Robert. 1982. *Acid Rain.* Minneapolis: Dillon Press.

Paarlberg, Don. 1980. *Farm and Food Policy.* Lincoln: University of Nebraska Press.

Page, Joseph, and Mary O'Brien. 1973. *Bitter Wages.* New York: Grossman.

Pape, Stuart M. 1982. "Legislative Issues in Food Safety Regulation." In Eugene Bardach and Robert A. Kagan, eds., *Social Regulation.* San Francisco: ICS Press, pp. 159–175.

Parsons, Donald O., and Edward J. Ray. 1975. "The United States Steel Consolidation." *Journal of Law and Economics* 18 (April), 181–220.

Pashigian, B. Peter. 1983. "How Large and Small Plants Fare Under Environmental Regulation." *Regulation* 7 (September–October), 19–23.

————. 1980. "Has Occupational Licensing Reduced Geographical Mobility and Raised Earnings?" In Simon Rottenberg, ed., *Occupational Licensure and Regulation.* Washington, D.C.: American Enterprise Institute, pp. 299–333.

————. 1979. "Occupational Licensing and Interstate Mobility of Professionals." *Journal of Law and Economics* 22 (April), 1–25.

Patterson, Samuel C. 1978. "The Semisovereign Congress." In Anthony King, ed., *The New American Political System.* Washington, D.C.: American Enterprise Institute, pp. 125–177.

Pauly, David. 1982. "A Deregulation Report Card." *Newsweek* (January 11), 50–52.

————, and Erik Ipsen. 1983. "The Saving of the Thrifts." *Newsweek* (April 18), 59.

————, and ————. 1984. "ITT: A Struggling Giant." *Newsweek* 103 (January 2), 49–50.

Peltzman, Sam. 1976. "Toward a More General Theory of Regulation." *Journal of Law and Economics* 19 (August), 211–240.

————. 1975. "The Effects of Automobile Safety Regulation." *Journal of Political Economy* (July–August), 667–735.

————. 1974. *Regulation of Pharmaceutical Innovation.* Washington, D.C.: American Enterprise Institute.

———. 1968. "Bank Stock Prices and the Effects of Regulation of the Banking Structure." *Journal of Business* 41 (October), 413–430.

Penn, J. B. 1981. "Economic Development in U.S. Agriculture During the 1970s." In D. Gale Johnson, ed., *Food and Agriculture Policy for the 1980s*. Washington, D.C.: American Enterprise Institute, pp. 3–47.

Penoyer, Ronald J. 1981. *Directory of Federal Regulatory Agencies*. St. Louis: Center for the Study of American Business, Washington University.

Perloff, Jeffrey M. 1980. "The Impact of Licensing Laws on Wage Changes in the Construction Industry." *Journal of Law and Economics* 23 (October), 409–428.

Pertschuk, Michael. 1980. "Needs and Licenses." In Simon Rottenberg, ed., *Occupational Licensing and Regulation*. Washington, D.C.: American Enterprise Institute, pp. 343–348.

———. 1982. *Revolt Against Regulation*. Berkeley: University of California Press.

Peskin, Henry M., Paul R. Portney, and Allen V. Kneese. 1981. *Environmental Regulation and the U.S. Economy*. Baltimore: Johns Hopkins University Press.

Peters, John G. 1978. "The 1977 Farm Bill: Coalitions in Congress." In Don F. Hadwiger and William P. Browne, eds., *The New Politics of Food*. Lexington, Mass.: Lexington Books, pp. 23–36.

Pettus, Beryl E. 1982. "OSHA Inspection Costs, Compliance Costs, and Other Outcomes." *Policy Studies Review* 1 (February), 596–614.

Pfeffer, Jeffrey. 1979. "Some Evidence on Occupational Licensing and Occupational Incomes." *Social Forces* 53 (September), 102–111.

Phelan, Jack. 1974. *Regulation of the Television Repair Industry in Louisiana and California: A Case Study*. Washington, D.C.: Federal Trade Commission.

Pitofsky, Robert. 1984. "Why *Dr. Miles* Was Right." *Regulation* 8 (January–February), 27–30.

Pittle, R. David. 1976. "The Consumer Product Safety Commission." In Robert N. Katz, ed., *Protecting the Consumer Interest*. Cambridge, Mass.: Ballinger, pp. 131–160.

Plott, Charles R. 1965. "Occupational Self-Regulation: A Case Study of the Oklahoma Dry Cleaners." *Journal of Law and Economics* 8 (October), 195–222.

Poole, Robert W. 1982. *Instead of Regulation*. Lexington, Mass.: Lexington Books.

Posner, Richard A. 1976. *Antitrust Law: An Economic Perspective*. Chicago: University of Chicago Press.

Posner, Richard A. 1974. "Theories of Economic Regulation." *Bell Journal of Economics and Management Science* 5 (Autumn), 337–352.

———. 1970. "A Statistical Study of Antitrust Enforcement." *Journal of Law and Economics* 13 (October), 371–390.

Pratt, Richard J. 1983. "Richard Pratt Goes to New York." *ABA Banking Journal* 75 (July), 97–100.

Pratt, Richard J. 1982. "The Savings and Loan Industry: Past, Present, and Future." *Federal Home Loan Bank Board Journal* 15 (November), 3–8.

Presidential Task Force on Regulatory Relief. 1983. *Reagan Administration Regulatory Achievements*. Washington, D.C. (August 11).

Puckett, Richard H. 1983. "Deregulation and the Principles of Regulation." *The Bankers Magazine* 166 (March–April), 86–88.

Quirk, Paul J. 1981. *Industry Influence in Federal Regulatory Agencies*. Princeton: Princeton University Press.

———. 1980. "The Food and Drug Administration." In James Q. Wilson, ed., *The Politics of Regulation*. New York: Basic Books, pp. 191–234.

Randal, Judith. 1984. "Is Aspartame Really Safe?" *Washington Post National Weekly Edition* (May 28), 7–8.

Redford, Emmette S. 1969. *Democracy and the Administrative State*. New York: Oxford University Press.

Renfrow, Patty D. 1980. "The New Independent Regulatory Commissions: The Politics of Establishment." Paper presented at the annual meeting of the Midwest Political Science Association, Chicago.

Report of the ABA Commission to Study the Federal Trade Commission. 1969. New York: American Bar Association.

Resources for the Future. 1980. *Public Opinion on Environmental Issues*. Washington, D.C.: U.S. Government Printing Office.

Ripley, Randall B., and Grace A. Franklin. 1980. *Congress, the Bureaucracy, and Public Policy*. Homewood, Ill.: Dorsey Press.

Romzek, Barbara S., and J. Stephen Hendricks. 1982. "Organizational Involvement and Representative Bureaucracy." *American Political Science Review* 76 (March), 75–82.

Rosenbaum, Walter A. 1973. *The Politics of Environmental Concern.* New York: Praeger.

Rottenberg, Simon. 1980. "Introduction." In Simon Rottenberg, ed., *Occupational Licensing and Regulation.* Washington, D.C.: American Enterprise Institute, pp. 1–10.

Rourke, Francis E. 1984. *Bureaucracy, Politics, and Public Policy.* Boston: Little, Brown.

Rowland, C. K., and Roger Marz. 1982. "Gresham's Law: The Regulatory Analogy." *Policy Studies Review* 1 (February), 572–580.

Ruff, Larry E. 1981. "Federal Environmental Regulation." In Leonard W. Weiss and Michael W. Klass, eds., *Case Studies in Regulation.* Boston: Little, Brown, pp. 235–261.

Sabatier, Paul A. 1983. "Toward a Strategic Interaction Framework of Policy Evaluation and Learning." Paper presented at the annual meeting of the Western Political Science Association.

———. 1977. "Regulatory Policy Making: Toward a Framework of Analysis." *National Resources Journal* 17 (July), 415–460.

Salamon, Lester B., and Gary L. Wamsley. 1975. "The Federal Bureaucracy: Responsive to Whom." In Leroy N. Rieselbach, ed., *People vs. Government.* Bloomington: Indiana University Press.

Scalia, Antonin. 1980. "The Legislative Veto." In Timothy B. Clark, Marvin H. Kosters, and James C. Miller, eds., *Reforming Regulation.* Washington, D.C.: American Enterprise Institute, pp. 55–61.

Scher, Seymour. 1960. "Congressional Committee Members as Independent Agency Overseers." *American Political Science Review* 54 (September), 911–920.

Schertz, Lyle P., and others. 1979. *Another Revolution in U.S. Farming?* Washington, D.C.: U.S. Department of Agriculture.

Schmitt, Harrison H. 1980. "Putting Democratic Controls on the Law of Bureaucrats." In Timothy B. Clark, Marvin H. Kosters, and James C. Miller, eds., *Reforming Regulation.* Washington, D.C.: American Enterprise Institute, pp. 51–54.

Schroeder, Frederick J. 1983. "Developments in Consumer Electronic Fund Transfer." *Federal Reserve Bulletin* 69 (June), 395–404.

Schubert, Glendon. 1960. *The Public Interest.* New York: Free Press.

Schuck, Peter R. 1980. "A Tool for Assessing Social Regulation." In Timothy B. Clark, Marvin H. Kosters, and James C. Miller, eds., *Reforming Regulation.* Washington, D.C.: American Enterprise Institute, pp. 117–122.

Schultze, Charles L. 1971. *The Distribution of Farm Subsidies: Who Gets the Benefits?* Washington, D.C.: Brookings.

Schutz, Howard G. 1983. "Effects of Increased Citizen Membership on Occupational Licensing Boards in California." *Policy Studies Journal* 11 (March), 504–516.

Schwartz, John E. 1983. *America's Hidden Success.* New York: Norton.

Schwartz, Warren F. 1981. *Private Enforcement of the Antitrust Laws.* Washington, D.C.: American Enterprise Institute.

Schwartzman, David. 1964. "The Effect of Monopoly on Price." *Journal of Political Economy* (August), 352–361.

Seidman, Harold. 1980. *Politics, Position, and Power.* New York: Oxford University Press.

Shaffer, Helen B. 1977. "Job Health and Safety." In *Earth, Energy and Environment.* Washington, D.C.: Congressional Quarterly, pp. 189–208.

Shapiro, Martin. 1982. "On Predicting the Future of Administrative Law." *Regulation* 6 (May/June), 18–25.

Shepard, Lawrence E. 1978. "Licensing Restrictions and the Cost of Dental Care." *Journal of Law and Economics* 21 (April), 187–201.

Shepherd, William G. 1975. *The Treatment of Market Power.* New York: Columbia University Press.

Shimberg, Benjamin, Barbara F. Esser, and Daniel H. Kruger. 1973. *Occupational Licensing: Practices and Policies.* Washington, D.C.: Public Affairs Press.

Shryock, Richard Harrison. 1967. *Medical Licensing in America, 1650–1965.* Baltimore: Johns Hopkins Press.

Sigelman, Lee, and Roland E. Smith. 1980. "Consumer Regulation in the American States." *Social Science Quarterly* 61 (June), 58–76.

Simon, Herbert A. 1969. *The Science of the Artificial.* Cambridge, Mass.: MIT Press.

———. 1957. *Administrative Behavior.* New York: Free Press.

Sinclair, Ward. 1984. "The Tobacco Lobby's Hot Potato." *Washington Post National Weekly Edition* (June 4), 18.

Singer, James W. 1976. "New OSHA Task Force." *National Journal* 8 (July 10), 973–975.

Smith, Adam. 1937. *Wealth of Nations.* New York: Random House.

Smith, Robert S. 1979. "The Impact of OSHA Inspections on Manufacturing Injury Rates." *Journal of Human Resources* 14 (Spring), 145–170.

———. 1976. *The Occupational Safety and Health Act.* Washington, D.C.: American Enterprise Institute.

———. 1974. "The Feasibility of an 'Injury Tax' Approach to Occupational Safety." *Law and Contemporary Problems* 38 (Summer–Autumn), 730–744.

Sobel, Stephen. 1977. "A Proposal for the Administrative Compensation of Victims of Toxic Substances Pollution." *Harvard Journal of Legislation* 14 (June), 683–824.

Spellman, Lewis J. 1982. *The Depository Firms and Industry.* New York: Academic Press.

Sprecher, Robert A. 1967. "Admission to Practice Law." *State Government* (Winter), 21–25.

Staelin, Richard, and R. David Pittle. 1978. "Consumer Product Safety." In Norman Kangun and Lee Richardson, eds., *Consumerism.* Chicago: American Marketing Association, pp. 53–70.

Stanfield, Rochelle L. 1984. "Ruckelshaus Casts EPA as 'Gorilla' in States' Enforcement Closet." *National Journal* 16 (May 26), 1034–1038.

Stewart, Charles T. 1979. *Air Pollution, Human Health and Public Policy.* Lexington, Mass.: Lexington Books.

Stewart, Joseph, James E. Anderson, and Zona Taylor. 1982. "Presidential and Congressional Support for Independent Regulatory Commissions." *Western Political Quarterly* 35 (September), 318–326.

Stigler, George J. 1971. "The Theory of Economic Regulation." *Bell Journal of Economics and Management Science* 2 (Spring), 3–21.

Stokey, Edith, and Richard Zeckhauser. 1978. *A Primer for Policy Analysis.* New York: Norton.

Stoll, Hans R. 1981. "Revolution in the Regulation of Securities." In Leonard W. Weiss and Michael W. Klass, eds., *Case Studies in Regulation.* Boston: Little, Brown, pp. 12–52.

Stone, Alan. 1982. *Regulation and Its Alternatives.* Washington, D.C.: Congressional Quarterly Press.

———. 1979. "New Directions in Banking and Its Regulation." Paper presented at the Symposium on Regulatory Policy, Chicago.

———. 1976. "Economic Regulation, the Free Market, and Public Ownership." In James E. Anderson, ed., *Economic Regulatory Policies.* Lexington, Mass.: Lexington Books, pp. 187–202.

Strelnick, Hal. 1983. "An Empirical Analysis of Institutional Patterns of Affirmative Action in American Medical Schools." Paper presented at the Hendricks Symposium on Affirmative Action, Lincoln, Nebraska.

———, and Richard Young. 1980. *Double Indemnity.* New York: Health Policy Advisory Center.

Strickland, Allyn Douglas. 1980. *Government Regulation and Business.* Boston: Houghton Mifflin.

Stubbs, Anne, and Leslie Cole. 1982. "Environmental Management." *Book of the States 1982–83.* Lexington, Ky.: Council of State Governments.

Sun, Marjorie. 1983. "Study Says U.S. Drug Firms Falling Behind." *Science* 221 (September 16), 1157–1158.

Swartzman, Daniel, Richard A. Liroff, and Kevin G. Croke. 1982. *Cost-Benefit Analysis and Environmental Regulation.* Washington, D.C.: The Conservation Foundation.

Talbot, Ross B., and Don F. Hadwiger. 1968. *The Policy Process in American Agriculture.* San Francisco: Chandler.

Tarbell, Ida. 1950. *The History of Standard Oil Company.* New York: Peter Smith.

Taylor, Carl C. 1953. *The Farmer's Movement, 1620–1920.* New York: American Book Company.

Teck, Alan. 1968. *Mutual Savings Banks and Savings and Loan Associations: Aspects of Growth.* New York: Columbia University Press.

Thompson, Frank J. 1982. "Deregulation by the Bureaucracy: OSHA and the Augean Quest for Error Correction." *Public Administration Review* 42 (May–June), 202–212.

Thompson, Fred, and L. R. Jones. 1982. *Regulatory Policy and Practices.* New York: Praeger.

Thompson, Mark S. 1980. *Benefit-Cost Analysis for Program Evaluation.* Beverly Hills: Sage.

Thompson, Roger. 1983. "Farm Policy's New Course." In Editorial Research Reports, *America's Economy.* Washington, D.C.: Congressional Quarterly Press, pp. 69–88.

Thorelli, Hans B. 1955. *The Federal Antitrust Policy.* Baltimore: Johns Hopkins Press.

Timberlake, Richard H., Jr. 1978. *The Origins of Central Banking in the United States.* Cambridge, Mass.: Harvard University Press.

Tobin, Richard J. 1984. "Revising the Clean Air Act." In Norman J. Vig and Michael E. Kraft, eds., *Environmental Policy in the 1980s.* Washington, D.C.: Congressional Quarterly Press, pp. 227–250.

———. 1982. "Recalls and the Remediation of Hazardous or Defective Consumer Products." *Journal of Consumer Affairs* 16 (Winter), 278–306.

Truman, David B. 1951. *The Governmental Process.* New York: Knopf.

Tucker, Harvey J. 1982. "Incremental Budgeting: Myth or Model." *Western Political Quarterly* 35 (September), 327–338.

Tweeten, Luther. 1981. "Prospective Changes in U.S. Agricultural Structure." In D. Gale Johnson, ed., *Food and Agricultural Policy for the 1980s.* Washington, D.C.: American Enterprise Institute, pp. 113–146.

———. 1979a. *Foundations of Farm Policy.* Lincoln: University of Nebraska Press.

———. 1979b. "Structure of Agriculture and Policy Alternatives to Preserve the Family Farm." Presented at the Farmer's Agricultural Policy Conference, Stillwater, Okla.

U.S. Department of Agriculture. *Agricultural Statistics 1982.* Washington, D.C.: U.S. Government Printing Office.

United States League of Savings Associations. 1982. *'82 Savings and Loan Sourcebook.* Chicago: U.S. League of Savings Associations.

Van Cise, Jerrold G. 1982. *The Federal Antitrust Laws.* Washington, D.C.: American Enterprise Institute.

Verba, Sidney, and Norman H. Nie. 1972. *Participation in America.* New York: Harper & Row.

Vig, Norman J., and Michael E. Kraft. 1984. "Environmental Policy from the Seventies to the Eighties." In Norman J. Vig and Michael E. Kraft, eds., *Environmental Policy in the 1980s.* Washington, D.C.: Congressional Quarterly Press, pp. 3–26.

Viscusi, W. Kip. 1983. *Risk By Choice.* Cambridge, Mass.: Harvard University Press.

———. 1982. "Health and Safety." *Regulation* 6 (January–February), 34–37.

Walton, Clarence C., and Frederick W. Cleveland, Jr. 1964. *Corporations on Trial: The Electric Cases.* Belmont, Calif.: Wadsworth.

Wardell, William M. 1973. "Introduction of New Therapeutic Drugs in the United States and Great Britain." *Clinical Pharmacology and Therapeutics* (September–October), 1022–1034.

———, et al. 1978. "The Rate of Development of New Drugs in the United States." *Clinical Pharmacology and Therapeutics* (May), 499–524.

Warren, Kenneth F. 1982. *Administrative Law in the American Political System.* St. Paul: West.

Weaver, Suzanne. 1977. *Decision to Prosecute.* Cambridge, Mass.: MIT Press.

Weidenbaum, Murray L. 1981. *Business, Government, and the Public.* 2d ed. Englewood Cliffs, N.J.: Prentice-Hall.

Weingast, Barry R. 1980. "Physicians, DNA Research, Scientists and the Market for Lemons." In Roger D. Blair and Stephen Rubin, eds., *Regulating the Professions.* Lexington: Lexington Books, pp. 81–96.

———, and Mark J. Moran. 1983. "Bureaucratic Discretion or Congressional Control? Regulatory Policymaking by the Federal Trade Commission." *Journal of Political Economy* 91:(5), 765–800.

———, and ———. 1982. "The Myth of the Runaway Bureaucracy: The Case of the FTC." *Regulation* 6 (May–June), 33–38.

Weiss, Leonard W. 1981. "Introduction: The Regulatory Reform Movement." In Leonard W. Weiss and Michael W. Klass, eds., *Case Studies in Regulation.* Boston: Little, Brown, pp. 1–11.

Welborn, David M. 1977. *The Governance of Federal Regulatory Agencies.* Knoxville: University of Tennessee Press.

Weller, Phil. 1980. *Acid Rain: The Silent Crisis.* Oshawa, Canada: Alger Press Limited.

Wenner, Lettie M. 1984. "Judicial Oversight of Environmental Regulation." In Norman J. Vig and Michael E. Kraft, eds., *Environmental Policy in the 1980s.* Washington, D.C.: Congressional Quarterly Press, pp. 181–200.

West, William F. 1982. "The Politics of Administrative Rulemaking." *Public Administration Review* 42 (September–October), 420–426.

White, Eugene Nelson. 1983. *The Regulation and Reform of the American Banking System, 1900–1929.* Princeton: Princeton University Press.

White, George C. 1980. "Payment Systems Today—and Tomorrow." *The Bankers Magazine* 163 (March–April), 26–31.

White, Lawrence. 1983. *Human Debris: The Injured Worker in America*. New York: Seaview/ Putnam.

White, Lawrence J. 1982. *The Regulation of Air Pollutant Emissions for Motor Vehicles*. Washington, D.C.: American Enterprise Institute.

———. 1981. *Reforming Regulation: Processes and Problems*. Englewood Cliffs, N.J.: Prentice-Hall.

White, Michael. 1982. "Barriers to Interstate Banking Begin to Crumble." *Savings and Loan News* 103 (January), 44–49.

White, William D. 1978. "The Impact of Occupational Licensure on Clinical Laboratory Personnel." *Journal of Human Resources* 13, 91–102.

———. 1980. "Mandatory Licensure of Registered Nurses: Introduction and Impact." In Simon Rottenberg, ed., *Occupational Licensing and Regulation*. Washington, D.C.: American Enterprise Institute, pp. 47–72.

Wilson, James Q. 1980. *The Politics of Regulation*. New York: Basic Books.

Wines, Michael. 1984. "Steel: Managing the Decline." *National Journal* 16 (March 31), 603–607.

———. 1983a. "It's Congress's Move." *National Journal* 15 (July 9), 1462.

———. 1983b. "Reagan Plan to Relieve Auto Industry of Regulatory Burden Gets Mixed Grades." *National Journal* 15 (July 23), 1532–1537.

———. 1983c. "From Doctors to Dairy Farmers, Critics Gunning for FTC." *National Journal* 15 (January 29), 221–223.

———. 1983d. "Doctors and FTC Eye Truce that Would Keep Most Antitrust Powers." *National Journal* 15 (March 23), 831, 859.

———. 1983e. "Legislative Veto Debate Threatens to Hogtie FTC Reauthorization Bill." *National Journal* 15 (September 10), 1830–1835.

———. 1983f. "McFadden Waiver Allows BankAmerica Expansion." *National Journal* 15 (April 30), 909.

———. 1983g. "Scandals at EPA May Have Done in Reagan's Move to Ease Cancer Controls." *National Journal* 15 (June 18), 1264–1269.

———. 1983h. "Less Milk Could Mean More Money for Dairy Farmers, Higher Federal Costs." *National Journal* 15 (December 31), 2666–2669.

———. 1983i. "Auchter's Record at OSHA Leaves Labor Outraged, Business Satisfied." *National Journal* 15 (October 10), 2008–2013.

———. 1983j. "Product Liability 'Reform'—Is It Only a Defense for Shoddy Products?" *National Journal* 15 (April 9), 748–752.

———. 1982a. "Reagan's Reforms Are Full of Sound and Fury, But What Do They Signify?" *National Journal* 14 (January 16), 92–98.

———. 1982b. "FTC About-Face Under Miller May Not Be Enough for Congressional Critics." *National Journal* 14 (June 2), 992–996.

———. 1982c. "Doctors, Dairymen Join in Effort to Clip Talons of the FTC." *National Journal* 14 (September 18), 1589–1594.

———. 1982d. "Banks, S&Ls, and the Securities Industry Scramble for Congressional Goodies." *National Journal* 14 (September 4), 1498–1502.

———. 1982e. "Reagan's Antitrust Line—Common Sense or Invitation to Corporate Abuse?" *National Journal* 14 (July 10), 1204–1209.

———. 1981. "The Financial Supermarket Is Here and Congress Is Trying to Catch Up." *National Journal* 13 (November 11), 2056–2062.

Wood, William C. 1978. "Pricing Behavior of Attorneys in Northern Virginia After *Goldfarb*." *The American Economist* 22, 56–68.

Worthley, John A., and Richard Torkelson. 1983. "Intergovernment and Public-Private Sector Relations in Hazardous Waste Management." In James P. Lester and Ann O'M. Bowman, eds., *The Politics of Hazardous Waste Management*. Durham, N.C.: Duke University Press, pp. 102–111.

Wright, Patrick J. 1978. *On a Clear Day You Can See General Motors*. New York: Avon.

Yandle, Bruce. 1982. "A Social Regulation Controversy." *Social Science Quarterly* 63 (March), 58–69.

Youngberg, Garth. 1976. "U.S. Agriculture in the 1970s: Policy and Politics." In James E. Anderson, ed., *Economic Regulatory Policies*. Lexington, Mass.: Lexington Books, pp. 51–68.

Zeigler, L. Harmon, and G. Wayne Peak. 1972. *Interest Groups in American Society*. Englewood Cliffs, N.J.: Prentice-Hall.

Zwick, David, and Marcy Benstock. 1971. *Water Wasteland*. New York: Grossman.

Court Cases Cited

Addyston Pipe and Steel Co. v. *United States*, 175 U.S. 211 (1899).
American Bankers Association v. *Connell*, 194 U.S. App. D.C. 80 (1980).
American Column and Lumber Co. v. *United States*, 257 U.S. 377 (1921).
American Medical Association v. *Federal Trade Commission*, 50 L.W. 4313 (1982).
American Textile Manufacturers v. *Donavan*, 452 U.S. 490 (1981).
Atlas Roofing v. *Occupational Safety and Health Review Commission*, 430 U.S. 442 (1977).
Baker v. *Carr*, 369 U.S. 186 (1962).
Bates v. *State Bar of Arizona*, 433 U.S. 350 (1977).
Brown Shoe Company v. *United States*, 370 U.S. 294 (1962).
Continental TV v. *GTE Sylvania*, 433 U.S. 365 (1977).
Federal Trade Commission v. *Consolidated Foods*, 360 U.S. 592 (1965).
Federal Trade Commission v. *Morton Salt*, 334 U.S. 37 (1948).
Federal Trade Commission v. *Procter & Gamble*, 386 U.S. 568 (1967).
Federal Trade Commission v. *Sperry and Hutchinson*, 405 U.S. 233 (1972).
Goldfarb v. *Virginia State Bar*, 421 U.S. 733 (1975).
Humphrey's Executor v. *United States*, 295 U.S. 602 (1935).
Illinois Brick Co. v. *Illinois*, 431 U.S. 720 (1977).
Immigration and Naturalization Service v. *Chadha*, 77 L. Ed. 2d 317 (1983).
Industrial Union Department, AFL-CIO v. *American Petroleum Institute*, 448 U.S. 607 (1981).
International Harvester v. *Ruckelshaus*, 478 F. 2d 615 (D.C. Cir. 1973).
International Salt Co. v. *United States*, 332 U.S. 392 (1947).
Loewe v. *Lawler*, 208 U.S. 274 (1908).
Marshall v. *Barlow's*, 436 U.S. 307 (1978).
Miles Medical Co. v. *John Park*, 220 U.S. 373 (1911).
Motor Vehicle Manufacturers Association v. *State Farm Mutual Automobile Insurance*, 77 L. Ed. 2d 443 (1983).
Northern Securities v. *United States*, 193 U.S. 197 (1904).
Packard Motor Co. v. *Webster*, 355 U.S. 822 (1957).
Philadelphia v. *Westinghouse Electric*, 210 F. Supp. 483 (1961).
Raladam v. *Federal Trade Commission*, 42 F.2d 430 (1930).
Siegal v. *Chicken Delight*, 448 F.2d 653 (1971).
Sierra Club v. *Ruckelshaus*, 489 F.2d 390 (5th Cir. 1974).
Standard Oil of California v. *United States*, 337 U.S. 293 (1949).
Standard Oil Company of New Jersey v. *United States*, 211 U.S. 1 (1911).

Tampa Electric Co. v. *Nashville Coal Co.*, 365 U.S. 320 (1961).
Times-Picayune Publishing Co. v. *United States*, 354 U.S. 594 (1953).
United Church of Christ v. *Federal Communications Commission*, 359 F.2d 994 (1966).
United States v. *Aluminum Company of America*, 148 F.2d 416 (2d Cir., 1945).
United States v. *American Tobacco Company*, 221 U.S. 106 (1911).
United States v. *Arnold, Schwinn and Co.*, 388 U.S. 365 (1949).
United States v. *Bethlehem Steel Corp.*, 168 F. Supp. 576 (1958).
United States v. *Butler*, 297 U.S. 1 (1936).
United States v. *Container Corporation of America*, 393 U.S. 333 (1969).
United States v. *E. C. Knight*, 156 U.S. 1 (1895).
United States v. *International Telephone and Telegraph*, 324 F. Supp. 19 (D. Conn., 1970).
United States v. *Jerrold Electronics*, 365 U.S. 567 (1961).
United States v. *Loew's Inc.*, 371 U.S. 38 (1962).
United States v. *Philadelphia National Bank*, 374 U.S. 321 (1963).
United States v. *Socony-Vacuum Oil Company*, 310 U.S. 150 (1940).
United States v. *United States Steel Corp.*, 251 U.S. 417 (1920).
United States v. *Trenton Potteries Co.*, 273 U.S. 392 (1927).
United States v. *Von's Grocery*, 384 U.S. 270 (1966).
Utah Pie v. *Continential Baking*, 386 U.S. 685 (1967).

Index

Abramson, Paul R., 20
Ackerman, Bruce A., 154
Additives, food, 90–92
Addyston Pipe v. *U.S.*, 245
Administrative law, 28–29
Administrative Procedure Act (APA, 1946),
  28, 208
Agency for Consumer Advocacy (proposed),
  291–92
Aggregate concentration, 261–62
  mergers and, 252–53
Agricultural Adjustment Acts (AAA), 81,
  129–30, 138
Agricultural Marketing Act (1929), 129
Agricultural Marketing Service (AMS), 94,
  125
Agricultural regulation, 119–38, 274–75,
  277
  agencies involved in, 123–24
  beneficiaries of, 135–37
  failure of farm policy, 134–35
  first efforts at, 129
  historical background of, 128–29
  New Deal, 129–30
  1973–1983 policies, 131–34
  party conflict on (1948–1973), 131
  politics of, 128–35
  price regulation, 124–26, 129–35
Agricultural Stabilization and Conservation
  Service (ASCS), 125
Agriculture (agricultural industries), 119–
  23. *See also* Agricultural regulation
  advocacy coalitions in, 122–23
  economic environment of, 126–27
  general description of agricultural sector,
    120
  individual industries in, 120–22
  subsystems of, 126
  technological environment of, 127
Agriculture and Consumer Protection Act
  (1973), 132
Agriculture, U.S. Department of (USDA),
  14, 112, 122–35, 141
  Extension Service of, 122, 128
  price regulation by, 124–26, 129–35
  in Progressive era, 78–80
Airbags, 98–99
Airline Deregulation Act (1978), 23
Air pollution. *See also* Clean Air Act
  (1963); Environmental regulation
  auto emissions controls and, 148–51
  bubble concept and, 155
  Carter administration and, 154–55
  from coal, 154
  early efforts at regulation of, 143

from lead, 155–56
  stationary sources of, 151–56
Air Pollution Control Act (1955), 143
Air Quality Act (1967), 143
Air quality standards, 151–53
Akers, Ronald L., 177, 178, 183
Alcoa (Aluminum Company of America),
  241
Aldrich, John H., 20
American Agriculture Movement (AAM),
  123
American Association of Medical Colleges,
  182
American Association of Retired Persons,
  112
American Bankers' Association (ABA), 38,
  63, 67, 69
American Bankers' Association v. *Connell*,
  63–65
American Bar Association (ABA), 108, 110,
  113, 192
American Column and Lumber v. *U.S.*, 246
American Enterprise Institute (AEI), 157,
  158
American Express, 72
American Farm Bureau, 122, 129, 131, 136
American Federation of Labor-Congress of
  Industrial Organizations (AFL-CIO),
  64, 207
American Home Economics Association, 80
American Medical Association (AMA), 79,
  80, 110, 112, 181–84, 191
American Medical Association v. *Federal
  Trade Commission*, 112
American Milk Producers, Inc., 112
American National Standards Institute, 211
American Nurses Association, 112
American Sugar Refining Company, 237
American Telephone and Telegraph (AT&T),
  242
American Textile Manufacturers v. *Dona-
  van*, 29
American Textile Workers v. *Donavan*,
  215, 218
American Tobacco Company, 236, 239–40
Anderson, Douglas D., 26, 32, 113, 275,
  281
Anderson, Harry, 246
Anderson, James E., 121–23, 125, 130,
  132, 142–44, 269
Andrews, Richard N. L., 144, 145, 152,
  161, 162, 164
Anthan, George, 135
Antitrust policy, 232–68, 271–72
  advocacy coalitions concerned with, 234

321

Carnes, Sam A., 161, 162
Carron, Andrew S., 32, 46, 67, 69
Carson, Rachel, 159
Carter, Jimmy (Carter administration), 25–27, 64, 67, 172, 287, 288, 292, 293
    air pollution control and, 154–55
    Consumer Product Safety Commission (CPSC) and, 104–5
    environmental protection and, 150
    Federal Trade Commission (FTC) and, 109–10
    Occupational Health and Safety Administration (OSHA) and, 209, 212, 214, 216, 217
Cash management account (CMA), 59–60, 71
Catalytic converters, 150
Celler-Kefauver Act (1950), 236, 248–53
Center for Auto Safety, 96
Cereal manufacturers, 246–47
Certification of occupations, 179–80
    all-comers examinations for, 195–96
    institutional, 198–99
    replacement of licensing with, 195
Chamber of Commerce, U.S., 107, 110
Chase, Stuart, 80
Checking accounts, interest payments on, 60–61
Chemical Manufacturers Association, 161, 162
Childproof caps for medicines and poisons, 105
Chrysler Corporation, 149
Citicorp (Citibank), 62, 73, 74
Civil Aeronautics Board, 24
Clark, Timothy B., 67, 296
Clarkson, Kenneth W., 108
Claybrook, Joan, 99, 293
Clayton, Henry D., 236
Clayton Antitrust Act (1914), 236, 266
    exclusionary practices and, 255–56
    price discrimination and, 253
Clean Air Act (1963), 140, 143, 164, 277
    cost-benefit analysis of, 167
    evaluation of, 155–56
    1970 amendments to, 146–47, 151
    1977 amendments to, 150, 154
    reauthorization of, 166
    stationary sources of air pollution and, 151–56
Clean Water Act, 140, 156–59, 167, 278
    evaluation of, 158–59
    reauthorization of, 166
Cleveland, Frederick W., 245
Clothing and Textile Workers Union, 214
Coal, air pollution and, 154
Coalitions, 19
    in agriculture, 122–23
    in antitrust area, 234
    automobile industry, 96
    breadth of, 21–22
    in consumer product safety area, 101

    in environmental protection, 141
    Federal Trade Commission (FTC)-related, 107, 110
    food-processing industry, 88
    Occupational Health and Safety Administration (OSHA) and, 203–4
    pharmaceutical industry, 82
Cochran, Thad, 65
Cochrane, Willard W., 131
Cohen, Richard E., 24
Cohen, Steven, 162
Cohesion
    as agency resource, 16
    of interest groups, 20
Cole, Leslie, 149, 162
Collective bargaining, workplace safety regulation through, 290
Collusion, 244–48, 271
Colton, Kent W., 48
Comanor, W. S., 285
Commercial banks, 38. See also Depository institutions
    checking accounts and, 60–61
    depression of 1930s and, 50–52, 55–56
    deregulation and, 63
    early history of regulation of, 48–52, 55–56
    interest on checking accounts and, 60–61
    interstate and branch banking and, 61–62
    in the 19th century, 49
Commodity Credit Corporation, 134
Commodity Futures Trading Commission (CFTC), 296
Competition, 234–35. See also Antitrust policy
    lack of, as justification of regulation, 271–72
    perfect, 270
    regulation as limiting, 281–82
Complexity, technological, 33. See also Technology
Comprehensive Environmental Response, Compensation and Liability Act (1980), 161
Comptroller of the Currency, Office of the, 41–42
Computerization of depository institutions, 47
Conglomerate mergers, 249, 251–52
Congress, 22–25. See also specified legislation
    authorization and appropriation process of, 23
    hearings, 23–24
    informal contact with members of, 25
    legislative process in, 23
    legislative veto power of, 24–25
    responsiveness of regulatory agencies to, 295–97
Connors, Helen V., 178, 179, 185
Consolidated Foods, 251–52